series

Advances in Reading Intervention

Research to Practice to Research

Advances in Reading Intervention

Research to Practice to Research

The Extraordinary Brain Series, XIV

edited by

Carol McDonald Connor, Ph.D.,
Arizona State University
Tempe

and

Peggy McCardle, Ph.D., M.P.H.
Peggy McCardle Consulting, LLC
Seminole, Florida

Baltimore • London • Sydney

Paul H. Brookes Publishing Co.
Post Office Box 10624
Baltimore, Maryland 21285–0624

www.brookespublishing.com

Typeset by Scribe Inc., Philadelphia, Pennsylvania.
Manufactured in the United States of America by
Sheridan Books, Chelsea, Michigan.

Library of Congress Cataloging-in-Publication Data

The Library of Congress has cataloged the printed edition as follows:

Connor, Carol McDonald.
Advances in reading intervention : research to practice to research / Carol McDonald Connor, Peggy McCardle.
pages cm.—(Extraordinary brain)
Summary: "This latest volume in the Extraordinary Brain series represents a joint effort between researchers and practitioners to shape the future of early reading intervention by taking stock of the present and making recommendations for the future"—Provided by publisher.
ISBN 978-1-59857-968-0 (paperback)—ISBN 978-1-59857-994-9 (hardcover)—ISBN 978-1-68125-042-7 (ebook)
1. Reading—Remedial teaching—Research. I. McCardle, Peggy D. II. Title.

LB1050.5.C656 2015
372.43—dc23 2015011410

British Library Cataloguing in Publication data are available from the British Library.

2019 2018 2017 2016 2015

10 9 8 7 6 5 4 3 2 1

Contents

About the Editors ix
About the Contributors xi
The Dyslexia Foundation and the Extraordinary Brain Series xxiii
Acknowledgments xxvii

Part I Introduction 1

Chapter 1 Research to Practice to Research: The Importance of Reciprocity to Building Better Interventions
Carol McDonald Connor and Peggy McCardle 3

Chapter 2 An Overview of Reading Intervention Research: Perspectives on Past Findings, Present Questions, and Future Needs
Maureen W. Lovett 7

Part II Basic Considerations for Reading Intervention: Behavior, Neurobiology, and Genetics 23

Chapter 3 The Growth of Self-Regulation in the Transition to School
Frederick J. Morrison 25

Chapter 4 Innovative Data Summary Measures Provide Novel Insights on Reading Performance
Christopher W. Bartlett, Andrew Yates, Judy F. Flax, and Linda M. Brzustowicz 37

Chapter 5 The Role of Rapid Automatized Naming in Reading Disruption: An Application of the Cusp Catastrophe
Georgios Sideridis, George K. Georgiou, Panagiotis G. Simos, Angeliki Mouzaki, and Dimitrios Stamovlasis 49

Chapter 6 Eye-Movement Research in Reading: Enhancing Focus on the Development of Reading and Reading Disabilities
Brett Miller 61

Chapter 7 Neurobiological Bases of Word Recognition and Reading Comprehension: Distinctions, Overlaps, and Implications for Instruction and Intervention
Laurie E. Cutting, Stephen Kent Bailey, Laura A. Barquero, and Katherine Aboud 73

Chapter 8 Integrating Neurobiological Findings in Search of a Neurochemical "Signature" of Dyslexia
Stephanie N. Del Tufo and Kenneth R. Pugh 85

Chapter 9 The Genetic Classroom: How Behavioral Genetics Can Inform Education
Sara A. Hart 99

Integrative Summary 1: The Future of Reading Research: New Concepts and Tools and the Need for Detailed Genetic and Neurobiological Contexts
Nadine Gaab 111

Part III Reading and Writing Interventions: Research to Inform Practice **117**

Chapter 10 What Practitioners Think and Want to Know
Joan A. Mele-McCarthy 119

Chapter 11 Literacy in the Early Grades: Research to Practice to Research
Carol McDonald Connor 129

Chapter 12 Addressing Dialect Variation in Early Reading Instruction for African American Children
Nicole Patton Terry 143

Chapter 13 Reading Development Among English Learners
Nonie K. Lesaux 155

Chapter 14 Students with Reading Difficulties Who Are English Learners
Melodee A. Walker, Philip Capin, and Sharon Vaughn 167

Chapter 15 The *Letra* Program: A Web-Based Tutorial Model for Preparing Teachers to Improve Reading in Early Grades
Juan E. Jiménez 181

Chapter 16 Struggling with Writing: The Challenges for Children with Dyslexia and Language Learning Difficulty When Learning to Write
Vincent Connelly and Julie E. Dockrell 197

Chapter 17 Fostering the Capabilities that Build Writing Achievement
Rui A. Alves and Teresa Limpo 209

Chapter 18 Effectiveness of a Beginning Reading Intervention: Compared with What? Examining the Counterfactual in Experimental Research
Michael D. Coyne 221

Integrative Summary 2: Translating Reading Research into Effective Interventions for All Children Who Struggle with Reading
Julie A. Washington 231

Part IV Finale: Looking to the Future **237**

Chapter 19 Innovation and Technology that Can Inform Reading Interventions
David J. Jodoin 239

Chapter 20 Reading Intervention in Perspective
Donald L. Compton and Laura M. Steacy 249

Chapter 21 Moving Forward in Reading Intervention Research and Practice
Peggy McCardle and Carol McDonald Connor 261

Index 273

About the Editors

Carol McDonald Connor, Ph.D., Senior Learning Scientist, Learning Sciences Institute, P.O. Box 872111, Arizona State University, Tempe, Arizona 85278

Carol McDonald Connor is a professor of psychology at Arizona State University and a distinguished research associate at the Florida Center for Reading Research. Her research focuses on examining the links between young children's language and their literacy development with the goal of illuminating reasons for the perplexing difficulties that children who are atypical and diverse learners have with developing basic and advanced literacy skills. Most recently, her research interests have focused on children's learning in the classroom—from preschool through fifth grade—and developing technology and interventions to improve teacher efficacy and students' reading outcomes. Awarded the Presidential Early Career Award for Scientists and Engineers (2008), the Society for Research in Child Development, Early Career Award (2009), and the Richard Snow Award (American Psychological Association, 2008), she is the principal investigator for studies funded by the U.S. Department of Education, Institute for Education Sciences, and the National Institute of Child Health and Human Development. She is also editor of the *Journal for Research in Educational Effectiveness* (Impact Factor 3.15) and associate editor for *Child Development* (Impact Factor 4.1).

Peggy McCardle, Ph.D., M.P.H., Owner, Peggy McCardle Consulting, LLC, 14465 86th Avenue, Seminole, Florida 33776

Peggy McCardle is a private consultant and an affiliated research scientist at Haskins Laboratories. She is the former chief of the Child Development and Behavior Branch of the *Eunice Kennedy Shriver* National Institute of Child Health and Human Development (NICHD), U.S. National Institutes of Health, where she also directed the Language, Bilingualism, and Biliteracy Research Program and developed various literacy initiatives. Dr. McCardle is a linguist, a former speech-language pathologist, and, in her remote past, a classroom teacher. The recipient of various awards for her work in federal government, including a 2013 NICHD Mentor Award, she also was selected in 2013 to receive the Einstein Award from The Dyslexia Foundation. Her publications address various aspects of public health and developmental psycholinguistics (e.g., language development, bilingualism, reading, learning disabilities). Dr. McCardle has taught scientific and technical writing and has extensive experience developing and coediting volumes and thematic journal issues.

About the Contributors

Katherine Aboud, M.F.A., Doctoral Candidate, Education and Brain Sciences Research Lab, Vanderbilt University, PMB 228, 230 Appleton Place, Nashville, Tennessee 37203

Katherine Aboud is a Ph.D. student in the educational neuroscience program at Vanderbilt University. She received her B.S. in mathematics and English at Virginia Tech University and her M.F.A. in poetry at George Mason University. Her current research focus is on the functional neural correlates of reading comprehension and their relationship with executive functions using magnetic resonance imaging (MRI).

Rui A. Alves, Ph.D., Assistant Professor, Universidade do Porto, Rua Alfredo Allen, 4200–135 Porto, Portugal

Rui A. Alves is an assistant professor of psychology at the University of Porto, where he lectures on writing, learning disabilities, and neuropsychology. His main research interests are writing and literacy development. His research group studies early text production and develops writing interventions. Since 2011, he has been the coordinator of the Special Interest Group on Writing of the European Association for Research on Learning and Instruction. He is also deeply engaged in editorial work and is an associate editor of the journal *Reading & Writing: An Interdisciplinary Journal*. Currently, he is also chairing the COST Action IS1401, which is establishing the European Literacy Network.

Stephen Kent Bailey, B.S., B.A., Doctoral Candidate, Educational Neuroscience, Education and Brain Sciences Research Lab, Vanderbilt University, PMB 328, 230 Appleton Place, Nashville, Tennessee, 37203

Stephen Bailey received a B.S. in chemistry and a B.A. in philosophy in 2011 from Samford University in Birmingham, Alabama. He is currently working toward a Ph.D. in educational neuroscience from the Peabody College of Education and Human Development at Vanderbilt University, advised by Laurie E. Cutting. His research interests include the investigation of neurocorrelates of reading ability using MRI techniques.

Laura A. Barquero, M.S., Doctoral Candidate, Special Education, Education and Brain Sciences Research Lab, Vanderbilt University, PMB 228, 230 Appleton Place, Nashville, Tennessee 37203

Laura Barquero is a doctoral candidate in special education at the Peabody College of Education and Human Development at Vanderbilt University. Her current research explores using functional MRI to explore responsiveness to reading intervention for children with reading difficulties.

Christopher W. Bartlett, Ph.D., Associate Professor of Pediatrics, Battelle Center for Mathematical Medicine, The Research Institute at Nationwide Children's Hospital and The Ohio State University College of Medicine, 575 Children's Crossroad, Columbus, Ohio 43215

Christopher Bartlett is an associate professor of pediatrics at Nationwide Children's Hospital and The Ohio State University College of Medicine. Dr. Bartlett researches the genetic basis of oral and written language impairments in populations with isolated impairments and language impairments that co-occur with autism spectrum disorders. He has published more than 40 peer-reviewed articles and has given invited oral presentations in Asia, Europe, and North America. He has been a special issue editor for the *Journal of Child Psychology and Psychiatry* and is currently editing a volume in the *Frontiers in Developmental Science* book series for Psychology Press. He serves as an associate editor for *BMC Bioinformatics.*

Linda M. Brzustowicz, M.D., Professor and Chair, Department of Genetics, Human Genetics Institute of New Jersey, Life Sciences Building, 145 Bevier Road, Piscataway, New Jersey 08854

Linda Brzustowicz received her A.B. in biochemistry and molecular biology from Harvard University (1982) and her M.D. from Columbia University (1987). After a pediatrics internship at Brown University's Rhode Island Hospital, she returned to Columbia University and completed residency training in psychiatry as well as postdoctoral training in molecular genetics and statistical genetics. She has been a faculty member at Rutgers University since 1994, running the Psychiatric Genetics Laboratory first at the Center for Molecular and Behavioral Neuroscience on the Newark Campus (1994–2001) and subsequently in the Department of Genetics on the Busch Campus, where she is professor and chair.

Philip Capin, M.A., Researcher, The Meadows Center for Preventing Educational Risk, University of Texas at Austin, 1912 Speedway D4900, Austin, Texas 78712

Philip Capin is a doctoral student at the University of Texas (UT) at Austin studying special education with a concentration in learning disabilities and behavior disorders. Before joining the Meadows Center for Preventing Educational Risk and UT, he planned and directed sustainable professional development initiatives to enhance reading instruction and assessment. Capin is also an experienced special education teacher and a certified school administrator. His research interests include empirically validated reading interventions, the measurement of reading comprehension, and response to intervention.

Donald L. Compton, Ph.D., Professor and Chair, Special Education Department, Peabody College, Vanderbilt University, P.O. Box 228, 110 Magnolia Circle, 313 OMC, Nashville, Tennessee 37203

Donald L. Compton is a professor and chair of the Special Education Department and a John F. Kennedy Center Investigator at Peabody College, Vanderbilt University. His research involves modeling individual differences in the development of children's reading skills and the identification of children with reading disabilities.

Vincent Connelly, Ph.D., Program Lead and Professor, Department of Psychology, Social Work and Public Health, Oxford Brookes University, Gipsy Lane, Oxford, OX3 0BP, United Kingdom

Vince Connelly is a professor of psychology at Oxford Brookes University in the United Kingdom. He has many years of experience in research on literacy. He has published work on the interaction between reading instruction and reading development but is more recently known for his work on the development of writing skills. He has published work studying the difficulties that children with language learning disorder and dyslexia have with learning to write. He has organized a number of workshops with teachers and educational professionals to exchange views on the teaching of writing in the United Kingdom. He is a joint coordinator of the European Special Interest Group on Writing with Rui Alves.

Michael D. Coyne, Ph.D., Professor, Special Education Program, Department of Educational Psychology, Neag School of Education, Unit 3064, University of Connecticut, Storrs, Connecticut 06269

Michael Coyne is a professor of special education in the Neag School of Education at the University of Connecticut. He is also a research scientist at the Center for Behavioral Education and Research. His research focuses on beginning reading and early vocabulary instruction and intervention, school-based experimental research, multitiered or response to intervention systems of support, and effective practices for students with learning disabilities.

Laurie E. Cutting, Ph.D., Patricia and Rodes Hart Endowed Chair and Professor, Peabody College of Education and Human Development, Vanderbilt University, Nashville, Tennessee 37203

Laurie Cutting holds faculty appointments in the Departments of Special Education, Psychology, Radiology, and Pediatrics at Vanderbilt University, is Senior Scientist at Haskins Laboratories, and has an adjunct faculty position at Johns Hopkins School of Medicine, Department of Neurology. Her research focuses on educational neuroscience—in particular, the neurobiological and behavioral underpinnings of reading, oral language, and dyslexia.

Stephanie N. Del Tufo, B.A., Doctoral Candidate, Department of Psychology, University of Connecticut, 406 Babbidge Road, Unit 1020, University of Connecticut, Storrs, Connecticut 06269

Stephanie N. Del Tufo is a doctoral candidate at the University of Connecticut and Haskins Laboratories, advised by Drs. Kenneth Pugh and Emily Myers. In her previous work as a technical assistant at the Massachusetts Institute of Technology, Del Tufo studied speech perception and reading in children and adults with and without dyslexia under Dr. John Gabrieli and Dr. Joanna Christodoulou. Del Tufo previously studied neuroscience and chemistry at Smith College. In her current work, she investigates the neurobiological basis of speech perception and reading that underlies developmental dyslexia.

Julie E. Dockrell, Ph.D., AcSS, FRCSLT, Professor of Psychology and Special Needs, Psychology and Human Development, Institute of Education, 20 Bedford Way, London WC1H 0AL, United Kingdom

Julie Dockrell is a qualified educational and clinical psychologist whose research focuses on the ways in which developmental difficulties affect children's learning and attainments. She was codirector of the Better Communication Research Programme, the largest U.K. study on the needs of children with language difficulties. She has been the editor of the *British Journal of Educational Psychology* and an associate editor of the *Journal of Speech Language and Hearing Research* and *Learning and Instruction.*

Judy F. Flax, Ph.D., Associate Research Professor, Department of Human Genetics, Rutgers University, 145 Bevier Road, Room 224, Piscataway, New Jersey 08854

Judy F. Flax is an associate research professor in the Brzustowicz Lab in the Department of Human Genetics and a former senior research scientist in the Infancy Studies Laboratory, Center for Molecular and Behavioral Neuroscience (CMBN) at Rutgers University. Over the past 20 years, her primary research interests have spanned the areas of normal speech and language acquisition; the behavioral, neural, and genetic bases of autism; and language-based learning disabilities (specific language impairment and dyslexia). As a licensed speech-language pathologist and learning consultant, she has more than 35 years of clinical expertise in language-based learning disabilities, autism, and special education.

Nadine Gaab, Ph.D., Associate Professor of Pediatrics, Boston Children's Hospital/Harvard Medical School, Department of Medicine/Division of Developmental Medicine, Laboratories of Cognitive Neuroscience, 1 Autumn Street, Boston, Massachusetts 02115

Nadine Gaab is an associate professor of pediatrics at Boston Children's Hospital/Harvard Medical School and a faculty member at the Harvard Graduate School of Education. Her current research focuses on auditory and language processing in the human brain and its applications for the development of typical and atypical language and literacy skills. The Gaab Lab is currently working on various topics with a main focus on early identification of developmental dyslexia in the prereading and infant brain. The Gaab Lab employs cross-sectional and longitudinal study designs and works closely with more than 20 private and public schools within the greater New England area.

George K. Georgiou, Ph.D., Associate Professor, Department of Educational Psychology, 6–102 Education North, University of Alberta, Edmonton-AB, T6G 2G5, Canada

George K. Georgiou is an associate professor in the Department of Educational Psychology at the University of Alberta. His interests include the examination of the role of rapid naming in reading across languages, ages, and populations. In addition, he specializes in the factors (cognitive and noncognitive) that impede or facilitate literacy development across languages.

Sara A. Hart, Ph.D., Assistant Professor, Department of Psychology, 1107 West Call Street, Florida State University, Tallahassee, Florida 32306

Sara A. Hart is an assistant professor of psychology and a member of the research faculty at the Florida Center for Reading Research at Florida State University. Broadly defined, her research interests focus on the sources of individual differences on cognitive ability and achievement development. She primarily focuses on how genetics and the environment interplay to influence the development of reading and math skills as well as general cognitive processing. In addition, she is interested in incorporating genetic and family environment information into practitioners' understanding of response to intervention.

Juan E. Jiménez, Ph.D., Professor of Learning Disabilities, Faculty of Psychology, Campus de Guajara 38200, Universidad de La Laguna, La Laguna, Tenerife, Canary Islands, Spain

Juan E. Jiménez, professor of learning disabilities, chaired the Scientific Committee of the Canary Institute and the Educational Quality Assessment. He served as the scientific advisor for the National Teacher Training Institute, Research and Education Innovation (Ministry of Education) in a study on students with dyslexia within the education system in Spain. In this capacity, he has participated as the Spanish coordinator responsible for cooperative programs of the Spanish Agency for International Development Cooperation (AECID) with the following Latin American countries: Guatemala, Mexico, Chile, and Ecuador. He has collaborated with the Technical Department of Humanities and Social Sciences of the Ministry of Science and Innovation. Jiménez serves as an expert appointed by United Nations Educational, Scientific, and Cultural Organization (UNESCO) for the project on Formative Assessment of Writing in Early Grades.

David J. Jodoin, B.A., Chief Technology Officer and Senior Vice President, CafeX Communications, 31 Milk Street, Boston, Massachusetts 02109

David J. Jodoin is an expert in innovation and runs a research and development team located in Boston, Massachusetts. His background as a serial entrepreneur has garnered him industry recognition as an authority on the open innovation process, leading the design, development, and introduction of several major high-technology products that are in widespread use today. Jodoin holds degrees from Harvard University and Dean College in social sciences, computer science engineering, and business management. He has performed extensive research concerning the impact of technology on the development of government, business, adults, and adolescents and the formation of social groups in virtual communities.

Nonie K. Lesaux, Ph.D., Juliana W. and William Foss Thompson Professor of Education and Society, Harvard Graduate School of Education, 14 Appian Way, Cambridge, Massachusetts 02138

Nonie K. Lesaux is the Juliana W. and William Foss Thompson Professor of Education and Society at the Harvard Graduate School of Education. She leads a research program that focuses on increasing opportunities to learn for students from diverse linguistic and economic backgrounds. Her studies on reading and vocabulary development, as well as instruction to prevent reading difficulties, have implications for practitioners, researchers, and policy makers. In 2009, she was a recipient of the Presidential Early Career Award for Scientists and Engineers, the highest honor given by the U.S. government to young independent researchers. A native of Canada, Lesaux earned her doctorate in educational psychology and special education from the University of British Columbia.

Teresa Limpo, Ph.D., Faculty Member, Psychology and Educational Sciences, Universidade do Porto, Rua Alfredo Allen, 4200–135 Porto, Portugal

Teresa Limpo completed her Ph.D. in psychology at the University of Porto in the Faculty of Psychology and Educational Sciences. Her primary research interest centers on writing from a cognitive perspective. In particular, she has been studying the role of transcription and self-regulation skills in writing as well as developing and testing intervention programs to promote them in school-age children. She also provides training for teachers interested in implementing these evidence-based practices in their classrooms. Currently, she is the junior coordinator of the Special Interest Group on Writing of the European Association for Research on Learning and Instruction.

Maureen W. Lovett, Ph.D., C.Psych., Professor of Pediatrics and Medical Sciences, University of Toronto; Senior Scientist, Neurosciences and Mental Health Program; and Director, Learning Disabilities Research Program, The Hospital for Sick Children, 555 University Avenue, Toronto, Ontario, M5G 1X8 Canada

Maureen W. Lovett is a senior scientist in the Neurosciences and Mental Health Program at The Hospital for Sick Children and a professor of pediatrics and medical sciences at the University of Toronto. Her research focuses on questions about the effective remediation of decoding, word identification, fluency, and reading comprehension impairments in struggling readers in elementary, middle, and high schools. As a Co-Principal Investigator of the Institute of Education Sciences–funded Center for the Study of Adult Literacy, she is developing interventions for adult literacy learners as well. She and her team are also involved in knowledge translation initiatives: Their Empower™ Reading intervention programs are now used to teach struggling readers in school districts in four Canadian provinces.

Joan A. Mele-McCarthy, D.A., Executive Director, Summit School, 664 East Central Avenue, Edgewater, Maryland 21037

Joan A. Mele-McCarthy is the executive director of The Summit School, a school designed for students who have dyslexia and other learning differences. Prior to this position, she served as a special assistant to the assistant secretary for special education/rehabilitation services in the U.S. Department of Education and worked on policy issues related to the connections between special education and general education and between English learners and disabilities. She also has served on university faculties in departments of communication sciences and disorders, owned and directed a private practice that provided direct intervention and school consultation, and worked in public schools. Her work is focused on language-based learning differences and special education policy.

Brett Miller, Ph.D., Program Director, *Eunice Kennedy Shriver* National Institute of Child Health and Human Development, 6100 Executive Boulevard, Suite 4B05, Rockville, Maryland 20852

Brett Miller oversees the Reading, Writing, and Related Learning Disabilities research portfolio at the National Institutes of Health, which focuses on developing and supporting research and training initiatives to increase knowledge relevant to the development of reading and written-language abilities for learners with and without disabilities. Dr. Miller also codirects the Language, Bilingualism, and Biliteracy Research Program, which focuses on language development and psycholinguistics from infancy through early adulthood, bilingualism and/or second-language acquisition, and reading in bilingual and/or English-language-learning children and youth.

Frederick J. Morrison, Ph.D., Professor of Psychology, Combined Program in Education and Psychology and Research Professor, Survey Research Center, Institute for Social Research, University of Michigan, 530 Church Street, Ann Arbor, Michigan 48109

Frederick J. Morrison is a professor of psychology and a professor in the Combined Program in Education and Psychology at the University of Michigan. In recent years, his research has focused on understanding the nature and sources of children's cognitive, literacy, and social development throughout the school transition period. His work ranges from conducting basic research studies utilizing natural experiments and large-scale, longitudinal, descriptive studies of children's developmental trajectories to developing, implementing, and evaluating two major interventions aimed at improving children's learning during the preschool and early school years. Recently, he has been exploring schooling effects on brain and behavior measures of children's self-regulation.

Angeliki Mouzaki, Ph.D., Assistant Professor of Learning Disabilities, Department of Primary Education, University of Crete, Gallos Campus, Rethymno 74100, Greece

Angeliki Mouzaki began her career as an elementary school teacher, earned a Ph.D. in educational psychology at the University of Houston, and worked at the Center for Academic and Reading Skills at the University of Texas Health and Science Center at Houston. Her primary research interests are reading and spelling skill development and disorders as well as issues related to reading instruction and interventions for diverse student populations.

Nicole Patton Terry, Ph.D., Associate Professor, Department of Educational Psychology and Special Education, and Director, The Urban Child Study Center, College of Education, Georgia State University, P.O. Box 3979, Atlanta, Georgia 30302

Nicole Patton Terry is the coordinator of the Behavior Learning Disabilities Program, a member of the Center for Research on Atypical Development and Learning and the Board of Regents Initiative on Research on the Challenges of Acquiring Language and Literacy, the director of the newly founded Urban Child Study Center in the College of Education, and a research scientist at Haskins Laboratories at Yale University. She is an associate editor of the *American Journal of Speech-Language Pathology.* Her research concerns children who struggle with language and literacy, in particular children from culturally and linguistically diverse backgrounds, who speak nonmainstream American English dialects and who live in low-income or working-class households.

Kenneth R. Pugh, Ph.D., President, Director of Research, and Senior Scientist, Haskins Laboratories, 300 George Street, Suite 900, New Haven, Connecticut 06511

In addition to his positions at Haskins Laboratories, a Yale University and University of Connecticut affiliated interdisciplinary institute that is dedicated to the investigation of the biological bases of language, Kenneth R. Pugh holds positions at the University of Connecticut, Yale University, and the Yale University School of Medicine. He directs the Yale Reading Center, is a member of the Scientific Advisory Board for the International Dyslexia Association and the Rodin Remediation Academy in Stockholm, and has served as a peer reviewer at the National Institutes of Health and as a panel member at the National Research Council of the National Academies. His research in cognitive neuroscience and psycholinguistics focuses on the neurobiology of typical and atypical language and reading development.

Georgios Sideridis, Ph.D., Assistant Professor, Harvard Medical School and Senior Survey Methodologist, Clinical Research Center, Boston Children's Hospital, 300 Longwood Avenue, Boston, Massachusetts 02115

Georgios Sideridis is an assistant professor of pediatrics at Harvard Medical School and a senior survey methodologist at Boston Children's Hospital. He has been a research associate professor at the University of Massachusetts, Boston, and an associate professor of research methods and statistics with the Department of Psychology at the University of Crete. His research interests include motivation and learning disabilities, an expansion of achievement goal theory, and investigation of systematic measurement error in the measurement of instruments in psychology and education.

Panagiotis G. Simos, Ph.D., Professor of Developmental Neuropsychology, School of Medicine, University of Crete, Vassilika Vouton, Herakleion 71003, Greece

Panagiotis G. Simos received his Ph.D. in experimental psychology-biopsychology (1995) from Southern Illinois University. He served as an assistant and associate professor with the Department of Neurosurgery at the University of Texas Health and Science Center at Houston and the Department of Psychology at the University of Crete, Greece. His research focuses on neuropsychological and brain imaging studies of reading and memory using magnetoencephalography and MRI with children and adults. Ongoing studies explore psychoeducational, emotional, and neurophysiological profiles associated with specific reading disability, attention-deficit/hyperactivity disorder, and neurodegenerative disorders.

Dimitrios Stamovlasis, Ph.D., Assistant Professor, Aristotle University of Thessaloniki, Department of Philosophy and Education, 54 124 Thessaloniki, Greece

Dimitrios Stamovlasis is an assistant professor of research methodology for social science at the Aristotle University in the Department of Philosophy and Education. His research interests are interdisciplinary, and they focus on methodological and epistemological issues of contemporary social sciences that improve theory building; on nonlinear dynamics (i.e., complexity, catastrophe theory, entropy, and related fields) and their application to social, behavioral, and life sciences; and on specific research endeavors in the areas of educational research concerning neo-Piagetian theories, learning, science education, problem solving, creativity, and group dynamics.

Laura M. Steacy, M.Ed., Doctoral Candidate, Department of Special Education, Vanderbilt University, 110 Magnolia Circle, Nashville, Tennessee 37203

Laura M. Steacy is a doctoral candidate in high-incidence disabilities in the Department of Special Education at Vanderbilt University. Her research interests include early predictors of reading achievement and early intervention for students who are at risk for reading disabilities.

Sharon Vaughn, Ph.D., H.E. Hartfelder/Southland Corp. Regents Chair in Human Development and Executive Director, The Meadows Center for Preventing Educational Risk, University of Texas at Austin, Sanchez Building, 1912 Speedway, Austin, Texas 78712

Sharon Vaughn is the executive director of The Meadows Center, an organized research unit at the University of Texas at Austin. She is the recipient of the American Education Research Association Special Interest Group Distinguished Researcher Award, the International Reading Association Albert J. Harris Award, the University of Texas Distinguished Faculty Award, and the Jeannette E. Fleischner Award for Outstanding Contributions in the Field of Learning Disabilities from the Council for Exceptional Children. She is the author of more than 35 books and 250 research articles. Vaughn is currently the principal investigator on several research grants from the Institute for Education Sciences, the National Institute of Child Health and Human Development, and the U.S. Department of Education.

Melodee A. Walker, M.Ed., Project Coordinator, The Meadows Center for Preventing Educational Risk, University of Texas at Austin, 1912 Speedway, Austin, Texas 78712

Melodee A. Walker is a doctoral student at the University of Texas at Austin studying learning disabilities and behavior disorders in the Department of Special Education. Prior to beginning her doctoral studies, Walker was a teacher in general and special education classrooms across diverse settings. Walker currently works as a member of a research team investigating the impact of multicomponent reading interventions. Her research interests include diagnosis and remediation of learning disabilities, effective reading instruction, multicultural issues in special education, and discourse as pedagogy.

Julie A. Washington, Ph.D., Professor, Department of Educational Psychology, Special Education and Communication Disorders, Georgia State University, 30 Pryor Street, Atlanta, Georgia 30302

Julie A. Washington is a professor in the communication sciences and disorders program at Georgia State University. She also holds a joint appointment in developmental psychology and is an affiliate faculty member in the Georgia Board of Regents' initiative, Research on the Challenges of Acquiring Language and

Literacy, a unique research initiative focused on both child and adult learners. Her work focuses on cultural dialect use in African American children, with a specific emphasis on the impact of dialectal variation on language assessment, literacy attainment, and academic performance. She is currently examining the role of cultural-linguistic variation and social factors on diagnosis of reading disabilities in African American students growing up in urban poverty.

Andrew Yates, M.S., Research Scientist, Facebook, 1 Hacker Way, Menlo Park, California 94025

Andrew Yates is a research scientist at Facebook. Following his doctoral training, Yates was a National Institutes of Health fellow and doctoral candidate at the Wexner Medical Center at The Ohio State University, where he published research on data mining methods and their applications on gene expression patterns in the human brain.

The Dyslexia Foundation and the Extraordinary Brain Series

The Dyslexia Foundation (TDF) began in the late 1980s. It was founded by William H. "Will" Baker in collaboration with notable researchers in dyslexia. Through the generosity of the Underwood and Baker families, funds were provided to support the establishment of the first dyslexia research laboratory at Beth Israel Hospital, Harvard Medical School, Boston, Massachusetts; the laboratory opened in 1982 with a goal of investigating the neural underpinnings of dyslexia. Baker became the director of research for the Orton Dyslexia Society, and at the urging of Dr. Albert Galaburda and others, he convened top researchers from cognition, neuroscience, and education in a 1987 meeting. That scientific symposium was held in Florence, Italy, under the auspices of the Orton Dyslexia Society with generous support from Emily Fisher Landau. At that symposium, ideas were presented and discussed, with sufficient time to disagree, to identify research challenges, and to brainstorm solutions. There, the concept of a dyslexia symposium series was born. In the Spring of 1989, the National Dyslexia Research Foundation (later renamed The Dyslexia Foundation; TDF) was formed to focus more specifically on research while the Orton Society continued its primary focus on treatment and education. In 1990, the new foundation sponsored the next symposium in Barcelona, Spain. With this second symposium—the first to be held under the foundation's auspices—the Extraordinary Brain Series was born.

This volume celebrates the 14th symposium in the Extraordinary Brain Series. These symposia result in volumes that reflect the papers presented and the discussion that is spurred by those presentations. The series volumes make accessible to all researchers the thoughts of scholars across various disciplines as they tackle various aspects of the behavior, neurobiology, and genetics of dyslexia and of learning to read and write. Below is a listing of TDF symposia and the related volumes:

I. June 1987. Florence, Italy. Symposium Director: Albert M. Galaburda.

   Galaburda, A.M. (Ed.). (1990). *From reading to neurons.* Cambridge, MA: Bradford Books/The MIT Press.

II. June 1990. Barcelona, Spain. Symposium Director: Albert M. Galaburda.

   Galaburda, A.M. (Ed.). (1992). *Dyslexia and development: Neurobiological aspects of extraordinary brains.* Cambridge, MA: Bradford Books/Harvard University Press.

III. June 1992. Santa Fe, NM. Symposium Director: Paula Tallal.

Chase, C., Rosen, G., & Sherman, G.F. (Eds.). (1996). *Developmental dyslexia: Neural, cognitive, and genetic mechanisms.* Mahwah, NJ: Lawrence Erlbaum Associates.

IV. June 1994. Kauai, Hawaii. Symposium Director: Benita Blachman.

Blachman, B.R. (Ed.). (1997). *Foundations of reading acquisition and dyslexia: Implications for early intervention.* Mahwah, NJ: Lawrence Erlbaum Associates.

V. June 1996. Kona, Hawaii. Symposium Director: Drake Duane.

Duane, D. (Ed.). (1998). *Reading and attention disorders: Neurobiological correlates.* Mahwah, NJ: Lawrence Erlbaum Associates.

VI. June 1998. Kona, Hawaii. Symposium Director: Barbara Foorman.

Foorman, B. (Ed.). (2003). *Preventing and remediating reading difficulties: Bringing science to scale.* Baltimore, MD: York Press.

VII. June 2000. Crete, Greece. Symposium Director: Maryanne Wolf.

Wolf, M. (Ed.). (2001). *Time, fluency, and dyslexia.* Baltimore, MD: York Press.

VIII. October 2001. Johannesburg, South Africa. Symposium Director: Frank Wood.

Multilingualism and dyslexia. No publication.

IX. June 2004. Como, Italy. Symposium Director: Glenn Rosen.

Rosen, G. (Ed.). (2005). *The dyslexic brain: New pathways in neuroscience discovery.* Mahwah, NJ: Lawrence Erlbaum Associates.

X. June 2007. Campos do Jordao, Brazil. Symposium Directors: Ken Pugh and Peggy McCardle.

Pugh, K., & McCardle, P. (Eds.). (2009). *How children learn to read: Current issues and new directions in the integration of cognition, neurobiology and genetics of reading and dyslexia research and practice.* New York, NY: Psychology Press, Taylor & Francis Group.

XI. January 2010. Taipei, Taiwan. Symposium Directors: Peggy McCardle, Ovid Tseng, Jun Ren Lee, & Brett Miller.

McCardle, P., Miller, B., Lee, J.R., & Tseng, O. (Eds.). (2011). *Dyslexia across languages: Orthography and the brain–gene–behavior link.* Baltimore, MD: Paul H. Brookes Publishing Co.

XII. June 2011. Cong, Ireland. Symposium Directors: April Benasich & Holly Fitch.

Benasich, April A., & Fitch, R. H. (Eds.). (2012). *Developmental dyslexia: Early precursors, neurobehavioral markers, and biological substrates.* Baltimore, MD: Paul H. Brookes Publishing Co.

XIII. June 2012. Talinn, Estonia. Symposium Directors: Brett Miller & Laurie Cutting.

Miller, B., Cutting, L. E., & McCardle, P. (Eds.). (2013). *Unraveling reading comprehension: Behavioral, neurobiological, and genetic components.* Baltimore, MD: Paul H. Brookes Publishing Co.

XIV. June 2014. Horta, Faial Island, The Azores. Symposium Directors: Carol Connor & Peggy McCardle.

Connor, C.M., & McCardle, P. (Eds.). (2015). *Advances in reading intervention: Research to practice to research.* Baltimore, MD: Paul H. Brookes Publishing Co.

Acknowledgments

A book such as this would not be possible without the hard work and goodwill of a number of individuals: First, we acknowledge the authors who traveled to a far-off destination and met, presented, discussed, thought deeply for 5 days, and then wrote and cheerfully revised chapters, often meeting stringent deadlines. In addition, we acknowledge the practitioners (teachers, educators, administrators), researchers, graduate students, and postdoctoral fellows who also traveled and not only listened attentively and thought deeply but discussed, questioned, commented, and helped us all accomplish, at least for that symposium, a research-to-practice-to-research reciprocity that informed this volume and that we hope will continue.

But underlying the very possibility of such a volume, and the meeting that formed its base, is The Dyslexia Foundation (TDF), which sponsored the entire effort. Without TDF Founder and President Will Baker and his daughter and able colleague, Amelia Baker, there would be no Extraordinary Brain Symposia (EBS) and thus no EBS series of volumes! Thank you, Will and Amelia. In addition, we and TDF wish to thank the following individuals, schools, and businesses that generously supported EBS XIV: AIM Academy, the Brehm School, the Carroll School, Cerebral Matters, the Charles Armstrong School, Eagle Hill School—Southport, the Howard School, Literacy Brain Connection, Joan McNichols, Purple Crayon, The Summit School, Wilson Language Training, and five individuals and two foundations that wish to remain anonymous. In addition, special thanks go to the following officials and individuals from the city of Horta and the lovely "blue island" of Faial in the Azores: Presidente da Câmara Municipal da Horta, Sr. José Leonardo Goulart da Silva (Mayor); Presidente da Assembleia Legislativa da Região Autónoma dos Açores, Dra. Ana Luísa Luís (Assembly President); the Direção Regional do Turismo dos Açores, Goretti Carreiro (SATA Airlines); and our friend and personal "ambassador," Antonio Americo da Silva Vargas, for all his efforts in putting together all of the special events to make our visit to Faial a very memorable one.

Thanks go also to the flexible, helpful, and extraordinarily capable editors at Paul H. Brookes Publishing Co., Astrid Pohl Zuckerman and Sarah Zerofsky, who guided us, supported us, and ensured a high-quality volume—and all this without having traveled to the Azores with the symposium group. We wish we could have had you there. Thank you for your help and patience on this book. We love working with you!

Finally, we want to thank each other: coediting a volume depends on having a solid working relationship—a true partnership in which when one partner needs a break, the other steps in. This was a mutually supportive and productive partnership, so Carol and Peggy want folks to know they appreciate each other!

This volume, reflecting the presentations and discussions that took place at The Dyslexia Foundation's 14th Extraordinary Brain Symposium (EBS XIV), is dedicated to Helen U. Baker. Without her unconditional support, the outstanding EBS XIV, and indeed the EBS series, would not have been possible. A private and selfless woman, Helen has always felt that the most important thing in life is a great education—making sure all her children and grandchildren received the support they needed, inside or outside the classroom, in order to have an excellent schooling experience. Therefore, it is fitting that the publication based on The Dyslexia Foundation's symposium on reading intervention be dedicated to Helen U. Baker, who has avidly supported the foundation's efforts to raise awareness of the importance of reading research and interventions. Her lifelong efforts and attention not only to the importance of education and its research but also to encouraging strong and mutual collaboration between research and practice continue to inspire the foundation's work. We cannot thank her enough for everything she has done to make EBS XIV and this volume possible.

I

Introduction

1

Research to Practice to Research

The Importance of Reciprocity to Building Better Interventions

Carol McDonald Connor and Peggy McCardle

Reading is essential to life success, including further education, overall health and well-being, and employability (Reynolds, Temple, Robertson, & Mann, 2002). It is key to gaining knowledge and information through the educational system and in society more generally through traditional media, such as books and newspapers; through information given by medical care and other service providers; or through more modern technologies, such as computers and smartphones. Even television viewing involves a certain amount of reading. All types of employment require some reading. Yet according to the National Assessment of Educational Progress (NAEP, 2013), at least one third of U.S. children in Grades 4, 8, and 12 do not read well enough to function in society. Research is ongoing about how individuals learn to read and write, how the brain processes written information, and the role genetics plays in reading and reading difficulties. Much less is known, however, about how to bring this information to the classroom, optimal ways to teach children to read considering all their individual differences, and how best to identify those who cannot read or who struggle with learning to read early enough to prevent the more serious sequelae of dyslexia.

Rigorously tested interventions exist for struggling readers (e.g., Al Otaiba et al., 2014; Foorman, Francis, Fletcher, Schatschneider, & Mehta, 1998; Mathes et al., 2005; Vaughn, Denton, & Fletcher, 2010) and more are coming to market regularly. Yet for many existing and new interventions, there is little evidence showing whether or not they actually work and if they work, which children might benefit from them. Accumulating evidence shows that not every solution works equally well for each individual child (Connor et al., 2013). Furthermore, it is important to know *how* and *why* some interventions work for some children and not for others. It appears to be more difficult to intervene successfully with older students—those in middle school and beyond—and for them, the intervention process seems to take longer (Hill, Bloome, Black, & Lipsey, 2008; Vaughn et al., 2012). Preschool and early elementary school–age children generally appear to respond more quickly to interventions (Hill et al., 2008), yet insufficient data exist on early identification and how best to target interventions for those with the most severe impairments or those with linguistic differences that may make the process more challenging, such as speaking a dialect or home language that is not the dialect or language of instruction in the school.

Although more research is needed, additional challenges exist: how best to get effective interventions into the hands of practitioners who can implement them in schools, how to move research into practice, and how to learn from practice. How do we find ways to improve existing interventions and innovatively design new ones to meet the changing demands of today's educational settings?

This volume is based on the 14th Extraordinary Brain Symposium, convened in June 2014 by The Dyslexia Foundation with the goal of mapping a realistic, actionable 5-year plan for reading intervention research. Intervening with children who struggle with reading is a topic that has been researched for several decades, more intensively in some periods than in others, but it has always included the challenges of forging strong links between research and practice. One key goal of this meeting was to forge a research agenda that could move the field forward innovatively in terms of how researchers can design and test interventions that are informed by input from the practice community regarding its needs and how best to move research into practice so that it can have a direct effect on the lives of struggling readers and their families. We see this as a reciprocal process whereby the research that leads to changes in or enhancements of practice will be further informed by what is learned as evidence-based practices are implemented in schools and classrooms and as further challenges are experienced—hence the title of this book, *Advances in Reading Intervention: Research to Practice to Research.*

The symposium began with presentations from teachers and educational leaders from independent schools that focus on serving children with learning differences and from individuals representing intervention programs or approaches. They presented their most pressing questions to the convened researchers, who, in their own presentations, addressed the implications of their research or future possibilities for research to affect practice—and the contributors have done so in this volume as well. The chapters are based on the presentations given at the symposium but are also informed by the rich discussion that took place there, including interactions with practitioners not only in the initial and final sessions but throughout the entire week. This process enriched the meeting, so all contributors were committed to have that same richness infuse this volume.

Section I, "Introduction," includes an overview of reading intervention research by Lovett (Chapter 2) and is followed by three sections: basic science considerations, intervention, and a finale that offers a look ahead. In Section II, "Basic Considerations for Reading Intervention: Behavior, Neurobiology, and Genetics," seven chapters address these key areas of science. Morrison (Chapter 3) addresses the issue of self-regulation, an aspect of executive function whose role in learning and education is drawing increasing attention and whose role should certainly be considered in reading intervention. Bartlett, Yates, Flax, and Brzustowicz (Chapter 4) offer an innovative, nonlinear model of reading comprehension that can increase the power of statistical inferences. Sideridis, Georgiou, Simos, Mouzaki, and Stamovlasis (Chapter 5) present information on why rapid automatized naming predicts reading performance with a new hypothesis (generic shutdown) that uses a new analytic approach; the authors provide an innovative view of reading performance as dynamic and determined by the complex interplay between cognitive abilities and affective/motivational states. Miller (Chapter 6) shares information about past and recent work on eye movement and looks toward its potential usefulness in studying reading intervention. Cutting, Bailey, Barquero, and Aboud (Chapter 7) and Del Tufo and Pugh (Chapter 8) discuss the underlying neurobiology of reading at various levels. Hart (Chapter 9) presents information on how behavioral genetics might be used to improve the education process in the classroom. Gaab then integrates thoughts about these six chapters as an ensemble.

Section III, "Reading and Writing Interventions: Research to Inform Practice," comprises nine chapters on intervention. This section is introduced by Mele-McCarthy (Chapter 10), who was one of the practice representatives at the symposium; she summarizes the key practice questions and issues that were raised by this group and discussed throughout the week. Connor (Chapter 11) offers a discussion on literacy intervention in the early grades. Three chapters address language issues that can affect reading development and intervention: Patton Terry (Chapter 12) discusses the issue of nonmainstream dialect, its potential impact on reading, and possibilities for instruction and intervention, and Lesaux (Chapter 13) and Walker, Capin, and Vaughn (Chapter 14) deal with English-learning students who struggle with English reading. Jiménez (Chapter 15) discusses teacher continuing education and Connelly and Dockrell (Chapter 16) and Alves and Limpo (Chapter 17) offer chapters on writing important aspects of literacy that have been neglected until recently. Finally, Coyne (Chapter 18) challenges us to consider how intervention effectiveness is approached. Washington provides an integrative summary of Chapters 10–18 with thoughts about future research.

In the last section, "Finale: Looking to the Future" (Chapter 19), Jodoin discusses innovation and technology from an outsider's perspective as one who is neither an interventionist nor a basic science researcher but whose thoughts on how researchers and practitioners all might think more innovatively and use technology more creatively should help us move forward. Compton and Steacy's perspectives chapter (Chapter 20) reflects on what we have learned and what we can learn from the various chapters in this volume. And we as coeditors (Chapter 21) offer thoughts on the next 5 years, summarizing future research directions in which the field might break important new ground not only in literacy intervention research but also in how best to build and maintain the reciprocal link that has become commonly discussed but too infrequently realized: research informing practice informing research.

REFERENCES

Al Otaiba, S., Connor, C.M., Folsom, J.S., Greulich, L., Wanzek, J., Schatschneider, C., & Wagner, R.K. (2014). To wait in Tier 1 or intervene immediately: A randomized experiment examining first grade response to intervention (RTI) in reading. *Exceptional Children, 81*(1), 11–27. doi: 10.1177/0014402914532234

Connor, C.M., Morrison, F.J., Fishman, B., Crowe, E.C., Al Otaiba, S., & Schatschneider, C. (2013). A longitudinal cluster-randomized controlled study on the accumulating effects of individualized literacy instruction on students' reading from first through third grade. *Psychological Science, 24*(8), 1408–1419. doi:10.1177/0956797612472204

Foorman, B.R., Francis, D.J., Fletcher, J.M., Schatschneider, C., & Mehta, P. (1998). The role of instruction in learning to read: Preventing reading failure in at risk children. *Journal of Educational Psychology, 90,* 37–55.

Hill, C., Bloome, H., Black, A.R., & Lipsey, M.W. (2008). Empirical benchmarks for interpreting effect sizes in research. *Child Development Perspectives,* 2(3), 172–177.

Mathes, P.G., Denton, C.A., Fletcher, J.M., Anthony, J.L., Francis, D.J., & Schatschneider, C. (2005). The effects of theoretically different instruction and student characteristics on the skills of struggling readers. *Reading Research Quarterly, 40*(2), 148–182.

National Assessment of Educational Progress. (2013). *The nation's report card.* Retrieved from http://nces.ed.gov/nationsreportcard

Reynolds, A.J., Temple, J.A., Robertson, D.L., & Mann, E.A. (2002). Age 21 cost-benefit analysis of the Title I Chicago child-parent centers. *Educational Evaluation and Policy Analysis, 24*(4), 267–303.

Vaughn, S., Denton, C.A., & Fletcher, J.M. (2010). Why intensive interventions are necessary for students with severe reading difficulties. *Psychology in the Schools, 47*(5), 432–444.

Vaughn, S., Wexler, J., Leroux, A., Roberts, G., Denton, C., Barth, A., & Fletcher, J. (2012). Effects of intensive reading intervention for eighth-grade students with persistently inadequate response to intervention. *Journal of Learning Disabilities, 45*(6), 515–525.

2

An Overview of Reading Intervention Research

Perspectives on Past Findings, Present Questions, and Future Needs

Maureen W. Lovett

Three decades of work in the relatively young science of reading intervention research have been productive, revealing many positive findings about how to intervene with children and adolescents who struggle to learn to read because of dyslexia, reading disabilities, or other causes. There appears to be compelling evidence that effective intervention for readers struggling with acquiring basic reading skills should include 1) explicit, systematic, phonologically based instruction with ample opportunities for practice and cumulative review; 2) systematic instruction on all levels of written language structure, from subsyllabic and sublexical dimensions to different text and discourse structures; 3) instruction and scaffolded practice to promote the application and transfer of newly acquired skills to new materials; 4) modeling, teaching, and mentoring of specific reading, self-regulation, and self-monitoring strategies; 5) an integration of decoding and spelling to stress the reciprocity of these activities; and 6) daily attention to vocabulary growth and comprehension development using a variety of appealing and complex texts. The amount of empirical evidence for these recommended ingredients of effective reading intervention decreases with list placement, although all can be considered to have good supporting evidence.

There are also data to suggest that improvement in reading skills may continue, with long-term investments in instruction and effort, into adulthood but that the "gap" between struggling and typical readers is rarely if ever completely closed for more severe cases of dyslexia. Some residual symptoms of reading disability (RD) tend to persist into adulthood, even with strong literacy and educational outcomes (Bruck, 1992; Shaywitz et al., 1999). We also know that early intervention for children at risk of reading-acquisition failure appears to be an excellent investment of time and resources, as it generally yields very positive outcomes (Denton, Fletcher, Taylor, Barth, & Vaughn, 2014; Foorman, Francis, Fletcher, Mehta, & Schnatschneider, 1998; Wanzek & Vaughn, 2007, 2008). Early intervention, with adequate infrastructure within the school and the availability of later "booster" interventions when needed, has been shown to be effective (Al Otaiba et al., 2014). Adolescents and adults with limited reading skills, in contrast, are far more difficult to remediate (Vaughn & Fletcher, 2010; Vaughn et al., 2012) and require a far greater investment of resources over time. It is important to recognize, however, that it is not too late for the remediation of older readers if effective intervention is available, along with group support and the reader's motivation to improve reading skills (Lovett, Lacerenza, De Palma, & Frijters, 2012).

Despite substantial advances, many aspects of effective treatment for dyslexia and other reading problems remain to be identified. There exists fairly strong evidence on how to teach decoding and word identification skills, but the field has not made sufficient progress in how to accelerate the growth of word-reading efficiency and text reading fluency. Research has revealed some general parameters of what constitutes effective comprehension instruction, but we still lack a comprehensive blueprint of how to help a struggling reader with poor oral language skills or a struggling English learner (EL) become a good comprehender and how to measure that end goal. There are gaps in which our understanding about RD and effective intervention falls short, gaps made more salient by new developments in related areas of cognitive, learning, and education sciences that could but have not influenced thinking and practices. Some areas of concern in intervention research and practice warrant closer scrutiny and discussion. These areas are summarized in the following sections and are also identified in others' contributions to this volume.

THEORY AND DATA TO PRACTICE: DO OUR THINKING AND OUR LANGUAGE ABOUT INTERVENTION NEED EXPANDING? WHAT IS THE ROAD MAP?

We, as researchers and practitioners, may be imposing constraints on our progress by the way in which we think and talk about reading intervention. It is important for the interventionist's perspective to encompass more than the desired growth of a reader on progress measures of instructional response. We may envision our end goal for struggling readers as construction of Perfetti's (1999) cognitive blueprint of the skilled reader (Figure 2.1) or Scarborough's (2001) intertwined rope of reading development (Figure 2.2) blending ever more tightly the automatized and strategic strands of oral and written language skill components. Regardless of the model that is embraced, it is important to ground instructional approaches and intervention programs in a coherent, evidence-based model of reading behavior. Effective instruction requires a detailed road map of where teachers and learners are headed.

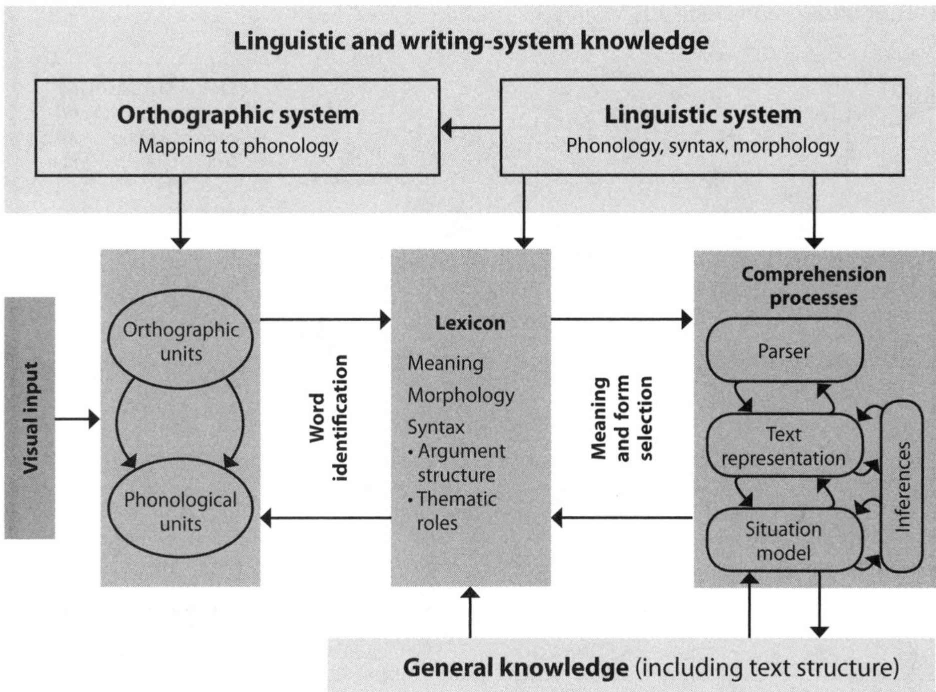

Figure 2.1. A blueprint of the skilled reader. (From Perfetti, C.A. [2000]. Comprehending written language: A blueprint of the reader. In C. Brown & P. Hagoort [Eds.], *The neurocognition of language* [p. 169]. Oxford, United Kingdom: Oxford University Press; reprinted by permission of Oxford University Press.)

Research has revealed that acquiring expertise on a complex skill requires thousands of hours of practice (Chi, Glaser, & Farr, 1988; Lesgold & Welch-Ross, 2012). Building a reading brain requires years of learning and practice. As Wolf (2007) and Dehaene (2009) both eloquently remind us, nothing in the course of human evolution equips humans to absorb language through the visual system. Yet neuroimaging studies show functional neural circuitry that, through learning and practice, has become beautifully attuned to the reading process (see for example, chapters by Cutting, Bailey, Barquero, & Aboud, Chapter 7; Del Tufo & Pugh, Chapter 8).

If we are working to help dyslexic readers build the same fundamental reading system and neural circuitry that typical readers have achieved, are there truly different instructional routes to that end? Are there multiple variations on the same routes to build the same cognitive system and its integrated neurobiological substrates? An effective intervention approach flows from a master plan that understands the architecture of the reading system that it is helping to build. And if there *is* a unified blueprint (or set of blueprints) for building a fluent reading system—one that produces optimal functionality—it is important to have a deep understanding of the learning processes necessary to become a skilled reader.

LANGUAGE COMPREHENSION

BACKGROUND KNOWLEDGE
(facts, concepts, etc.)

VOCABULARY
(breadth, precision, links, etc.)

LANGUAGE STRUCTURES
(syntax, semantics, etc.)

VERBAL REASONING
(inference, metaphor, etc.)

LITERACY KNOWLEDGE
(print concepts, genres, etc.)

WORD RECOGNITION

PHONOLOGICAL AWARENESS
(syllables, phonemes, etc.)

DECODING
(alphabetic principle, spelling-sound correspondences)

SIGHT RECOGNITION
(of familiar words)

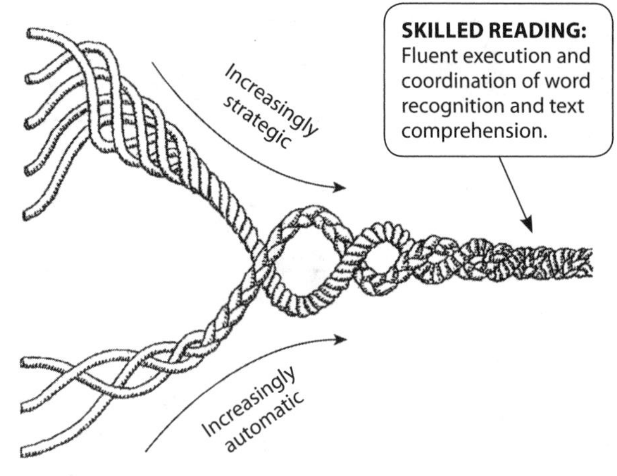

Figure 2.2. Learning that is multidimensional with a focus that changes over time. (Republished with permission of Guilford Press, from Scarborough, H.S. [2001]. Connecting early language and literacy to later reading [dis]abilities: Evidence, theory, and practice. In S.B. Neuman & D.K. Dickinson [Eds.], *Handbook of early literacy research* [p. 98]. New York, NY: Guilford Press; permission conveyed through Copyright Clearance Center, Inc.)

HOW WELL DO WE UNDERSTAND THE LEARNING MECHANISMS INVOLVED IN TYPICAL READING ACQUISITION, COMPREHENSION DEVELOPMENT, AND THE ATTAINMENT OF SKILLED READING?

Compton and colleagues recently suggested that we may have forsaken reading theory in the name of "quick-fix" interventions for children with RD (Compton, Miller, Elleman, & Steacy, 2014). They specifically argue that the skills and knowledge we set as intervention goals are quite different from the inductive and generative learning processes that characterize typical reading development. Interventions for dyslexia have focused on the response to explicit instruction on language structures and language patterns, with scant attention paid to implicit learning inside and outside of the instructional context. But how could instructional variables be manipulated to facilitate implicit learning in a population that is speculated to be deficient in aspects of implicit learning that impact early reading development (Vicari et al., 2005)? Some have suggested that it is a failure in the *interaction* of implicit lexical learning and explicit learning about phonology–grapheme mappings that underlies atypical reading development (Folia et al., 2008).

Insufficient attention in intervention to implicit learning and building robust lexical representations may account for the frequent postintervention finding of solid gains in word-reading accuracy but not in word-reading efficiency. Compton and colleagues contend that

> skilled readers develop and rely on complex "context-dependent" decoding rules to build fully specified lexical representations, whereas children with RD tend to develop and rely on simplistic "context-independent" decoding rules that fail to promote fully specified lexical representations. We define context-independent connections as subword orthographic-phonological connections that are insensitive to word position and surrounding letters, less implicit, and slow and arduous to apply. (2014, p. 60)

Rapid, efficient word recognition is the foundation of skilled reading and requires the establishment of a robust system of lexical representations. Many foundational skills become integrated with reading development (Ehri, 2005, 2014; Rosenthal & Ehri, 2008; Scarborough & Parker, 2003) to allow efficient word recognition, which in turn allows the development of higher order comprehension and fluency (Perfetti, 2007; Perfetti & Stafura, 2014). Although there exists strong evidence of effective strategies for teaching word identification to struggling readers, our exclusive focus on explicit instruction may have caused us to overlook aspects of intervention that could be important to achieving gains in the quality of lexical representations and greater word-reading efficiency.

THE DEVELOPMENT OF READING COMPREHENSION IN STRUGGLING READERS: PROBLEMS IN DEFINITION, MEASUREMENT, AND SCALE

Although more remains to be discovered about effective practices in the remediation of word reading problems, many more basic questions remain unresolved regarding intervention for reading comprehension difficulties. Expectations have increased throughout the last 20 years for the literacy skills required in today's job markets; understanding and learning from a broad array of texts is critical for postsecondary education and employment. Yet imprecision remains in how we think about and address reading comprehension difficulties. This is not surprising given that comprehension processes are as inherently complex as any aspect of higher order thinking and reasoning.

Cognitive definitions of reading comprehension focus on active, ongoing *construction* processes of considerable complexity: The work of comprehension is to construct a coherent mental representation of what is read. Cognitive and discourse processing research have specified that both an explicit text-based model and a "situation" model appear to be built mentally by the reader, the latter combining text-based information with other knowledge (e.g., background knowledge; Graesser & McNamara, 2011). For informational text, the situation model is the informational content or subject matter being discussed. Text comprehension requires the reader to integrate his or her relevant world knowledge, and the situation model will include inferences activated by the text-based information, which are incorporated into this model (Graesser, Singer, & Trabasso, 1994; Kintsch, 1998). It is within this situation model building that learning from text occurs; thus the building of a rich, integrated situation model is critical to reading comprehension. Individual readers vary widely, however, on different central components of text comprehension that may limit their processing of text meaning and curtail the representations they build at both text-based and situational levels. These components include an individual reader's standards for coherence (i.e., the degree of coherence one needs during ongoing reading), his or her ability to create a coherent representation of text information, his or her ability to make inferences, and his or her sensitivity to structural centrality (i.e., the degree to which he or she allocates attention to information central to the author's message; Helder, van den Broek, Van Leijenhorst, & Beker, 2013). All these sources of individual differences contribute to comprehension breakdown in reading, but these very important elements of comprehension have rarely been targets of reading comprehension instruction and intervention. This is an omission of real concern.

Comprehension theorists distinguish between "online" and "offline" products of text comprehension, the former being the construction and representation processes and the latter being what is recalled or available to the reader after a text is read. Different general sources of comprehension breakdown are recognized by researchers, including weak language skills, deficient background knowledge, and limited processing resources of the individual reader (Cain, 2013; Compton et al., 2014), as well as a failure to implement effective reading practices (Helder et al., 2013; Vaughn, Klinger, et al., 2011) and a poor understanding of how texts are structured.

Assessment instruments to identify some of these central components of comprehension and measures to evaluate the growth of comprehension processes and products are still lacking. This makes it difficult to design and implement effective comprehension interventions: If the sources of reading comprehension difficulties cannot be identified through assessment, it is very difficult to target remediation of those core areas and tailor instruction so that it will be most effective in improving comprehension skills in that struggling reader. Traditional measures assess somewhat crudely the *products* of reading comprehension, or what is understood after a text is read. Some of the limitations of these standardized reading comprehension tests, including inadequate content validity and concurrent validity, have been well documented (Keenan, Betjemann, & Olson, 2008).

Attempts to assess the online *processes* of comprehension remain experimental at this point and include eye-movement tracking (Rayner, Chace, Slattery, & Ashby, 2006; see also Miller, Chapter 6), think-aloud tasks (Ericsson & Simon, 1993; McMaster et al., 2012), and neuroimaging measures (Ferstl, Neumann, Bogler, & von Cramon, 2008; Perfetti & Fishkoff, 2008). Critical comprehension processes, including generating different types of inferences, making connections across paragraphs and texts, sensitivity to structural centrality (van den Broek, Helder, & Van Leijenhorst, 2013), and building coherence (Linderholm & van den Broek, 2002), are not routinely assessed and are only occasionally targeted in reading comprehension interventions.

Finally, recent research has illuminated the extent to which comprehension processing is shaped by three different major influences: characteristics of the reader, properties of the text being read, and the instructional context of the reader (McNamara & Kendeou, 2011; Snow, 2002; van den Broek, Young, Tzeng, & Linderholm, 1999; van den Broek et al., 2013). There has been limited research and development in assessment and intervention that has operated from models at this level of specificity. This is despite their promise to support instruction tailored to the individual needs of readers with different purposes, different comprehension profiles, and in different contexts. Studies of reading comprehension development have just begun to investigate individual differences at this level of detail (Barth, Tolar, Fletcher, & Francis, 2014; Miller et al., 2014), and investigations of this type have yet to extend to research on reading disabilities.

VOCABULARY AND BACKGROUND KNOWLEDGE IN READING COMPREHENSION INTERVENTION

The language vulnerability most often associated with poor reading comprehension is limited vocabulary knowledge. Reading ability has been well documented to be substantially correlated with estimates of vocabulary knowledge (Baumann, Kame'enui, & Ash, 2003; Kamil, 2004; Nagy, 2007), and reading interventions that target vocabulary development also tend to improve reading comprehension scores (e.g., the RAVE-O [retrieval, automaticity, vocabulary, engagement with language, orthography] Program, Morris et al., 2012; Wolf, Miller, & Donnelly, 2000).

The importance of vocabulary knowledge has been made even more salient by some theoretical accounts of reading comprehension. The landscape model of text comprehension (Rapp, van den Broek, McMaster, Kendeou, & Espin, 2007) paints a picture of multiple complex, ongoing processes occurring *simultaneously* during text reading—described as a *landscape* of fluctuating patterns of activation:

> During reading, concepts continually fluctuate in the amount of attention they receive and hence in their activation. . . . These fluctuations in activation form the basis for the representation of the text in memory. *Patterns of . . . simultaneous activations of concepts* [emphasis added] determine the presence or strength of connections between the concepts in memory. (van den Broek, Lorch, & Thurlow, 1996; van den Broek, 2010)

The need for *simultaneous* activation of semantic representations and rapid access to background knowledge is critical for struggling readers, whose reading is characterized by slowed retrieval and representations of poor lexical quality (Perfetti, 2007). Van den Broek's emphasis on simultaneous and presumably rapid activation of concepts during text comprehension is congruent with evidence of brain-based reading comprehension networks that encompass several brain regions (Miller et al., 2014; Landi, Frost, Mencl, Sandak, & Pugh, 2013). The idea of comprehension depending on a network of simultaneous fluctuating activations is but one example of a potentially central component of reading comprehension that requires an expanded focus in assessment and intervention efforts and greater study in future research. A better understanding of how reading comprehension develops for able readers will inform the road map for intervention with struggling readers and facilitate better outcomes.

In a parallel vein, Compton and colleagues emphasize the need for greater appreciation of the role of background knowledge in reading comprehension problems. They review evidence, suggesting that "poor readers tend to have less well-developed knowledge structures as well as problems accessing and using their knowledge to make inferences and build coherent representations of text" (Compton et al., 2014, p. 65). These authors advocate for the next generation of reading comprehension interventions to incorporate three instructional components: 1) the provision of background knowledge about the topic prior to reading, thus allowing "microworld" (i.e., passage-specific) knowledge building during reading, 2) clustering texts around a theme to build background knowledge, and 3) providing explicit instruction in inference making and the use of background knowledge to make text inferences (Compton et al., 2014; Compton, Miller, Gilbert, & Steacy, 2013). Some of these components have been used in practice with anecdotal success, but the disciplined manner suggested here for their implementation could lead to a potentially greater impact from reading comprehension instruction.

Background knowledge is a construct with many parallels to vocabulary knowledge, and vocabulary itself involves the naming and representation of concepts (Pearson, 2010). Reading comprehension is thought to depend on an array of both automatic and strategic processes, and for the skilled reader, many inferences are made automatically—the by-product of solid networks of knowledge structures that are easily accessed and facilitate inference making (Kintsch & Kintsch, 2005). Although Figures 2.1 and 2.2 offer somewhat different conceptualizations of reading development, in both, vocabulary knowledge (the lexicon in Perfetti's model) sits reliably next to general knowledge.

Existing work offers some indications as to how reading comprehension interventions might incorporate systematic instruction and implicit learning opportunities that target the building of cohesive and well-elaborated knowledge structures and vocabulary representations. Retrieval practice and the building of flexible knowledge about words are important foci in Wolf's RAVE-O Program that are realized through engaging instruction and playful activities with multiple-meaning words, morphological structures, and speeded games (Wolf et al., 2000; Wolf, Barzillai, Gottwald, Miller, Spencer, et al., 2009). Classroom and small-group discussions can be designed to establish, elaborate, use, and connect vocabulary and knowledge representations: the Collaborative Strategic Reading approach of Vaughn and colleagues (2011) is one example.

The Word Generation Programs of Snow and colleagues, through the Strategic Education Research Partnership (SERP), provide excellent demonstrations of evidence-based principles of effective vocabulary development and knowledge acquisition applied to comprehension instruction for youth with language impairments or limited English language experience (Snow, Lawrence, & White, 2009). Focusing on controversial topics to stimulate engagement (e.g., the pros and cons of drug legalization and animal testing; see http://wordgen.serpmedia.org), the program has demonstrated efficacy with native English-speaking and language-minority youth (Snow et al., 2009).

IMPLEMENTATION AND PSYCHOSOCIAL FACTORS: THE BROADER CONTEXT OF WHAT WORKS AND WHY

Implementation and psychosocial factors play a critical role in intervention outcomes; among the most important are motivation and the individual's perception of his or her self-efficacy as a learner—effects that are likely reciprocal. Struggling readers have complex social-cognitive histories that shape their experiences of intervention and their trajectories of reading growth. We have found that interventions that target maladaptive attributions and motivational profiles *during* reading intervention result in improved reading outcomes *and* positive changes in motivation in adolescents with RD (Frijters, Lovett, Sevcik, Donohue, & Morris, in preparation). In fact, the interweaving of motivational and attributional retraining, cognitive strategy instruction, and reading remediation characterizes both our Phonological and Strategy Training (PHAST) and our Empower™ Reading intervention programs at every developmental level, from the early grades (Lovett, Lacerenza, Steinbach, & De Palma, 2014; Morris et al., 2012) through middle school (Frijters, Lovett, Sevcik, & Morris, 2013; Lovett et al., 2008) and into high school (Lovett et al., 2012).

With motivational issues in mind, our reading interventions are deliberately designed for group implementation; we have witnessed over three decades the positive impact for struggling readers of dealing with literacy learning problems in the company of peers. The impact of the instructional group is substantial, but this is an aspect of findings that is not often interpreted in intervention research reports. Instructional group effects point to the need to study how group factors can mobilize change for learners and how teacher–student and student–student affiliations contribute to outcomes. Small-group versus one-to-one intervention ratios are not a major factor in predicting response, and there is no empirical basis for advocating one-to-one intervention over small-group instruction in most cases (Vaughn, Swanson, & Solis, 2013). Neglecting instructional group dynamics, teacher–student and student–student affiliation, and the ways in which group factors can mobilize change for struggling learners limits our understanding of the contexts that facilitate the best outcomes for learners.

Systems-level factors have received some research attention in the past two decades and include teacher preparation and support, instructional coaching, teacher quality, and systemic investment in literacy intervention (Moats & Foorman, 2003). In 2008, Faggella-Luby and Deshler issued a challenge for researchers who wanted their findings to be of use to practitioners:

> Researchers must carefully describe the types of learners for whom an intervention is designed, the context within which it should be taught, the content of the intervention, the pedagogy used to teach it, the fidelity required to achieve the desired outcomes, and the intensity required. (2008, p. 71)

These authors and others have reviewed the available evidence on reading comprehension instruction for adolescents with RD and identified four areas for future research efforts: 1) the need to be informed and guided by theory and theoretical models—an issue of urgent need already identified in the present chapter; 2) implementation needs, specifically a better understanding of instructional dosage requirements (i.e., length of sessions, frequency, and overall duration); 3) development of a continuum of service delivery beyond the early grades and into high school; and 4) the factors needed for successful scale-up of evidence-based interventions (Denton et al., 2010; Klinger, Boardman, & McMaster, 2013).

INTERVENTION RESEARCH PROGRAM: AN OVERVIEW

My own experience spans more than 30 years of conducting RD intervention research, work undertaken both with my group at the Hospital for Sick Children in Toronto on our own and in collaboration with our longstanding colleagues Robin Morris and Maryanne Wolf. Reference is made subsequently to a range of studies conducted with struggling readers of different ages.

In early studies comparing phonological skill-based and strategy-training approaches to the remediation of severe RD, we found that faster learning and better reading outcomes were attained when a multidimensional intervention approach was adopted—one combining direct and dialogue-based instruction, explicitly teaching children different levels of subsyllabic segmentation and training them in the acquisition, use, and monitoring of multiple decoding strategies (Lovett et al., 2000). Strategy instruction, attributional retraining, and the promotion of a flexible approach to word identification and text reading appear to be critical for achieving generalization and maintenance of intervention gains; these findings led to the development of the PHAST Reading Program (Lovett, Lacerenza, & Borden, 2000; since revised and updated to be part of the Empower™ Reading intervention programs).

The PHAST Reading Program was first evaluated as one part of a large multisite intervention study conducted with Robin Morris and Maryanne Wolf. The results indicated that the PHAST Reading Program and the RAVE-O Program (paired with a phonological program, Phonological Analysis and Blending/Direct Instruction [PHAB/DI]) were associated with improved reading outcomes for second and third graders with RD who varied in socioeconomic status and in intellectual functioning (Morris et al., 2012). The two multiple-component programs were associated with rates of learning and achievement gains of equivalent magnitude for children from disadvantaged circumstances and for those with IQs estimated to fall between 70 and 89 (i.e., below the average range), a demonstration of the generalizability of these results (Morris et al., 2012). Both the PHAST Reading Program and the RAVE-O Program, combined with the PHAB/DI Program, were confirmed to yield significant benefits immediately following intervention, and gains were maintained even a full year after instruction ended.

In a subsequent study, we evaluated 125 hours of small-group intervention for children with RD receiving remediation in first, second, or third grade. Robust intervention effects were obtained with effect sizes (Cohen's *d*) ranging from 0.63 to 2.08 and a median effect size of 0.89. Developmental and individual differences in response to intervention were examined, and questions about the timing of early intense intervention were considered. We learned that although earlier intervention results in greater "normalization" of reading scores, developmental effects are qualified by differential rates of growth among control participants of different ages. In addition, intervention effects on some reading outcomes are qualified by specific grade × treatment and individual differences × treatment interactions, with particular implications for lower IQ and lower vocabulary children with RD (Lovett, Frijters, Wolf, et al., in preparation). As always, interpretation of reading comprehension outcomes is dependent on the quality and adequacy of measurement, and varying rates of normalization were observed on different measures, highlighting the problems identified earlier in measuring reading comprehension and intervention-related comprehension growth.

We also evaluated intensive middle school intervention in a study of adolescents with RD, who were in Grades 6–8. Robust, positive intervention results were revealed, with effect sizes ranging from 0.34 to 0.94 on different reading outcomes. Few overall differences emerged between a PHAST intervention that combined decoding strategy training and reading comprehension instruction and one that combined decoding strategy training and multilevel fluency training (i.e., PHAST-comprehension versus PHAST-fluency focus). The program variations were developed to explore different paths to improved comprehension in adolescents with poor decoding and RD. Individual differences were examined to assess predictors of responsiveness. For adolescents with RD who have lower IQ scores or vocabulary knowledge or are more impaired in reading at entry, the type of intervention appeared to be particularly critical (Frijters et al., 2013; Lovett, Frijters, Steinbach, Sevcik, & Morris, in preparation).

We have also reported results from an intervention study with struggling high school readers (Lovett et al., 2012). Significant gains on standardized word attack, word reading, and passage comprehension tests were demonstrated following only one semester of PHAST PACES (predicting, activating prior knowledge, clarifying, evaluating through questioning, and summarizing), a reading intervention designed specifically for struggling readers in high school. Following the decoding and comprehension strategy instruction, significant gains in letter-sound knowledge and multisyllabic word reading were revealed for those involved with PHAST PACES relative to control group participants, confirming that adolescence is not too late to address basic decoding gaps. Effect sizes ranged from 0.35 to 1.21 with a median effect size of 0.63 across measures. At follow-up, passage comprehension showed continued growth among PHAST PACES graduates a full year after intervention had ended.

CONCLUSION

There is much to celebrate in the advances made in both research and practice regarding thoughtful well-designed interventions for RD and in the encouraging evidence that continued intervention for older, struggling readers can yield positive outcomes. The need for multifaceted reading interventions, with a firmer grounding in theory and evidence and more attention paid to instructional needs beyond the literacy-related ones, is obvious. As demands for literacy competencies in youth have escalated, so too have demands to design instructional programs that address the long-term learning, motivational, social-cognitive, and self-efficacy needs of today's struggling readers. These remarks end with a wish list. After more than 30 years of intervention research experience, from my perspective, the following areas require focused attention and renewed effort. We need the following:

1. Better-developed, comprehensive, cohesive road maps for providing intervention and instruction that allow for the construction of an efficient reading system. This would involve scaled remedial scaffolding for learners' different needs.
2. More evidence on how to build deeper comprehension skills in learners with vocabulary weaknesses and limited language experiences.
3. More implementation studies on reading intervention that will allow an understanding of the social and motivational contexts that promote optimal reading growth for different struggling readers.
4. An ability to harness new technologies to engage struggling readers in much more reading practice, thus providing some of the reading experience needed to achieve reading fluency and deeper comprehension.
5. Useful assessment instruments both to measure growth in vocabulary knowledge—in terms of breadth, depth, and connections—and to measure online and offline comprehension processes and their growth over time.

REFERENCES

Al Otaiba, S., Connor, C.M., Folsom, J.S., Greulich, L., Wanzek, J., Schatschneider, C., & Wagner, R.K. (2014). To wait in Tier 1 or intervene immediately: A randomized experiment examining first grade response to intervention (RTI) in reading. *Exceptional Children, 81*(11), 11–27. http://ecx.sagepub.com/content/81/1/11

Barth, A.E., Tolar, T.D., Fletcher, J.M., & Francis, D. (2014). The effects of student and text characteristics on the oral reading fluency of middle-grade students. *Journal of Educational Psychology, 106*(1), 162–180.

Baumann, J.F., Kame'enui, E.J., & Ash, G.E. (2003). Research on vocabulary instruction. In J. Flood, J.M. Jensen, D. Lapp, & J.R. Squire (Eds.), *Handbook of research in teaching the English language arts* (2nd ed., pp. 752–785). New York, NY: MacMillan.

Bruck, M. (1992). Persistence of dyslexics' phonological awareness deficits. *Developmental Psychology, 28*(5), 874–886.

Cain, K. (2013). Reading comprehension difficulties in struggling readers. In B. Miller, L.E. Cutting, & P. McCardle (Eds.), *Unraveling reading comprehension: Behavioral, neurobiological, and genetic components* (pp. 54–65). Baltimore, MD: Paul H. Brookes Publishing Co.

Chi, M.T.H., Glaser, R., & Farr, M.J. (1988). *The nature of expertise.* Mahwah, NJ: Lawrence Erlbaum Associates.

Committee on Learning Sciences: Foundations and Applications to Adolescent and Adult Literacy. (2012). *Improving adult literacy: Options for practice and research.* Washington, DC: National Academies Press.

Compton, D.L., Miller, A.C., Elleman, A.M., & Steacy, L.M. (2014). Have we forsaken reading theory in the name of "quick fix" interventions for children with reading disability? *Scientific Studies of Reading, 18*(1), 55–73.

Compton, D.L., Miller, A.C., Gilbert, J.K., & Steacy, L.M. (2013). What can be learned about the reading comprehension of poor readers through the use of advanced statistical modeling techniques? In B. Miller, L.E. Cutting, & P. McCardle (Eds.), *Unraveling reading comprehension: Behavioral, neurobiological, and genetic components* (pp. 135–147). Baltimore, MD: Paul H. Brookes Publishing Co.

Dehaene, S. (2009). *Reading in the brain: The new science of how we read.* New York, NY: Penguin.

Denton, C.A., Fletcher, J.M., Taylor, W.P., Barth, A.E., & Vaughn, S. (2014). An experimental evaluation of guided reading and explicit interventions for primary-grade students at-risk for reading difficulties. *Journal of Research on Educational Effectiveness, 7*(3), 268–293. doi: 10.1080/19345747.2014.906010

Denton, C.A., Nimon, K., Mathes, P.G., Swanson, E.A., Kethley, C., Kutz, T.B., & Shih, M. (2010). Effectiveness of a supplemental early reading intervention scaled up in multiple schools. *Exceptional Children, 76*(4), 394–416.

Ehri, L.C. (2005). Learning to read words: Theory, findings, and issues. *Scientific Studies of Reading, 9*(2), 167–188.

Ehri, L.C. (2014). Orthographic mapping in the acquisition of sight word reading, spelling memory, and vocabulary learning. *Scientific Studies of Reading, 18*(1), 5–21.

Ericsson, K.A., & Simon, H.A. (1993). *Protocol analysis: Verbal reports as data* (Rev. ed.). Cambridge, MA: MIT Press.

Faggella-Luby, M.N., & Deshler, D., D. (2008). Reading comprehension in adolescents with LD. *Learning Disabilities Research and Practice, 23*(2), 70–78.

Ferstl, E.C., Neumann, J., Bogler, C., & von Cramon, D.Y. (2008). The extended language network: A meta-analysis of neuroimaging studies on text comprehension. *Human Brain Mapping, 29*(5), 581–593.

Folia, V., Uddén, J., Forkstam, C., Ingvar, M., Hagoort, P., & Petersson, K.M. (2008). Implicit learning and dyslexia. *Annals of the New York Academy of Sciences, 1145,* 132–150.

Foorman, B.R., Francis, D.J., Fletcher, J.M., Schatschneider, C., & Mehta, P. (1998). The role of instruction in learning to read: Preventing reading failure in at-risk children. *Journal of Educational Psychology, 90*(1), 37–55.

Frijters, J.C., Lovett, M.W., Sevcik, R.A., Donohue, D., & Morris, R. (in preparation). Change in attributions for reading success and failure associated with intensive reading intervention.

Frijters, J.C., Lovett, M.W., Sevcik, R.A., & Morris, R.D. (2013). Four methods of identifying change in the context of a multiple component reading intervention for struggling middle school readers. *Reading and Writing: An Interdisciplinary Journal, 26*(4), 539–563.

Graesser, A.C., & McNamara, D.S. (2011). Computational analyses of multilevel discourse comprehension. *Topics in Cognitive Science, 3*(2), 371–398.

Graesser, A.C., Singer, M., & Trabasso, T. (1994). Constructing inferences during narrative text comprehension. *Psychological Review, 101*(3), 371–395.

Helder, A., van den Broek, P., Van Leijenhorst, L., & Beker, K. (2013). Sources of comprehension problems during reading. In B. Miller, L.E. Cutting, & P. McCardle (Eds.), *Unraveling reading comprehension: Behavioral, neurobiological, and genetic components* (pp. 43–53). Baltimore, MD: Paul H. Brookes Publishing Co.

Kamil, M.L. (2004). The current state of quantitative research. *Reading Research Quarterly, 39*(1), 100–108.

Keenan, J.M., Betjemann, R.S., & Olson, R.K. (2008). Reading comprehension tests vary in the skills they assess. *Scientific Studies of Reading, 12*(3), 281–300.

Kintsch, W. (1998). *Comprehension: A paradigm for cognition.* Cambridge, UK: Cambridge University Press.

Kintsch, W., & Kintsch, E. (2005). Comprehension. In S.G. Paris & S.A. Stahl (Eds.), *Children's reading comprehension and assessment* (pp. 71–92). Mahwah, NJ: Lawrence Erlbaum Associates.

Klinger, J., Boardman, A., & McMaster, K. (2013). What does it take to scale up and sustain evidence-based practices? *Exceptional Children, 79*(2), 195–211.

Landi, N., Frost, S.J., Mencl, W.E., Sandak, R., & Pugh, K.R. (2013). Neurobiological bases of reading comprehension. *Reading and Writing, 29*(2), 145–167.

Linderholm, T., & van den Broek, P. (2002). The effects of reading purpose and working memory capacity on the processing of expository text. *Journal of Educational Psychology, 94*(4), 778–784.

Lovett, M.W., De Palma, M., Frijters, J.C., Steinbach, K.A., Temple, M., Benson, N.J., & Lacerenza, L. (2008). Interventions for reading difficulties: A comparison of response to intervention by ELL and EFL struggling readers. *Journal of Learning Disabilities, 41*(4), 333–352.

Lovett, M.W., Frijters, J.C., Steinbach, K.A., Sevcik, R.A., & Morris, R.D. (in preparation). Paths to improving reading fluency and reading comprehension in adolescents with reading disabilities: Program effects and individual differences in reading outcomes.

Lovett, M.W., Frijters, J.C., Wolf, M.A., Steinbach, K.A., Sevcik, R.A., & Morris, R.D. (in preparation). Early intervention for children at risk for reading disability: The impact of grade at intervention and individual differences on intervention outcomes.

Lovett, M.W., Lacerenza, L., & Borden, S.L. (2000). Putting struggling readers on the PHAST track: A program to integrate phonological and strategy-based remedial reading instruction and maximize outcomes. *Journal of Learning Disabilities, 33*(5), 458–476.

Lovett, M.W., Lacerenza, L., Borden, S.L., Frijters, J.C., Steinbach, K.A., & De Palma, M. (2000). Components of effective remediation for developmental reading disabilities: Combining phonological and strategy-based instruction to improve outcomes. *Journal of Educational Psychology, 92*(2), 263–283.

Lovett, M.W., Lacerenza, L., De Palma, M., & Frijters, J.C. (2012). Evaluating the efficacy of remediation for struggling readers in high school. *Journal of Learning Disabilities, 45*(2), 151–169.

Lovett, M.W., Lacerenza, L., Steinbach, K.A., & De Palma, M. (2014). Development and rollout of a research-based intervention program for children with reading disabilities. *Perspectives on Language and Literacy, 40,* 21–31. Baltimore, MD: IDA.

McMaster, K.L., van den Broek, P.V., Espin, C.A., White, M.J., Rapp, D.N., Kendeou, P., . . . Carlson, S. (2012). Making the right connections: Differential effects of reading intervention for subgroups of comprehenders. *Learning and Individual Differences, 22*(1), 100–111.

McNamara, D.S., & Kendeou, P. (2011). Translating advances in reading comprehension research to educational practice. *International Electronic Journal of Elementary Education, 4*(1), 33–46.

Miller, A.C., Davis, N., Gilbert, J.K., Cho, S.J., Toste, J.R., Street, J., & Cutting, L.E. (2014). Novel approaches to examine passage, student, and question effects on reading comprehension. *Learning Disabilities Research and Practice, 29*(1), 25–35.

Moats, L.C., & Foorman, B.R. (2003). Measuring teachers' content knowledge of language and reading. *Annals of Dyslexia, 53*(1), 23–45.

Morris, R.D., Lovett, M.W., Wolf, M.A., Sevcik, R.A., Steinbach, K.A., Frijters, J.C., & Shapiro, M. (2012). Multiple-component remediation for developmental reading disabilities: IQ, socioeconomic status, and race as factors in remedial outcome. *Journal of Learning Disabilities, 45*(2), 99–127.

Nagy, W.E. (2007). Metalinguistic awareness and the vocabulary-comprehension connection. In R.K. Wagner, A.E. Muse, & K.R. Tannenbaum (Eds.), *Vocabulary acquisition: Implications for reading comprehension* (pp. 52–77). New York, NY: Guilford Press.

Pearson, P.D. (2010, January). *Vocabulary: Words make a comeback in reading pedagogy.* Presentation at the University of California, Berkeley, Naperville, IL.

Perfetti, C.A. (2000). Comprehending written language: A blueprint of the reader. In C. Brown & P. Hagoort (Eds.), *The neurocognition of language* (pp. 167–208). Oxford, UK: Oxford University Press.

Perfetti, C.A. (2007). Reading ability: Lexical quality to comprehension. *Scientific Studies of Reading, 11*(4), 357–383.

Perfetti, C.A., & Frishkoff, G.A. (2008). The neural bases of text and discourse processing. In B. Stemmer & H. Whitaker (Eds.), *Handbook of the neuroscience of language* (pp. 165–174). London, UK: Elsevier.

Perfetti, C.A., & Stafura, J. (2014). Word knowledge in a theory of reading comprehension. *Scientific Studies of Reading, 18*(1), 22–37.

Rapp, D.N., van den Broek, P., McMaster, K., Kendeou, P., & Espin, C. (2007). Higher-order comprehension processes in struggling readers. *Scientific Studies of Reading, 11*(4), 289–312.

Rayner, K., Chace, K.H., Slattery, T., & Ashby, J. (2006). Eye movements as reflections of comprehension processes in reading. *Scientific Studies of Reading, 10*(3), 241–255.

Rosenthal, J., & Ehri, L.C. (2008). The mnemonic value of orthography for vocabulary learning. *Journal of Educational Psychology, 100*(1), 175–191.

Scarborough, H.S. (2001). Connecting early language and literacy to later reading (dis)abilities: Evidence, theory, and practice. In S. Neuman & D. Dickinson (Eds.), *Handbook for research in early literacy* (pp. 97–110). New York, NY: Guilford Press.

Shaywitz, S.E., Fletcher, J.M., Holahan, J.M., Schneider, A.E., Marchione, K.E., Stuebing, K.K., . . . Shaywitz, B.A. (1999). Persistence of dyslexia: The Connecticut longitudinal study at adolescence. *Pediatrics, 104*(6), 1351–1359.

Snow, C.E. (2002). *Reading for understanding: Toward an R&D program in reading comprehension.* Santa Monica, CA: RAND Reading Study Group.

Snow, C.E., Lawrence, J.F., & White, C. (2009). Generating knowledge of academic language among urban middle school students. *Journal of Research on Educational Effectiveness, 2*(4), 325–344.

van den Broek, P. (2010). Using texts in science education. *Science, 328*(5977), 453–456.

van den Broek, P., Helder, A., & Van Leijenhorst, L. (2013). Sensitivity to structural centrality. In M.A. Britt, S.R. Goldman, & J.-F. Rouet (Eds.), *Reading: From words to multiple texts* (pp. 132–146). New York, NY: Routledge.

van den Broek, P., Lorch, E.P., & Thurlow, R. (1996). Children's and adults' memory for television stories: The role of causal factors, story-grammar categories, and hierarchical level. *Child Development, 67*(6), 3010–3028.

van den Broek, P., Young, M., Tzeng, Y., & Linderholm, T. (1999). The landscape model of reading: Inferences and the on-line construction of a memory representation. In H. van Oostendorp & S.R. Goldman (Eds.), *The construction of mental representations during reading* (pp. 71–98). Mahwah, NJ: Lawrence Erlbaum Associates.

Vaughn, S., & Fletcher, J.M. (2010). Thoughts on rethinking response to intervention with secondary students. *School Psychology Review, 39*(2), 296–299.

Vaughn, S., Klingner, J.K., Swanson, E.A., Boardman, A.G., Roberts, G., Mohammed, S.S., & Stillman-Spisak, S.J. (2011). Efficacy of collaborative strategic reading with middle school students. *American Educational Research Journal, 48*(4), 938–964.

Vaughn, S., Swanson, E.A., & Solis, M. (2013). Reading comprehension for adolescents with significant reading problems. In H.L. Swanson, K.R. Harris, & S. Graham (Eds.), *Handbook of learning disabilities* (2nd ed., pp. 375–387). New York, NY: Guilford Press.

Vaughn, S., Wexler, J., Leroux, A., Roberts, G., Denton, C.A., Barth, A., & Fletcher, J.M. (2012). Effects of intensive reading intervention for eighth-grade students with persistently inadequate response to intervention. *Journal of Learning Disabilities, 45*(6), 515–525.

Vaughn, S., Wexler, J., Roberts, G., Barth, A., Cirino, P.T., Romain, M.A., . . . Denton, C.A. (2011). Effects of individualized and standardized interventions on middle school students with reading disabilities. *Exceptional Children, 77*(4), 391–407.

Vicari, S., Finzi, A., Menghini, D., Marotta, L., Baldi, S., & Petrosini, L. (2005). Do children with developmental dyslexia have an implicit learning deficit? *Journal of Neurology, Neurosurgery & Psychiatry, 76*(10), 1392–1397.

Wanzek, J., & Vaughn, S. (2007). Research-based implications from extensive early reading interventions. *School Psychology Review, 36*(4), 541–561.

Wanzek, J., & Vaughn, S. (2008). Response to varying amounts of time in reading intervention for students with low response to intervention. *Journal of Learning Disabilities, 41*(2), 126–142.

Wolf, M. (2007). *Proust and the squid: The story and science of the reading brain.* New York, NY: Harper.

Wolf, M., Barzillai, M., Gottwald, S., Miller, L., Spencer, K., Norton, E., Lovett, M., & Morris, R. (2009). The RAVE-O intervention: Connecting neuroscience to the classroom. *Mind, Brain, and Education, 3*(2), 84–94.

Wolf, M., Miller, L., & Donnelly, K. (2000). Retrieval, automaticity, vocabulary elaboration, orthography (RAVE-O): A comprehensive, fluency-based reading intervention program. *Journal of Learning Disabilities, 33*(4), 375–386.

II

Basic Considerations for Reading Intervention

Behavior, Neurobiology, and Genetics

3

The Growth of Self-Regulation in the Transition to School

Frederick J. Morrison

Over the last two decades, a sizable body of research has documented the importance of the early childhood years as a critical foundation not only for successful transition to school but for success in elementary school and beyond (for a review, see Morrison, Bachman, & Connor, 2005). Furthermore, a complex set of factors in the child, family, school, and larger sociocultural context, both independently and in interaction, shape the growth of early literacy skills over that crucial time period. Attention has increasingly focused on a set of skills, called self-regulation (also executive function or effortful control), that has been shown to uniquely impact children's academic growth across the school years as well as their success in adult life (Moffit et al., 2011). This chapter will focus on four central questions about self-regulation, a skill set essential to learning. First, how have scientists conceptualized self-regulation? As this chapter will show, there are multiple perspectives on the definition of self-regulation as well as on its measurement. Second, what are the extent and nature of individual differences in self-regulation during the transition to school? Third, what is the unique impact of self-regulation on early literacy and later academic achievement? Finally, can self-regulation be modified by appropriate environmental stimulation, especially in the school environment?

CONCEPTUALIZATIONS OF SELF-REGULATION

On a common-sense level, self-regulation refers to one's ability to control his or her thoughts, emotions, and behaviors in the service of achieving goals or otherwise acting appropriately. On a theoretical level, self-regulation has been conceptualized as a complex skill, comprising three fundamental components:

attention control and/or flexibility, working memory, and response inhibition. Understandably, this skill set has been the object of much attention from scientists across a broad range of disciplines. Developmental scientists have focused on the growth of executive functioning from infancy to early adulthood (Welsh, 2001). Along with education researchers, they have sought to understand the interplay between the maturational and environmental factors that shape the development of executive skills; the role of variability in children's self-control, which emerges even before children start school; and the impact of this interplay on American children's poor academic achievement (Duckworth & Seligman, 2006; Matthews, Ponitz, & Morrison, 2009). From a different perspective, neuroscientists have noted distinct differences between brain areas subserving basic cognitive functions (e.g., attention, memory) and those involved in integrating and coordinating attentional and memory skills, and they have more recently explored differences in the neural bases of these skills in children as compared with adults (Welsh, Friedman, & Spieker, 2006). In addition, cognitive scientists have been analyzing the underlying components of executive functioning (e.g., attentional control/flexibility, working memory, response inhibition, planning) to ascertain their structure and function (Zelazo, Craik, & Booth, 2004).

Until recently, each discipline has been working in relative isolation from the others; consequently, what the skill is called and how it is measured varies widely. The dominant labels are *executive function* (from neurophysiological and cognitive researchers), *self-regulation* (from educational and developmental scientists), and *effortful control* (from early childhood researchers). Likewise, the methods of measurement range from highly constrained tasks with simple responses (needed for neurophysiological and cognitive studies) to more child-friendly tasks that mimic real-world behaviors to more global assessments derived from parent and teacher rating scales. The proliferation of constructs and tasks has created a kind of "conceptual clutter" and "measurement mayhem" as these disciplines begin to integrate their efforts (Morrison & Grammer, in press). At present, it is not clear whether these varying terms refer to distinctly different underlying skills or simply reflect the same construct across disciplines. Likewise, little is known about how the various measures of self-regulation relate to each other or to real-world behaviors (Morrison & Grammer, in press).

EARLY VARIABILITY

As for many skills important for academic success, variability in children's self-regulation emerges early and can remain stable throughout their school years and beyond without explicit intervention (Morrison, Ponitz, & McClelland, 2010). For example, in one study (Matthews et al., 2009), a sample of middle-class children was tested at the beginning of kindergarten on two measures: a direct assessment of their response inhibition and a teacher report of their overall self-regulation in the classroom. The direct assessment utilized the head-toes-knees-shoulders (HTKS) task, in which children, after following a researcher's example of touching their head, toes, and so forth on command, are then instructed to do the opposite—for example, touch their toes when told to touch their head. The Child Behavior Rating Scale (Bronson, Tivnan, & Seppanen, 1995) was given to teachers, one subscale of which was utilized as a measure of self-regulation.

Children's performance on HTKS is illustrated in Figure 3.1. Depicted is a frequency distribution of the number of participants at various levels of accuracy on the task. Several things should be noted. First, there is substantial variability in levels of accuracy across children, confirming that individual differences in self-regulation emerge before the start of formal schooling. Second, girls not only outperform boys overall, but their scores are more closely bunched together. Finally, and perhaps most significantly, the lowest performing children are almost exclusively boys.

Results from the teacher ratings are depicted in Figure 3.2. The findings mirror closely those of HTKS. Substantial variability in children's self-regulation ratings in the fall semester of kindergarten emerged across teachers. Girls were rated higher than boys and more similar to each other. Strikingly, teachers also rated a small but notable cluster of boys, appearing at the bottom of the distribution, as lowest in self-regulation.

The pattern of results from this study and others (see Morrison et al., 2010, for review) corroborate recent findings that meaningful variation in important academic skills, including self-regulation, emerge early in development. Furthermore, gender differences in self-regulation favoring girls are evident in early childhood and may have long-term implications for later development. In that regard, it is noteworthy that a major underlying reason for the gender gap may reside with a group of particularly low-performing boys. Keep in mind

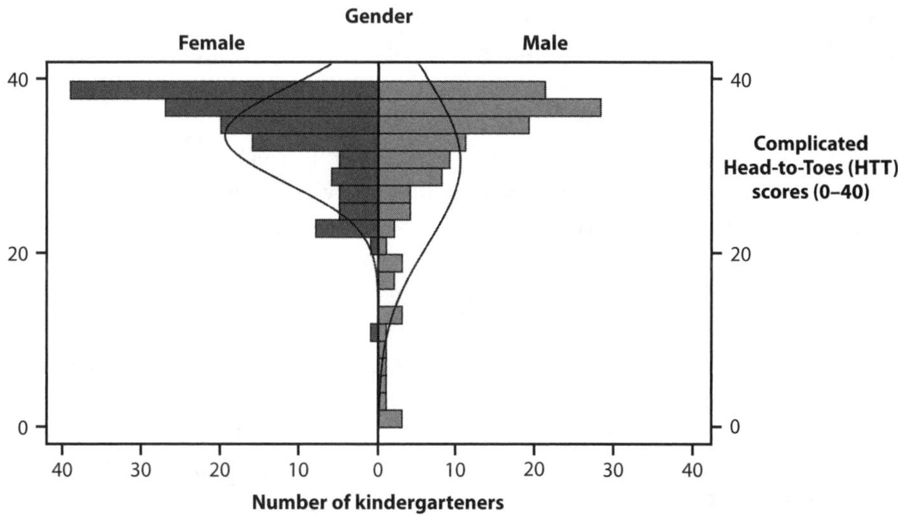

Figure 3.1. Frequency distribution of performance on the head-toes-knees-shoulders task for males and females in the fall semester of kindergarten. (*Key:* HTT, head to toes.) (From Matthews, J.S., Ponitz, C., & Morrison, F.J. [2009]. Early gender differences in self-regulation and academic achievement. *Journal of Educational Psychology, 101*, 689–704. Washington, DC: American Psychological Association; reprinted by permission.)

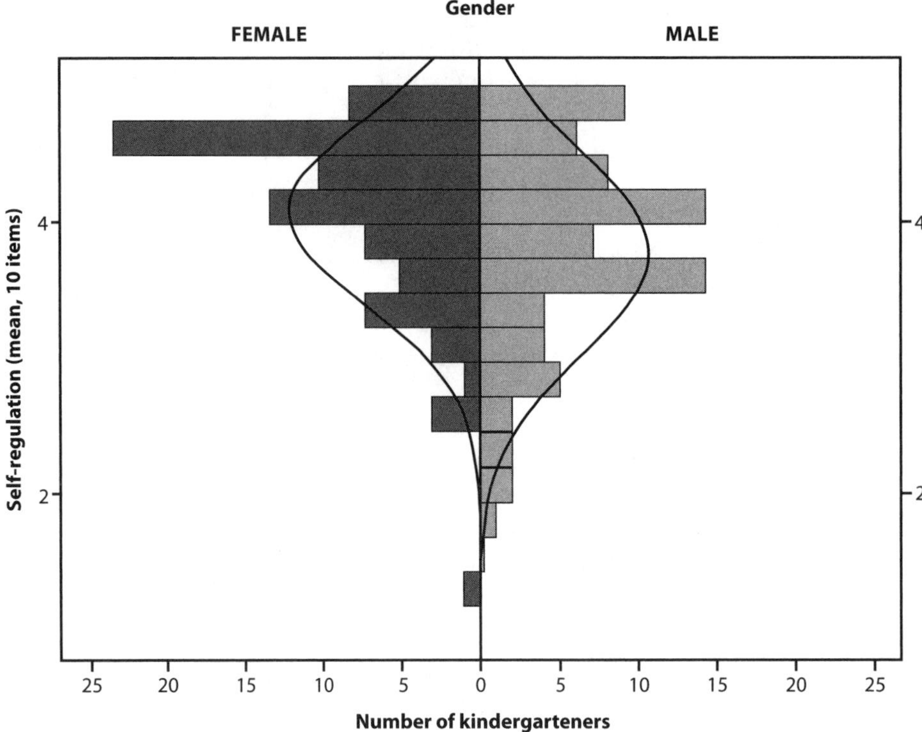

Figure 3.2. Frequency distribution of teacher ratings of self-regulation for males and females in the fall semester of kindergarten. (From Matthews, J.S., Ponitz, C., & Morrison, F.J. [2009]. Early gender differences in self-regulation and academic achievement. *Journal of Educational Psychology, 101*, 689–704. Washington, DC: American Psychological Association; reprinted by permission.)

that the children in this study all came from middle-class backgrounds. Including more disadvantaged children would arguably have increased the proportion of low-performing boys. Finally, the close agreement between the direct measure and teacher ratings not only reinforces the overall patterns found but also reveals that teacher ratings are not inherently biased.

A recent partial replication of this study was undertaken by Bell-Weixler et al. (in review). In that study, two groups of closely matched Chinese and American kindergartners were tested on a direct measure of attention control, taken from the Woodcock-Johnson III (WJIII) Complete Battery (Woodcock, McGrew, & Mather, 2001). The findings for the U.S. children (shown in Figure 3.3) replicated those of Matthews et al. (2009), revealing significant variability across children in attention control skills and most strikingly, the identical pattern of gender differences favoring girls, including the appearance of almost exclusively boys performing at the lowest level. In contrast, although Chinese children did show substantial variability in the fall semester of kindergarten, no evidence of a gender gap was apparent (see Figure 3.4). This latter finding has been replicated by Wanless et al. (2011), who found gender differences in self-regulation in a U.S. sample but no differences in samples of children from Beijing, Taiwan, and South Korea.

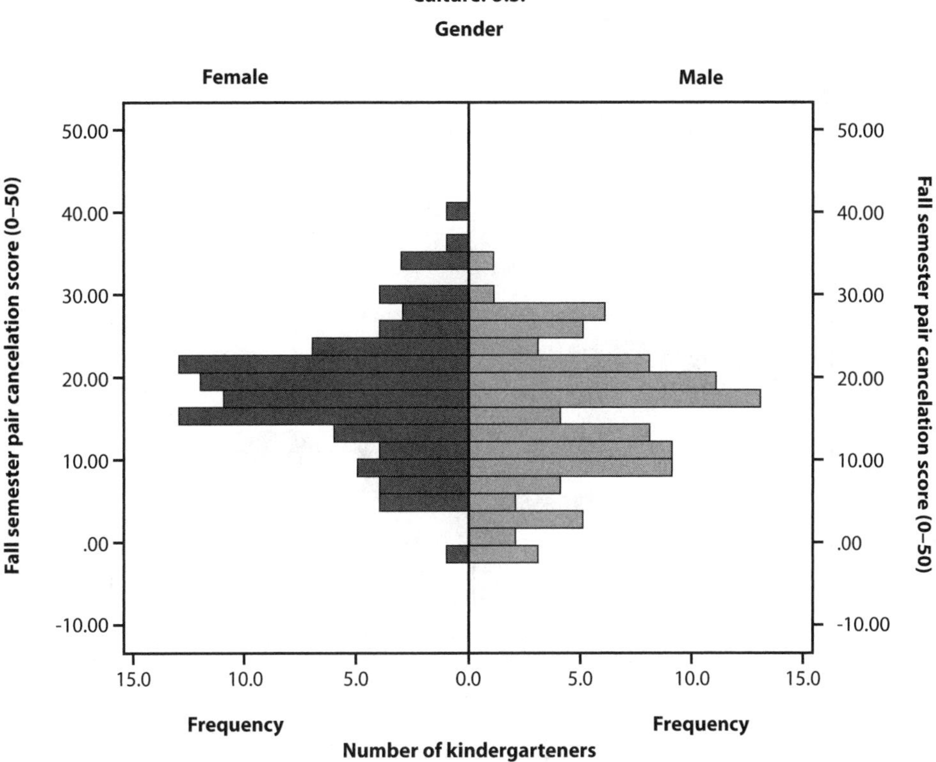

Figure 3.3. Frequency distribution of performance on pair cancelation for U.S. males and females in the fall semester of kindergarten.

PREDICTION OF ACADEMIC ACHIEVEMENT

Beyond the discovery of early variability in self-regulation, accumulating evidence has demonstrated that differences in self-regulation uniquely predict children's emergent literacy skills (Blair & Razza, 2007) as well as their academic achievement throughout elementary school (McClelland, Acock, & Morrison, 2006; see Morrison et al., 2010 for review). Some, but not all, studies have shown that self-regulation predicts performance on math tasks more strongly than on reading tasks. This difference may stem, in part, from the fact that elementary math tasks, especially word problems, engage working memory to a greater degree than beginning reading tasks that focus primarily on single-word decoding.

The sweep of self-regulation is not limited to academic domains or to childhood. A recent study by Moffit et al. (2011) found that a measure of self-control in early childhood predicted patterns of health, wealth, and criminality in adults decades later. Clearly, growth of self-regulation across one's life-span exerts broad influence on many domains that underlie life success.

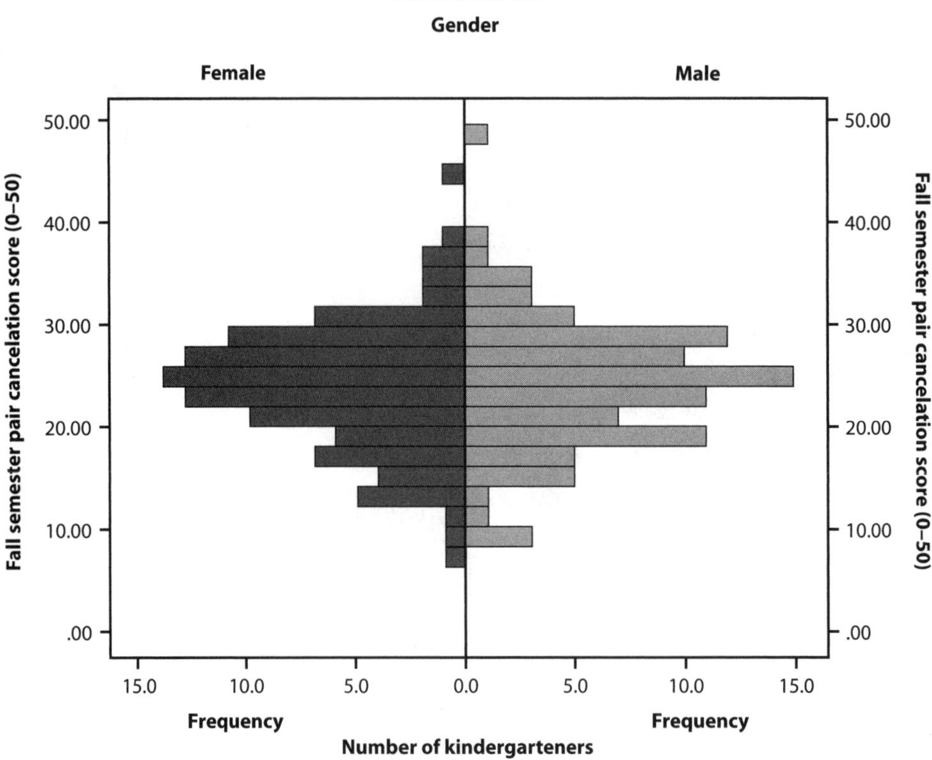

Figure 3.4. Frequency distribution of performance on pair cancelation for Chinese males and females in the fall semester of kindergarten.

SCHOOLING INFLUENCES ON GROWTH OF SELF-REGULATION

For that reason, in part, scientists have been interested in the degree to which self-regulation can be modified. Until recently, self-regulation has been viewed as primarily under maturational control. Schools themselves seem to have adopted this view implicitly because there has been little effort to explicitly teach self-regulation skills in the classroom as part of the school curriculum. This is changing gradually as schools recognize the potential power of self-regulation in enhancing children's life chances inside and outside of the classroom.

Does schooling have a direct effect on the growth of self-regulation? Clearly self-regulation improves as children progress through school, and spurts in self-regulation can be seen from preschool to early elementary school. But these changes could all be driven by maturation. We have tried to address the causal connection between experiences in school and the growth of self-regulation using a natural experiment called *school cutoff* (Morrison et al., 2005). Each year, school districts admit students to kindergarten based on a birthdate cutoff that varies widely across localities. Children born prior to the cutoff date are permitted to enter kindergarten, whereas those born after the date must wait until the following year. By selecting children who cluster very closely around the school cutoff date (by one or two months), we can effectively equate children according to age and compare their growth by using a pre-post design. Differences in growth rates throughout the school year can be legitimately attributed to schooling-related experiences, though the exact nature of the experience responsible for the differences needs to be separately determined.

Across a number of studies, evidence has accumulated that schooling does in fact have a significant impact on a variety of cognitive, language, and academic skills during the school transition period (Morrison et al., 2005). Furthermore, research has documented that the extent and timing of the schooling effect varies across different skills (Christian, Morrison, Frazier, & Massetti, 2000). For example, simple word decoding is influenced both during kindergarten and first grade, but phonemic awareness is uniquely impacted by schooling experiences much more strongly in first grade. In contrast, receptive vocabulary, surprisingly, is minimally changed by schooling experiences alone.

In an effort to examine schooling effects on the growth of self-regulation skills, Burrage et al. (2008) employed the school cutoff method to compare groups of younger kindergarten children and older prekindergarten (pre-K) children on two self-regulation skills: working memory (from the WJIII battery) and response inhibition (HTKS). They also included a measure of word decoding from the WJIII as a manipulation check. The groups did not differ on background variables.

The results for word decoding (in Figure 3.5) revealed that kindergarten children outperformed pre-K children at fall testing, revealing a schooling

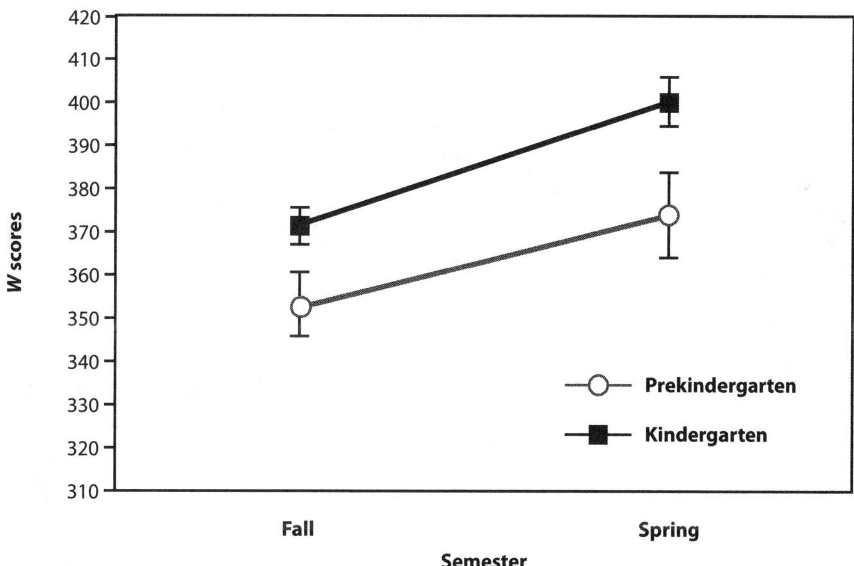

Figure 3.5. Performance on word decoding (*W* scores from the Woodcock-Johnson III) of young kindergartners and old pre-K children in the fall and spring semesters of the school year. (From Burrage, M., Ponitz, C.C., Shah, P., McCready, E.M., Sims, B.C., & Morrison, F.J. [2008]. A natural experiment of schooling effects on executive functions. *Child Neuropsychology, 14,* 510–524. Washington, DC: American Psychological Association; reprinted by permission.)

effect during the pre-K year. In addition, a separate effect of the kindergarten year was revealed in a significant group difference favoring kindergarten children in the spring semester.

The outcomes for working memory (Figure 3.6) demonstrated a strong schooling effect during the pre-K year (compare fall and spring semesters), and although there was not an independent schooling effect during the kindergarten year, the kindergarten children maintained their advantage on the spring semester posttest.

The findings for response inhibition were quite different (see Figure 3.7). Here, there is a marginally significant effect of schooling during the pre-K year but no evidence of a schooling effect in kindergarten and, in reality, minimal evidence of growth in response inhibition throughout the 2-year period.

Taken together, the results for self-regulation mirror those for the other skills studied. Schooling experiences do produce significant, unique growth in working memory skills in preschool, but not in response inhibition, in these data. Although the reasons for these different patterns remain to be studied, some evidence points to the potential role of classroom experiences. Specifically, Cameron, Connor, and Morrison (2005), using direct classroom observations in first grade, examined teachers' use of orienting and organizing language in directing children's actions. This variable, labeled *orient–organize* consisted of instructions to the children about what would be happening in the next half-hour, day, or week and what the children needed to do to prepare. They found that the more time teachers spent in orient–organize instructions, the less time children took to make transitions between activities. Furthermore,

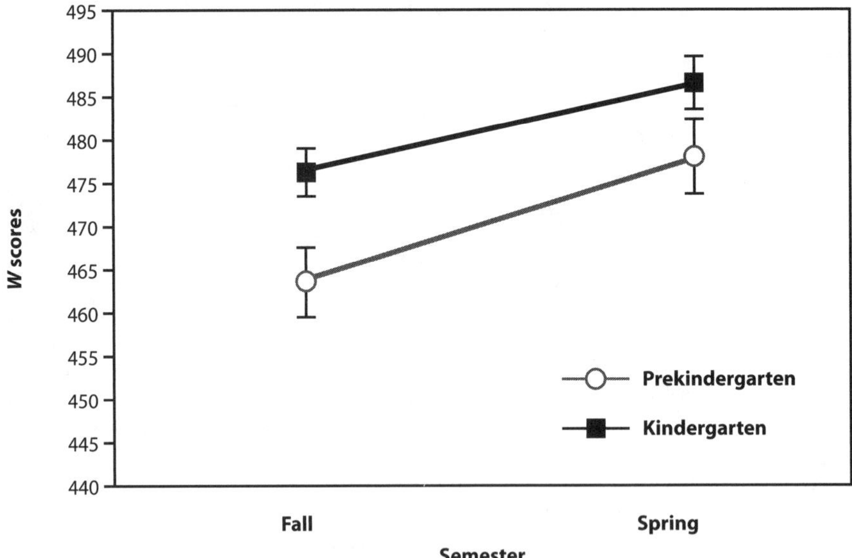

Figure 3.6. Performance on working memory (W scores on the Woodcock-Johnson III) of young kindergartners and old pre-K children in the fall and spring semesters of the school year. (From Burrage, M., Ponitz, C.C., Shah, P., McCready, E.M., Sims, B.C., & Morrison, F.J. [2008]. A natural experiment of schooling effects on executive functions. *Child Neuropsychology, 14,* 510–524. Washington, DC: American Psychological Association; reprinted by permission.)

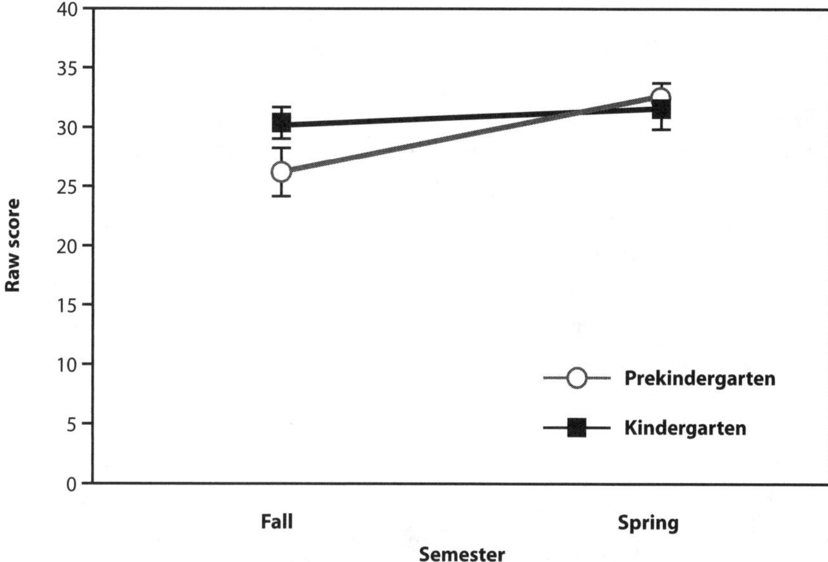

Figure 3.7. Performance on response inhibition of young kindergartners and old pre-K children in the fall and spring semesters of the school year. (From Burrage, M., Ponitz, C.C., Shah, P., McCready, E.M., Sims, B.C., & Morrison, F.J. [2008]. A natural experiment of schooling effects on executive functions. *Child Neuropsychology, 14*, 510–524. Washington, DC: American Psychological Association; reprinted by permission.)

teachers who spent more time in orient–organize instructions in the fall semester had children who spent more time managing their own activities in the spring semester. More recently, Connor and colleagues (Connor et al., 2010) found that classroom management that included clear expectations for self-regulated learning led to greater gains in self-regulation for students with initially weaker skills.

Finally, recent efforts have extended our work to include a neurobiological perspective. We (Grammer, Carrasco, Gehring, & Morrison, in press) developed a Go/No-go task that involved recording event-related potentials that could be used with children as young as 4 years of age. Furthermore, the study was conducted entirely within the children's school, utilizing portable electroencepholographic equipment. We found clear, measurable neurophysiological changes in self-regulation in children 4–7 years of age that predicted academic achievement. This study paves the way for a more comprehensive approach to understanding growth of self-regulation, combining brain and behavior perspectives.

CONCLUSION

Like many other skills underlying success in school and later life, individual differences in self-regulation emerge early in development before children enter formal schooling. Of particular concern is a subset of males who comprise the lower end of the distribution of self-regulation skills and who may be at risk for poor developmental outcomes. Mounting evidence documents the strong, unique effect of self-regulation on success in school and in later life. Despite these strong associations, self-regulation has been shown to be malleable during early development, raising the hope that appropriately timed interventions could improve the self-regulation skills of children at increased risk for poor academic and psychological outcomes. In fact, in the past 5 years, some promising interventions have been developed and evaluated. For example, one program called "Tools of the Mind" utilizes common classroom activities (shared book reading, pretend play activities) to focus children's attention on waiting one's turn and paying attention to another's reading efforts. The success of these interventions (see Diamond & Lee, 2011; Jacob, Jones, & Morrison, in review, for examples) will spawn new research on how self-regulation develops and when and how it can be modified to help children grow.

REFERENCES

Bell Weixler, L., Li, S., & Morrison, F.J. (in review) The Chinese-US gap in executive functioning: Associations with socioeconomic status, gender, and preschool attendance.

Blair, C., & Razza, R. (2007). Relating effortful control, executive function, and false belief understanding to emerging math and literacy ability in kindergarten. *Child Development, 78,* 647–663.

Burrage, M., Ponitz, C.C., Shah, P., McCready, E.M., Sims, B.C., & Morrison, F.J. (2008). A natural experiment of schooling effects on executive functions. *Child Neuropsychology, 14,* 510–524.

Bronson, M.B., Tivnan, T., & Seppanen, P.S. (1995). Relations between teacher and classroom activity variables and the classroom behaviors of preschool children in Chapter 1 funded programs. *Journal of Applied Developmental Psychology, 16,* 253–282.

Cameron, C.E., Connor, C.M., & Morrison, F.J. (2005). Effects of variation in teacher organization on classroom function. *Journal of School Psychology, 43,* 61–85.

Christian, K., Morrison, F.J., Frazier, J.A., & Massetti, G. (2000). Specificity in the nature and timing of cognitive growth in kindergarten and first grade. *Journal of Cognition and Development, 1,* 429–448. doi:10.1207/S15327647JCD0104_04

Connor, C.M., Ponitz, C.E.C., Phillips, B., Travis, Q.M., Day, S.G., & Morrison, F.J. (2010). First graders' literacy and self-regulation gains: The effect of individualizing instruction. *Journal of School Psychology, 48,* 433–455.

Diamond, A., & Lee, K. (2011). Interventions shown to aid executive function development in children 4–12 years old. *Science, 333*(6045), 959–964. doi:10.1126/science.1204529

Duckworth, A., & Seligman, M.P. (2006). Self-discipline gives girls the edge: Gender in self-discipline, grades, and achievement test scores. *Journal of Educational Psychology, 98,* 198–208. doi:10.1037/0022-0663.98.1.198

Grammer, J.K., Carrasco, M., Gehring, W.G., & Morrison, F.J. (in press) Age-related changes in error processing in young children. *Journal of Developmental Cognitive Neuroscience.*

Jacobs, R., Jones, S., & Morrison, F.J. (in review) Evaluating the impact of a self-regulation intervention (SECURe) on growth of self-regulation and academic achievement.

Matthews, J.S., Ponitz, C., & Morrison, F.J. (2009). Early gender differences in self-regulation and academic achievement. *Journal of Educational Psychology, 101,* 689–704. doi:10.1037/a0014240

McClelland, M.M., Acock, A.C., & Morrison, F.J. (2006). The impact of kindergarten learning-related skills on academic trajectories at the end of elementary school. *Early Childhood Research Quarterly, 21,* 471–490.

Moffitt, T.E., Arseneault, L., Belsky, D., Dickson, N., Hancox, R.J., Harrington, H., . . . Caspi, A. (2011). A gradient of childhood self-control predicts health, wealth, and public safety. *Proceedings of the National Academy of Sciences, USA, 108,* 2693–2698. doi:10.1073/pnas.1010076108

Morrison, F.J., & Grammer, J.K. (in press) Conceptual clutter and measurement mayhem: Proposals for cross disciplinary integration in conceptualizing and measuring executive function. In J. Griffin, P. McCardle, & L. Freund. (Eds., Forthcoming), *Research directions in preschool executive functions: Integrating measurement, neurodevelopment and translational research.* Washington, DC: American Psychological Association.

Morrison, F.J., Bachman, H.J., & Connor, C.M. (2005). *Improving literacy in America: Guidelines from research.* New Haven, CT: Yale University Press.

Morrison, F.J., Ponitz, C.C., & McClelland, M.M. (2010). Self-regulation and academic achievement in the transition to school. In S. Calkins & M. Bell (Eds.), *Child development at the intersection of emotion and cognition* (pp. 203–224). Washington, DC: American Psychological Association.

Wanless, S.B., McClelland, M.M., Lan, X., Son, S.-H., Cameron, C.E., Morrison, F.J., Chen, F.-M., . . . Sung, M. (2013). Gender differences in behavioral regulation in four societies: The U.S., Taiwan, South Korea, and China. *Early Childhood Research Quarterly, 28,* 621–633. doi:10.1016/j.ecresq.2013.04.002.

Welsh, M.C. (2001). The prefrontal cortex and the development of executive functions. In A. Kalverboer & A. Gramsbergen (Eds.), *Handbook of brain and behaviour development* (pp. 767–789). Amsterdam, The Netherlands: Wolters-Kluwer Co.

Welsh, M.C., Friedman, S.L., & Spieker, S.J. (2006). Executive functions in developing children: Current conceptualizations and questions for the future. In K. McCartney & D. Phillips (Eds.), *Blackwell handbook of early childhood development* (pp. 167–187). Malden, MA: Blackwell.

Woodcock, R.W., McGrew, K.S., & Mather, N. (2001). *Woodcock-Johnson-III tests of achievement.* Itasca, IL: Riverside.

Zelazo, P., Craik, F.M., & Booth, L. (2004). Executive function across the life span. *Acta Psychologica, 115,* 167–183.

4

Innovative Data Summary Measures Provide Novel Insights on Reading Performance

Christopher W. Bartlett, Andrew Yates, Judy F. Flax, and Linda M. Brzustowicz[1]

Investigation of reading comprehension has successfully enumerated the basic components of the framework (including single-word reading and listening comprehension) and defined the major sources of interactions among those components. The next level of inquiry is to understand those interactions, but the relationships at the next level are more subtle and generally of smaller effect sizes, which hampers the development of a unified reading comprehension theory. Although researchers are constantly incorporating new statistical tools and concepts into their research, such as hierarchical linear modeling (Raudenbush & Bryk, 2002) and quantile regression (Koenker, 2005), these new methods all rely on the same assumption: Variables relate to each other primarily through straight lines (i.e., the linear model assumption). Though intuitive and often effective, this model misses or underestimates the effect of nonlinear relationships. Proper quantification of nonlinear relationships increases power for statistical inference; we therefore explore one type of nonlinear model in the context of reading comprehension.

After discussing the basics of the statistical approach, we present a series of motivating, real data examples to show the new associations between reading and language that can be found and discuss the implications of those associations. These data relate to reading comprehension using the Simple View of Reading (Gough & Tunmer, 1986), which incorporates listening comprehension and word decoding as the two major contributors to reading comprehension as

1. We thank the families for participating in this research, Carol McDonald Connor for suggesting quantile regression as a method to further understand threshold correlations, and funding from the New Jersey Autism Center of Excellence.

a construct. We present data on those two components and use novel methods to further understand their relationship. Finally, we discuss the use of quantile regression, which more readers may be familiar with, and compare and contrast the use of that tool with other methods.

Please note that throughout this chapter, we assume that the reader is an informed consumer of basic statistics and understands the concepts of mean, variance, correlation, and regression. No statistical theory is required to gain an informed outlook on modern statistical methods. Statistically savvy readers should refer to the references for a more formal discussion of the mathematical details.

DISTANCE CORRELATION IS SENSITIVE TO NONLINEAR DEPENDENCE

The traditional correlation metric for quantitative measures of reading is the Pearson product–moment correlation (Pearson's *r;* Pearson, 1896), which measures the degree of linear dependence between pairs of variables. As if to highlight the importance of the best-fit line in data analysis, scatterplots are often shown with both the regression line and the value of Pearson's *r.* Pearson's *r* ranges from –1 to 1, in which negative or positive numbers imply a straight-line relation that is negative or positive, respectively, and in which 0 implies no linear relation. The distinction of the term *linear* here is important: Pearson's *r* does *not* necessarily assess independence. When Pearson's $r = 0$, the data are inconsistent with a linear relation, but no further conclusions can be made. Therefore, an assessment of independence requires a different tool not based on linearity.

Distance Correlation as a Measure of General Dependence

Recently, several novel methods have been developed to assess the relation between two quantitative variables. These include distance correlation (*dCor;* Székely et al., 2007; Székely & Rizzo, 2009) and maximal information coefficient (MIC; Reshef et al., 2011). We focus on *dCor,* which has a strong statistical foundation and an analytically and computationally tractable formula and has been shown to be robust in many different contexts (Yates et al., 2014).

Although Pearson's *r* is calculated using variability relative to the mean of each variable, *dCor* is calculated using all possible pairwise distances in the data. Rather than thinking of *dCor* as a measure of the aggregation of points around a line, *dCor* can be thought of as assessing the deviation of data from a random configuration. Using this math, Pearson's *r* is a special case of the more general *dCor* formula (Székely & Rizzo, 2009), and *dCor* is roughly equal to r^2 in the Gaussian, linear case. Thus the application of *dCor* is methodologically consistent with past work based on Pearson's *r.*

Classifying the Types of Nonlinear Relations

Pearson's *r*'s linearity limitation makes it easy to interpret ($r = 0$ means no correlation, $r > 0$ means some degree of positive correlation, and $r < 0$ means some degree of negative correlation). When assessing relations quantified by *dCor,* an additional classification step can be helpful for interpreting the many new relations that may be detected. Of particular interest are naturally the straight-line relations (Figure 4.1A & B) but also what here we call *threshold relations* (Figure 4.1C–F), in which two variables have a minimal relation until a certain value in one variable is reached (e.g., Figure 4.1C). (As used here, the term *threshold relation* refers to the appearance of the association observed in data and does not necessarily imply the existence of an underlying biological threshold.) Considered from an alternative point of view, this type of relation is characterized by an insufficiency of data in one imaginary quadrant of the scatterplot. The process of classifying observed dependencies is discussed elsewhere (Yates et al., 2014) and is based on assessing how many data are in each quadrant, although depending on the research topic and the nature of the data being processed, other types of relations could be classified, too. As in Figure 4.1, superimposed glyphs can be used as shorthand to display the various relations and highlight the form of the relation detected by *dCor.*

READING COMPREHENSION EXAMPLES

Here we present a series of real data analyses to highlight what threshold relations look like in real behavioral data commonly used in studies of reading and to discuss the implications of threshold relations in reading research. We are interested in reading comprehension and have used the simple-view-of-reading

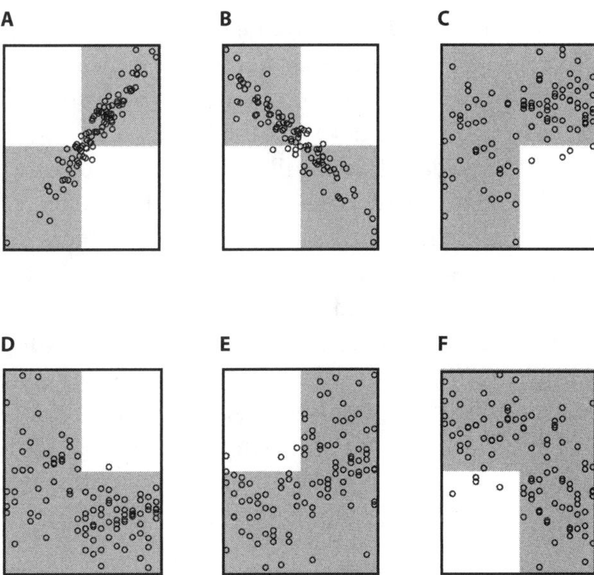

Figure 4.1. Six types of relations between variables. Each dataset was simulated using a random number generator in R® that was constrained to fit the familiar linear correlations (A & B) or one of the four types of threshold models (C–F).

model (Gough & Tunmer, 1986) described earlier as our framework. Specifically, we plot oral language from the Clinical Evaluation of Language Fundamentals, Fourth Edition (CELF-4; Semel, Wiig, & Secord, 2003; Wiig, Secord, & Semel, 2004) versus decoding assessed by the Word Identification subtest from the Woodcock Reading Mastery Test–Revised–Normative Update (Woodcock, 1997). Together, these two processes (oral language use and decoding) make substantial and independent contributions to reading comprehension, and we wished to explore this relation in greater detail. To assess this relation, we calculated *dCor* in the freely available R® statistical software (R Core Team, 2014) using a library from one of the authors (described in Yates et al., 2014; Glyph SPLOM, https://github.com/andrewdyates/gsplom.rpackage); *dCor* is not yet commonly implemented in commercial statistical packages.

Participants

The example dataset is from the New Jersey Language–Autism Genetic Study (NJLAGS), described in greater detail elsewhere (Bartlett et al., 2012, 2014). Briefly, 54 families were enrolled in the study after being ascertained for having both at least one family member with a specific language impairment (defined by a CELF-4 core score that is less than 85 and a nonverbal IQ that is greater than 85 and excluding autism or other neurological conditions that can explain language difficulties) and at least one separate family member meeting criteria for autistic disorder (who may or may not have also had language impairment) using the *Diagnostic and Statistical Manual of Mental Disorders, Fourth Edition* (*DSM-IV*; American Psychiatric Association, 2000), the Autism Diagnostic Observation Schedule (ADOS; Lord et al., 1989), and the Autism Diagnostic Interview–Revised (ADI-R; Lord, Rutter, & Le Couteur, 1994) diagnostic criteria. This study focused on finding molecular genetic modifiers of language ability in the general population and those factors unique to autism. There were 345 individuals with these phenotypes distributed within the families, including parents, siblings, and any additional family members who were willing to participate, including, in some cases, cousins and grandparents. All participants provided informed consent in a process approved by Rutgers University.

The test battery included a variety of language, reading, and cognitive measures, and included in this study were 1) age-appropriate versions of the CELF-4 (Semel et al., 2003; Wiig et al., 2004), 2) single-word reading (Word Identification subtest) from the Woodcock Reading Mastery Test–Revised–Normative Update (Woodcock, 1997), and 3) nonword repetition from the Comprehensive Test of Phonological Processing (CTOPP; Wagner, Torgesen, & Rashotte, 1999). These measures assess oral language, word decoding, phonological short-term memory, and three domains related to reading comprehension and general language ability.

In the course of assessing the properties of the NJLAGS families, we considered hyperlexia. Within the autism literature, this typically refers to an extreme phenotype in which decoding skills are far stronger than comprehension and most often far stronger than oral language ability in general. Of note, hyperlexic children are considered rare, though formal epidemiology has not been rigorously assessed. We began by examining whether anyone within the NJLAGS could be considered hyperlexic, positing that the prevalence of persons with hyperlexia could be enriched in our sample given that every family in the study has at least one person diagnosed with autism. However, upon examination of the scatterplot (Figure 4.2A), it is clear that not only does the NJLAGS lack anyone who could be considered hyperlexic, who would appear in the lower right-hand corner of the scatterplot, but there is also a conspicuous absence of data in that quadrant.

Single-Word Reading and Oral Language

Although single-word reading and oral language are linearly correlated, the data resemble that of Figure 4.1C, which is statistically quantified by calculating *dCor* = 0.29 ($P < .001$) and classified using the glyph assignment procedure of Yates and colleagues (2014). As we have often observed with threshold relations, Pearson's r is also significant ($r = 0.48$, $P < .001$). However, the linear correlation is at least partially driven by the absence of data in the lower right quadrant (i.e., the threshold relationship). Statistical interpretation of a threshold relation that is varied by *dCor* is straightforward. As seen in Figure 4.2A, single-word reading does not show a strong correlation if we are only examining the left side of the plot. However, single-word reading values near or greater than the population mean of 100 are associated with higher CELF-4 core scores. Hence the relation between single-word reading and oral language is greater for above-average readers than for below-average readers.

Placing a threshold relation into the larger context of reading research requires nuances, and we interpret the result in terms of reading providing *support* and *compensation*. Reading may provide support for gaining oral language mastery later in life, whereas language ability may act as a vehicle to develop compensation strategies for difficulties in mastering decoding skills. The observed decoupling of oral language and decoding at lower values of decoding ability indicates that high language ability is not sufficient to compensate for difficulties in decoding. Phrased differently, because there does not appear to be an excess of students who experience both language and reading difficulties, it may be that decoding difficulty can be due to reasons other than language impairments. Therefore a simple way to frame these findings is that there are many ways to have difficulties with reading but fewer ways to be above the population mean in language ability, and reading is an important component of that ability. The upper-right quadrant in Figure 4.2A shows a high degree of association between oral language and decoding, making hyperlexic people quite rare. This suggests that single-word reading is a (surrogate) marker for mastering language, probably because reading can provide support to language mastery such that good readers, regardless of individual differences in language, may learn language better than below-average readers. It is

A

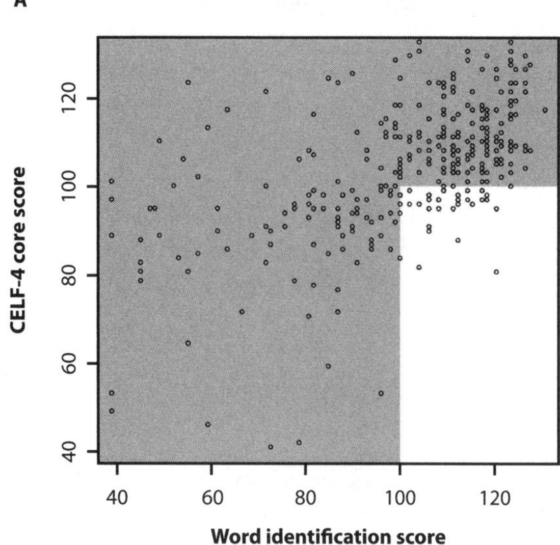

B

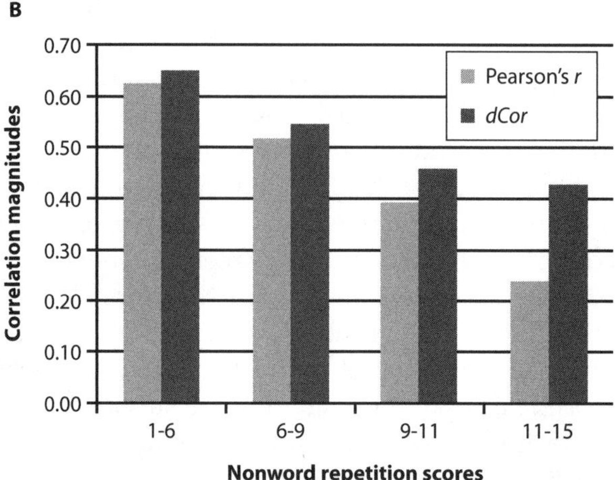

Figure 4.2. Components of reading comprehension show a threshold relation. A) In the New Jersey Language–Autism Genetic Study dataset, single-word reading fails to predict oral language below the population mean of 100 (uncorrelated in this range). However, above-average single-word reading strongly predicts near or above-average language ability; note the largely empty lower right quadrant (white space) where poor comprehenders with above-average reading would appear. The threshold for this relationship appears to be near the population mean of single-word reading. B) The strength of the threshold effect is moderated by nonword repetition performance. With increasing nonword repetition scores (x-axis categories), the linear dependence from Pearson's *r* drops off much faster than *dCor* (correlation magnitudes on y-axis). This indicates a nonlinear association with nonword repetition on the reading comprehension threshold effect. (*Key: dCor,* distance correlation; CELF-4, Clinical Evaluation of Language Fundamentals, Fourth Edition.)

possible that without the invention of reading, there would be more language-impaired people, though it is equally possible that people with good reading ability are naturally more resistant to language difficulties as a benefit of some other factor that is correlated with both oral language and single-word reading in that group.

At present, this discussion is firmly rooted in speculation. To understand if support and compensation are the correct constructs for interpreting these data, longitudinal datasets are needed. This would enable quantifying the changes in language growth as moderated by reading. Although early conversational language has been examined in the Western Reserve Reading Project's longitudinal twin cohort (DeThorne, Petrill, Schatschneider, & Cutting, 2010), the children were too young to exhibit more than 2 years of reading growth, and this question was not explicitly examined. For the data studied therein, however, the group with a history of poor expressive language showed a correlation between the mean length of expressive language utterance in early childhood and single-word reading, whereas children without an early expressive impairment did not. This may indicate, in those data, an underlying threshold relationship between reading and language that should be explored.

Nonword Repetition and the Simple View of Reading

The goal of the NJLAGS is to find behavioral and genetic biomarkers for structural language development, particularly with regard to autism (Bartlett et al., 2014). Nonword repetition, often recognized as a measure of phonological short-term memory, has shown to be a marker for structural language impairments in specific language impairment and autism; it has been suggested that the mechanism for poor performance differs between the two disorders (Whitehouse, Barry, & Bishop, 2008).

In the previous section, we explored the relation between the oral language and decoding data in Figure 4.2A. Now we consider Figure 4.2B to tie nonword repetition into the relation between oral language and decoding. For below-average scores in nonword repetition (CTOPP nonword repetition has a mean of 10 and a standard deviation of 3), the correlation between oral language and decoding is quite high. In contrast with the lack of correlation at low levels of decoding in Figure 4.2A, incorporating nonword repetition identifies the subset of individuals with deficits in both oral language and single-word reading, as 55% of the participants in this subset are doubly impaired. This induces the strong correlation observed with both Pearson's r and *dCor* (Figure 4.2B).

At the other extreme of nonword repetition, consisting of only participants with above-average performance, the linear Pearson's r correlation is much attenuated at only a third of the value seen in the below-average group. In this case, 75% of the participants are above average in both oral language and decoding; the linear correlation fails to detect a relation due to the restriction of range phenomena, whereby strong correlations when viewing the whole range of values are diminished when only examining a narrow range of one variable. However, *dCor* continues to quantify a strong relationship between oral language and decoding in this group of participants with high nonword repetition performance and does so across the range of nonword repetition subgroups. High scores on nonword repetition are clearly associated with high scores in both oral language and decoding. The use of *dCor* for inference is a more sensitive tool for correctly detecting this detail.

The use of nonword repetition strengthens the relation between oral language and decoding, the two components of the Simple View of Reading. However, the use of linear modeling (i.e., regression) underestimates this association. In a stepwise linear regression, we found that nonword reading only accounted for an extra 2% of the variance in reading comprehension on top of the 18% of this variance accounted for by decoding. This occurred despite nonword repetition successfully separating out language-impaired poor readers from non-language-impaired poor readers and inducing a correlation of 0.6 in that group. This finding underscores the need for models that adequately capture associations, especially strong associations as noted here. We have not applied nonlinear regression to model the relation detected by *dCor,* although the results in Figure 4.2B indicate that additional research should assess which of the three highly correlated components (oral language, decoding, and nonword reading) may moderate or mediate the other(s).

QUANTILE REGRESSION AS AN ADJUNCT TO DISTANCE CORRELATION

Quantile regression is a form of regression developed largely independent of classical (i.e., least squares) regression (Koenker & Bassett, 1978). Rather than regressing along the mean of the y-axis variable relative to the x-axis variable, quantile regression uses the median (i.e., the 50th percentile) or any other specified quantile (i.e., percentile). There are two main advantages to quantile regression: robustness to outliers and insight gained by examining regression from a range of quantiles. Robustness to outliers follows directly from use of the median instead of the mean; the mean (as used in classical linear regression) does not have this robustness. Analysis from a family of quantile regressions will be discussed in the example data associated with Figure 4.3.

Quantile regression has made greater inroads into mainstream behavioral research than *dCor* (e.g., Logan et al., 2011; see a more general discussion in Petscher & Logan, 2014). As many researchers are comfortable using and interpreting results from quantile regression, we present a discussion about how quantile regression could be used to detect threshold relationships and why it is not ideal for this purpose. Quantile regression does, however, provide additional insight by estimating the value of the threshold under some circumstances.

To illustrate the insight that a series of quantile regressions can offer, here we compute quantile regressions in R® (package version 5.05) with the *quantreg* library (http://CRAN.R-project.org/package=quantreg). (Note that quantile regression is available in commercial packages, such as SAS and Stata.) Datasets were simulated using a mixture of random, normally distributed numbers, in which up to the 75th percentile of the data came from a normal distribution with *M* = 0.25 and *SD* = 1.25 and the remaining 25 percentiles of the data came from a normal distribution with *M* = 1.25 and *SD* = 0.74. The advantage of simulated datasets is that these so-called Monte Carlo experiments have known properties (i.e., a known threshold relationship and a known threshold value) such that novel procedures can be evaluated against the known parameter values (i.e., the truth). Simulation procedures also allow us to assess sampling variability and statistical power.

Figure 4.3 shows a series of quantile regressions on one simulated dataset. Due to the nature of the simulation, the threshold relationship is readily apparent by visual inspection but still holds sufficient random noise to have some degree of ecological validity relative to real datasets. Scanning from left to right, after the 75th percentile, the threshold occurs and the lower right quadrant largely shows an absence of data. The threshold relationship is confirmed with an estimated *dCor* of 0.30 ($P < 2.2 \times 10^{-16}$). In Figure 4.3A, the series of quantile regressions is shown, with the median (50th percentile) regression line highlighted in a darker color (very similar to a classical regression line). The other lines, however, show an increasing y-intercept and decreasing slope, proceeding from the bottom of the plot upward. This fan-like pattern visually tracks with the pattern of data in the scatterplot. Hence quantile regression detects the threshold relationship.

Additional information is obtained when interpreting all of the slopes from the series of regression lines. Figure 4.3B plots the slopes of each line (y-axis) versus the percentile of the data in the quantile regression. Where the quantile regression slopes cross the average of all of the slopes, this point coincides with the simulated threshold. For reasonably sized datasets (*N* = 200 or greater), we observed that most simulated datasets yielded a threshold estimate close to the true value when the threshold was within the 40th–60th percentiles; with *N* = 400, the correct threshold is often inferred within the 20th–80th percentile range. Unfortunately, power dropped precipitously outside this range, with datasets greater than *N* = 10,000 still failing to estimate thresholds as far out as the 10th or 90th percentiles. We note that our proof-of-concept simulations are not a proper estimation procedure, nor is the concept of a point estimate for the threshold relationship statistically validated. Yet, as a heuristic for understanding the data, it appears sound and can be reasonably inferred under at least some circumstances. We will await further developments in estimating the threshold to assess power across the range of the quantiles for various sample sizes and magnitudes of *dCor.*

CONCLUSION

We have presented a correlation metric that is new to the field of reading research. This metric, known as distance correlation, or *dCor,* quantifies the dependence of two variables without assuming a linear relationship. We examined components

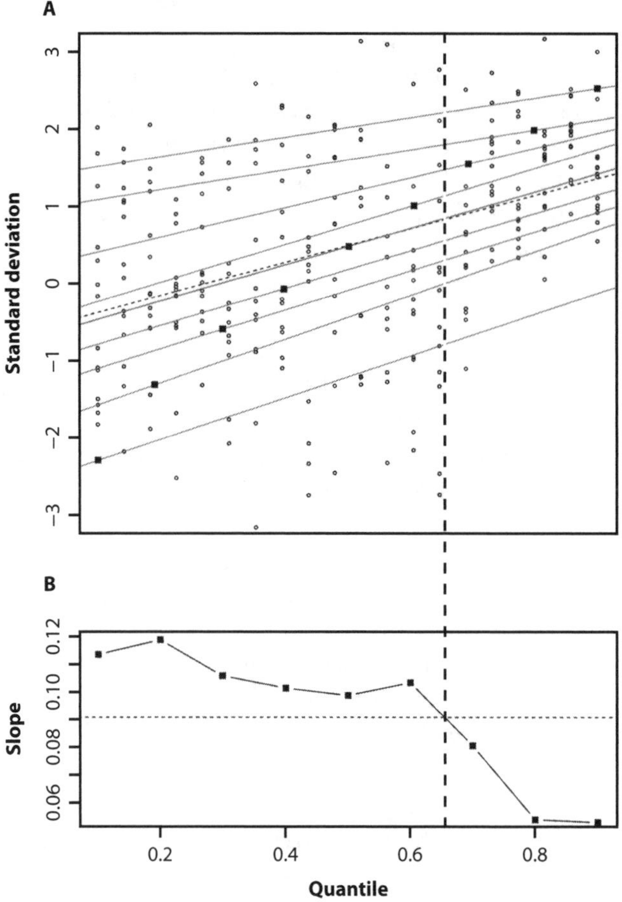

Figure 4.3. Quantile regression used to characterize simulated data exhibiting a threshold relationship between two variables. A) Simulated data with reduced variability in the largest quartile (right 25% of the data). Regressions by decile (gray lines) show increasing y-intercepts with larger values on the x-axis, indicating that the data are less linearly related toward the top of the scatterplot. B) As the intercepts increase, the slope of the regression lines decrease. Black dots on regression lines correspond to the ten data points in panel B. Where the slope of the quantile regression lines equal the average regression slope, the crossing over point is the threshold in the dataset (vertical dotted line).

of reading comprehension from the Simple View of Reading (i.e., comprehension built up from oral language and decoding) and showed that these two domains exhibit a linear correlation that is partially driven by an underlying threshold relationship, a term we introduced in this study. Specifically, below-average scores in decoding only weakly predict language, but above-average scores strongly predict above-average language. Additional studies, preferably using longitudinal cohorts, will be helpful in understanding the nature of this threshold relationship. Last, we showed that although quantile regression can detect threshold relationships, it does not quantify the strength of that relation nor does it provide the formal statistical test of independence available with *dCor.* We have, however, shown that under some circumstances, quantile regression can estimate the value of the threshold in which one variable makes a transition from being unrelated to related, though the simple estimation procedure presented here is not powerful for extreme thresholds. Overall, we conclude that nonlinear models provide a novel avenue for research into reading comprehension and that the relationship between oral language and decoding includes additional factors such as phonological short-term memory.

REFERENCES

American Psychiatric Association. (2000). *Diagnostic and statistical manual of mental disorders* (4th ed.). doi:10.1176/appi.books.9780890423349

Bartlett, C.W., Hou, L., Flax, J.F., Hare, A., Cheong, S.Y., Fermano, Z., . . . Brzustowicz, L.M. (2014). A genome scan for loci shared by autism spectrum disorder and language impairment. *American Journal of Psychiatry, 171*(1), 72–81. doi:10.1176/appi.ajp.2013.12081103

Bartlett, C.W., Flax, J.F., Fermano, Z., Hare, A., Hou, L., Petrill, S.A., . . . Brzustowicz, L.M. (2012). Gene × gene interaction in shared etiology of autism and specific language impairment. *Biological Psychiatry, 72,* 692–699. doi:10.1016/j.biopsych.2012.05.019

DeThorne, L.S., Petrill, S.A., Schatschneider, C., & Cutting, L. (2010). Conversational language use as a predictor of early reading development: Language history as a moderating variable. *Journal of Speech, Language, and Hearing Research, 53,* 209–223. doi:10.1044/1092-4388(2009/08-0060)

Gough, P.B., & Tunmer, W.E. (1986). Decoding, reading, and reading disability. *Remedial and Special Education, 7,* 6–10. doi:10.1177/074193258600700104

Koenker, R. (2005). *Quantile Regression* (No. 38). Cambridge University Press.

Koenker, R., & Bassett, G. (1978). Regression quantiles. *Econometrica, 46,* 33–50.

Logan, J.A.R., Petrill, S.A., Hart, S.A., Schatschneider, C., Thompson, L.A., Deater-Deckard, K., . . . Bartlett, C. (2011). Heritability across the distribution: An application of quantile regression. *Behavioral Genetics, 42,* 256–267. doi:10.1007/s10519-011-9497-7

Lord, C., Rutter, M., & Le Couteur, A. (1994). Autism diagnostic interview-revised: A revised version of a diagnostic interview for caregivers of individuals with possible pervasive developmental disorders. *Journal of Autism and Developmental Disorders, 24*(5), 659–685. doi:10.1007/BF02172145

Lord, C., Rutter, M., Goode. S., Heemsbergen, J., Jordan, H., Mawhood, L., & Schopler, E. (1989). Autism diagnostic observation schedule: A standardized observation of communicative and social behavior. *Journal of Autism and Developmental Disorders, 19*(2), 185–212. doi:10.1007/BF02211841

Pearson, K. (1896). Mathematical contributions to the theory of evolution. III. Regression, heredity and panmixia. *Philosophical Transactions of the Royal Society of London, 187,* 253–318.

Petscher, Y., & Logan, J.A.R. (2014). Quantile regression in the study of developmental sciences. *Child Development, 85,* 861–881. doi:10.1111/cdev.12190

R Core Team. (2014). *R: A language and environment for statistical computing.* Vienna, Austria: R Foundation for Statistical Computing. Retrieved from http://www.r-project.org

Raudenbush, S.W., & Bryk, A.S. (2002). *Hierarchical linear models: Applications and data analysis methods* (Vol. 1). Thousand Oaks, CA: Sage Publications.

Reshef, D.N., Reshef, Y.A., Finucane, H.K., Grossman, S.R., McVean, G., Turnbaugh, P.J., . . . & Sabeti, P.C. (2011). Detecting novel associations in large data sets. *Science, 334*(6062), 1518–1524.

Semel, E., Wiig, E., & Secord, W. (2003). *Clinical evaluation of language fundamentals* (4th ed.). Toronto: The Psychological Corporation.

Székely, G.J., & Rizzo, M.L. (2009). Brownian distance covariance. *The Annals of Applied Statistics, 3,* 1236–1265. doi:10.1214/09-AOAS312

Székely, G.J., Rizzo, M.L., & Bakirov, N.K. (2007). Measuring and testing dependence by correlation of distance. *Annals of Statistics, 35,* 2769–2794. doi:10.1214/009053607000000505

Yates, A., Webb, A., Sharpnack, M., Chamberlin, H., Huang, K., & Machiraju, R. (2014). Visualizing multidimensional data with glyph SPLOMs. *Computer Graphics Forum, 33,* 301–310. doi:10.1111/cgf.12386

Wagner, R., Torgesen, J., & Rashotte, C. (1999). *Comprehensive Test of Phonological Processing.* Austin, TX: PRO-ED.

Whitehouse, A.J.O., Barry, J.G., & Bishop, D.V.M. (2008). Further defining the language impairment of autism: Is there a specific language impairment subtype? *Journal of Communication Disorders, 41,* 319–336. doi:10.1016/j.jcomdis.2008.01.002

Wiig, E., Secord, W., & Semel, E. (2004). *Clinical Evaluation of Language Fundamentals—Preschool* (2nd ed.). Toronto: The Psychological Corporation.

Woodcock, R. (1997). *Woodcock Reading Mastery Tests revised/Normative Update.* Circle Pines, MN: American Guidance Service.

5

The Role of Rapid Automatized Naming in Reading Disruption

An Application of the Cusp Catastrophe

Georgios Sideridis, George K. Georgiou,
Panagiotis G. Simos, Angeliki Mouzaki, and Dimitrios Stamovlasis

A plethora of studies have established that rapid automatized naming (RAN) speed is a strong predictor of reading performance across languages (e.g., Lervåg & Hulme, 2009; Nag & Snowling, 2012; Protopapas, Altani, & Georgiou, 2013), ages (e.g., van den Bos, Zijlstra, & Spelberg, 2002), and reading ability levels (e.g., Cardoso-Martins & Pennington, 2004). Importantly, the predictive value of RAN persists even after controlling for other correlates of reading, such as letter knowledge (e.g., Kirby, Parrila, & Pfeiffer, 2003), phonological awareness (e.g., Manis, Doi, & Bhadha, 2000), and orthographic processing (e.g., Georgiou, Parrila, & Kirby, 2009). Researchers concur, however, on the lack of a clear understanding as to why RAN performance predicts reading performance (e.g., Norton & Wolf, 2012). In this chapter, we aim to shed some light on this question by examining the validity of a novel hypothesis, the *generic shutdown hypothesis,* using a new analytic approach (i.e., the cusp catastrophe model; Thom, 1975).

The relationship between RAN and reading was originally attributed to a common phonological processing element because they both rely on quick access to stored phonological information in long-term memory (e.g., Wagner & Torgesen, 1987). Several studies have established, however, that RAN accounts for variance in reading performance beyond the variance explained by direct measures of phonological processing (e.g., Kirby et al., 2003; Manis et al., 2000; Powell, Stainthorp, Stuart, Garwood, & Quinlan, 2007). Bowers and Wolf (1993) in turn proposed that if letter identification is laborious, letter representations in words may not be activated at rates sufficient to promote the development of adequate sensitivity to commonly occurring orthographic patterns. Recent studies, however, have provided contradictory results showing that RAN performance is not strongly related to measures of orthographic processing (e.g., Cutting & Denckla, 2001; Georgiou et al., 2009) and that children exhibiting slow naming speed may have unimpaired orthographic learning (Powell, Stainthorp, & Stuart, 2014).

A critical feature of RAN is that it involves a large number of component processes (i.e., attentional, perceptual, lexical, phonological, motor, and articulatory) and that efficient naming requires timely integration of information within and across these subprocesses (see Georgiou, 2010, for the object naming model and Wolf & Bowers, 1999, for the letter naming model). Slow RAN performance consequently may be caused by 1) a breakdown in any one specific subprocess, 2) a failure to integrate information across subprocesses, or 3) rate deficits either in a single subprocess or across multiple subprocesses (Wolf, Bowers, & Biddle, 2000). This componential property of RAN renders it suitable to assess specific predictions of the generic shutdown hypothesis. The need for an alternative hypothesis to account for the strong association between reading ability and RAN is underlined by contradictory results pertaining to the existing theoretical accounts mentioned in the previous paragraph.

According to the generic shutdown hypothesis, there may be additive and interactive effects of cognitive difficulties, negative affectivity, and dysfunctional motivational attributes on students' ability to self-regulate their reading behavior. The hypothesis implies a critical level of individual, reading-related cognitive ability below which the combination of cognitive, emotional, and motivational difficulties overwhelms students who already experience academic difficulties (evidenced in this study by poor reading comprehension). *Shutdown* is therefore viewed as a breakdown of the mechanism typically responsible for cognitive and emotional self-regulation. In this context, shutdown may occur if students attempt to allocate already insufficient cognitive resources to coping with the emotional concomitants of academic challenges and failures. This learned tendency pulls resources away from planning and execution of adaptive academic behaviors, such as the reading of relatively unfamiliar words and extracting meaning from text (Elias, 2004).

There are several reasons to believe that a generic shutdown may explain the detrimental effects of slow RAN performance on word reading. First, according to Wolf and colleagues (2000), if there are general timing deficits, RAN performance may represent, at once, both the combined effects of impaired lower level visual, auditory, perceptual, and/or motor processes and an additional source of further disruption in reading fluency. Thus disruption of the ability to process information within and across subprocesses (indexed by slow RAN performance) could lead to a snowball effect in which both reading fluency and comprehension are compromised. Second, there is evidence that RAN is related to motivational factors, such as task avoidance (e.g., Georgiou, Manolitsis, Nurmi, & Parrila, 2010) and task orientation (e.g., Lepola, Poskiparta, Laakkonen, & Niemi, 2005), thus fulfilling one of the premises of the generic shutdown hypothesis. Finally, in order to explain why RAN performance is related more strongly to reading in poor readers than in good readers, some researchers have argued that there might be a "threshold" level in RAN performance beyond which additional increases in naming speed do not lead to further gains in reading (e.g., Savage et al., 2005). This hypothesis predicts that there is a discontinuity in the impact of RAN scores on word-reading scores, which is more evident among students who struggle with reading than among those who do not. The presence of such a discontinuity, which could mark a critical level of cognitive capacity at the point in which the postulated shutdown takes place, is assessed here using the cusp catastrophe model.

THE PRESENT STUDY

Three hypotheses were examined concerning the relation between RAN and psychoemotional and between RAN and motivational status and their functional roles in reading. The first hypothesis states that emotional status and motivational attributes impact RAN performance so that the latter can be predicted by a linear combination of the former variables. The second hypothesis is that the well-established linear association between word-reading and pseudoword decoding does not hold across all levels of RAN performance but that a critical value exists, beyond which word-reading performance may drop dramatically in a nonlinear fashion. Hypothesis 2 was tested using a cusp catastrophe model with RAN as the bifurcation factor; we predicted that the hypothesized catastrophe effect would fit the data of students displaying poor reading-comprehension ability, who are therefore considered at risk for later school failure, although word reading may still be predicted linearly by basic reading skills (pseudoword decoding) among students who score above average on text comprehension. Finally, one salient prediction of the third hypothesis, termed the *generic shutdown hypothesis,* was that when psychoemotional and motivational variables are partialed out from RAN performance, the cusp model would no longer be supported (i.e., the residualized RAN term would relate only linearly to the outcome variable).

Method: Participants and Procedures

Children in Grades 2–4 were grouped by their reading-comprehension ability: a low ability group scoring at least 1 *SD* below the population mean ($N = 93$; 42 girls and 51 boys; mean age = 105.19 months, $SD = 11.07$) and a high ability group scoring at least 1 *SD* above the population mean ($N = 84$; 46 girls and 38 boys; mean age = 104.39, $SD = 10.84$). All participants were fluent speakers of Greek and had never been referred for psychoeducational or psychiatric evaluation. School selection involved a strict, stratified, randomized protocol representative of urban, rural, and semiurban schools. Following school randomization, students were also selected randomly from each classroom with the final participants representing only those who returned signed consent forms. Participants were individually tested in two 40-minute sessions by trained examiners on measures of reading, rapid automatized naming of digits, and psychoemotional variables (see Table 5.1).

Table 5.1. Outline of measures used in the present study

	Stimuli	Stopping rule	Scoring	A
TORP word reading	Forty 3–13-letter words	Six consecutive errors	0 (inaccurate pronunciation), 1 (phonologically correct but inaccurate stress), 2 (correct stress & phonology)	0.82
TORP pseudoword reading	Nineteen 4–8-letter pseudowords	—	—	0.90
TORP reading comprehension	Six 19–97-word passages; two to four 4-choice comprehension questions	Four consecutive errors	—	0.80
RAN	Fifty single digits (1, 2, 5, 7, 9) in five rows	—	Total time to name one page (seconds)	—
PANAS	Ten items for negative affect	Self-report	1–4	0.89
RCMAS	Twenty-eight items for physiological anxiety and worry	Self-report	0–2	0.64–0.72
CDI	Twenty-six items	Self-report	0–2	0.72
Achievement goals questionnaire—performance avoidance scale[a]	Four items (e.g., "Are you worried that you may not do as well as the others on these puzzles?")	Self-report	1–4	0.65

Key: A, alpha; TORP, Test of Reading Performance (Padeliadu & Sideridis, 2000); RAN, Rapid Automatized Naming Test; PANAS, Positive and Negative Affective Schedule (Watson, Clark, & Tellegen, 1988); RCMAS, Revised Children's Manifest Anxiety Scale (Reynolds & Richmond, 1978); CDI, Children's Depression Inventory (Kovacs, 1992).

[a] Elliot and Church (1997).

Statistical Analyses

Hypothesis 1 was assessed through multiple linear regression with RAN as the dependent variable. Positive and Negative Affective Schedule (PANAS), Revised Children's Manifest Anxiety Scale (RCMAS), Children's Depression Inventory (CDI), and performance avoidance total scores were entered together in the equation.

Hypothesis 2 was assessed using a cusp model, based on a maximum likelihood method performed in R® (Grassman, van der Maas, & Wagenmakers, 2009). The R® procedure uses the potential function of the cusp surface:

$$\text{Cusp } Y(a,b) = \mathbf{a}y + 1/2\mathbf{b}y^2 - 1/4y^4$$

It then estimates the asymmetry (*a*) and bifurcation factors (*b*), which in the present work correspond to pseudoword decoding and RAN performance, respectively (see Figure 5.1). The dependent variable *y* was the word-reading accuracy score. The cusp data–model fit was compared with alterative linear and logistic models. The cusp model was deemed superior to the competing models because all coefficients for the cusp model were statistically significant, the Akaike Information Criterion (AIC) and Bayesian Information Criterion (BIC) indices were lower than they were for the competing models, and because the chi-square difference test favored the cusp model. A well-fitting catastrophe model is further suggested by the presence of bimodality in the response function. Each model was applied separately to the two comprehension achievement groups. Hypothesis 2 specified that the interaction between cognitive and affective variables would exert an abrupt, nonlinear effect on word-reading ability in the at-risk group of students (low achievers).

Hypothesis 3 (within the *generic shutdown framework*) predicted that after statistically removing the contribution of psychoemotional and motivational components from RAN scores, the residual variance would not emerge as a significant bifurcating variable in the cusp model.

Results

The results of multiple regression indicated that the linear combination of motivational, emotional, and psychopathological variables explained 26.1% of the variability in RAN performance [$F(6,78) = 4.586$, $p < .01$], justifying the testing of models on the association of RAN with these independent variables.

The results of the cusp analysis are shown in Table 5.2 for the group at risk for reading failure. This model indicated excellent fit, predicting changes in word-reading accuracy, with pseudoword decoding acting as the asymmetry variable and RAN as the bifurcation factor. All parameter estimates were within their 95% confidence intervals. Bimodality was evident in the bifurcation area as well as substantial skew in the areas adjacent to the bifurcation (Figure 5.1). Comparisons between the cusp model and the competing models suggested the superiority of the former. The chi-square test for the difference between the linear and cusp models was significant (χ^2 [2] = 357.800, $p < .001$),

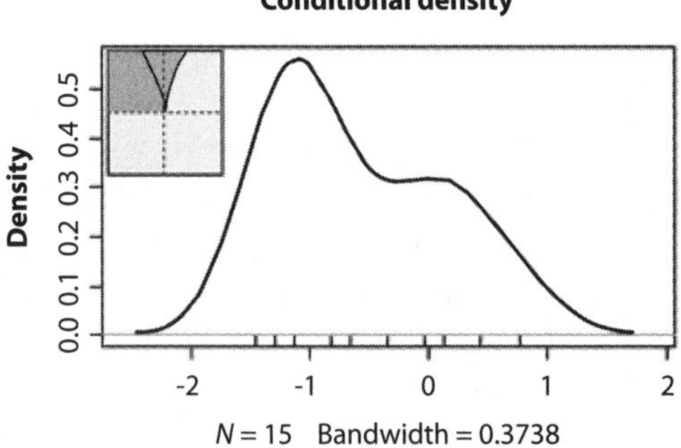

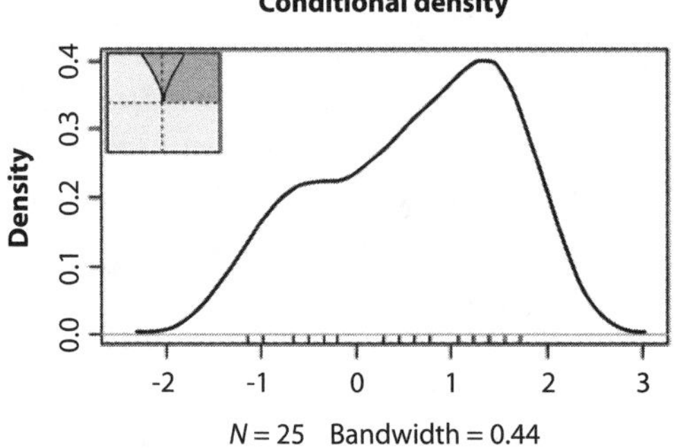

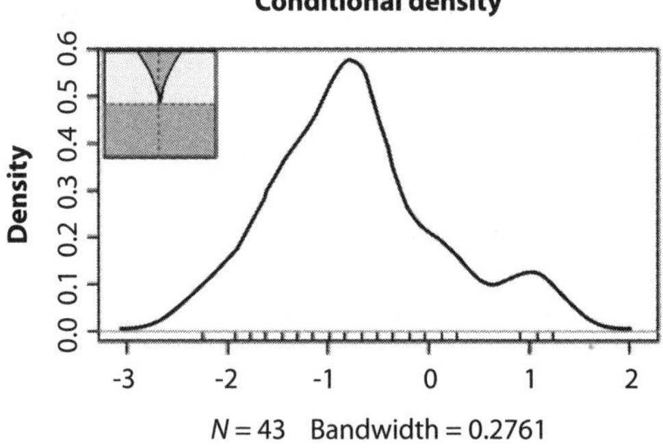

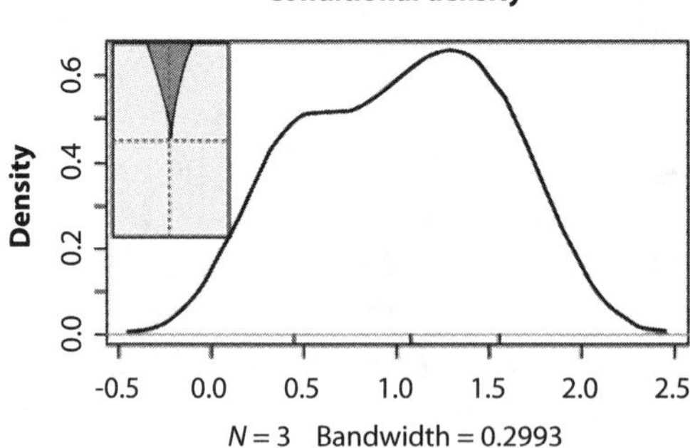

Figure 5.1. Visual display of the lower surface of the control space with distributions of responses per area. The recommended positive and negative skews in the areas to the left and right of the bifurcation area are satisfied (upper two panels). Bimodality is also evident within the bifurcation area (bottom panel). Last, the distribution of the responses in areas away from the bifurcation is approximately normal as posited by the cusp model.

Table 5.2. Predicting word-reading accuracy as a function of pseudoword decoding (asymmetry variable) and rapid automatized naming (bifurcation factor) for the group at risk for reading failure using the cusp model

Parameter estimates	*B*	*SE*	*z* score	*p*
a (Intercept)	−13.594	2.494	−5.450	< 0.001***
a (Pseudoword decoding)	0.189	0.034	5.542	< 0.001***
b (Intercept)	3.554	1.527	2.328	0.019*
b (RAN)	−0.129	0.061	−2.095	0.036*
w (Intercept)	−4.311	0.350	−12.327	< 0.001***
w (Word reading)	0.159	0.012	13.383	< 0.001***

***$p < .001$, **$p < .01$, *$p < .05$.

Key: B, unstandardized slope; *SE,* standard error; *a,* asymmetry; *b,* bifurcation; *w,* dependent variables.

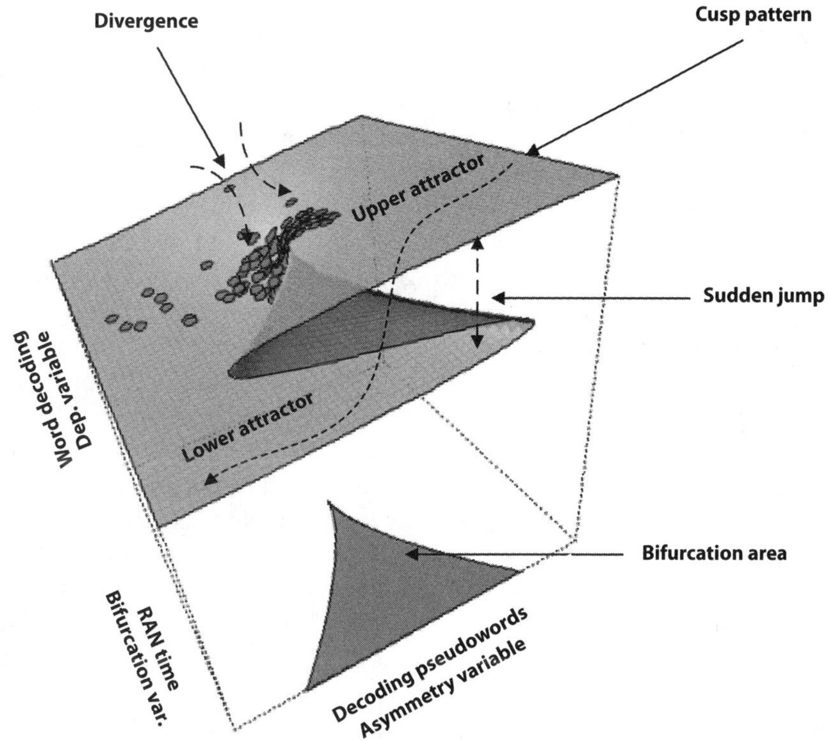

Figure 5.2. Cusp model explaining the relationship between pseudoword decoding and rapid automatized naming performance for the prediction of word-reading accuracy. The shaded area represents the area of unpredictability.

whereas the AIC and BIC indices for the linear, logistic, and cusp models were 522.5 and 532.3, 499.4 and 511.8, and 168.7 and 183.4, respectively. Collectively, these findings point to the superiority of the cusp model to all competing models. Figure 5.2 shows the behavior change between the two modes as a function of pseudoword decoding and RAN.

The corresponding cusp model for the high achievement group revealed that the RAN coefficient failed to reach significance. That is, RAN was not a valid bifurcation factor in this ability group, and its effect on word-reading accuracy was better described by a linear function (linear slope for $b_{RAN} = -.264$, $p < .05$).

Support for Hypothesis 3 was provided by the results of additional cusp models including the residualized RAN scores (after partialing out PANAS, RCMAS, CDI, and performance avoidance total scores). The residualized RAN as a bifurcation factor was indeed no longer significant in predicting nonlinear changes in word reading (b_{RAN} = -0.07, p =.102). Thus individual variability in RAN, which did not include variance attributed to psychoemotional and motivational characteristics, was not associated with nonlinearity and unpredictability of word-reading ability.

Discussion

The present study introduced a novel function of RAN performance as a correlate of word-level reading ability. While confirming the extant literature on RAN performance as a (linear) predictor of word-reading ability for students with above-average reading comprehension scores, our results revealed that RAN digits may function as a nonlinear moderator of the association between basic reading skills (decoding) and word reading. Thus the normally linear predictability of word-reading accuracy from decoding ability was disrupted for students who displayed slow digit naming and struggled in reading comprehension. In functional terms, this finding implies that in this group of students, word-reading ability ceased to be systematically related to RAN. Pending replication with different samples, this is a remarkable phenomenon in view of the well-established, strong causal link between decoding and word-reading accuracy, especially in the age range studied here (Grades 2–4).

The study was designed to provide some clues toward an explanation of this finding. A key element of the account proffered here concerns the nature of the RAN task itself as well as the outcome variable used. The RAN digits task possesses considerable independence from other key contributors to reading ability, such as phonological and orthographic processing skills (Georgiou et al., 2009; Georgiou, Papadopoulos, Fella, & Parrila, 2012). Moreover, RAN appears to engage a multitude of cognitive operations and related skills, requiring speeded visual recognition, access to stored representations, and efficient retrieval of lexical and phonological entities (Georgiou et al., 2009; Lervåg & Hulme, 2009). Importantly, RAN requires effective integration of information across subprocesses (Wolf et al., 2000), itself a hallmark of cognitive and/or attentional control. In this light, RAN is expected to be highly susceptible to affective and motivational states (Eysenck, Derakshan, Santos, & Calvo, 2007; Georgiou et al., 2010; Lepola et al., 2005). This notion was corroborated by the finding that more than 26% of the variance in RAN scores reflected the unique contribution of psychoemotional and motivational variables. Moreover, we have presented evidence that this unique variance determined, at least in part, the moderating role of RAN performance as a bifurcating variable. It should be pointed out, however, that total RAN variance (without partialing out emotional "components") remained a significant linear predictor of word reading accuracy among students scoring in the above-average range on reading comprehension. In this group, apparently cognitive and emotional/motivational components of RAN contributed jointly and uniformly to word-reading ability along with more basic reading skills (decoding). Among the struggling readers, however, emotional/motivational components were the critical determinants of the postulated disruption of the reading process by RAN.

Another important element of the study design concerns the outcome variable that did not involve speeded reading, rendering the function of RAN as bifurcation variable all the more notable (see also Sheppes & Gross, 2011). The present findings also shed light on earlier findings that the contribution of RAN to reading behavior is more pronounced among struggling students or those at risk for reading failure (Scarborough, 1998) and is linked to a disruption of timing processes (Catts, Gillispie, Leonard, Kail, & Miller, 2002).

CONCLUSION: READING AND THE NONLINEAR DYNAMIC SYSTEMS PERSPECTIVE

The account of these results was founded on a relatively novel analytic tool, the cusp catastrophe model, and supports a potentially innovative view of reading performance as a dynamic phenomenon grounded on crystalized knowledge of linguistic and print-related information and determined each time by the complex interplay between cognitive abilities and affective/motivational states. Application of the cusp model to describe behavior (performance) is founded on *self-organization theory* and represents an *epistemological shift* to widely used statistical approaches, including moderated regression or other nonlinear forms of analysis. The concept of bifurcation is unique to this technique as a means to describe the function of *self-organizing systems* (Nicolis & Nicolis, 2007). Within this framework, reading is considered as a *self-organizing function* driven by the constant interplay between cognitive and affective/motivational components. Cognitive components, such as working memory, speed of processing, attention, crystallized knowledge, strategic verbal retrieval, phonological decoding, and visuomotor coordination, are engaged as needed during each step of the reading process. The interplay among these operations determines the next state of the system. Negative affect experienced situationally as a result of external conditions (e.g., class climate, negative or inappropriate feedback from teacher) and internal stimuli (e.g., fixed cognitive schemas of inadequacy, dysfunctional beliefs) can trigger physiological manifestations of anxiety, which, together with negative automatic thoughts, could interfere with the more demanding processing steps. In principle, tasks that require constant, controlled integration of resources and cognitive operations will be more vulnerable to such disruptions, leading to lower performance or even to overload or shutdown phenomena. The system may be robust to such disruptions 1) under moderate levels of negative affect and intensity of dysfunctional thoughts, 2) at manageable levels of task difficulty, and 3) when sufficient cognitive resources have developed through systematic instruction and reading experience. When one or more of these prerequisites are not met, nonetheless, a general breakdown in the function of reading may take place. This phenomenon may explain the disruption in the predictability of word reading from pseudoword decoding ability in the present study among struggling readers.

One of the limitations of the present study concerns the use of linear regression in order to "extract" emotion/motivation-related variance from RAN scores. Thus, although the independence of RAN from other cognitive resources has been demonstrated (Sideridis, Morgan, Botsas, Padeliadu, & Fuchs, 2006), this procedure may have removed shared variance containing such cognitive attributes. A second limitation is that RAN ability was measured through a single task involving digits presented in a serial format, which may have inflated the degree of association with the reading measures (Georgiou, Parrila, Cui, & Papadopoulos, 2013). Future studies should explore more direct measures of the postulated cognitive components of RAN within a more comprehensive model of reading performance (Pauly et al., 2011). In addition, given the heterogeneity of struggling readers (Mazzocco & Grimm, 2013), it is important to apply the cusp catastrophe model to various subpopulations of students at risk for reading failure.

REFERENCES

Bowers, P.G., & Wolf, M. (1993). Theoretical links among naming speed, precise timing mechanisms and orthographic skill in dyslexia. *Reading and Writing: An Interdisciplinary Journal, 5,* 69–85.

Cardoso-Martins, C., & Pennington, B.F. (2004). The relationship between phoneme awareness and rapid serial naming skills and literacy acquisition: The role of developmental period and reading ability. *Scientific Studies of Reading, 8,* 27–52.

Catts, H.W., Gillispie, M., Leonard, L.B., Kail, R.V., & Miller, C.A. (2002). The role of speed of processing, rapid naming, and phonological awareness in reading achievement. *Journal of Learning Disabilities, 35,* 509–524.

Cutting, L.E., & Denckla, M.B. (2001). The relationship of rapid automatized naming and word reading in normally developing readers. *Reading and Writing: An Interdisciplinary Journal, 14,* 673–704.

Elias, M. (2004). The connection between social emotional learning and learning disabilities: Implications for intervention. *Journal of Learning Disabilities, 27,* 53–63.

Elliot, A.J., & Church, M.A. (1997). A hierarchical model of approach and avoidance achievement motivation. *Journal of Personality and Social Psychology, 72,* 218–232.

Eysenck, M.W., Derakshan, N., Santos, R., & Calvo, M.G. (2007). Anxiety and cognitive performance: Attentional control theory. *Emotion, 7,* 336–353.

Georgiou, G. (2010). PASS cognitive processes: Can they explain the RAN-reading relationship? *Psychological Science (Chinese), 33,* 1291–1298.

Georgiou, G., Manolitsis, G., Nurmi, J.E., & Parrila, R. (2010). Does task-focused versus task-avoidance behavior matter for literacy development in an orthographically consistent language. *Contemporary Educational Psychology, 35,* 1–10.

Georgiou, G., Papadopoulos, T.C., Fella, A., & Parrila, R. (2012). Rapid naming speed components and reading development in a consistent orthography. *Journal of Experimental Child Psychology, 112,* 1–17.

Georgiou, G., Parrila, R., & Kirby, J. (2009). RAN components and reading development from Grade 3 to Grade 5: What underlies their relationship? *Scientific Studies of Reading, 13,* 508–534.

Georgiou, G., Parrila, R., Cui, Y., & Papadopoulos, T. (2013). Why is rapid automatized naming related to reading? *Journal of Experimental Child Psychology, 115,* 218–225.

Grassman, R.P., van der Maas, H.L., & Wagenmakers, E.J. (2009). Fitting the cusp catastrophe in R: A cusp package primer. *Journal of Statistical Software, 32,* 1–27.

Kirby, J., Parrila, R., & Pfeiffer, S. (2003). Naming speed and phonological awareness as predictors of reading development. *Journal of Educational Psychology, 95,* 453–464.

Kovacs, M. (1992). *Children's depression inventory* (CDI). North Tonawanda, NY: Multi-health systems.

Lepola, J., Poskiparta, E., Laakkonen, E., & Niemi, P. (2005). Development of and relationship between phonological and motivational processes and naming speed in predicting word recognition in grade 1. *Scientific Studies of Reading, 9,* 367–399.

Lervåg, A., & Hulme, C. (2009). Rapid naming (RAN) taps a basic constraint on the development of reading fluency. *Psychological Science, 20,* 1040–1048.

Manis, F., Doi, L., & Bhadha, B. (2000). Naming speed, phonological awareness, and orthographic knowledge in second graders. *Journal of Learning Disabilities, 33,* 325.

Mazzocco, M., & Grimm, K. (2013). Growth in rapid automatized naming from grades K to 8 in children with math or reading disabilities. *Journal of Learning Disabilities, 46,* 517–533.

Nag, S., Snowling, M.J. (2012). School underachievement and specific learning difficulties. In J.M. Rey (Ed.), *IACAPAP E-textbook of child and adolescent mental health.* Geneva: International Association for Child and Adolescent Psychiatry and Allied Professions.

Nicolis, G., & Nicolis, C. (2007). *Foundations of complex systems.* New York, NY: World Scientific.

Norton, E., & Wolf, M. (2012). Rapid automatized naming (RAN) and reading fluency: Implications for understanding and treatment of reading disabilities. *Annual Review of Psychology, 63,* 427–452.

Padeliadu, S., & Sideridis, G. (2000). Discriminant validation of the test of reading performance (TORP) for identifying children at risk of reading difficulties. *European Journal of Psychological Assessment, 16,* 139–146.

Pauly, H., Linkersdorfer, J., Lindberg, S., Woerner, W., Hasslhorn, M., & Lonnemann, J. (2011). Domain-specific rapid automatized naming deficits in children at risk for learning disabilities. *Journal of Neurolinguistics, 24,* 602–610.

Powell, D., Stainthorp, R., & Stuart, M. (2014). Deficits in orthographic knowledge in children poor at rapid automatized naming (RAN) tasks? *Scientific Studies of Reading, 18,* 192–207.

Powell, D., Stainthorp, R., Stuart, M., Garwood, H., & Quinlan, P. (2007). An experimental comparison between rival theories of rapid automatized naming performance and its relationship to reading. *Journal of Experimental Child Psychology, 98,* 46–68.

Protopapas, A., Altani, A., & Georgiou, G.K. (2013). Development of serial processing in reading and rapid naming. *Journal of Experimental Child Psychology 116,* 914–929.

Reynolds, C.R., & Richmond, B.O. (1978). What I think and feel: A revised measure of children's manifest anxiety. *Journal of Abnormal Child Psychology, 6,* 271–280.

Savage, R.S., Frederickson, N., Goodwin, R., Patni, U., Smith, N., & Tuersley, L. (2005). Relationship among rapid digit naming, phonological processing, motor automaticity, and speech perception in poor, average, and good readers and spellers. *Journal of Learning Disabilities, 38*(1), 12–28.

Scarborough, H.S. (1998). Predicting the future achievement of second graders with reading disabilities: Contributions of phonemic awareness, verbal memory, rapid naming, and IQ. *Annals of Dyslexia, 48,* 115–136.

Sheppes, G., & Gross, J.J. (2011). Is timing everything? Temporal considerations in emotion regulation. *Personality and Social Psychology Review, 15,* 319–331.

Sideridis, G.D., Morgan, P., Botsas, G., Padeliadu, S., & Fuchs, D. (2006). Predicting LD on the basis of motivation, metacognition and psychopathology: An ROC analysis. *Journal of Learning Disabilities, 39,* 215–229.

Thom, R. (1975). *Structural stability and morphogenesis.* Reading, MA: W.A. Benjamin.

van den Bos, K.P., Zijlstra, B.J.H., & Spelberg, H.C. (2002). Life-span data on continuous-naming speeds of numbers, letters, colors, and pictured objects, and word-reading speed. *Scientific Studies of Reading, 6,* 25–49.

Wagner, R.K., & Torgesen, J.K. (1987). The nature of phonological processing and its causal role in the acquisition of reading skills. *Psychological Bulletin, 101,* 192–212.

Watson, D., Clark, L.A., & Tellegen, A. (1988). Development and validation of brief measures of positive and negative affect: The PANAS scales. *Journal of Personality and Social Psychology, 47,* 1063–1070.

Wolf, M., & Bowers, P. (1999). The question of naming-speed deficits in developmental reading disabilities: An introduction to the double-deficit hypothesis. *Journal of Learning Disabilities, 33,* 322–324.

Wolf, M., Bowers, P.G., & Biddle, K. (2000). Naming-speed processes, timing, and reading: A conceptual review. *Journal of Learning Disabilities, 33,* 387–407.

6

Eye-Movement Research in Reading

Enhancing Focus on the Development of Reading and Reading Disabilities

Brett Miller[1]

Eye movements provide an exquisitely sensitive lens into the reading process of adults and children. This fine-grained lens reveals the temporal and spatial specificity of the data provided through eye-tracking equipment and offers a unique view into the moment-by-moment unfolding of the processes involved in reading (e.g., Rayner, 1998, 2009). Despite the potential of this tool, eye-movement technology has been infrequently utilized to examine developing readers and young readers at risk for or diagnosed with a reading disability. This chapter focuses on some of the potential reasons for a historic focus on skilled adult readers, provides a description of the development of research based on developmental reading disabilities, and discusses lessons learned from other domains that could speed the effective utilization of this tool in diverse settings (i.e., lab and field).

SENSITIVITY: COSTS AND BENEFITS

Eye-movement technologies provide both temporally and spatially reliable data related to eye gaze position (see Rayner, 1998, 2009; Rayner, Ardoin, Binder, 2013). Although the exact specifications vary according to the particular

1. The opinions and assertions presented in this chapter are those of the author and do not purport to represent those of the *Eunice Kennedy Shriver* National Institute of Child Health and Human Development, the U.S. National Institutes of Health, or the U.S. Department of Health and Human Services.

eye-tracking equipment used, historically these systems sampled at rates of up to 1000 HZ, or once every millisecond, although higher sampling rates are available today. The output provided by these systems includes eye-gaze position at each sample. From these data, one can extract information such as what point, object, or word a person is looking at; how long he or she gazes at it; and when and to where his or her eyes move next. The flexibility of the systems permits accurate monitoring of eye-gaze position in a more natural context (e.g., sentence, paragraph, integrated text, and images) than is technologically feasible through many other technologies (e.g., electroencephalography) or presentation approaches, such as rapid, serial visual presentations in which one word (or group of words) is presented at a time (e.g., Schotter, Tran, & Rayner, 2014). Despite this advantage of collecting rich temporal information about a reader's gaze while reading text (generally silently), technical and other aspects related to the systems historically have limited their viability for examining reading development and developmental reading disabilities in children.[2]

These limitations largely involve two major categories: the cost of acquiring these systems and challenges related to technical or system limitations. Prior to approximately the beginning of the 21st century and the widespread availability of high-speed, highly spatially accurate video-based eye trackers, eye-tracking systems were often prohibitively expensive for many investigators, particularly those without significant start-up funds from their institution or independent grant support. Fortunately, with the increased availability of video-based systems, the cost of eye trackers has decreased substantially—often cited in the $5,000–$40,000 range (e.g., Kumar, 2006), with higher sampling models appropriate for reading research in the upper half of this price range.

Second, the most advanced systems were difficult to use and, in some cases, prone to mechanical problems (for discussion, see Rayner et al., 2013). Arguably the dominant system in the 1980s and 1990s in reading research was the Dual Purkinje Image (DPI) eye tracker. This system allowed for interfacing with PCs and provided excellent spatial and temporal resolution; however, these systems required extensive operator training, and gaining expertise remained quite challenging, particularly when running gaze-contingent paradigms. Also, as Rayner et al. (2013) point out, these systems utilized a series of mechanical parts to move the systems into place and to physically track the eye gaze, making them more prone to mechanical problems. Both factors limited their widespread usage.

Eye trackers before circa 2000 generally required permanent installations (e.g., DPI systems) and thus were not capable of being transported to different sites (e.g., schools) for data collection purposes. Elaborate programming and

2. The focus of this chapter is on developmental reading disabilities rather than on acquired forms of reading disability (i.e., via brain injury); therefore, work on acquired forms of reading disabilities is generally not reviewed in this chapter.

data synthesis routines to facilitate quick experimental prototyping were not widely available from vendors—although programming routines were available in numerous labs.

In addition to these limitations, the ability to accurately monitor eye gaze, or "track," an individual was impacted by individual differences among participants. Given the specific interest in this chapter in developing readers, I focus on limitations that directly affected children's participation. Some common limitations included 1) the need for participants to remain quite still while reading (not an easy task for young children); 2) the difficulty or inability to track individuals with glasses or hard contact lenses; and 3) the limitations on usage with individuals possessing built-in retainers, braces, or other dental appliances.[3] Fortunately, many of these limitations have been significantly reduced with newer systems.

Enhanced Flexibility for Studies with Developing Readers

Features of many of the recently developed, video-based eye-tracking systems (e.g., SR Research's equipment) overcome numerous technical and feasibility limitations. These systems can allow for simultaneous tracking of head position and eye gaze, allowing for a more natural, less intrusive experimental setting. With the addition of head-position monitoring, these systems can accommodate modest head movements and retain tracking of participants' gaze position, facilitating studies with children. Remember that with some previous installations of systems, such as the DPI imaging systems, experimenters used "bite bars" and other methods to maintain a fixed head position, which had the unfortunate consequence of limiting the involvement of individuals with permanent dental fixtures (e.g., children with braces). Also, many systems no longer require permanent installations and can be set up for use outside of the laboratory with relative ease. Video-based systems also generally allow for monitoring eye-gaze position for both eyes simultaneously; previous systems generally tracked eye position on a single eye and would require two separate physical systems to track binocular eye movements. In the context of reading studies, this is generally a minor limitation because most experiments and designs do not make explicit predictions about differences in eye-gaze position (although see as examples Blythe, Liversedge, Joseph, White, Findlay, & Rayner, 2006; Bucci, Brémond-Gignac, & Kapoula, 2008; Kirkby, Blythe, Drieghe, & Liversedge, 2011). Finally, the temporal resolution of video-based systems has increased to be comparable to or exceed those of systems such as the Dual Purkinje systems; this sampling resolution permits designs that

3. This limitation depends upon the mechanism used to help participants remain in a fixed position during a trial. This is not an inherent limitation of the equipment per se. For example, bite bars were molded in some labs for each individual and the individual was asked to rest his/her mouth on this bar while reading, generally with the aid of head pads as well (for additional discussion, see Rayner et al., 2013).

involve gaze-contingent display changes and provides accuracy of measurement sufficient for reading research. Critically, vendors recently have begun supporting extensive software libraries for creating experiments as well as supporting the output of common eye-tracking measures for analyses. These technical advances, enhanced software platforms for experimentation and analyses, mobility, and overall reduction in cost should permit more rapid adoption and usage of fast-sampling eye-tracking equipment to study the development of reading and reading disabilities.

EYE MOVEMENTS AND DEVELOPING READERS

In order to contextualize the need for research, I next describe some of what is known about eye-movement behavior generally and what has been learned about eye movements during reading, with a particular focus on developing readers and those with developmental reading disabilities (for reviews, see Rayner, 1998, 2009; Rayner et al., 2013).

Contrary to intuition, readers often do not move their eyes smoothly across the page while reading; readers instead make ballistic eye movements from one location to the next (see Rayner, 1998, 2009, for discussion). During silent reading, these eye movements, or *saccades,* are followed by time periods of relative stability as the eyes gaze at a particular location (*fixation*). Eye movements occur while readers' eyes move forward or backward in the text; backward saccades are referred to as *regressions* and tend to constitute about 10%–15% of fixations in skilled adult readers. Saccades average roughly seven to nine letter spaces in English with significant range in length. For adult skilled readers, fixations last on average between approximately 175 and 350 milliseconds, with most lasting 200–250 milliseconds for silent reading. General indicators of relative processing difficulties include longer fixation durations, larger numbers of fixations, and more interword regressions. Easier text, in contrast, is often fixated on for less time, with more frequent skips and with fewer regressions (see Rayner, 1998, 2009, for review).

Also belying intuition, readers can only extract information useful for text processing from a relatively small "window," or perceptual span (e.g., McConkie & Rayner, 1975; Rayner, 1986; Rayner & Bertera, 1979). In English, this span is roughly 14–15 characters to the right of fixation and approximately 3–4 characters to the left of fixation; this region is asymmetric and the direction of the asymmetry will shift depending on the language being read (e.g., Pollatsek, Bolozky, Well, & Rayner, 1981). Importantly for our broader context of developing reading, a reader's perceptual span is not fixed but can reduce in size, particularly in response to reading challenging text (e.g., Inhoff, Pollatsek, Posner, & Rayner, 1989; Rayner, 1986).

In the case of children who are developing their reading skills, differences in eye-movement patterns are generally differences of scale rather than kind (e.g., Blythe & Joseph, 2011; Rayner, 1986; Reichle et al., 2013). Consistent with this argument, children generally exhibit longer fixation durations, shorter saccade movements, greater numbers of fixations, and more frequent regressions backward in text (e.g., McConkie et al., 1991; Rayner, 1985b; for a review, see Blythe, 2014). This is generally a pattern of reading that suggests more difficulty and/or less expertise in the process than skilled adult readers. Developing young readers also have smaller perceptual spans relative to skilled adult readers, and this span increases with skill development (e.g. Häikiö, Bertram, Hyönä, & Niemi, 2009; Rayner, 1986; see also Häikiö, Bertram, & Hyönä, 2010). In Rayner's (1986) studies, which were conducted in English, for instance, letter feature information was extracted seven characters to the right of fixation in second-grade children and then plateaued at 11–12 characters during fourth grade. If one looks at word-length information, this reaches adult-level performance at around sixth grade, when readers are able to obtain information out to about 14 characters to the right of fixation. Note that these changes in perceptual span likely reflect developmental changes in attentional allocation related to age and/or experience with reading text rather than changes in visual acuity (e.g., Blythe, 2014).

Although perhaps more stark than the change in perceptual span, developing readers also show a rapid decrease in the percentage of short saccades that are made during silent reading (McConkie et al., 1991). McConkie and colleagues specifically found that young readers (approximately 6–7 years of age) very often execute short saccades (i.e., two characters or less)—roughly 90% of all saccades. The frequency of these short saccades drops precipitously with reading experience and age, with 10–11-year-olds executing these short saccades only about 4% of the time. The performance level is not quite that of a skilled adult reader, in which this type of saccade is very infrequent, but it does show rapid developmental movement toward this pattern of performance. Finally, there is some suggestion that there may be individual differences in the likelihood of an intraword regression, which is a regressive eye movement to an earlier part of the word on which the reader is currently fixating. Valle, Binder, Walsh, Nemier, and Bangs (2013) report higher intraword regressive saccades for average, compared with highly skilled, second-grade readers. This finding, if it holds, could suggest individual differences in word processing, even among those performing at or above grade standard; this difference may be exacerbated for students at weaker reading skill levels.

In addition, there are some data suggesting that young readers are sensitive to various linguistic aspects of text in a way that is similar to adult readers. Young readers show expected word-length effects, with readers spending more time on gaze duration (or the time spent on one's first pass reading a word), the number of fixations during first pass, and so forth (e.g., Blythe, Liversedge, Joseph, White, & Rayner, 2009; Huestegge, Radach, Corbic, & Huestegge, 2009; Hyönä & Olson, 1995; Joseph, Liversedge, Blythe, White, & Rayner, 2009), with some indication that this effect may be modulated by word familiarity (Rau, Moeller, & Landerl, 2014). Children also display expected word-frequency effects similar to those of adult readers, with longer fixation durations on low- compared with high-frequency words—although these effects may be more pronounced with children than with adults (e.g., Blythe et al., 2009; Joseph, Nation, & Liversedge, 2013; Valle et al., 2013). There is also early evidence about the development of syntactic and pragmatic processing of text. Joseph et al. (2008) found children's anomaly detection—in this case, thematic relationships (e.g., "using a radio to play a *mouse*")—to occur on a time frame similar to that of adults, but children showed a somewhat later detection of implausible or unlikely relationships in text (e.g., "using a hook to catch a *mouse*"); essentially, children showed signs of detecting the anomaly on a measure that encompassed all of the reading time on a region of text (i.e., initial and later rereading) rather than first-pass reading times. A plausible interpretation here, as proposed by Joseph and colleagues, could be that young readers are less efficient in utilizing world knowledge when processing sentence meaning; however, Connor, Radach, Vorstius, Day, and Morrison (2015) found fifth-grade readers often detected implausible words in text during their first pass on the word. Interestingly, they found individuals with more highly rated academic language scores had inflated rereading of the target word in implausible, as compared with plausible, text than did those with lower academic language scores. Additional data will be needed to home in on the time course of this issue. Joseph and Liversedge (2013) similarly demonstrated that children showed parsing preferences similar to those of adults when reading syntactically ambiguous text—that is, children (ages 6–9) showed similar garden path effects to those commonly seen in adult readers.

Finally, eye movements have recently been used to look at comprehension processing in children. The field is in the early stages of this utilization (e.g., Ablinger, Huber, & Radach, 2014; Connor et al., 2015; Joseph et al., 2008; Vorstius, Radach, Mayer, & Lonigan, 2013), particularly in response to intervention; nevertheless, this approach holds promise for analyzing viewing patterns related to overall comprehension and response to intervention. For instance, one might make specific predictions about order and attentional emphasis within text based on the comprehension strategy taught to a reader. Along this line, Foster, Ardoin, and Binder (2013) asked second-grade readers to reread text using repeated reading approaches—similar to what occurs in classrooms. Consistent with previous research, they found faster reading rates for children's subsequent reading of text. Critically though, the improved reading times were due to shorter reading times on low-frequency words and were interpreted to be due to improvements in the readers' familiarity with these words. This improvement was not due to skipping previously read text; readers continued to fixate on low- and high-frequency words throughout their rereadings.

In sum, we are beginning to develop a research base that investigates the development of reading utilizing eye tracking. Some foundational data related to eye-movement behavior and linguistic effects (e.g., word frequency effects) have been collected, but some of the data await replication and extension and/or examine effects for a limited range of readers (i.e., skill level), languages studied, and ages. There is also a dearth of data on developmental changes that utilize longitudinal data (e.g., McConkie et al., 1991), which in concert with cross-sectional data, could provide a more comprehensive lens through which to consider the variability within reader groups.

Eye Movements: Examining Struggling Readers or Those Diagnosed with Dyslexia

In this section, I focus on some of the emerging research utilizing eye movements specifically to study dyslexia. The emphasis in this section is primarily on developmental, rather than acquired, forms of dyslexia, and it focuses primarily on studies that examine reading directly.[4] Individuals with dyslexia generally show longer fixation durations and a larger number of fixations and, correspondingly, fewer skipped words, shorter saccades, and sometimes more regressions back in text (e.g., De Luca, Di Pace, Judica, Spinelli, & Zoccolotti, 1999; Hawelka, Gagl, & Wimmer, 2010; Hutzler & Wimmer, 2004). There is also some initial suggestion that patterns may differ somewhat for children with dyslexia compared with those who have dyslexia and comorbid attention deficits. In a study by Thaler et al. (2009), dyslexic children spent more time reading words presented to them and had higher numbers of fixations; in comparison, children with dyslexia and comorbid attention deficit problems had fewer fixations but had the longest fixations and highest naming error rate for the target word. This interesting study needs to be replicated and extended before firm conclusions can be made on possible differences between these groups.

A more extensive line of research has examined the possible link between poor oculomotor control and dyslexia (see Blythe, 2014; Kirkby, Webster, Blythe, & Liversedge, 2008; Miller & O'Donnell, 2013; Rayner, 1985a, for extended discussions)—the general consensus from this research is that the poor oculomotor control seen in dyslexic readers is not causally related to dyslexia itself but is likely a consequence of it, at least initially. Researchers similarly have examined potential discrepancies between the fixation position of both eyes when looking at a word or text. It is important to note here that there are binocular fixation disparities for skilled adult readers and that discrepancies tend to be larger for children (e.g., Blythe et al., 2006; although see Kirkby et al., 2011); note that the discrepancy tends to occur with the eyes uncrossed. In the case of children with dyslexia, the discrepancy tends to be larger than for typically developing readers matched for age, and in one study, the average size of the binocular fixation disparity for typically developing readers was approximately twice as large as that of individuals with dyslexia (Kirkby et al., 2011; see also Bucci et al., 2008). To date, I am unaware of any actively manipulated reading

---

4. Within the eye-movement community (and outside), there has been an ongoing debate about the role of visual attention deficits and dyslexia. A full discussion of this issue is beyond the scope of the chapter, but the interested reader may wish to consider a 2013 review by Bellocchi, Muneaux, Bastien-Toniazzo, and Ducrot as well as data from neuroimaging techniques (e.g., Olulade, Napoliello, & Eden, 2013).

intervention study for children with developmental dyslexia that utilizes eye movements, although there have been some initial efforts with individuals who have acquired dyslexia that offer promise that this approach may be used to ascertain the underlying strategic processing involved for readers with developmental dyslexia (e.g., Ablinger et al., 2014).

MOVING FORWARD: THE NEED FOR TRANSDISCIPLINARY RESEARCH MODELS

An enhanced focus on developing readers, including those at risk for or diagnosed with a reading disability, necessitates a transition to a more team-based approach to science. As a bit of history, research utilizing eye movements to examine reading originated largely from labs in cognitive and/or vision sciences and focused predominately on general mechanisms involved in skilled adult reading (although see Rayner et al., 2013). This focus formed our foundational understanding of both the cognitive and ocular motor processes involved in skilled reading, including readers' ability to access and use word-level, sentence-level, and text-based information to extract meaning from text. To link this work to the emergent literature on studies of eye movement and reading development, a stronger developmental lens is likely necessary. Connecting these disparate literatures depends on bringing together teams composed of researchers with a firm understanding of literature on the role of eye movements in reading and individuals with an understanding of the developmental processes involved in reading and reading disabilities. Much remains to be learned about eye-movement behavior related to the basic developmental trajectories of reading and reading disabilities, but as this happens, the field should emphasize the design of experimental questions and methodologies that are complementary to other behavioral and neurobiological data. This is critical if researchers are to move forward in discovering what eye movements can uniquely tell them about reading and reading development. In addition, team-based approaches should facilitate richer examinations of individual differences across experiments and facilitate the involvement of well-described and well-characterized samples, permitting easier comparison to existing literatures, especially for struggling readers or those with learning disabilities. Teams that understand the complexities of working in school settings and understand intervention design, delivery, and appropriate targeted outcomes should work hand in hand with the eye-movement research community, particularly as interest increases for the use of eye-movement technology in school settings or to examine intervention response.

Increased attention to integrating eye movements with other complementary experimental paradigms to provide converging information about reading development (e.g., electroencephalography [EEG], functional magnetic resonance imaging [fMRI]) also holds promise. Moving from models in which eye movements are largely measured to control for artifacts to ones in which they are an integrated data source, along with other neuroimaging data, could help us overcome some of the challenges of presenting extended text within an MRI scanner or linking behavioral indices (i.e., eye-movement data) to time-sensitive neural signatures of language and reading processes via EEG. Finally, although it is rarely framed this way, working with data scientists, eye-movement researchers may be able to capitalize on the rich, often millisecond-by-millisecond, data by utilizing statistical modeling approaches beyond analysis of variance (ANOVA), multivariate analysis of covariance (MANCOVA), and traditional general linear models (e.g., Feng, 2009; Matsuki, Kuperman, & Van Dyke, in progress).

In summary, despite the significant impact of eye-movement work on the field's conceptualization of skilled reading, there has been, and remains, a relative paucity of such research to examine the development of reading and reading disabilities. This approach, used as a convergent data source, should help form a strong foundation that informs our understanding of reading as a developmental process for those with and without reading disabilities. The time is right for eye-movement research to be more fully integrated into transdisciplinary developmental studies of reading.

REFERENCES

Ablinger, I., Huber, W., & Radach, R. (2014). Eye movement analyses indicate the underlying reading strategy in the recovery of lexical readers. *Aphasiology, 28*(6), 640–657.

Bellocchi, S., Muneaux, M., Bastien-Toniazzo, M., & Ducrot, S. (2013). I can read it in your eyes: What eye movements tell us about visuo-attentional processes in developmental dyslexia. *Research in Developmental Disabilities, 34,* 452–460.

Blythe, H. (2014). Developmental changes in eye movements and visual information encoding associated with learning to read. *Current Directions in Psychological Science, 23*(3), 201–207.

Blythe, H., & Joseph, H. (2011). Children's eye movements during reading. In S.P. Liversedge, I.D. Gilchrist, & S. Everling (Eds.), *Oxford handbook on eye movements* (pp. 643–662). Oxford, UK: Oxford University Press.

Blythe, H., Liversedge, S., Joseph, H., White, S., & Rayner, K. (2009). Visual information capture during fixations in reading for children and adults. *Vision Research, 49,* 1583–1591.

Blythe, H., Liversedge, S., Joseph, H., White, S., Findlay, J., & Rayner, K. (2006). The binocular coordination of eye movements during reading in children and adults. *Vision Research, 46,* 3898–3908.

Bucci, M.P., Brémond-Gignac, D., & Kapoula, Z. (2008). Poor binocular coordination of saccades in dyslexic children. *Graefes Archives of Clinical and Experimental Ophthalmology, 246,* 417–428.

Connor, C.M., Radach, R., Vorstius, C., Day, S., & Morrison, F.J. (2015). Individual differences in fifth graders' literacy and academic language predict their comprehension monitoring development: An eye-movement study. *Scientific Studies of Reading, 19,* 114–134.

De Luca, M., Di Pace, E., Judica, A., Spinelli, D., & Zoccolotti, P. (1999). Eye movement patterns in linguistic and non-linguistic tasks in developmental surface dyslexia. *Neuropsychologia, 37*(12), 1407–1420.

Feng, G. (2009). Time course and hazard function: A distributional analysis of fixation duration in reading. *Journal of Eye Movement Research, 3,* 1–23.

Foster, T., Ardoin, S., & Binder, K. (2013). Underlying changes in repeated reading: An eye movement study. *School Psychology Review, 42,* 140–156.

Häikiö, T., Bertram, R., & Hyönä, J. (2010). Development of parafoveal processing within and across words in reading: Evidence from the boundary paradigm. *The Quarterly Journal of Experimental Psychology, 63*(10), 1982–1998.

Häikiö, T., Bertram, R., Hyönä, J., & Niemi, P. (2009). Development of the letter identity span in reading: Evidence from the eye movement moving window paradigm. *Journal of Experimental Child Psychology, 102*(2), 167–181.

Hawelka, S., Gagl, B., & Wimmer, H. (2010). A dual-route perspective on eye movements of dyslexic readers. *Cognition, 115,* 367–379.

Huestegge, L., Radach, R., Corbic, D., & Huestegge, S. (2009). Oculomotor and linguistic determinants of reading development: A longitudinal study. *Vision Research, 49,* 2948–2959.

Hutzler, F., & Wimmer, H. (2004). Eye movement of dyslexic children when reading in a regular orthography. *Brain and Language, 89,* 235–242.

Hyönä, J., & Olson, R. (1995). Eye fixation patterns among dyslexic and normal readers: Effects of word-length and word-frequency. *Journal of Experimental Psychology: Learning, Memory, and Cognition, 21,* 1430–1440.

Inhoff, A., Pollatsek, A., Posner, M., & Rayner, K. (1989). Covert attention and eye movements during reading. *Quarterly Journal of Experimental Psychology Section A: Human Experimental Psychology, 41*(1), 63–89.

Joseph, H., & Liversedge, S. (2013). Children's and adults' on-line processing of syntactically ambiguous sentences during reading. *PLOS ONE, 8*(1), e54141.

Joseph, H., Liversedge, S., Blythe, H., White, S., & Rayner, K. (2009). Word length and landing position effects during reading in children and adults. *Vision Research, 49,* 2078–2086.

Joseph, H., Liversedge, S., Blythe, H., White, S., Gathercole, S., & Rayner, K. (2008). Children's and adults' processing of anomaly and implausibility during reading: Evidence from eye movements. *The Quarterly Journal of Experimental Psychology, 61,* 708–723.

Joseph, H., Nation, K., & Liversedge, S. (2013). Using eye movements to investigate word frequency effects in children's sentence reading. *School Psychology Review, 42,* 207–222.

Kirkby, J., Blythe, H., Drieghe, D., & Liversedge, S. (2011). Reading text increases binocular disparity in dyslexic children. *PLOS ONE, 6*(11), e27105. doi:10.1371/journal.pone.0027105

Kirkby, J., Webster, L., Blythe, H., & Liversedge, S. (2008). Binocular coordination during reading and non-reading tasks. *Psychological Bulletin, 134*(5), 742–763.

Kumar, M. (2006, April). *Reducing the cost of eye tracking systems* (Stanford Tech Report CSTR 2006–08). Retrieved from http://hci.stanford.edu/cstr/reports/2006–08.pdf

Matsuki, K., Kuperman, V., & Van Dyke, J. (in progress). Individual differences during sentence reading: An analysis using random forests.

McConkie, G., & Rayner, K. (1975). The span of the effective stimulus during a fixation in reading. *Perception & Psychophysics, 17,* 578–586.

McConkie, G., Zola, D., Grimes, J., Kerr, P., Bryant, N., & Wolff, P. (1991). Children's eye movements during reading. In J.F. Stein (Ed.), *Vision and visual dyslexia* (pp. 251–262). London, UK: Macmillan Press.

Miller, B., & O'Donnell, C. (2013). Opening a window into reading development: Eye movements' role within a broader literacy research framework. *School Psychology Review, 42,* 123–139.

Olulade, O., Napoliello, E., & Eden, G. (2013). Abnormal visual motion processing is not a cause of dyslexia. *Neuron, 79,* 180–190.

Pollatsek, A., Bolozky, S., Well, A., & Rayner, K. (1981). Asymmetries in the perceptual span for Israeli readers. *Brain and Language, 14,* 174–180.

Rau, A., Moeller, K., & Landerl, K. (2014). The transition from sublexical to lexical processing in a consistent orthography: An eye-tracking study. *Scientific Studies of Reading, 18*(3), 224–233.

Rayner, K. (1985a). Do faulty eye movements cause dyslexia? *Developmental Neuropsychology, 1,* 3–15.

Rayner, K. (1985b). The role of eye movements in learning to read and reading disability. *Remedial and Special Education, 6*(6), 53–60.

Rayner, K. (1986). Eye movements and the perceptual span in beginning and skilled readers. *Journal of Experimental Child Psychology, 41,* 211–236.

Rayner, K. (1998). Eye movements in reading and information processing: 20 years of research. *Psychological Bulletin, 124,* 372–422.

Rayner, K. (2009). The thirty-fifth Sir Frederick Bartlett lecture: Eye movements and attention in reading, scene perception, and visual search. *Quarterly Journal of Experimental Psychology, 62,* 1457–1506.

Rayner, K., Ardoin, S., & Binder, K. (2013). Children's eye movements in reading: A commentary. *School Psychology Review, 42,* 223–233.

Rayner, K., & Bertera, J. (1979). Reading without a fovea. *Science, 206,* 468–469.

Reichle, E., Liversedge, S., Drieghe, D., Blythe, H., Joseph, H., White, S., & Rayner, K. (2013). Using E-Z Reader to examine the concurrent development of eye-movement control and reading skill. *Developmental Review, 33,* 110–149.

Schotter, E., Tran, R., & Rayner, K. (2014). Don't believe what you read (only once): Comprehension is supported by regressions during reading. *Psychological Science, 25,* 1218–1226.

Thaler, V., Urton, K., Heine, A., Hawelka, S., Engl, V., & Jacobs, A. (2009). Differential behavioral and eye movement patterns of dyslexic readers with and without attentional deficits during single word reading. *Neuropsychologia, 47,* 2436–2445.

Valle, A., Binder, K., Walsh, C., Nemier, C., & Bangs, K. (2013). Eye movements, prosody, and word frequency among average- and high-skilled second-grade readers. *School Psychology Review, 42,* 171–190.

Vorstius, C., Radach, R., Mayer, M., & Lonigan, C. (2013). Monitoring local comprehension in sentence reading. *School Psychology Review, 42,* 191–206.

7

Neurobiological Bases of Word Recognition and Reading Comprehension

Distinctions, Overlaps, and Implications for Instruction and Intervention

Laurie E. Cutting, Stephen Kent Bailey, Laura A. Barquero, and Katherine Aboud

A primary goal of education is to enable students to learn through reading, a skill required within all academic subjects and one that is widely used in everyday life. The National Assessment of Educational Progress (NAEP), however, reports that more than 30% of fourth graders and 20% of eighth graders score at below-basic levels in reading (NAEP, 2013). Reading disabilities likely contribute to these disappointing numbers, with estimates of 5%–17.5% of the population exhibiting word-level reading deficits (WRD) and 3%–10% showing specific reading comprehension deficits (S-RCD) in which comprehension is poor despite adequate word-level skills (see Aaron, Joshi, & Williams, 1999; Catts, Hogan, & Fey, 2003; Leach, Scarborough, & Rescorla, 2003; Nation, Marshall, & Snowling, 2001; Torppa et al., 2007). Better understanding comprehension difficulties requires an understanding of the components of reading comprehension as well as the underlying neurobiology that may facilitate or impede the processes of deriving meaning from text.

The Simple View of Reading conceptualizes reading comprehension as an intertwining of two levels of processing: 1) word-level reading processes, including phonological awareness, decoding, and sight word recognition and 2) language comprehension processes not specific to reading, including vocabulary, semantics, syntax, and sentence processing (Hoover & Gough, 1990; Scarborough, 2001). The two strands are useful not only in categorizing reading problems (Catts, Nielsen, Bridges, Liu, & Bontempo, 2013; Spencer, Quinn, & Wagner,

2014) but also in viewing reading within a developmental context: Younger children begin to develop word-level reading skills (e.g., alphabetic knowledge and automaticity in decoding) somewhat independently of developing language comprehension (e.g., background knowledge, vocabulary, language structure). To obtain the eventual goal of deriving meaning from text, however, students must be able to negotiate the intertwining of the two strands. Students who cannot readily do so face difficulties, particularly when instruction shifts from "learning to read" to "reading to learn" and when text comprehension becomes paramount; however, how all these skills weave together in order for children to become successful readers and solid comprehenders is a complex endeavor that likely requires more than word-level and language comprehension skills and one that researchers are still only beginning to understand. As illustrated in Figure 7.1, which is an adaptation of Scarborough's (2001) original rope illustration, there is an increasing realization that, in addition to linguistic skills, executive function—or "a family of [effortful] top-down processes [that] are needed when you have to concentrate and pay attention, when 'going on automatic' or relying on instinct or intuition would be ill-advised, insufficient, or impossible" (Diamond, 2013, p. 7)—may play an important role in facilitating reading

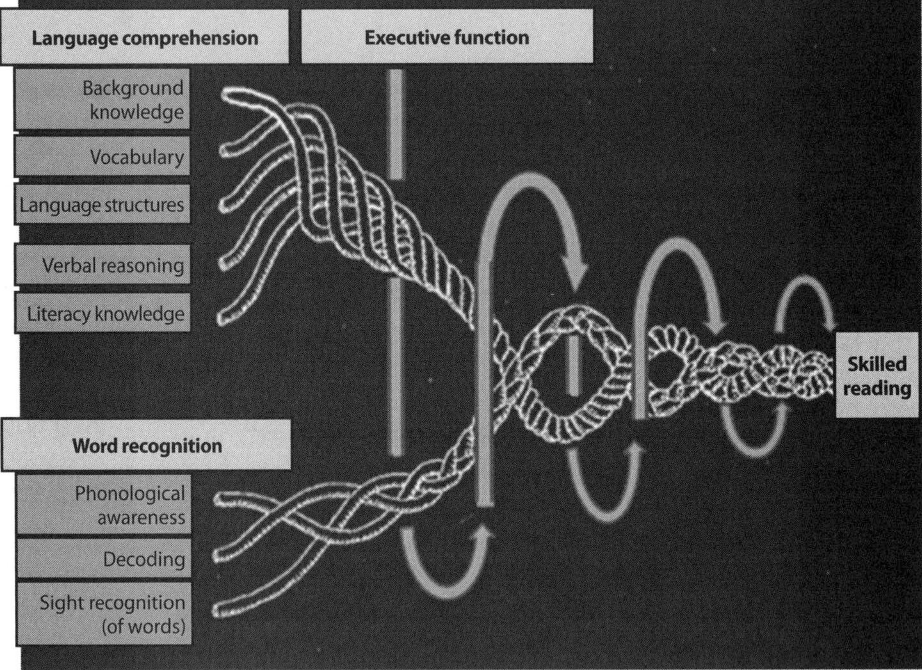

Figure 7.1. Expanded simple view of reading. This illustration shows aspects hypothesized to be the building blocks of reading. The lower strand illustrates the subcomponents that support word recognition. The upper strand illustrates the components needed for higher level aspects of reading, and the curved lines surrounding the ropes represent the potential role of executive functioning in integrating these skills. (Adapted with permission of Guilford Press, from Scarborough, H.S. [2001]. Connecting early language and literacy to later reading [dis]abilities: Evidence, theory, and practice. In S.B. Neuman & D.K. Dickinson [Eds.], *Handbook of early literacy research* [p. 98]. New York, NY: Guilford Press; permission conveyed through Copyright Clearance Center, Inc. As adapted in Cutting, L.E. [2013, November]. *From words to text: Behavioral and neurobiological correlates of reading*. Paper presented at the annual meeting of the International Dyslexia Association, New Orleans, LA.)

growth. Indeed, our studies have shown that executive function plays an important role beyond that of word-level and linguistic processes (Eason, Goldberg, Young, Geist, & Cutting, 2012; Locascio, Mahone, Eason, & Cutting, 2010; Rimrodt et al., 2009; Sesma, Mahone, Levine, Eason, & Cutting, 2009).

Within this context, this chapter reviews the cognitive and neurobiological components of reading comprehension, first focusing on word-level processes, then examining both cognitive and neurobiological findings "beyond" the word level (i.e., reading comprehension). Finally, we discuss our findings within the context of implications for practice.

WORD-LEVEL READING AND DISCOURSE COMPREHENSION

Successful reading comprehension has long been known to be a complex and multifaceted process. The existing body of knowledge about early reading acquisition identifies word-level processes as the primary contributors to reading comprehension, yet much remains to be understood about what other processes impact a child's reading ability.

Neurobiological models of reading have focused on both word- and comprehension-level processes, with comprehension-level findings consistently (and not surprisingly) showing that comprehension elicits a more extensive network of activation of both domain-specific (i.e., language) and domain-general (i.e., executive function) regions than processing isolated words. Nevertheless, most studies have focused on comprehension in typically developing readers, especially at the sentence level; fewer studies have focused on discourse processing in the context of educational gain and reading impairment. Rimrodt et al. (2009) found that during sentence processing, readers with dyslexia show greater activation of language and attention areas when reading incongruent sentences, suggesting more effortful processing. The study additionally found that word- and text-level fluency correlated with increased activation in the left occipitotemporal area (Rimrodt et al., 2009; see Figure 7.2). This study and others on discourse and sentence processing, however, are restricted to children with word-decoding deficits. No studies that we are aware of have examined sentence or discourse processes in struggling readers with typical word processing ability. Understanding the neural correlates of comprehension, particularly discourse processing, in older (adolescents) and impaired readers with a wider range of deficits is a critical area in need of more extensive exploration. Older readers generally are more resistant to intervention and often have profiles that are heterogeneous, with varied reasons for poor comprehension. Therefore, it is not surprising that successful intervention is more challenging in this population. Thus insights into word- and comprehension-level processes using neurobiological measures may be especially informative with regard to understanding the best methods of instruction and intervention for those who struggle with reading. In this section, we first review the neuroimaging literature relevant to word-level and comprehension-level processing and then discuss work examining the distinctions and overlaps between the

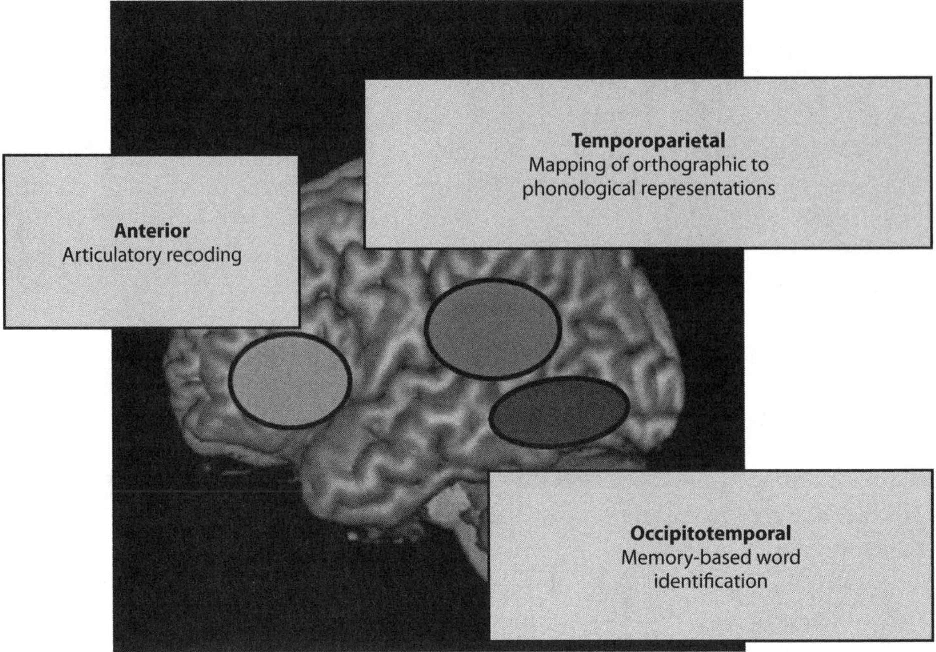

Figure 7.2. Left-hemisphere brain regions associated with single-word reading. (Reprinted from Pugh, K.R., Einar Mencl, W., Jenner, A.R., Katz, L., Frost, S.J., Lee, J.R., Shaywitz, S.E., & Shaywitz, B.A. [2001]. Neurobiological studies of reading and reading disabilities. *Journal of Communication Disorders, 34*[6], 479–492. Copyright 2001, with permission from Elsevier.)

two. Of particular potential relevance for intervention and responsiveness are the areas in which word and comprehension processing overlap; recent findings suggest that these areas may be key nodes that support overall reading, and therefore it follows that anomalies in these regions could potentially result in highly intractable reading difficulty (Bailey et al., 2014; Swett et al., 2013).

Word-Level Processes

Research on the neurobiological bases of word recognition using functional neuroimaging has consistently revealed that skilled readers recruit a distributed network of brain regions to read, including activation in left-hemisphere language regions, particularly the left occipitotemporal (OT) area (Figure 7.2; Richlan, 2012). In particular, left OT activation has been shown to correlate with increasing print proficiency (Shaywitz et al., 2004). Differences have also been noted in semantic versus phonological processing (Price, 2012). Conversely, neural correlates of those with word-reading deficits show left-hemisphere *dysfunction,* including prominent underactivation in left occipitotemporal regions, as well as left inferior parietal and inferior frontal regions (Richlan, 2012). Studies have also revealed neural predictors of reading growth (Hoeft et al., 2011) that add power to predicting outcomes as well as those areas that show increased activation following intervention (Barquero, Davis, & Cutting, 2014).

In addition to functional underactivation, the left OT region has shown aberrant functional connectivity patterns in children and adults with WRD (Finn et al., 2013; van der Mark et al., 2011). Compared with typically developing (TD) readers, those with WRD showed less connectivity (underconnectivity) between the left OT and language regions, including temporoparietal regions. In contrast, WRD exhibited overconnectivity between the left OT and visual processing regions. In congruence with the functional imaging findings, our work using diffusion tensor imaging (DTI), a measurement of the structural integrity of white matter tracts, highlights the importance of the left OT in WRD. Examining five posterior–anterior gradient regions of interest in the left OT region showed different structural connectivity patterns in children with WRD compared with TD readers (Fan, Davis, Anderson, & Cutting, 2014). Results indicated that readers with WRD exhibit underconnectivity between the left OT and several other regions involved in reading, including the left inferior temporal gyrus (ITG), middle temporal gyrus (MTG), superior temporal gyrus (STG), and left inferior parietal regions, while showing overconnectivity between the OT and primary visual regions. Such approaches may be fruitful for expanding our prediction of response to treatment; indeed, studies have shown that DTI measures may help predict treatment response and reading growth (Davis et al., 2010; Myers et al., 2014).

Comprehension

Many imaging studies have examined the neurobiological correlates of comprehension (e.g., Fletcher et al., 1995; Horowitz-Kraus, Vannest, & Holland, 2013; Maguire, Frith, & Morris, 1999; Price, 2012; Speer, Reynolds, Swallow, & Zacks, 2009; Xu, Kemeny, Park, Frattali, & Braun, 2005). Patterns of activation emerge when processing discourse that cannot be predicted from models of reading single words, or even single sentences, in isolation (Xu et al., 2005). Areas that consistently appear to be unique to processing narrative texts include the dorsomedial prefrontal cortex (dmPFC); bilateral temporal poles/anterior temporal lobe (see Figure 7.3), thought to play a role in generating semantic associations in connected text; and posterior-medial structures, including the posterior cingulate cortex (PCC) and precuneus (PCU; Figure 7.3), which have been associated with updates in and integration of the reader's mental model (e.g., Price, 2012; Speer et al., 2009; Whitney et al., 2009; Yarkoni, Speer, & Zacks, 2008). Only a handful of studies using fMRI, including ours, have examined, how the neural correlates of discourse processing change during the temporal progression of the discourse (Speer et al., 2009; Xu et al., 2005; Yarkoni, Speer, & Zacks, 2008). Consistent with others' findings, Swett et al. (2013) found that regions in the posterior parietal cortex associated with visuospatial updating and attention are involved in the construction of a reader's mental model, yet language in the temporal lobe areas are more involved in its maintenance. Also, temporal-lobe language activation that initially started as overlapping between words and discourse diverges over time. Overall, existing studies support theoretical

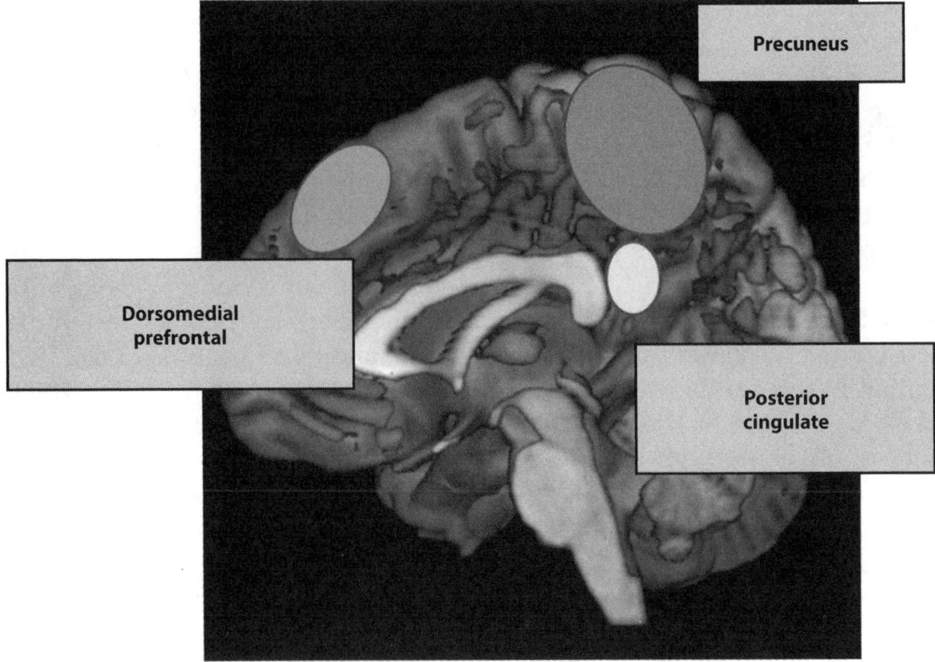

Figure 7.3. Regions outside the language network that are implicated in text reading.

models that suggest that building a mental representation of text is a dynamic process in which the cognitive demands shift.

Also consistent with the existing literature, our findings indicate that reading comprehension involves processes that are distinct from, as well as overlap, those required in isolated word reading (Bailey et al., 2014; Swett et al., 2013). In terms of distinct areas, studies have shown greater activation in prefrontal regions for comprehension tasks (Figure 7.3; also see Price, 2012) as well as classic language-related regions compared with isolated word processing (Figure 7.4); although there are areas in common, the question is how they function when the requirements are to read words (i.e., word-level processing) versus read words and comprehend them in context. Interestingly, Horowitz-Kraus et al. (2013) reported that during a listening comprehension task for 5–7-year-olds, neural activation was linked to reading comprehension outcomes at age 11 and included both classic temporal language regions and areas that overlap with word-level processing, as well as prefrontal cortices.

Whereas it is clear that word and comprehension processes take place in overlapping regions, few studies have actually examined the areas of overlap between word and discourse processing in the same experiment, and in children. This may be important, as, behaviorally, a large amount of variance in predicting reading is *shared* between word- and (listening) comprehension-level processes (Cutting & Scarborough, 2009). Therefore, understanding the neurobiological origins of this overlap (and distinction) may provide insight

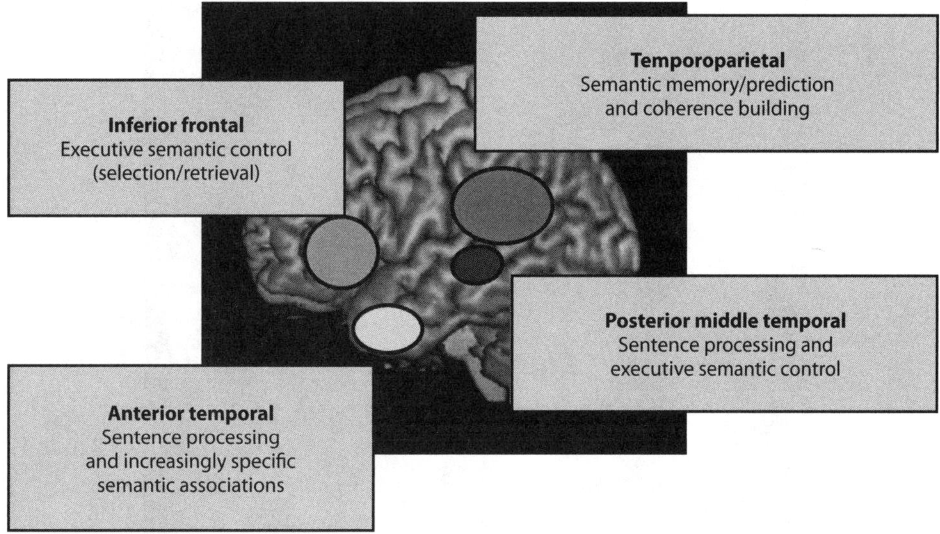

Figure 7.4. Left-lateralized brain regions associated with semantic processing.

into which aspects of reading are the most problematic for different children, thus allowing for greater tailoring of instruction. For example, Bailey et al. (2014) conducted functional connectivity analyses using areas showing strong overlapping variance between word and discourse processing (i.e., the left dorsal inferior frontal gyrus [LdIFG]; the left posterior middle temporal gyrus [LpMTG]; the left temporal pole; and left medial prefrontal cortex [LmPFC]) as seed regions. Results showed that during isolated word reading, both the LdIFG and the LpMTG seed regions exhibited strong overlapping connections (for each seed) to the bilateral ventral IFG (vIFG) and right insula (Figure 7.5, light arrows), and the strength of connectivity *increased with greater word-recognition proficiency;* no connectivity findings for left temporal pole reached significance. In contrast, passages showed strong and overlapping connections to the angular gyrus for all three seed regions (Figure 7.5, dark arrows; temporal pole not shown), and the strength of connectivity *increased with greater reading comprehension proficiency.*

Our initial connectivity findings on words versus passages therefore suggest that connections from key nodes during isolated word processing may be important for precise meaning and/or semantic retrieval and top-down control, but during passage reading, connections are made to areas in which information is combined and integrated. Importantly, an area known to elicit more activation for connected text as compared with isolated words, the left temporal pole, showed no significant areas of connectivity for words but showed connectivity to the same left angular gyrus (AG) region for passages. Also, the LmPFC showed connectivity patterns to language regions, specifically the LdIFG and left temporal pole, for passages but not for words. This suggests that

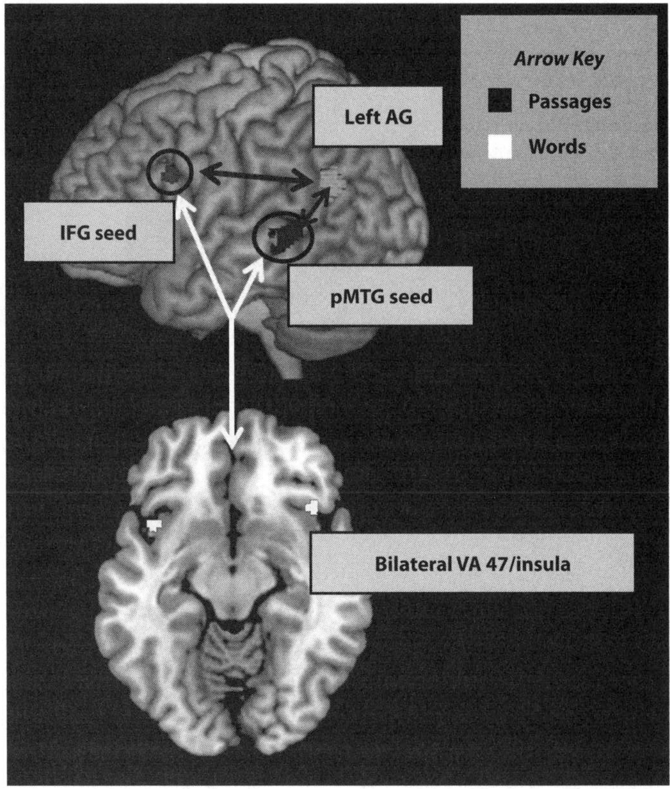

Figure 7.5. Semantic processing regions (black regions) functionally correlate with different regions (white regions) during passage reading (dark arrows) and word reading (light arrows). (*Key:* pMTG, posterior middle temporal gyrus; AG, angular gyrus; IFG, interior frontal gyrus.)

the LmPFC may play a specific role in reading comprehension, an observation consistent with our behavior findings showing that executive function contributes specifically to reading comprehension (Sesma et al., 2009). In sum, findings suggest that words and passages (reading comprehension) activate key nodes in overlapping neural areas; however, these nodes diverge in that they *connect* to different areas depending on which type of processing is happening (i.e., word- or discourse-level processing). Thus this network appears to have a role in both word-level and discourse-level processing and, therefore, may be important for predicting responsiveness to intervention, especially for older readers whose reading difficulties are heterogeneous and often include both word- and discourse-level difficulties.

An additional aspect of reading comprehension that our research group has introduced involves the neurobiological correlates of identifying a text's most central ideas (Swett et al., 2013). Behaviorally, skilled readers form connections among a text's semantically related ideas as they read. Some ideas are causally or logically connected to many other ideas and, as a result, emerge as being *central* to the overall meaning of the text, whereas others have relatively few connections and fall out as being less important, or *peripheral* (Trabasso & van den Broek, 1985; van den Broek, 1988). A robust finding in the behavioral reading comprehension literature is that skilled readers are more likely to recognize and recall ideas that are more central to the text's meaning, regardless of genre (van den Broek, 1988). Thus *sensitivity to centrality* is an important indicator of reading-comprehension ability. We examined these processes neurobiologically, showing that central ideas elicit greater activation in various areas, including the PCC and PCU, compared with peripheral ideas (Swett et al., 2013).

Of final note are the differential demands of various types of texts; behaviorally, researchers know that narrative and expository text differ in cognitive demands, with expository texts placing greater demands on executive function (Eason et al., 2012). Nevertheless, how this may manifest neurobiologically is unknown, but it is a topic that our lab is currently investigating. Such approaches to examining the nuances of text features (i.e., central–peripheral and narrative–expository) may have implications for intervention and the development of treatment protocols.

IMPLICATIONS FOR PRACTICE

Of primary interest in our current line of research are the practical implications of the brain regions discussed and whether neuroimaging can offer insights into treatment for reading disabilities. It is often the case that individuals with significant and/or treatment-resistant reading problems have difficulties at both the word and comprehension levels. This inherently makes sense: If one has difficulty in either words or comprehension, but not both, then it seems logical that he or she could use compensatory mechanisms to become a better reader. In contrast, if one is "hit" in both areas, then it would seem more difficult for him or her to overcome reading difficulty. Such logic led us to examine, using other data from an intervention study, profiles of responders and nonresponders on the percentage of signal change extracted from these key overlap regions, illustrated in Figure 7.5. These very preliminary findings provided some suggestion that these overlap regions would indeed play a role in predicting response. Of course, what researchers ultimately want to be able to test is whether oral discourse comprehension and word-level processing have these key areas of overlap and, if so, whether they predict intervention response. Nevertheless, initial findings have led us to an interesting thought process: Perhaps researchers need to be examining where the two strands in Figure 7.1 overlap—not where they are distinct.

Other areas of investigation that seem potentially applicable to understanding everyday practice include utilizing structural connectivity analyses (from DTI data) to predict responsiveness; indeed, studies are increasingly suggesting that neurobiological data may have utility in predicting response to intervention (Hoeft et al., 2011; Myers et al., 2014). Furthermore, our very preliminary data analyses on the overlap regions in our intervention dataset also suggest that neurobiological data can more accurately predict those who will be responders versus those who will not. Finally, examining aspects of text such as the processing of central versus peripheral ideas and narrative versus expository text, may offer further opportunities for the application of neurobiological knowledge to practice. Such investigations may prove fruitful in understanding more about those who struggle with reading in substantial ways.

SUMMARY

There are many neuroimaging studies that have illuminated the neurobiological correlates with word- and comprehension-level processing. Much work remains, however, in using these tools to identify the neural foundations of reading difficulties. Our research group's current and future research is particularly interested in exploring the implications of distinct versus common substrates of these processes. Identifying neural regions that are critical to multiple levels of text comprehension could help specify the field's understanding of struggling readers, particularly those resistant to interventions currently available and older struggling readers for whom the origins of reading difficulties are heterogeneous. In addition, the examination of aspects of text that have been behaviorally implicated in comprehension difficulty, for instance readers' sensitivity to textual centrality and text genre, will help better identify the role these regions of the brain play in reading. Isolating regions that are predictive of specific reading outcomes for multiple populations of struggling readers will ultimately hone the definition of reading difficulties, as well as interventional and instructional strategies, and perhaps allow for more tailored treatment to individual profiles. These are the key components of reading that our lab is seeking to address in our current line of reading research.

REFERENCES

Aaron, P., Joshi, M., & Williams, K. (1999). Not all reading disabilities are alike. *Journal of Learning Disabilities, 31*(2), 12–137.

Bailey, S.K., Swett, K., Burns, S.S., Sefcik, A., Barquero, L.A., & Cutting, L.E. (2014, March). *Expository text comprehension and executive function: An fMRI study of adolescent reading.* Poster presented at the annual meeting of the Cognitive Neuroscience Society, Boston, MA.

Barquero, L.A., Davis, N., & Cutting, L.E. (2014). Neuroimaging of reading intervention: A systematic review and activation likelihood estimate meta-analysis. *PLOS ONE, 9*(1), e83668. doi:10.1371/journal.pone.0083668

Catts, H.W., Hogan, T.P., & Fey, M.E. (2003). Subgrouping poor readers on the basis of individual differences in reading-related abilities. *Journal of Learning Disabilities, 36*(2), 151–164. doi:10.1177/002221940303600208

Catts, H.W., Nielsen, D., Bridges, M.S., Liu, Y., & Bontempo, D. (2013). Early identification of reading disabilities within an RTI framework. *Journal of Learning Disabilities.* doi: 0022219413498115

Cutting, L.E. (2013). *From Words to Text: Behavioral and Neurobiological Correlates of Reading.* Presented at the annual meeting of the International Dyslexia Association, New Orleans, LA.

Cutting, L.E., & Scarborough, H.S. (2009). Prediction of reading comprehension: Relative contributions of word recognition, language proficiency, and other cognitive skills can depend on how comprehension is measured. *Scientific Studies of Reading, 10*(3), 37–41. doi:10.1207/s1532799xssr1003

Davis, N., Fan, Q., Compton, D.L., Fuchs, D., Fuchs, L.S., Cutting, L.E., . . . Anderson, A.W. (2010). Influences of neural pathway integrity on children's response to reading instruction. *Frontiers in Systems Neuroscience, 4*(October), 150. doi:10.3389/fnsys.2010.00150

Diamond, A. (2013). Executive functions. *Annual Review of Psychology, 64,* 135–168. doi:10.1146/annurev-psych-113011-143750

Eason, S.H., Goldberg, L.F., Young, K.M., Geist, M.C., & Cutting, L.E. (2012). Reader-text interactions: How differential text and question types influence cognitive skills needed for reading comprehension. *Journal of Educational Psychology, 104*(3), 515–528. doi:10.1037/a0027182

Fan, Q., Davis, N., Anderson, A.W., & Cutting, L.E. (2014). Structural connectivity patterns of the visual word form area and children's reading ability. *Brain Research, 1586,* 118–129. doi: 10.1016/j.brainres.2014.08.050.

Finn, E.S., Shen, X., Holahan, J.M., Scheinost, D., Lacadie, C., Papademetris, X., . . . Constable, R.T. (2013). Disruption of functional networks in dyslexia: A whole-brain, data-driven analysis of connectivity. *Biological Psychiatry, 76*(5), 397–404. doi:10.1016/j.biopsych.2013.08.031

Fletcher, P., Happé, F., Frith, U., Baker, S., Dolan, R., Frackowiak, R., & Frith, C. (1995). Other minds in the brain: A functional imaging study of "theory of mind" in story comprehension. *Cognition, 57*(2), 109–128. Retrieved from http://www.ncbi.nlm.nih.gov/pubmed/8556839

Hoeft, F., McCandliss, B.D., Black, J.M., Gantman, A., Zakerani, N., Hulme, C., . . . Gabrieli, J.D.E. (2011). Neural systems predicting long-term outcome in dyslexia. *Proceedings of the National Academy of Sciences, USA, 108*(1), 361–366. doi:10.1073/pnas.1008950108

Hoover, W.A., & Gough, P.B. (1990). The simple view of reading. *Reading and Writing, 2,* 127–160. doi:10.1007/BF00401799

Horowitz-Kraus, T., Vannest, J.J., & Holland, S.K. (2013). Overlapping neural circuitry for narrative comprehension and proficient reading in children and adolescents. *Neuropsychologia, 51*(13), 2651–2662. doi:10.1016/j.neuropsychologia.2013.09.002

Leach, J.M., Scarborough, H.S., & Rescorla, L. (2003). Late-emerging reading disabilities. *Journal of Educational Psychology, 95*(2), 211–224. doi:10.1037/0022-0663.95.2.211

Locascio, G., Mahone, E.M., Eason, S.H., & Cutting, L.E. (2010). Executive dysfunction among children with reading comprehension deficits. *Journal of Learning Disabilities, 43*(5), 441–454. doi:10.1177/0022219409355476.Executive

Maguire, E.A., Frith, C.D., & Morris, R.G. (1999). The functional neuroanatomy of comprehension and memory: The importance of prior knowledge. *Brain: A Journal of Neurology, 122* (Pt 10), 1839–1850. Retrieved from http://www.ncbi.nlm.nih.gov/pubmed/10506087

Myers, C.A., Vandermosten, M., Farris, E.A., Hancock, R., Gimenez, P., Black, J.M., . . . Tumber, M. (2014). White matter morphometric changes uniquely predict children' s reading acquisition. *Psychological Science,* 1–14. doi:10.1177/0956797614544511

Nation, K., Marshall, C.M., & Snowling, M.J. (2001). Phonological and semantic contributions to children's picture naming skill: Evidence from children with developmental reading disorders. *Language and Cognitive Processes, 16*(2), 241–259.

National Assessment of Educational Progress. (2013). *Nation's Report Card.* U.S. Department of Education, Institute of Education Sciences, National Center for Education Statistics.

Price, C.J. (2012). A review and synthesis of the first 20 years of PET and fMRI studies of heard speech, spoken language and reading. *NeuroImage, 62*(2), 816–847. doi:10.1016/j.neuroimage.2012.04.062

Richlan, F. (2012). Developmental dyslexia: Dysfunction of a left hemisphere reading network. *Frontiers in Human Neuroscience, 6*(May), 120. doi:10.3389/fnhum.2012.00120

Rimrodt, S.L., Clements-Stephens, A.M., Pugh, K.R., Courtney, S.M., Gaur, P., Pekar, J.J., & Cutting, L.E. (2009). Functional MRI of sentence comprehension in children with dyslexia: Beyond word recognition. *Cerebral Cortex, 19*(2), 402–413. doi:10.1093/cercor/bhn092

Scarborough, H.S. (2001). Connecting early language and literacy to later reading disabilities: Evidence, theory, and practice. In F. Fletcher-Campbell, J. Soler, & G. Reid (Eds.), *Approaching Difficulties in Literacy Development: Assessment, pedagogy and programmes* (pp. 23–28). Milton Keyes, UK: Sage Publications. Retrieved from http://books.google.com/books?hl=en&lr=&id=sfKpsYBGX2MC&pgis=1

Sesma, H.W., Mahone, E.M., Levine, T., Eason, S.H., & Cutting, L.E. (2009). The contribution of executive skills to reading comprehension. *Child Neuropsychology, 15*(3), 232–246. doi:10.1080/09297040802220029.

Shaywitz, B.A., Shaywitz, S.E., Blachman, B.A., Pugh, K.R., Fulbright, R.K., Skudlarski, P., . . . Gore, J.C. (2004). Development of left occipitotemporal systems for skilled reading in children after a phonologically-based intervention. *Biological Psychiatry, 55*(9), 926–933. doi:10.1016/j.biopsych.2003.12.019

Speer, N.K., Reynolds, J.R., Swallow, K.M., & Zacks, J.M. (2009). Reading stories activates neural representations of visual and motor experiences. *Psychological Science, 20*(8), 989–999. doi:10.1111/j.1467-9280.2009.02397.x

Spencer, M., Quinn, J.M., & Wagner, R.K. (2014). Specific reading comprehension disability: Major problem, myth, or misnomer? *Learning Disabilities Research & Practice, 29*(1), 3–9. doi:10.1111/ldrp.12024

Swett, K., Miller, A.C., Burns, S., Hoeft, F., Davis, N., Petrill, S.A., & Cutting, L.E. (2013). Comprehending expository texts: The dynamic neurobiological correlates of building a coherent text representation. *Frontiers in Human Neuroscience, 7*(December), 1–14. doi:10.3389/fnhum.2013.00853

Swett, K.E., Burns, S., Petrill, S., Bailey, S.K., & Cutting, L.E. (in progress). Comprehending text versus recognizing words in typical and struggling adolescent readers: Distinct patterns of functional connectivity from common semantic hubs. *Developmental Science.*

Torppa, M., Tolvanen, A., Poikkeus, A.-M., Eklund, K., Lerkkanen, M.-K., Leskinen, E., & Lyytinen, H. (2007). Reading development subtypes and their early characteristics. *Annals of Dyslexia, 57*(1), 3–32. doi:10.1007/s11881-007-0003-0

Trabasso, T., & van den Broek, P. (1985). Causal thinking and the representation of narrative events. *Journal of Memory and Language, 24,* 612–630.

van den Broek, P. (1988). The effects of causal relations and hierarchical importance of story statements. *Journal of Memory and Language, 27,* 1–22.

Van der Mark, S., Klaver, P., Bucher, K., Maurer, U., Schulz, E., Brem, S., . . . Brandeis, D. (2011). The left occipitotemporal system in reading: Disruption of focal fMRI connectivity to left inferior frontal and inferior parietal language areas in children with dyslexia. *NeuroImage, 54*(3), 2426–2436. doi:10.1016/j.neuroimage.2010.10.002

Whitney, C., Huber, W., Klann, J., Weis, S., Krach, S., & Kircher, T. (2009). Neural correlates of narrative shifts during auditory story comprehension. *NeuroImage, 47*(1), 360–366. doi:10.1016/j.neuroimage.2009.04.037

Xu, J., Kemeny, S., Park, G., Frattali, C., & Braun, A. (2005). Language in context: Emergent features of word, sentence, and narrative comprehension. *NeuroImage, 25,* 1002–1015. doi:10.1016/j.neuroimage.2004.12.013

Yarkoni, T., Speer, N., & Zacks, J. (2008). Neural substrates of narrative comprehension and memory. *NeuroImage, 41*(4), 1408–1425. doi:10.1016/j.neuroimage.2008.03.062.

8

Integrating Neurobiological Findings in Search of a Neurochemical "Signature" of Dyslexia

Stephanie N. Del Tufo and Kenneth R. Pugh

Dyslexia is a hereditable disorder that is estimated to affect 5%–17.5% of the population (Shaywitz & Shaywitz, 2008). Researchers and clinicians characterize this developmental disorder based on a failure to read at grade level, regardless of instruction, socioeconomic status, intelligence, or motivation (Snowling, 2000). Dyslexia is primarily characterized by profound difficulties with phonological awareness (Bradley & Bryant, 1978; Liberman, Shankweiler, & Liberman, 1989). Remediation programs for individuals with dyslexia focus largely on phonological awareness but often only show short-term gains for 1–2 years following treatment (Peterson & Pennington, 2012). Many individuals with dyslexia also experience severe emotional repercussions—that is, these individuals view academic environments as "threatening" and often have higher rates of depression, frustration, and anxiety. Individuals with dyslexia develop avoidance behaviors and have higher rates of entry into the juvenile justice system (Sideridis, Mouzaki, Simos, & Protopapas, 2006). Despite these facts and the ability to identify dyslexia through standardized assessments, debate remains as to its underlying etiology.

In this chapter, we briefly review the core neuroimaging findings on reading development and dyslexia that indicate a replicable and robustly divergent brain activation network. We provide an introduction to the gray and white matter differences that have monopolized the attention of researchers for the last decade. Despite the enormous gains in functional and structural imaging, there is a clear gap in the neurobiology of dyslexia: the role of neurochemistry.

We give an overview of the sparse literature on the neurochemical signature of dyslexia from in vivo studies of magnetic resonance spectroscopy (MRS) and attempt to provide a broad understanding of genetic research and the key findings of these studies. We also briefly explain how a nonreading animal is used as a reading disorder model to investigate protein expression. Finally, we discuss studies that are bringing these diverse fields and methods together to gain a more complete understanding of the complex neurobiological systems that underlie developmental dyslexia.

FUNCTIONAL MAGNETIC RESONANCE IMAGING

The most basic neural model of the adult reading circuit is composed of three primary regions: left occipitotemporal, left temporoparietal, and left inferior frontal regions (Pugh et al., 2010). These have been confirmed by numerous studies that show robust functional activation for reading-related tasks: the left occipitotemporal region, which includes the visual word form area (VWFA) in word-reading tasks (e.g., orthography); the left temporoparietal region in tasks focusing on the integration of oral language with reading-relevant orthographic information (e.g., phonology, morphology, and semantics); and the left inferior frontal regions, which include the *pars triangularis* and *pars opercularis* for tasks focused on naming, phonological processing, and phonetic identification and, in conjunction with temporoparietal networks, when learning to read.

Throughout development, individuals with dyslexia show differing patterns of functional activation when compared with age- and reading-matched peers. Even in infancy, for example, typically developing infants' show increased activation in the primary reading network. In infants at hereditary risk for dyslexia, this increase in activation is not seen. During childhood, typically developing children become more automatic readers; they transition to using the VWFA for fast word recognition (McCandliss, Cohen, & Dehaene, 2003). This milestone is not seen in dyslexic children (Shaywitz et al., 2007). Although it is easy to assume that dyslexic children don't use the VWFA for fast word recognition due to a failure to reach automaticity, the evidence from infant prereaders clearly emphasizes the biological nature of dyslexia.

Adults with dyslexia also consistently show aberrant functional activation (e.g., reduced or absent activation in brain regions known to be involved in reading). This reduction in activation is seen in response to phonological tasks in the left temporoparietal cortex (see Démonet, Taylor, & Chaix, 2004, for review) and orthography in the VWFA activation (Shaywitz et al., 2007). Reduction in activation is thought to reflect an immature or disconnected functional reading network. However, disruptions in the functional reading network are not simple or straightforward. Increased or dispersed activation is also often seen in dyslexic readers, particularly in the right superior temporal gyrus and the right inferior frontal gyrus. Increases in activation have been suggested to reflect a compensatory mechanism.

FUNCTIONAL CONNECTIVITY

Functional connectivity analysis typically describes studies in which an a priori region of activation is temporally associated with other regions throughout the brain; these regions, in essence, activate together in time during an in-scanner (e.g., functional magnetic resonance imaging [fMRI]) task. In an early study, Pugh and colleagues (2000) found that dyslexic readers showed less robust phonological representations: Disruptions were found between the left angular gyrus, the superior temporal gyrus, and the VWFA on a non-word-rhyming phonological task. Many studies have since reported that dyslexic readers show divergent temporal connectivity—the correlations typically found among remote brain regions are irregular or absent during an in-scanner fMRI task. Findings include decreased temporal connectivity between the superior temporal gyrus and VWFA and increased temporal connectivity, bilaterally, between the left and right superior temporal gyri. Koyama et al. (2013) suggest that in children, the functional connections among the regions involved in speech production and speech perception are predictive of reading ability. Regardless of how dyslexia is studied, as a unidimensional disorder (i.e., across a spectrum of reading ability from good to very impaired) or as a multidimensional disorder (i.e., subtyping based on differences in reading-task performance), evidence seems to indicate that dyslexic readers use a divergent pathway for reading, one not as well suited to fluent, automatized reading.

STRUCTURAL DIFFERENCES

Dyslexic individuals evince cortical structural differences in both gray and white matter. Gray matter is composed of neuron cell bodies, glial cells used for support and protection, and unmyelinated axons. Dyslexic individuals have gray matter decreases bilaterally in the fusiform and temporoparietal regions, in the left occipitotemporal region, in the right lingual gyrus (Eliez et al., 2000), and throughout the cerebellum (Eckert et al., 2003). Increases in gray matter have been found in the precentral and postcentral gyri, the superior and medial frontal gyri, and the precuneus, as well as the posterior, temporal, and inferior temporal gyri (Kronbichler et al., 2008). Structural differences align very closely with functional activation differences (Linkersdörfer, Lonnemann, Lindberg, Hasselhorn, & Fiebach, 2012).

White matter is composed of glial cells and axons myelinated by glial cells. White matter structural images are acquired through a magnetic resonance imaging (MRI) sequence called diffusion tensor imaging (DTI). White matter is typically separated into tracts—myelinated axons grouped into bundles and assessed through a measurement of fractional anisotropy. Fractional anisotropy describes the diffusion of water along the path of least resistance. In the cortex, this dispersion occurs largely in and around white matter tracts. Increased myelination causes faster signal transmission across the cortex and will result in higher levels of fractional anisotropy. Lower levels of fractional anisotropy are indicative of decreased myelination. In adults with dyslexia, fractional anisotropy has been found to be lower in two tracts: the left arcuate fasciculus (Klingberg et al., 2000) and the longitudinal fasciculus (Steinbrink et al., 2008). This indicates that individuals with dyslexia have smaller or less tightly bundled white matter tracts.

Fractional anisotropy measures in the left arcuate and longitudinal fasciculus positively correlate with increased performance on standardized reading measures (Gold, Powell, Xuan, Jiang, & Hardy, 2007; Klingberg et al., 2000; Rimrodt, Peterson, Denckla, Kaufmann, & Cutting, 2010). Differences in fractional anisotropy have been seen between age-matched typical readers and dyslexic readers. No differences were found, however, between typical readers and dyslexic readers matched on reading ability rather than age (Krafnick, Flowers, Luetje, Napoliello, & Eden, 2014). As mentioned previously, increased myelination results in faster signal conduction; however, increased myelination also results in bigger tracts that take up more brain space. Throughout one's lifetime, pruning occurs in which some axons are left to grow and develop and other axons are eliminated. During childhood, a period of intensive neuronal pruning occurs. Yeatman, Dougherty, Ben-Shachar, and Wandell (2012) found that in an age-matched sample, above-average readers initially showed lower levels of fractional anisotropy and a longitudinal increase, whereas below-average readers showed high levels of fractional anisotropy and a longitudinal decrease. This longitudinal trajectory of fractional anisotropy suggests either that dyslexic children initially have white matter tracts that their brain is unable to support or that dyslexic children show inappropriate pruning throughout development. It is also possible that dyslexic children have both white matter tracts that cannot be supported and inappropriate developmental pruning.

PROTON MAGNETIC RESONANCE IMAGING: THE ROLE OF NEUROMETABOLITES IN READING

MRS is a noninvasive in vivo technique that measures biochemical concentrations in the brain using neurometabolite resonance frequencies. Proton (1H) MRS is specifically aimed at determining neurotransmitter concentrations, calculated from a composite of neurometabolite levels. MRS is generally collected for a single voxel or region, determined a priori to prevent signal distortion (Rothman, 1994). Neurotransmitter findings are now reported as a ratio to an internal reference to control for potential drift in the spectra during acquisition. Creatine (Cr) is currently recommended as an MRS internal reference (Li, Babb, Soher, Maudsley, & Gonen, 2002). Here we discuss known functions of neurotransmitters and examine findings from proton MRS studies of dyslexia.

CHOLINE AND *N*-ACETYLASPARTATE: PROTON MAGNETIC RESONANCE IMAGING

The neurotransmitter choline (Cho) is integral to cell membrane synthesis and degradation as well as the direct precursor of acetylcholine. Choline is also involved in metabolic pathways, cholinergic neurotransmission, and transmembrane signaling. MRS studies of developmental disorders have found atypically high concentrations of cortical choline in individuals with attention-deficit/hyperactivity disorder (Perlov et al., 2009) and autism (see Baruth, Wall, Patterson, & Port, 2013). Given the number of metabolic pathways and transport mechanisms that influence choline, many theories have been suggested to explain elevated choline. These theories include increased cellular density, increased signal intensity, cell membrane synthesis, and degradation resulting in membrane turnover and changes in white matter organization.

A number of studies have investigated the role of choline in reading ability. In an early study, Rae and colleagues (1998) investigated choline differences between adults with dyslexia and age-matched typical readers (*n* = 29, 14 dyslexic). They found that dyslexic adults had a decreased ratio of Cho:NAA (Choline:N-acetylaspartate) in the left temporoparietal lobe and the right cerebellum. These researchers also investigated brain laterality (right versus left) in the individuals with dyslexia (*n* = 14) and found a decrease in Cho:NAA in the left temporoparietal lobe and decreased Cr:NAA in the right cerebellum. A decade later, Laycock and colleagues (2008) investigated choline differences between a small sample of adults with dyslexia, controlled for brain volume–, age-, and intelligence-matched typical readers (*n* = 12, 6 dyslexic). They found that dyslexic adults had a decreased ratio of NAA:Cho in the right cerebellum and increased Cho:Cr in the left cerebellum. Given that we now know NAA is an unstable internal reference (Jung et al., 2005), the results of the choline and NAA ratios are difficult to parse; however, NAA is typically thought to correspond with cognitive abilities, which were only controlled for in Laycock and colleagues' work. The increase of Cho:Cr, also found in the left cerebellum (Laycock et al., 2008), suggests that dyslexics have an increase in choline concentration rather than a decrease in NAA concentration.

Bruno, Lu, and Manis (2013) further parsed the relationships between reading ability and choline and NAA. First, the more stable internal creatine reference was used for each neurotransmitter. Second, they studied adults with equated cognitive ability that ranged across a spectrum of reading ability (*n* = 30, 10 dyslexic). Bruno and colleagues (2013) found that although lower phonological ability was associated with increased Cho:Cr in the left angular gyrus, no association was found between NAA:Cr and reading ability. This suggests that previous results may have been indicative of an increased choline concentration.

Pugh and colleagues (2014) investigated choline and NAA in a temporoparietal-to-occipitotemporal region in children (*n* = 75, mean age = 7.68) whose reading skills ranged from good to very weak (i.e., dyslexic). Even in children, increased choline concentration was found to be indicative of poorer reading. A group comparison between a subsample of typical and dyslexic readers (*n* = 47, 10 dyslexic) found that dyslexic readers had higher concentrations of Cho:Cr. These researchers also reported a replication of their finding using a separate sample of pediatric readers from the National Institutes of

Health (NIH) MRI Study of Normal Brain Development.[1] The NIH database includes MRS data collected from a midline occipital region as well as standardized assessments of reading ability. In this sample, children (n = 85) across a wide age range (i.e., 5–18 years) had increased Cho:Cr that was correlated with poorer reading assessment scores. Again, no association was found between NAA:Cr and reading ability. Based on the combined findings from these studies, we conclude that elevated levels of choline indicate poorer reading ability in both children and adults.

GLUTAMATE AND GAMMA-AMINOBUTYRIC ACID: PROTON MAGNETIC RESONANCE SPECTROSCOPY

Glutamate is an amino acid found in high concentrations throughout the brain. Glutamate is the principal excitatory neurotransmitter involved in many metabolic pathways and can be used to indicate metabolic activity—or system excitability. In MRS, glutamate (Glu) concentration is a composite of both glutamate and glutamine, reflecting tightly coupled neuroenergetics. Like choline, elevated glutamate concentrations have been reported in attention-deficit/hyperactivity disorder (Perlov et al., 2009) and autism (Brown, Singel, Hepburn, & Rojas, 2013). Theories aimed at explaining elevated levels of glutamate have focused on hyperexcitability, networks involved in learning and consolidation, and neural plasticity.

Pugh and colleagues (2014) also investigated glutamate and gamma-aminobutyric acid (GABA) in a temporoparietal-to-occipitotemporal region in children (n = 75, mean age = 7.68), whose reading skills ranged from good to very weak (i.e., dyslexic). Increased Glu:Cr was indicative of poorer reading ability and vocabulary scores. In the subsample group, comparison of typically developing readers and dyslexic readers (n = 47, 10 dyslexic) resulted in dyslexic readers with higher Glu:Cr. No significant relationship was found between GABA and reading ability. The association between reading ability and Glu:Cr concentration was robust enough to indicate reading ability at a follow-up assessment 24 months later (n =45, mean age = 10.1). Although further studies and replications are needed, given the resilience of this association, we suggest that adult dyslexics may also show elevated levels of Glutamate.

LACTATE: PROTON MAGNETIC RESONANCE SPECTROSCOPY

Many early MRS studies focused on the relation of lactate to reading ability (Richards et al., 2002, 2000, 1999). Lactate, in addition to glutamate oxidation and glycolysis, contributes to the energy demands of excitatory neurotransmission. Low lactate levels are typically coupled with low glutamine. Although clearly relevant, early MRS studies of lactate are often overlooked because of potential

---

1. http://pediatricmri.nih.gov, release 5.

confounds, such as the inability to stabilize lactate concentration, given that lactate crosses the blood–brain barrier (Dienel & Cruz, 2009). Although results should therefore be interpreted with caution, we can clearly gain direction from some of the findings.

Richards and colleagues (1999) found increased lactate:NAA along the Sylvian fissure in dyslexic children (n = 6) compared to age-matched, typically developing readers (n = 7). In a replication with an added phonological intervention, Richards and colleagues (2000) found that prior to intervention, there was an increase in lactate:NAA in dyslexic readers (n = 8) compared with age-matched, typically developing readers (n = 7) in a very large region encompassing frontal and parietal lobe regions. Following intervention, dyslexic readers (n = 6) were found to have either elevated or typical levels of lactate:NAA. Richards and colleagues (2002) investigated a large area that encompassed the frontal operculum and the posterior portion of the superior temporal gyrus in dyslexic children and age-matched, typically developing readers (n = 8). Between scans, dyslexic readers were randomly assigned to either a morphological or phonological intervention. Prior to intervention, dyslexic readers had significantly elevated levels of lactate:NAA. Following the morphological intervention, five of the six dyslexic readers showed decreased but still elevated levels of lactate:NAA (compared with typical readers). All four dyslexic readers who had received the phonological intervention continued to show elevated lactate:NAA. Richards and colleagues' work suggests that lactate:NAA levels in dyslexic readers tend to be elevated when compared with typically developing peers. We caution that the small sample and the inability to stabilize lactate concentration during MRS acquisition make these results very hard to interpret. They appear to demonstrate, however, that a link between reading and lactate in MRS is relevant and worthy of further investigation.

PHOSPHORUS MAGNETIC RESONANCE SPECTROSCOPY: THE NEUROMETABOLIC SIGNATURE

Phosphorus MRS is clinically used to determine metabolic abnormalities, primarily in chronic cerebrovascular disease but also in schizophrenia, depression, chronic fatigue syndrome, and dyslexia (see Puri, 2006, for review). The phosphorus MRS reflects a composite of metabolic energy sources, primarily adenosine triphosphate (ATP), phosphocreatine (PCr), and several other low-weighted molecules that contain phosphate (Qiao, Zhang, Zhu, Du, & Chen, 2006). Results of phosphorus MRS studies are also reported as a ratio (e.g., PCr:ATP) to control for inhomogeneity during image acquisition. To prevent signal distortion, the phosphorus MRS is also collected for a single voxel or region determined a priori.

A limited amount of research using phosphorus MRS has focused on the link between cortical metabolic levels and reading ability. Rae and colleagues (1998) further hypothesized that differences in the phosphorus MR spectra would be coupled with changes in Choline, as Choline was known to be indicative of cellular density. This pilot study investigated a region in the frontal lobe that extended onto both sides of the intrahemispheric fissure as well as into the parietal lobe. No significant differences between dyslexic and typical adult readers were found, although the reported ratios of PCr:ATP are interesting; however, Rae and colleagues admittedly state that the results are inconclusive due to limited statistical power.

A year prior, Richardson, Cox, Sargentoni, and Puri (1997) investigated an area centered in the basal ganglia in dyslexic (n = 12) and age- and intelligence-matched, typically reading adults (n = 10) and found an increase in dyslexic readers' phosphomonoesters as compared with typically developing readers. This phosphomonoester peak included phosphocholine, phosphoethanolamine, and L-phosphoserine as well as smaller sugar phosphates. The internal references, nucleotide triphosphates, contain spectral contributions from ATP, PCr, and inorganic phosphate and may therefore result in an increase in phosphomonoesters; however, because the majority of the phosphorus MR signal is the result of ATP and PCr, the results are more likely a reflection of decreases in ATP, PCr, and/or inorganic phosphate. The results of these initial studies, though they require additional confirmation, suggest that there may be a deviant metabolic signature in individuals with dyslexia.

THE GENETICS OF READING DISABILITY

Early genetic research on dyslexia relied primarily on heritability due to the anecdotal evidence of dyslexia in family lines. Heritability studies investigate the proportion of disorder, disease, or trait that can be assigned to genetic influences. The results of these initial genetic studies found that a large portion of reading performance is accounted for by genetic influences. Although these studies were highly replicable and confirmed dyslexia heritability, to date there remains no answer as to the biological loci of dyslexia.

Linkage and association studies are used to determine susceptibility genes—genes with possible causal variants resulting in a disorder. To begin to localize genetic effects within a family, linkage studies trace the segregation of a trait and the segregation of one or more chromosomes, allowing a comparison between segregated traits (e.g., reading difficulty) and the selected chromosomes. Linkage studies often use single-nucleotide polymorphisms (SNPs) for better genetic resolution. Although association studies follow the same pattern of analysis, they focus on a sample across families. These techniques were used to identify the first chromosomes associated with reading difficulty: chromosomes 1, 2, 3, 6, 15, and 18.

In dyslexia, the links between genes and reading ability (genotype) and among genes, environment, and reading ability (phenotype) do not result from a direct correspondence. Candidate gene studies begin with the selection of proposed genes based on chromosomal regions from linkage and association studies or mechanisms relevant to the disorder. The first series of candidate dyslexia genes, *DYX1C1, ROBO1, KIAA0319,* and *DCDC2,* resulted from proposed genes based on findings from linkage studies. It is of note that at least 10 additional candidate genes have been purported. Gialluisi and colleagues (2014) reported the results of a genome-wide association study (GWAS) focused on reading ability. A GWAS is a partial survey that results from genotyping large numbers of common SNPs. Novel associations were found for the *RBFOX2* gene (chromosome 22) as well as *CCDC136* and *FLNC* (chromosome 7). Each of these candidate genes and association genes plays a complex role in the development of the nervous system. These genetic associations have been found in both neurons and glial cells. Glial cells contribute to cell migration, plasticity, organization, structure, and widespread protein synthesis. In short, dyslexia is the result of extremely complex neurobiology that is interacting and changing throughout development.

ANIMAL MODELS OF DYSLEXIA

The *dyslexic rodent* is a candidate gene rodent model of dyslexia and underlies much of what researchers know about protein expression in dyslexia. Although there was initially much conjecture regarding a "reading" rodent, the increased, cross-disciplinary knowledge of genetics has resulted in a slow acceptance across the fields of psychology and education. There are four primary types of rodent models of dyslexia. The first two rodent models focus on stopping candidate gene expression. In these models, the candidate gene is stopped from directing the assembly of a protein (see Galaburda, LoTurco, Ramus, Fitch, & Rosen, 2006, for review). Rodent knockout models are genetically engineered never to express a particular gene. No part of the knockout rodent's development occurs with typical gene expression. The third rodent model consists of rodents with ribonucleic acid interference, commonly called RNAi rodents. RNAi rodents begin gestation normally. Following typical neural tube and brainstem development, RNAi stops gene expression. Both of these rodent models of dyslexia reported behavioral deficits in nonspatial and spatial discrimination learning, auditory processing, and memory.

Rodent models of dyslexia reported anatomical abnormalities—focal microgyria and molecular layer ectopias (small structural malformations in the brain) that are associated with failures in neuronal migration. These abnormalities closely resemble early postmortem evidence found in humans with dyslexia (Galaburda, Sherman, Rosen, Aboitiz, & Geschwind, 1985). Based on these findings, a fourth rodent model of dyslexia was created with experimentally induced neuronal microgyria but with no underlying genetic manipulation (Fitch, Tallal, Brown, Galaburda, & Rosen, 1994). In rodents with induced microgyria that have normal gene expression, deficits were still seen in auditory processing, learning, and memory. This suggests that some of the deficits commonly seen in dyslexia may be associated with, rather than dependent on, neuronal migration failures.

THE NEUROBIOLOGY OF DYSLEXIA: STUDIES LINKING GENES, ANIMAL MODELS, AND NEUROIMAGING

As mentioned previously, studies investigating white matter in dyslexic adults have reported lower levels of fractional anisotropy (i.e., decreased strength of water diffusion in and around axonal fibers). White matter density is tightly linked to a number of neurotransmitters, including Glutamate and GABA in the corpus callosum and cerebellum and Choline and NAA in the cortex. Decreased white matter has been found to correspond to decreased levels of both NAA and Choline in individuals with multiple sclerosis and traumatic brain injury (Gustafsson, Dahlqvist, Jaworski, Lundberg, & Landtblom, 2007). Darki, Peyrard-Janvid, Matsson, Kere, and Klingberg (2012) and Marino and colleagues (2014) found *KIAA0319* and *DCDC2* to be associated with regions in the superior longitudinal fasciculus and corpus callosum, tracts that connect the middle temporal gyrus to the angular gyrus and supramarginal gyri. The middle temporal gyrus and the angular gyrus are involved in lexical–semantic processing, whereas the supramarginal gyrus is involved in speech-sound processing. Darki and colleagues (2012) also reported that *DYX1C1* was associated bilaterally with the cingulum, a white matter bundle that connects temporoparietal regions. The left temporoparietal regions integrate many levels of auditory language with orthographic information. This finding emphasizes the need for the investigation of white matter tract formation, particularly at the level of gene expression.

DCDC2 expression in gray matter has been found to be widespread and robust across lobes and throughout the reading network, composed of the inferior temporal cortex, superior temporal cortex, superior parietal cortex, frontal cortex, and prefrontal cortex. Meda and colleagues (2008) investigated gray matter structure in typically developing individuals who showed variants of the *DCDC2* genotype. They found that for the *DCDC2* dyslexia variant, there was an increase in gray matter in the superior temporal, medial temporal, and inferior temporal cortex; the fusiform; the hippocampal gyrus; the inferior occipitoparietal, inferior, and middle frontal gyri; and the parahippocampal gyrus. As mentioned previously, increased and decreased gray matter have now been reported in dyslexic readers. Given the small sample size (n = 56), replication on a larger scale is needed, but these results are intriguing. It is worth considering the source of differences in gray matter structural imaging.

Typically, voxel-based morphometry (VBM) is used in neuroimaging to identify differences in gray matter concentration. These VBM changes have a complex relation with neuronal density. Animal work suggests that changes seen in VBM may be largely due to neuron rebuilding through processes such as the growth of dendritic spines (see Thomas & Baker, 2013, for review). Szalkowski and colleagues (2013) reported that RNAi *DYX1C1* rodents had a gray matter volume increase in the medial geniculate nucleus. Galaburda, Menard, and Rosen (1994) reported postmortem reductions in the number of "large cells" in the medial geniculate nucleus of dyslexic readers. Szalkowski and colleagues (2013) reported RNAi *DYX1C1* rodents with an increased number of "small cells" and a smaller number of "large cells"—specifically in the medial geniculate nucleus. This suggests that there is much more to gray matter differences than simply a measure of more or less gray matter.

CONCLUSION

Dyslexia presents as a failure to achieve adequate reading ability. There are other behavioral difficulties seen in dyslexia, yet only reading failure has been robustly shown to have severe emotional and educational repercussions. The day-to-day repercussions of dyslexia may seem far removed from the complex neurobiology underlying dyslexia. There is currently no direct, noninvasive way to detect and assess the expression, transfer, and therapeutic changes of genes in living humans. This makes it difficult to create and monitor pharmacological interventions and reinforces the need for rodent models of dyslexia. Linking research to practice and practice to research is not easy, but there are large repercussions of nontargeted practice and research. Future dyslexia practice focused on identification and intervention must be grounded in genetic and animal model research, in neurochemistry, and in neuroimaging studies. Future dyslexia research must not lose sight of identification, intervention, and clinical practice.

REFERENCES

Baruth, J.M., Wall, C.A., Patterson, M.C., & Port, J.D. (2013). Proton magnetic resonance spectroscopy as a probe into the pathophysiology of autism spectrum disorders (ASD): A review. *Autism Research, 6*(2), 119–133.

Bradley, L., & Bryant, P.E. (1978). Difficulties in auditory organisation as a possible cause of reading backwardness. *Nature, 271,* 746–747.

Brown, M.S., Singel, D., Hepburn, S., & Rojas, D.C. (2013). Increased glutamate concentration in the auditory cortex of persons with autism and first-degree relatives: A 1H-MRS study. *Autism Research, 6,* 1–10.

Bruno, J.L., Lu, Z.-L., & Manis, F. (2013). Phonological processing is uniquely associated with neuro-metabolic concentration. *NeuroImage, 67,* 175–181.

Darki, F., Peyrard-Janvid, M., Matsson, H., Kere, J., & Klingberg, T. (2012). Three dyslexia susceptibility genes, *DYX1C1, DCDC2,* and *KIAA0319,* affect temporo-parietal white matter structure. *Biological Psychiatry, 72*(8), 671–676.

Démonet, J.-F., Taylor, M.J., & Chaix, Y. (2004). Developmental dyslexia. *The Lancet, 363*(9419), 1451–1460.

Dienel, G.A., & Cruz, N.F. (2009). Exchange-mediated dilution of brain lactate specific activity: Implications for the origin of glutamate dilution and the contributions of glutamine dilution and other pathways. *Journal of Neurochemistry, 109*(s1), 30–37.

Eckert, M.A., Leonard, C.M., Richards, T.L., Aylward, E.H., Thomson, J., & Berninger, V.W. (2003). Anatomical correlates of dyslexia: Frontal and cerebellar findings. *Brain, 126*(2), 482–494.

Eliez, S., Rumsey, J.M., Giedd, J.N., Schmitt, J.E., Patwardhan, A.J., & Reiss, A.L. (2000). Morphological alteration of temporal lobe gray matter in dyslexia: An MRI study. *Journal of Child Psychology and Psychiatry, 41*(5), 637–644.

Fitch, R.H., Tallal, P., Brown, C.P., Galaburda, A.M., & Rosen, G.D. (1994). Induced microgyria and auditory temporal processing in rats: A model for language impairment? *Cerebral Cortex, 4*(3), 260–270.

Galaburda, A.M., LoTurco, J., Ramus, F., Fitch, R.H., & Rosen, G.D. (2006). From genes to behavior in developmental dyslexia. *Nature Neuroscience, 9*(10), 1213–1217.

Galaburda, A.M., Menard, M.T., & Rosen, G.D. (1994). Evidence for aberrant auditory anatomy in developmental dyslexia. *Proceedings of the National Academy of Sciences, 91*(17), 8010–8013.

Galaburda, A.M., Sherman, G.F., Rosen, G.D., Aboitiz, F., & Geschwind, N. (1985). Developmental dyslexia: Four consecutive patients with cortical anomalies. *Annals of Neurology, 18*(2), 222–233.

Gialluisi, A., Newbury, D.F., Wilcutt, E.G., Olson, R.K., DeFries, J.C., Brandler, W.M., . . . Simpson, N.H. (2014). Genome-wide screening for DNA variants associated with reading and language traits. *Genes, Brain and Behavior, 13*(7), 686–701.

Gold, B.T., Powell, D.K., Xuan, L., Jiang, Y., & Hardy, P.A. (2007). Speed of lexical decision correlates with diffusion anisotropy in left parietal and frontal white matter: Evidence from diffusion tensor imaging. *Neuropsychologia, 45*(11), 2439–2446.

Gustafsson, M., Dahlqvist, O., Jaworski, J., Lundberg, P., & Landtblom, A.-M. (2007). Low choline concentrations in normal-appearing white matter of patients with multiple sclerosis and normal MR imaging brain scans. *American Journal of Neuroradiology, 28*(7), 1306–1312.

Jung, R.E., Haier, R.J., Yeo, R.A., Rowland, L.M., Petropoulos, H., Levine, A.S., . . . Brooks, W.M. (2005). Sex differences in *N*-acetylaspartate correlates of general intelligence: An 1H-MRS study of normal human brain. *NeuroImage, 26*(3), 965–972.

Klingberg, T., Hedehus, M., Temple, E., Salz, T., Gabrieli, J.D., Moseley, M.E., & Poldrack, R.A. (2000). Microstructure of temporo-parietal white matter as a basis for reading ability: Evidence from diffusion tensor magnetic resonance imaging. *Neuron, 25*(2), 493–500.

Koyama, M.S., Di Martino, A., Kelly, C., Jutagir, D.R., Sunshine, J., Schwartz, S.J., . . . Milham, M.P. (2013). Cortical signatures of dyslexia and remediation: An intrinsic functional connectivity approach. *PLOS ONE, 8*(2), e55454.

Krafnick, A.J., Flowers, D.L., Luetje, M.M., Napoliello, E.M., & Eden, G.F. (2014). An investigation into the origin of anatomical differences in dyslexia. *The Journal of Neuroscience, 34*(3), 901–908.

Kronbichler, M., Wimmer, H., Staffen, W., Hutzler, F., Mair, A., & Ladurner, G. (2008). Developmental dyslexia: Gray matter abnormalities in the occipitotemporal cortex. *Human Brain Mapping, 29*(5), 613–625.

Laycock, S.K., Wilkinson, I.D., Wallis, L.I., Darwent, G., Wonders, S.H., Fawcett, A.J., . . . Nicolson, R.I. (2008). Cerebellar volume and cerebellar metabolic characteristics in adults with dyslexia. *Annals of the New York Academy of Sciences, 1145*(1), 222–236.

Li, B.S., Babb, J.S., Soher, B.J., Maudsley, A.A., & Gonen, O. (2002). Reproducibility of 3D proton spectroscopy in the human brain. *Magnetic Resonance in Medicine, 47*(3), 439–446.

Liberman, I.Y., Shankweiler, D., & Liberman, A.M. (1989). The alphabetic principle and learning to read. In D. Shankweiler, & I.Y. Liberman (Eds.), *Phonology and reading disability: Solving the reading puzzle.* (pp. 1–33). Ann Arbor, MI: University of Michigan Press.

Linkersdörfer, J., Lonnemann, J., Lindberg, S., Hasselhorn, M., & Fiebach, C.J. (2012). Grey matter alterations co-localize with functional abnormalities in developmental dyslexia: An ALE meta-analysis. *PLOS ONE, 7*(8), e43122.

Marino, C., Scifo, P., Della Rosa, P.A., Mascheretti, S., Facoetti, A., Lorusso, M.L., . . . Molteni, M. (2014). The *DCDC2* intron 2 deletion and white matter disorganization: Focus on developmental dyslexia. *Cortex, 57,* 227–243.

McCandliss, B.D., Cohen, L., & Dehaene, S. (2003). The visual word form area: Expertise for reading in the fusiform gyrus. *Trends in Cognitive Sciences, 7*(7), 293–299.

Meda, S.A., Gelernter, J., Gruen, J.R., Calhoun, V.D., Meng, H., Cope, N.A., & Pearlson, G.D. (2008). Polymorphism of DCDC2 reveals differences in cortical morphology of healthy individuals—A preliminary voxel based morphometry study. *Brain Imaging and Behavior, 2*(1), 21–26.

Perlov, E., Philipsen, A., Matthies, S., Drieling, T., Maier, S., Bubl, E., . . . Ebert, D. (2009). Spectroscopic findings in attention-deficit/hyperactivity disorder: Review and meta-analysis. *World Journal of Biological Psychiatry, 10*(4–2), 355–365.

Peterson, R.L., & Pennington, B.F. (2012). Developmental dyslexia. *The Lancet 379,* 1997–2007.

Pugh, K.R., Frost, S.J., Rothman, D.L., Hoeft, F., Del Tufo, S.N., Mason, G.F., . . . Fulbright, R.K. (2014). Glutamate and choline levels predict individuals differences in reading ability in emergent readers. *Journal of Neuroscience, 34*(11), 4082–4089.

Pugh, K.R., Frost, S.J., Sandak, R., Landi, N., Moore, D., Della Porta, G., . . . Pugh, K. (2010). Mapping the word reading circuitry in skilled and disabled readers. *The Neural Basis of Reading,* 281–305.

Pugh, K.R., Mencl, W.E., Shaywitz, B.A., Shaywitz, S.E., Fulbright, R.K., Constable, R.T., . . . Fletcher, J.M. (2000). The angular gyrus in developmental dyslexia: Task-specific differences in functional connectivity within posterior cortex. *Psychological Science, 11*(1), 51–56.

Puri, B.K. (2006). Proton and 31-phosphorus neurospectroscopy in the study of membrane phospholipids and fatty acid intervention in schizophrenia, depression, chronic fatigue syndrome (myalgic encephalomyelitis) and dyslexia. *International Review of Psychiatry, 18*(2), 145–147.

Qiao, H., Zhang, X., Zhu, X.-H., Du, F., & Chen, W. (2006). In vivo 31P MRS of human brain at high/ultrahigh fields: A quantitative comparison of NMR detection sensitivity and spectral resolution between 4 T and 7 T. *Magnetic Resonance Imaging, 24*(10), 1281–1286.

Rae, C., Lee, M.A., Dixon, R.M., Blamire, A.M., Thompson, C.H., Styles, P., . . . Stein, J.F. (1998). Metabolic abnormalities in developmental dyslexia detected by 1H magnetic resonance spectroscopy. *The Lancet, 351*(9119), 1849–1852.

Richards, T.L., Berninger, V.W., Aylward, E.H., Richards, A.L., Thomson, J.B., Nagy, W.E., . . . Abbott, R.D. (2002). Reproducibility of proton MR spectroscopic imaging (PEPSI): Comparison of dyslexic and normal-reading children and effects of treatment on brain lactate levels during language tasks. *American Journal of Neuroradiology, 23*(10), 1678–1685.

Richards, T.L., Corina, D., Serafini, S., Steury, K., Echelard, D.R., Dager, S.R., . . . Berninger, V.W. (2000). Effects of a phonologically driven treatment for dyslexia on lactate levels measured by proton MR spectroscopic imaging. *American Journal of Neuroradiology, 21*(5), 916–922.

Richards, T.L., Dager, S.R., Corina, D., Serafini, S., Heide, A.C., Steury, K., . . . Craft, S. (1999). Dyslexic children have abnormal brain lactate response to reading-related language tasks. *American Journal of Neuroradiology, 20*(8), 1393–1398.

Richardson, A.J., Cox, I.J., Sargentoni, J., & Puri, B.K. (1997). Abnormal cerebral phospholipid metabolism in dyslexia indicated by phosphorus-31 magnetic resonance spectroscopy. *NMR in Biomedicine, 10*(7), 309–314.

Rimrodt, S.L., Peterson, D.J., Denckla, M.B., Kaufmann, W.E., & Cutting, L.E. (2010). White matter microstructural differences linked to left perisylvian language network in children with dyslexia. *Cortex, 46*(6), 739–749.

Rothman, D. (1994). 1H NMR studies of human brain metabolism and physiology. In R.J. Gillies (Ed.), *NMR in Physiology and Biomedicine.* (pp. 353–372). San Diego, CA: Academic Press.

Shaywitz, S.E., & Shaywitz, B.A. (2008). Paying attention to reading: The neurobiology of reading and dyslexia. *Development and Psychopathology, 20*(4), 1329–1349.

Shaywitz, B.A., Skudlarski, P., Holahan, J.M., Marchione, K.E., Constable, R.T., Fulbright, R.K., . . . Shaywitz, S.E. (2007). Age-related changes in reading systems of dyslexic children. *Annals of Neurology, 61*(4), 363–370.

Sideridis, G.D., Mouzaki, A., Simos, P., & Protopapas, A. (2006). Classification of students with reading comprehension difficulties: The roles of motivation, affect, and psychopathology. *Learning Disability Quarterly, 29*(3), 159–180.

Snowling, M. J. (2000). *Dyslexia.* Oxford, UK: Blackwell.

Steinbrink, C., Vogt, K., Kastrup, A., Müller, H.-P., Juengling, F., Kassubek, J., & Riecker, A. (2008). The contribution of white and gray matter differences to developmental dyslexia: Insights from DTI and VBM at 3.0 T. *Neuropsychologia, 46*(13), 3170–3178.

Szalkowski, C.E., Booker, A.B., Truong, D.T., Threlkeld, S.W., Rosen, G.D., & Fitch, R.H. (2013). Knockdown of the candidate dyslexia susceptibility gene homolog Dyx1c1 in rodents: Effects on auditory processing, visual attention, and cortical and thalamic anatomy. *Developmental Neuroscience, 35*(1), 50–68.

Thomas, C., & Baker, C.I. (2013). Teaching an adult brain new tricks: A critical review of evidence for training-dependent structural plasticity in humans. *NeuroImage, 73,* 225–236.

Yeatman, J.D., Dougherty, R.F., Ben-Shachar, M., & Wandell, B.A. (2012). Development of white matter and reading skills. *Proceedings of the National Academy of Sciences, 109*(44), E3045–E3053.

9

The Genetic Classroom

How Behavioral Genetics Can Inform Education

Sara A. Hart

The field of behavioral genetics has a long history of examining educationally relevant outcomes, especially in the areas of reading achievement, reading development, and reading difficulties. As a group, reading researchers across disciplines have accepted and supported behavioral genetics research in reading (for one recent example, see Olson, Keenan, Byrne, & Samuelsson, 2014); however, it is not clear exactly how behavioral genetics has actually informed reading research and perhaps more importantly, educational practice. This chapter will first broadly review the previous behavioral genetics literature on reading component skills, reading development, and reading disability. It will then explain how behavioral genetics can make a concrete contribution to education science and practice.

Behavioral genetic methodology offers an important and unique opportunity to examine the genetic and environmental influences on reading and reading-related component skills. In particular, twin and adoption study methodologies allow for the examination of the proportion of variance attributable to additive genetic influences (or heritability; h^2), shared environmental influences (i.e., nongenetic influences that make siblings more similar; c^2), and nonshared environmental influences (i.e., nongenetic effects that make siblings different, plus error; e^2) on any given measure. The twin study methodology involves comparing the within-twin-pair similarities of monozygotic (MZ) twins and dizygotic (DZ) twins. Because MZ twins share 100% of their segregating alleles and DZ twins share, on average, only 50% of their segregating alleles, the extent to which MZ twins are more similar to each other than DZ twins is assumed to represent additive genetic influences. The extent to which MZ twins are not at least twice as similar to each other as DZ twins is thus assumed to represent shared environmental influences (e.g., books in the home, being in the same classroom, having the same peers). Finally, the extent to which the MZ twin similarity is not perfect is assumed to represent the nonshared environmental influences (e.g., being in different classrooms, having different peers, measurement error; Plomin, DeFreis, Knopik, & Neiderhiser, 2013).

Twin studies have been used for more than 30 years to examine the genetic and environmental influences on reading, with research suggesting that genetic influences are important (Smith, Kimberling, Pennington, & Lubs, 1983; Stevenson, Graham, Fredman, & Mcloughli, 1987). Some of the first point estimates of "reading ability" suggested genetic influences .44, on average, with lower estimates of shared environmental influences at around .27 (Stevenson et al., 1987). Since 1987, the literature has moved away from this initial interest in simply measuring overall reading ability and has recognized the importance of studying the genetic and environmental influences on the component skills of reading, such as phonological awareness, decoding, reading fluency, and reading comprehension. These are described in more detail in the following discussion.

Phonological awareness (*PA*) is one of the most important predictors of early reading (see National Reading Panel [NICHD], 2000, for review and meta-analysis). PA is the ability to isolate and manipulate phonemes in speech. Twin studies of preschool through kindergarten readers have suggested that genetic influences are important for PA, with heritability estimates that are moderate and significant—$h^2 = .37 - .60$ across studies (Byrne et al., 2005; Kovas et al., 2005; Petrill, Deater-Deckard, Thompson, DeThorne, & Schatschneider, 2006a; Taylor & Schatschneider, 2010)—although one follow-up study in first grade found nonsignificant estimates of heritability ($h^2 = .20$; Byrne et al., 2007). Estimates of shared environmental influences ranged greatly in magnitude ($c^2 = .06 - .43$) with only some studies reporting significant estimates (Petrill et al., 2006a; Taylor & Schatschneider, 2010).

Decoding refers to the ability to read individual printed words. This component skill can be measured by real-word or nonword reading measures, with nonword measures intending to control for sight word recognition. Decoding is widely accepted as one of the most important skills needed for reading for understanding (Hoover & Gough, 1990), with much of early literacy instruction focused on learning to fluently and accurately decode (Ehri, 1992). Twin studies have generally indicated that decoding is moderately genetically influenced, with estimates of heritability ranging from .51 to .68 and low shared environmental influence ranging from .00 to .34 (Byrne et al., 2008; Petrill et al., 2007).

Reading fluency is the ability to accurately and quickly read words and/or connected text (Jenkins, Fuchs, van den Broek, Espin, & Deno, 2003; Stanovich, 1980). Reading fluency is an efficient measure of reading skill in the primary grades (Roehrig, Petscher, Nettles, Hudson, & Torgesen, 2008) and is considered a good predictor of reading comprehension (Fuchs, Fuchs, Hosp, & Jenkins, 2001). Behavioral genetics research examining the etiology of reading fluency has indicated that reading fluency is highly genetically influenced (h^2 = .62 – .82) with a low proportion of shared environmental influences (c^2 = .00 – .22; Byrne et al., 2005; Harlaar, Dale, & Plomin, 2007; Hart, Petrill, & Thompson, 2010; Petrill et al., 2012; Taylor & Schatschneider, 2010).

Reading comprehension is typically considered the end goal of learning to read and is most relevant to older readers (Chall, 1983). Reading comprehension is a complex process and, interestingly, does not have an agreed-on definition or method of measurement (e.g., Keenan, Betjemann, & Olson, 2008). The Simple View of Reading indicates that reading comprehension is a combination of decoding and listening comprehension (Hoover & Gough, 1990); however, other component skills, such as fluency (Joshi & Aaron, 2000) and background knowledge (Pearson, Hansen, & Gordon, 1979), also have been suggested as important predictors of reading comprehension. The behavioral genetic literature indicates that the heritability of reading comprehension is moderate to high (h^2 = .50 – .76) with corresponding low estimates of shared environmental influences (c^2 = .03 – .21; Byrne et al., 2007; Hart, Soden et al., 2013; Petrill et al., 2007).

Three themes have emerged from the behavioral genetics literature examining the component skills of reading. First, a common theme across the differing component skills is that genetics plays a significant role in reading, irrespective of age. In contrast, the significance of shared environmental influences is less consistent, although work from the more racially and economically diverse Florida Twin Project on Reading consistently indicates significant shared environmental influences (Taylor, Hart, Mikolajewski, & Schatschneider, 2013; Taylor & Schatschneider, 2010). A second theme across the literature is that timed aspects of reading tend to have higher estimates of heritability than the other component skills of reading (Hart et al., 2010; Petrill et al., 2012). Finally, the magnitude and significance of the estimated influence of shared environment on reading skills varies depending on age and, presumably, the amount of formal reading instruction required for mastery. Shared environmental effects tend to be moderate and significant in preschool and early-school-age twins only (Byrne et al., 2002; Petrill et al., 2006b), tapering off after a few years of schooling. The next section of this chapter expands on this third theme and explores the literature on the development of reading.

Initial work from twin studies began to explore the developmental nature of reading using a longitudinal Cholesky decomposition, a model that estimates all possible genetic and environmental relationships among time points (e.g., Petrill et al., 2007). More recent work has explored genetically sensitive developmental models, such as latent growth curve modeling and simplex models. In the first of these studies, Petrill et al. (2010), using a linear latent growth curve model, suggested that significant genetic and shared environmental influences affect initial reading status, and weak and mostly statistically nonsignificant genetic and strong shared environmental influences affect the growth of reading. Logan et al. (2013), using the same sample, extended this linear model to examine curvilinear growth and found that the change and deceleration of word-reading skills were influenced by both genetic and environmental influences. In a 2013 study, growth curve models with correlated residuals were used to examine the growth of word-reading fluency, reading comprehension, and spelling in early grade school (Christopher et al., 2013a). This work suggested genetic effects on the intercept and linear slope factors, with nonsignificant effects due to the shared environment. Results were similar for a study examining word-reading fluency in young readers in twin samples across the United States, Australia, and Scandinavia. In this study, genetic influences were indicated for both the intercept and linear slope, and depending on the country, shared environmental influences were also indicated (particularly for Scandinavia; Christopher et al., 2013b). Finally, in the largest and most diverse twin study to date to publish a developmental model, results from latent growth curve modeling indicated both genetic and shared environmental influences on intercept, linear slope, and quadratic slope for the development of connected text fluency (oral reading fluency [ORF]) across first through fifth grade (Hart, Logan et al., 2013). In addition, using the same data, a simplex model (exploring dynamic change) indicated that novel genetic influences are important for Grades 1, 2, and 3, with general genetic influences also transmitted across all the years of primary school (see Figure 9.1). For the shared environment, general influences were indicated, coming online in first grade and transmitted across the following school years.

The general trend from these results indicates that genetics and the shared environment are important for beginning reading skill and that genetics and likely the shared environment influence students' growth in reading. This is coupled with the common finding that genetic influences increase as children get older and that shared environmental influences subsequently decrease. Although much more work is needed before conclusions can be drawn, these results may indicate that in the first few years of formal instruction, individual

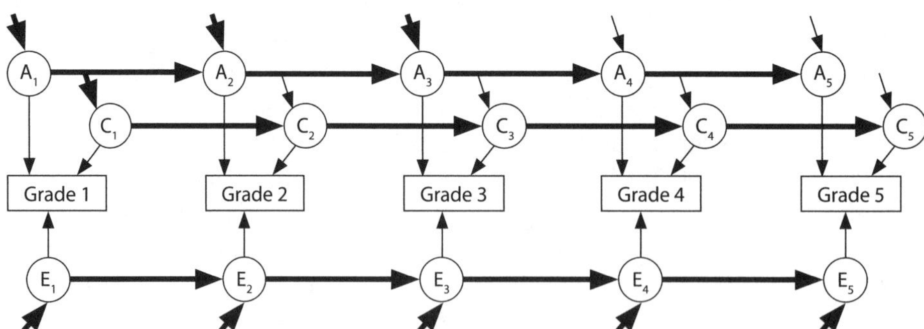

Figure 9.1. Simplex model of genetic (A), shared environmental (C), and nonshared environmental (E) influences on oral reading fluency (ORF) across Grades 1–5 (g1–g5, respectively). Bolded lines indicate significant influences.

differences among children are reflective of a wider variability in the skills first learned at home (e.g., being read to) and therefore represent shared environmental influences in addition to genetically driven abilities. As more children learn the fundamental aspects of reading through formal instruction, the variability related to these shared environmental effects may diminish, leading to larger genetic estimates. The shared environment is still important for students' growth in skills and especially for the active, instructional environment needed for them to learn to read, but it does not contribute to their individual differences to the same extent that genetic influences do.

In addition to examining reading skills and development across the range of ability, researchers have examined the genetic and environmental etiology of reading disability. Several methods have been employed to measure and classify disability, but a common method is the DeFries-Fulker (DF; DeFries & Fulker, 1985) analysis. DF analysis compares cotwins' scores to determine the etiology of the extremes of reading ability. This technique mirrors the continuous ability theories of dyslexia, which allow for a quantitative rather than qualitative method of defining reading disability (Vellutino, Fletcher, Snowling, & Scanlon, 2004). This type of definition of dyslexia, or reading disability, assumes that reading ability is a continuous distribution with a continuous distribution of genes that interact with the environment underlying it. The further toward the left tail on the ability spectrum an individual is, the greater his or her chance of having a reading disability. With the DF analysis, when a twin is selected for low ability (i.e., 10th percentile cutoff), the cotwin's score will regress toward the mean of the sample (i.e., will tend to be higher than the cotwin score). Greater regression to the mean in dizygotic twins compared with monozygotic twins is suggestive of genetic influences. Equal regression to the mean (i.e., the twins' scores remain highly similar) is suggestive of shared environmental effects.

Results across the literature of examining the genetic influences on reading disability have indicated two themes: 1) The genetic influences on reading disability are moderate to high (group heritability typically ranges .50–.73; Harlaar, Spinath, Dale, & Plomin, 2005; Hart, Petrill, & Kamp Dush, 2010; Hawke, Wadsworth, Olson, & DeFries, 2007; Light & DeFries, 1995), and 2) the magnitude of the genetic influences are similar to those of the entire typical range of reading ability. This is consistent with the hypothesis that the genes responsible for reading disability are the same genes that are responsible for reading ability (Plomin & Kovas, 2005).

In total, if a rule of thumb were to be given for the results from twin studies on reading, across constructs, across ages, and across ability, approximately 50% of individual differences in reading achievement is attributable to additive genetic influences, approximately 30% to shared environmental influences, and the remaining approximately 20% to nonshared environmental influences. As mentioned earlier, however, there are notable differences, especially based on construct and age.

The evidence from this large body of behavioral genetics research offers suggestions for the research and practice of education. For example, a book by Asbury and Plomin (2013) gives suggestions for changes to U.K.-specific educational practices based on the findings of a large twin study conducted in the United Kingdom. Some of these recommendations, such as personalizing learning, starting to teach early and equally to all, and working on student self-confidence, are clear and would not sound outlandish to education practitioners. Some recommendations, such as teaching teachers about genetics, may sound odd but are not entirely out of the scope of practicality. However, many of recommendations would surely change the core of how we practice education; these include getting rid of disability labels, putting all children in an individualized education program, and dismissing the idea that all children can and should be on grade level. No matter how well educators would accept these recommendations, based on observations of educational practice in the United States, it is difficult to see how or where behavioral genetics has actually informed educational research or practice. Admittedly, these recommendations (and other similar ones) are not simple or inexpensive, yet there is little happening to *apply* the findings of behavioral genetics. Given this, I propose a way that we can bring behavioral genetics to education research, and subsequently to practice, that would not require an overhaul of the entire education system. By following the path of personalized medicine, personalized education plans based on risk profiles that are informed by behavioral genetics can be made for children in schools.

Although the idea of individual differences affecting response to classroom instruction was proposed at least 30 years ago as *aptitude-by-instruction interactions* (Cronbach & Snow, 1977), and more recently as *child characteristic-by-instruction interactions* (Connor, Morrison, & Petrella, 2004), this model is still not commonly used in education research. By simple extension of the child-by-instruction-interaction model, individual characteristics of the child should interact with educationally based interventions just as they do with typical instruction (e.g., Peterson & Janicki, 1979). Instruction and interventions, however, are typically applied using the same method across all students, with the only consideration toward individualization typically being an attempt to change the intensity of the instruction or intervention for students who are experiencing difficulty with reading (e.g., Fuchs, Mock, Morgan, & Young, 2003). There are many explanations for why individualized instruction and interventions are not commonly found, including methodological and practical considerations; however, there is mounting evidence that many different sources of influence on the child entering into the classroom can influence the results of the instruction (Connor et al., 2004). Importantly, the sources of individual differences can be directly informed by behavioral genetics.

As reviewed previously, twin results across reading component skills, age, and ability levels indicate that genetic influences account for approximately 50% of the variance in reading outcomes. Although there have been advances in molecular genetics, the evidence from this field is not at the point of identifying specific molecular genetic risk factors (i.e., genes) for reading difficulties that could contribute to a measurable source of variance in reading outcomes (Maher, 2008). It is also likely the case that the general public is not yet willing to accept that a child's education should be based on genetic markers measured via spitting in a tube upon entering kindergarten (see an attempt to do this in an educational setting in Kegel, Bus, & van Ijzendoorn, 2011); however, familial risk—in which some families tend to have reading problems or other closely related problems, such as language difficulties, running through generations—puts children at greater risk for dyslexia than children of families without familial risk. Prospective familial risk studies have indicated that children of parents with dyslexia are at an increased risk for being diagnosed with dyslexia themselves, and even if their reading difficulties are not so severe as to be diagnosed, these children generally do more poorly than control peers with no familial risk (e.g., Pennington & Lefly, 2001; Snowling, Gallagher, & Frith, 2003). Similar to personalized medicine, in which family risk of diseases, such as cancer and heart disease, is taken into account when making primary care decisions (e.g., medicine use, behavior changes), family risk of learning disabilities should be taken into account when making education decisions. By using a child's family history as a proxy for genetic influences, a familial genetic risk index can be formed that is predictive of how that child is going to perform in school. This familial genetic risk index can then be used as a base for recommending treatment—the beginnings of personalized education (in the medical sense; Uher, 2011).

It has been stated before that a complete family history should be included in the diagnosis of a learning disability to create an appropriate intervention plan (Fletcher et al., 2002); however, familial genetic risk status is rarely, if ever, taken into account during educational interventions and even less so in typical classroom instruction. The behavioral genetics literature indicates that familial genetic risk is an important diagnostic marker that is being ignored. Quantifying the influence of familial genetic risk on a child's response to instruction and/or intervention is key to optimizing, or personalizing, educational learning opportunities for that child. For instance, it is likely the case that a child with reading difficulties entering into a reading intervention should immediately be placed into a more intensive framework if he or she has a family history of reading difficulties, whereas a child who presents with similar reading deficits but does not have a family history of reading difficulties should receive (and would need) a less intensive regimen. Previous work has begun to explore this, including studies that assigned children with familial risk of reading problems to receive a literacy intervention (Duff et al., 2014; Elbro & Petersen, 2004; Hindson et al., 2005; Regtvoort & van der Leij, 2007; van Otterloo, van der Leij, & Henrichs, 2009). In general, this work has shown short-term effects on the literacy skills that were the target of direct intervention in the at-risk group, with one study showing long-term generalized effects on other reading skills (Elbro & Petersen, 2004) and one randomized controlled intervention trial unfortunately showing no overall intervention impact (Duff et al., 2014).

CONCLUSION

In general, the literature examining the role of personalized intervention for children based on familial risk is just starting to grow. Indeed, I recently started Project KIDS, which examines familial genetic risk status as a moderator of response to intervention. This project is based on the findings of behavioral genetics and reading and uses what is known from the rich history of this field in an applied way. With this work, familial risk (and other risk factors not explored here, such as familial environment) will be examined to determine which children will not respond to effective interventions. The next step will be to conduct a prospective randomized controlled trial, similar to that of Duff and colleagues (Duff et al., 2014), in which children are chosen to receive specialized dosages of interventions based on familial risk. It is with this type of work that the field can take steps toward genetically informed, individualized education.

An educational system based on the findings of behavioral genetics should include personalized education. Mirroring a trip to one's doctor's office, at school entrance, parents would fill out a questionnaire that would include family history of learning disabilities. The "results" from this questionnaire would be used by school professionals to "prescribe" further testing, progress monitoring, and/or treatment. Schools would be able to use any treatments, or interventions, that are evidence based and successful in their particular environment in dosages, depending on the child's risk status. This does not mean that all children would have to receive completely different treatment plans (which would surely be taxing to teachers and expensive); instead, further research should be done to determine whether similarities among student profiles might be identified so that students with similar profiles might be grouped together to receive similar intervention regimens (see Connor, Chapter 11). Using the metaphor of personalized medicine, the long-standing findings of behavioral genetics can be integrated directly into education science and practice via the biological classroom.

REFERENCES

Asbury, K., & Plomin, R. (2013). *G is for genes: The impact of genetics on education and achievement* (Vol. 14). London, UK: John Wiley & Sons.

Byrne, B., Coventry, W.L., Olson, R.K., Hulslander, J., Wadsworth, S., DeFries, J.C., . . . Samuelsson, S. (2008). A behaviour-genetic analysis of orthographic learning, spelling and decoding. *Journal of Research in Reading, 31*(1), 8–21.

Byrne, B., Delaland, C., Fielding-Barnsley, R., Quain, P., Samuelsson, S., Hoien, T., . . . Olson, R.K. (2002). Longitudinal twin study of early reading development in three countries: Preliminary results. *Annals of Dyslexia, 52*, 49–73.

Byrne, B., Samuelsson, S., Wadsworth, S., Hulslander, J., Corley, R., DeFries, J.C., . . . Olson, R.K. (2007). Longitudinal twin study of early literacy development: Preschool through grade 1. *Reading and Writing, 20*(1–2), 77–102.

Byrne, B., Wadsworth, S., Corley, R., Samuelsson, S., Quain, P., DeFries, J.C., . . . Olson, R.K. (2005). Longitudinal twin study of early literacy development: Preschool and kindergarten phases. *Scientific Studies of Reading, 9*(3), 219–235.

Chall, J.S. (1983). *Stages of reading development.* New York, NY: McGraw-Hill.

Christopher, M.E., Hulslander, J., Byrne, B., Samuelsson, S., Keenan, J.M., Pennington, B., . . . Olson, R.K. (2013a). Modeling the etiology of individual differences in early reading development: Evidence for strong genetic influences. *Scientific Studies of Reading, 17*(5), 350–368.

Christopher, M.E., Hulslander, J., Byrne, B., Samuelsson, S., Keenan, J.M., Pennington, B., . . . Olson, R.K. (2013b). The genetic and environmental etiologies of individual differences in early reading growth in Australia, the United States, and Scandinavia. *Journal of Experimental Child Psychology, 115*(3), 453–467.

Connor, C.M., Morrison, F.J., & Petrella, J.N. (2004). Effective reading comprehension Instruction: Examining child x instruction interactions. *Journal of Educational Psychology, 96*(4), 682–698.

Cronbach, L., & Snow, R. (1977). Individual differences and instructional theory. *Educational Researcher, 6*(10), 11–15.

DeFries, J.C., & Fulker, D.W. (1985). Multiple regression analysis of twin data. *Behavior Genetics, 15*(5), 467–473.

Duff, F.J., Hulme, C., Grainger, K., Hardwick, S.J., Miles, J.N.V., & Snowling, M.J. (2014). Reading and language intervention for children at risk of dyslexia: A randomised controlled trial. *Journal of Child Psychology and Psychiatry, 55*(11), 1234–1243. doi: 10.1111/jcpp.12257

Ehri, L.C. (1992). Reconceptualizing the development of sight word reading and its relationship to recoding. In P.E. Gough, L.C. Ehri, & R. Trieman. (Eds.), *Reading acquisition* (pp. 107–143). Mahwah, NJ: Lawrence Erlbaum Associates.

Elbro, C., & Petersen, D.K. (2004). Long-term effects of phoneme awareness and letter sound training: An intervention study with children at risk for dyslexia. *Journal of Educational Psychology, 96*(4), 660.

Fletcher, J.M., Foorman, B.R., Boudousquie, A., Barnes, M.A., Schatschneider, C., & Francis, D.J. (2002). Assessment of reading and learning disabilities a research-based intervention-oriented approach. *Journal of School Psychology, 40*(1), 27–63.

Fuchs, D., Mock, D., Morgan, P.L., & Young, C.L. (2003). Responsiveness-to-intervention: Definitions, evidence, and implications for the learning disabilities construct. *Learning Disabilities Research & Practice, 18*(3), 157–171.

Fuchs, L.S., Fuchs, D., Hosp, M.K., & Jenkins, J.R. (2001). Oral reading fluency as an indicator of reading competence: A theoretical, empirical, and historical analysis. *Scientific Studies of Reading, 5*(3), 239–256.

Harlaar, N., Dale, P.S., & Plomin, R. (2007). Reading exposure: A (largely) environmental risk factor with environmentally-mediated effects on reading performance in the primary school years. *Journal of Child Psychology and Psychiatry, 48*(12), 1192–1199.

Harlaar, N., Spinath, F.M., Dale, P.S., & Plomin, R. (2005). Genetic influences on early word recognition abilities and disabilities: A study of 7-year-old twins. *Journal of Child Psychology and Psychiatry, 46*(4), 373–384.

Hart, S.A., Logan, J.A.R., Soden-Hensler, B., Kershaw, S., Taylor, J., & Schatschneider, C. (2013). Exploring how nature and nurture affect the development of reading: An analysis of the Florida Twin Project on Reading. *Developmental Psychology, 49*(10), 1971.

Hart, S.A., Petrill, S.A., & Kamp Dush, C.M. (2010). Genetic influences on language, reading, and mathematics skills in a national sample: An analysis using the National Longitudinal Survey of Youth. *Language, Speech, and Hearing Services in Schools, 41*(1), 118.

Hart, S.A., Petrill, S.A., & Thompson, L.A. (2010). A factorial analysis of timed and untimed measures of mathematics and reading abilities in school aged twins. *Learning and Individual Differences, 20*(2), 63–69.

Hart, S.A., Soden, B., Johnson, W., Schatschneider, C., & Taylor, J. (2013). Expanding the environment: Gene x school-level SES interaction on reading comprehension. *Journal of Child Psychology and Psychiatry, 54*(10), 1047–1055.

Hawke, J.L., Wadsworth, S.J., Olson, R.K., & DeFries, J.C. (2007). Etiology of reading difficulties as a function of gender and severity. *Reading and Writing, 20*(1–2), 13–25.

Hindson, B., Byrne, B., Fielding-Barnsley, R., Newman, C., Hine, D.W., & Shankweiler, D. (2005). Assessment and early instruction of preschool children at risk for reading disability. *Journal of Educational Psychology, 97*(4), 687–704.

Hoover, W.A., & Gough, P.B. (1990). The simple view of reading. *Reading and Writing, 2*(2), 127–160.

Jenkins, J.R., Fuchs, L.S., van Den Broek, P., Espin, C., & Deno, S.L. (2003). Sources of individual differences in reading comprehension and reading fluency. *Journal of Educational Psychology, 95*(4), 719.

Joshi, R.M., & Aaron, P.G. (2000). The component model of reading: Simple view of reading made a little more complex. *Reading Psychology, 21*(2), 85–97.

Keenan, J.M., Betjemann, R.S., & Olson, R.K. (2008). Reading comprehension tests vary in the skills they assess: Differential dependence on decoding and oral comprehension. *Scientific Studies of Reading, 12*(3), 281–300.

Kegel, C.A.T., Bus, A.G., & van Ijzendoorn, M.H. (2011). Differential susceptibility in early literacy instruction through computer games: The role of the dopamine D4 receptor gene (DRD4). *Mind, Brain, and Education, 5*(2), 71–78.

Kovas, Y., Hayiou-Thomas, M.E., Oliver, B., Dale, P.S., Bishop, D.V.M., & Plomin, R. (2005). Genetic influences in different aspects of language development: The etiology of language skills in 4.5 year-old twins. *Child Development, 76*(3), 632–651.

Light, J.G., & DeFries, J.C. (1995). Comorbidity of reading and mathematics disabilities: Genetic and environmental etiologies. *Journal of Learning Disabilities, 28*(2), 96–106.

Logan, J.A.R., Hart, S.A., Cutting, L., Deater-Deckard, K., Schatschneider, C., & Petrill, S. (2013). Reading development in young children: Genetic and environmental influences. *Child Development, 84*(6), 2131–2144.

Maher, B. (2008). The case of the missing heritability. *Nature, 465*(6), 18–21.

National Institute of Child Health and Development. (2000). *Report of the National Reading Panel. Teaching children to read: An evidence-based assessment of the scientific research literature on reading and its implications for reading instruction* (NIH Pub. No. 00-4769). Washington, DC: Government Printing Office.

Olson, R.K., Keenan, J.M., Byrne, B., & Samuelsson, S. (2014). Why do children differ in their development of reading and related skills? *Scientific Studies of Reading, 18*(1), 38–54.

Pearson, P.D., Hansen, J., & Gordon, C. (1979). The effect of background knowledge on young children's comprehension of explicit and implicit information. *Journal of Literacy Research, 11*(3), 201–209.

Pennington, B.F., & Lefly, D.L. (2001). Early reading development in children at family risk for dyslexia. *Child Development, 72*(3), 816–833.

Peterson, P.L., & Janicki, T.C. (1979). Individual characteristics and children's learning in large-group and small-group approaches. *Journal of Educational Psychology, 71*(5), 677–687.

Petrill, S.A., Deater-Deckard, K., Thompson, L.A., DeThorne, L.S., & Schatschneider, C. (2006a). Genetic and environmental effects of serial naming and phonological awareness on early reading outcomes. *Journal of Educational Psychology, 98*(1), 112–121.

Petrill, S.A., Deater-Deckard, K., Thompson, L.A., DeThorne, L.S., & Schatschneider, C. (2006b). Reading skills in early readers: Genetic and shared environmental influences. *Journal of Learning Disabilities, 39*(1), 48–55.

Petrill, S.A., Deater-Deckard, K., Thompson, L.A., Schatschneider, C., DeThorne, L.S., & Vandenbergh, D.J. (2007). Longitudinal genetic analysis of early reading: The Western Reserve Reading Project. *Reading and Writing, 20*(1–2), 127–146.

Petrill, S.A., Hart, S.A., Harlaar, N., Logan, J., Justice, L.M., Schatschneider, C., . . . Cutting, L. (2010). Genetic and environmental influences on the growth of early reading skills. *Journal of Child Psychology and Psychiatry, 51*(6), 660–667.

Petrill, S.A., Logan, J., Hart, S., Vincent, P., Thompson, L., Kovas, Y., & Plomin, R. (2012). Math fluency is etiologically distinct from untimed math performance, decoding fluency, and untimed reading performance: Evidence from a twin study. *Journal of Learning Disabilities, 45*(4), 371–381.

Plomin, R., & Kovas, Y. (2005). Generalist genes and learning disabilities. *Psychological Bulletin, 131*(4), 592–617.

Plomin, R., DeFries, J.C., Knopik, Valerie, S., & Neiderhiser, J.M. (2013). *Behavioral Genetics* (6th ed.). New York, NY: Worth Publishers.

Regtvoort, A.G.F.M., & van der Leij, A. (2007). Early intervention with children of dyslexic parents: Effects of computer-based reading instruction at home on literacy acquisition. *Learning and Individual Differences, 17*(1), 35–53.

Roehrig, A.D., Petscher, Y., Nettles, S.M., Hudson, R.F., & Torgesen, J.K. (2008). Accuracy of the DIBELS oral reading fluency measure for predicting third grade reading comprehension outcomes. *Journal of School Psychology, 46*(3), 343–366.

Smith, S.D., Kimberling, W.J., Pennington, B.F., & Lubs, H.A. (1983). Specific reading disability: Identification of an inherited form through linkage analysis. *Science, 219*(4590), 1345–1347.

Snowling, M.J., Gallagher, A., & Frith, U. (2003). Family risk of dyslexia is continuous: Individual differences in the precursors of reading skill. *Child Development, 74*(2), 358–373.

Stanovich, K.E. (1980). Toward an interactive-compensatory model of individual differences in the development of reading fluency. *Reading Research Quarterly*, 32–71.

Stevenson, J., Graham, P., Fredman, G., & Mcloughli, V. (1987). A twin study of genetic influences on reading and spelling ability and disability. *Journal of Child Psychology and Psychiatry, 28*(2), 229–247.

Taylor, J., & Schatschneider, C. (2010). Genetic influence on literacy constructs in kindergarten and first grade: Evidence from a diverse twin sample. *Behavior Genetics, 40*(5), 591–602.

Taylor, J., Hart, S.A., Mikolajewski, A.J., & Schatschneider, C. (2013). An update on the Florida State Twin Registry. *Twin Research and Human Genetics, 16*(1), 471–475.

Uher, R. (2011). Genes, environments, and individual differences in responding to treatment for depression. *Harvard Review of Psychiatry, 19*(3), 109–124.

van Otterloo, S.G., van der Leij, A., & Henrichs, L.F. (2009). Early home-based intervention in the Netherlands for children at familial risk of dyslexia. *Dyslexia, 15*(3), 187–217.

Vellutino, F.R., Fletcher, J.M., Snowling, M.J., & Scanlon, D.M. (2004). Specific reading disability (dyslexia): What have we learned in the past four decades? *Journal of Child Psychology and Psychiatry, 45*(1), 2–40.

Integrative Summary 1

The Future of Reading Research: New Concepts and Tools and the Need for Detailed Genetic and Neurobiological Contexts

Nadine Gaab

Reading intervention is one of the most debated topics in the fields of developmental dyslexia and general reading research. Researchers, educators, and clinicians debate not only about who should get intervention and when to intervene but also about how to intervene, the duration of the intervention, the appropriate tools for quantifying intervention effects, and so forth. Researchers, educators, and clinicians in the field have reached a point at which most agree there is no magic all-fits-all intervention for children with reading disabilities, and the field is moving toward a customized intervention strategy similar to the concept of personal medicine; however, we still have a long way to go before we can apply effective "personal education" with strong outcome success in a way that is cost efficient. The 2014 meeting of The Dyslexia Foundation focused, as does this volume, on reading intervention and the construction and maintenance of a bidirectional bridge between neurobiological, genetic, and behavioral research and educational practice in the classroom. Section II (Chapters 3–9) focuses on basic considerations for reading intervention research and spans several disciplines. These basic considerations are important concepts, tools, and perspectives for the development and evaluation of effective interventions and should carefully be considered both when designing research studies that evaluate existing intervention strategies and during the development of new customized reading interventions.

Morrison, in Chapter 3, addresses the important construct of self-regulation—its significance during the early childhood years and its relationship to reading acquisition and long-term academic outcomes. Self-regulation (often also termed *executive functions* or *effortful control*), with its central components of attention control, working memory, and response inhibition, shows high variability before the start of formal schooling, and there seems to be a prominent gender effect, with boys showing lower performance on self-regulation tasks than girls. Self-regulation abilities predict not only later academic achievement but also general health and economic well-being, and it is surprising that self-regulation skills are not a fundamental part of current school curricula. There seems to be a relationship, however, between general schooling and both specific teaching strategies and an improvement in certain aspects of self-regulation skills. Given the relationship between self-regulation skills and later academic achievement and the reported strong link between executive function and literacy skills (especially comprehension skills), improving self-regulation skills seems to be a promising early intervention strategy for children at risk for poor academic and psychological outcomes.

In Chapter 4, Bartlett and colleagues introduce new statistical tools that will help to detangle some of the most pressing questions in reading research. The chapter shows that the common tools employed in reading research (e.g., Pearson's correlation) may often underestimate the effects of nonlinear relationships. Using a distance correlation (*dCor*), they were able to show that the relationship between listening comprehension and word decoding, the two major contributors to reading comprehension as indicated in the Simple View of Reading (Hoover & Gough, 1990; Scarborough, 2001), indicates a far more complex relationship than previously anticipated. This *dCor* quantifies the dependence of two variables without assuming a linear relationship. Employing a large data set from the New Jersey Language–Autism Study, for example, the authors could show that the relationship between single-word reading and oral language is greater for above-average readers than for struggling readers. They further introduce quantile regression, a statistical tool that determines regressions from a range of quantiles rather than the whole data set and therefore shows better robustness to outliers. Using these techniques, their results suggest that below-average scores in word decoding only weakly predict oral language performance but that high word-decoding scores strongly predict superior oral language performance. These important "threshold relationships" are not detectable with conventional statistical methods, and it will be exciting to see what new relationships emerge once these toolboxes are used more widely within the field of reading research.

Sideridis and colleagues, in Chapter 5, address the role of the reading subskill known as *rapid automatized naming* (*RAN*) and aim to answer the research question of why it is predictive of reading performance. They present a novel hypothesis of "generic shutdown," using a new analytic approach that they also introduce us to: the cusp catastrophe model (Thom, 1975). In generic shutdown, they explain, cognitive difficulties, negative affect, and dysfunctional motivation can interact additively to interfere with a student's ability to self-regulate while reading. They present data that argue convincingly for RAN as a correlate of word reading but that also indicate that the predictive ability of RAN is lessened for students with slow digit naming and poor reading comprehension. Thus they conclude that 1) RAN is a nonlinear moderator of word reading and that 2) decoding is far more complex than has been previously considered. The cusp model presents reading as a self-organizing function (Nicolis & Nicolis, 2007) that engages various cognitive components (e.g., working memory, processing speed, attention, decoding) as needed during reading. This system, Sideridis and colleagues point out, is robust unless levels of task difficulty or negative affect and dysfunctional thoughts get too great; it also fails when there are insufficient cognitive resources (which are developed through reading instruction and experience). This fresh look at RAN offers intriguing possibilities, and similar to Morrison and Cutting and colleagues in their chapters, Sideridis's group invokes the importance of an integrated look at the components of reading and executive and cognitive functions.

Miller convincingly claims in Chapter 6 that eye tracking is an underappreciated tool in reading (intervention) research, especially within a developmental frame. He provides a brief historic time line of eye trackers and the technique's limitations, and he describes its foundation in experimental psychology and behavioral neuroscience. The potential for reading intervention research quickly becomes evident in his summary of the role of eye-movement research in developing readers. Prominent changes in various eye-movement parameters are observed throughout the developmental time course, especially in perceptual span, which is defined as the vertical and horizontal spans within which the human eye has sharp enough vision to read connected text. Furthermore, eye movement research suggests that younger readers show significant word-length, word-familiarity, and frequency effects that are less efficient for utilizing word knowledge (as indicated by a delayed detection of implausible text) while reading connected text. There is also a line of research that investigates the possible link between poor oculomotor control and developmental dyslexia. In his outline of the potential impact of eye tracking on reading intervention research, Miller suggests its use as an outcome measure. For instance, the effectiveness of various comprehension strategies could be evaluated using eye tracking in typical as well as struggling readers. Not many researchers are trained, however, in how to effectively use an eye tracker; interdisciplinary teams will be needed if researchers are to implement eye tracking as part of the toolbox for reading research.

Cutting and colleagues emphasize the importance of disentangling distinct versus common neural substrates for various reading processes in Chapter 7. Understanding the neurobiological origins of overlapping activation during various reading processes may provide insights into which aspects of reading are most problematic. Identifying areas that are impaired during many different reading processes, lower level as well as higher level, may provide the perfect target areas for reading intervention. The authors discuss the specific reading comprehension deficit (S-RCD) and review the literature on the Simple View of Reading, its relationship to executive functions, and its developmental time course. They then give an overview of the neural correlates of reading and reading disability, especially related to word-level processes and comprehension, strongly emphasizing white matter connectivity and functional networks. They conclude that reading comprehension involves both processes that are distinct and processes that overlap with those utilized in single-word reading and argue that overlapping areas of activation in key nodes change function and functional connectivity depending on the dynamic shifts in cognitive demands during the construction of mental representations of text, especially specific text genres. Furthermore, the authors emphasize that a stronger focus on textual centrality and text genre will help to identify areas of weakness and strength in typical and struggling readers, which will further support the development of customized intervention strategies for (new) subtypes of struggling readers.

In Chapter 8, Del Tufo and Pugh present another neurobiological context essential for the development of integrated theories of developmental dyslexia and targeted intervention strategies. The authors review the neurobiological and genetic foundations of reading, including the typical and atypical reading network, compensatory mechanisms, and functional and structural connectivity, and then convincingly argue that a model of a neurobiological foundation of developmental dyslexia requires the inclusion of neurochemical correlates of perception and cognition. They review research using magnetic resonance spectroscopy, a noninvasive technique to quantify the brain's metabolic activity, which has shown atypical metabolic activity in the brains of individuals with developmental dyslexia. Del Tufo and Pugh offer a working hypothesis for the role of neurometabolites in reading and its connection to various other neurobiological, genetic, and behavioral findings. For example, elevated choline has been linked to alterations in white matter connectivity, although the exact mechanisms are still unclear. In addition, elevated glutamate levels have been connected to hyperexcitability, which has a negative impact on various brain processes essential for learning and cognition. Intensive research linking in vivo studies and brain imaging, led by combined teams of behavioral neuroscientists, cognitive neuroscientists, biochemists, geneticists, and molecular biologists, is needed to integrate the various neurobiological, genetic, and biochemical findings into interventions with individuals with dyslexia. This line of research will have important implications for the development of unique interventions and the evaluation of existing intervention strategies.

In Chapter 9, Hart gives us an overview of genetic and environmental influences on reading and its components, and she argues that behavioral genetics can make concrete contributions to research on typical and atypical reading and reading intervention. She reviews the heritability estimates for various reading components (i.e., phonological awareness, decoding, reading fluency, and reading comprehension) and summarizes shared and nonshared environmental influences. One can surmise that genetics plays a significant role (with, at times, aspects of reading showing the highest heritability estimates) and that the magnitude and significance of one's environment varies depending on his or her age—having more influence in one's early years before basic reading is successfully mastered. This can be explained with strong, early influences in the toddler–preschool years (e.g., rich home literacy environment), which become less important during the later stages of reading development. Hart also presents data to suggest that genetic influences on reading disability are of similar magnitude to those of the full range of reading ability and that similar genes are responsible for both reading ability and reading disability. Further research, taking into account the evidence from neurobiological and neurochemical studies, is needed to more fully examine this hypothesis. Hart provides some concrete examples of how behavioral genetics can inform decisions in education. She strongly pleads for customized interventions and intervention dosages based on familial (genetic) risk, proposing the inclusion of familial risk profiles in individualized education and intervention plans. She also states, however, that the general public may not (yet) be ready to accept a genetics-based, personalized intervention and education plan.

In summary, the chapters in Section II, "Basic Considerations for Reading Intervention: Behavior, Neurobiology, and Genetics," provide unique perspectives, tool sets, and constructs that should be considered in the design, implementation, and analysis of studies evaluating reading interventions, as well as in the design of new "personalized" intervention strategies and in the integration of behavioral, cognitive, neurobiological, and neurochemical aspects of reading. Such a multidisciplinary integration will ensure a multifaceted view of reading, reading disability, and reading interventions, and it will help the field critically evaluate (and hopefully replace) many of the so-called brain-based interventions with theory-driven, multicomponential intervention strategies grounded in neurobiological and neurochemical mechanisms and further enriched by the various additional elements and constructs that compose successful reading.

REFERENCES

Hoover, W.A., & Gough, P.B. (1990). The simple view of reading. *Reading and Writing, 2,* 127–160. doi:10.1007/BF00401799

Nicolis, G., & Nicolis, C. (2007). *Foundations of complex systems.* Singapore: World Scientific.

Scarborough, H.S. (2001). Connecting early language and literacy to later reading (dis) abilities: Evidence, theory, and practice. In S. Neuman & D. Dickinson (Eds.), *Handbook for research in early literacy* (pp. 97–110). New York, NY: Guilford Press.

Thom, R. (1975). *Structural stability and morphogenesis.* Reading, MA: W.A. Benjamin.

III

Reading and Writing Interventions

Research to Inform Practice

10

What Practitioners Think and Want to Know

Joan A. Mele-McCarthy

Every day, educators and academic practitioners[1] work with students who struggle with dyslexia and other reading difficulties. Every day, many children improve their reading skills, but some do not—or at least not enough to make a difference in their academic growth and, perhaps, the array of choices they will have beyond high school. Practitioners therefore look to the scientific literature to seek reasons why some students improve their reading skills and others do not and which interventions would be effective for which students. Practitioners also scour the products of publishing companies that offer the latest materials to use for students with reading deficits, hoping to find that best intervention program that will prove successful for those particular students.

Practitioners also understand the importance of individualized assessments for students with reading and academic deficits and that accurate assessments drive instruction. Yet they also seek ways to understand a student's overall learning profile, which goes beyond the traditional, behavioral pencil-and-paper batteries. Once again, practitioners turn to scientific literature to seek information and generate ideas that can make a difference in the lives of students with reading challenges and other learning issues. There is an implicit partnership, then, between those who deliver instruction (practitioners) and those who pose questions and answer them scientifically (researchers). Why not expand this partnership from an implicit one to an explicit one? How beneficial it would be to students if the field were to adopt an active research-to-practice-to-research partnership in which practitioners utilized available information and expanded it by proposing additional questions for scientific exploration!

1. For convenience, the term *practitioner* will be used henceforth.

That's what practitioners think, and in this chapter, I offer many ideas for what I and other practitioners would like to know.

TREATMENT RESPONDERS VERSUS TREATMENT NONRESPONDERS

One often-asked question among practitioners concerns "treatment nonresponders." There are students who begin an intervention program with similar skill levels, similar cognitive abilities, and similar processing abilities, yet Student A responds beautifully to intervention and Student B does not. Practitioners may use a diagnostic tree approach to work through Student B's weak progress. The branches on the tree, which represent possible next steps in the student's intervention, include 1) changing or not changing the intervention method, 2) increasing or not increasing the intensity and frequency of intervention, and 3) adding other strategies or keeping strategies constant based on existing or new assessment data.

Neuroscience and education research have provided insights into intervention effectiveness for children who have dyslexia and other reading difficulties, as evidenced in several chapters of this book and many other published works, yet to date, I know of no data that are *predictive* in nature—that tell who will respond well and who will not respond well to reading interventions. It is this *predictive* data that practitioners seek. Predictive data could provide the evidence for implementing high- versus low-intensity intervention. In typical mainstream public schools, students are often placed in a multitiered system of support or a response to intervention (RTI) programming sequence that uses data to monitor progress and drive subsequent programming decisions; school personnel could do this more efficiently if given predictive information about who would respond best to which types of intervention and at what levels of intensity. Independent schools designed to meet the needs of struggling learners would also benefit from this predictive research, of course. If research could provide behavioral indices, genetic predispositions, or neurobiological markers for determining which students would progress slowly through intervention regimens, then the time taken to move through an RTI sequence could be decreased; students could be placed directly into the appropriate tiered level of programming intensity without having to work through every tier and presumably would progress more rapidly. If research could determine the components of intervention strategies needed for the most affected learner, coupled with ways to predict who is at risk for being a "treatment nonresponder," then, theoretically, the most challenged reader could improve to a greater degree and at a faster rate. To this end, and in the spirit of a research-to-practice-to-research partnership, practitioners would like answers to the following questions:

- Can neural signatures discriminate between responders and nonresponders?
- Can genetic markers, family history, and behavior measures predict who will be a responder or a nonresponder to intervention?

SUBTYPING READING DISABILITY

Related to the issue of treatment response is the issue of reading disability subtyping. Certainly, the field at large is comfortable with understanding the difference between readers who struggle with decoding and are described as having dyslexia and readers who can determine the individual words but struggle with comprehending what they read (see discussion in Lovett, Chapter 2). Many students demonstrate difficulties with both reading decoding and reading comprehension. Practitioners would presume, and most likely have experienced, that deficits in both areas yield a less-than-hardy response to intervention; however, effective intervention for some students might require these two domains of reading performance to be differentiated, with specific components in each domain delineated. This, in turn, could lead to targeted interventions that would hypothetically result in greater reading skill improvements. Therefore, practitioners have questions about potential subtypes of dyslexia and of reading comprehension difficulties.

Some scientific literature has presented the concept of surface versus phonological subtypes of dyslexia (Castles & Coltheart, 1993; Zeigler, 2011). On a very basic level, individuals with surface dyslexia demonstrate difficulties reading sight words (i.e., words that often do not follow predictable phonics rules), and their reading profiles are similar to those of younger readers, whereas individuals with phonological dyslexia perform more poorly when reading *nonwords* (i.e., fabricated words that follow predictable phonics rules). If this research and the research expanding upon this finding (Manis, Seidenberg, Doi, McBride-Chang, & Peterson, 1996) were not carefully reviewed, this subtyping nomenclature presents the danger of being misunderstood and misused for intervention purposes. For example, a practitioner could assume that teaching only sight words to an individual classified as having surface dyslexia would be the intervention of choice, whereas implementing a phonological-awareness and explicit-phonics approach with an individual who demonstrates phonological dyslexia would be sufficient; however, Castles and Coltheart (1993), Manis and colleagues (Manis et al., 1996), and Zeigler (2011) also demonstrated that children with surface and phonological dyslexia exhibited difficulty reading sight words *and* nonwords when compared with their same-age peers. Subtypes themselves encompass heterogeneity and do not necessarily represent prescriptions for intervention.

In addition, listservs and blogs abound with conversations that talk about visual versus auditory dyslexia and consonant versus vowel dyslexia, just to name a few. Needless to say, the nomenclature can be confusing, is frequently inaccurate, and can be detrimental to the main task of teaching struggling readers how to read based on scientific data. This example illustrates the idea that practitioners are reading what is available to them as they seek to understand the scientific evidence for subtypes of dyslexia as well as the implications for interventions, and what is available is not always rigorous. Much-repeated questions of what will work, for whom, and with what intensity pointedly relate to this issue of dyslexia subtypes. These questions also cycle us back to the question of who will respond well versus who will not. The answer is important to those of us who work with children in the classroom or the clinic for obvious reasons: Practitioners want to provide instruction that is relevant, meaningful, and specifically designed to meet individual areas of difficulty to close the gap between struggling readers and their neurotypical peers, and they want to do so with expediency. With this in mind, practitioners would like to know whether they can clarify and substantiate subtypes of dyslexia through research findings in neurobiology, genetics, and behavior measures, and they would like to know how this can improve their practice.

Practitioners who work with children with reading deficits know well that many children struggle with reading comprehension as well as decoding. Reading comprehension, like decoding, is not a unidimensional construct; rather, competent reading comprehension relies on a multitude of intertwined factors (Cutting, Materek, Cole, Levine, & Mahone, 2009; Cutting et al., 2013; Cutting, Bailey, Barquero, & Aboud, Chapter 7; Scarborough, 2009), including, but not limited to, vocabulary and background knowledge, an understanding of syntax and grammar, the ability to understand inference, executive functions related to working memory, sequencing, cognitive organization, and text characteristics. Again, although poor comprehenders may not be categorized as having dyslexia, it seems logical that research on subtyping reading comprehension difficulties has the potential to be equally informative and helpful to practitioners, as also noted by Lovett (Chapter 2). Perhaps scientific inquiry could verify, for example, the sources of difficulty, such as oral language (e.g., discourse and listening comprehension), language in general (e.g., vocabulary, syntax, grammar), executive function components (e.g., working memory, sequencing, organization, attention), and/or decoding or reading fluency. These broad categories are noted by many practitioners. How does text structure interact with each of these categories? Practitioners seek clarification about how to conceptualize reading comprehension difficulties diagnostically and then, of course, instructionally:

- Are there subtypes of profiles for reading comprehension difficulties, and how are these subtypes determined?
- How might motivation, topic interest, stress, and self-confidence interact with anticipated subtypes of reading comprehension difficulties, and how might these inform effective interventions?
- What specific components are foundational to effective reading comprehension instruction, and how should these components be delivered to students who struggle with reading comprehension?

READING FLUENCY, DECODING, COMPREHENSION, AND COGNITIVE INFORMATION PROCESSING

A discussion of decoding and reading comprehension is not complete without a discussion of reading fluency. Children often improve their phonological, word-attack, and word-identification skills, yet text-level reading fluency remains problematic. For many children, it is this issue that impedes reading comprehension, whereas others manage to comprehend despite word-level inaccuracies and slow reading speeds. Practitioners seek scientific evidence for instructional strategies for reading fluency, even when reading accuracy and comprehension improve. Practitioners and researchers know that decoding can improve in adolescents who are struggling readers (Scammacca et al., 2007) and in adults (Eden et al., 2004; Tighe, Barnes, Connor, & Steadman, 2013). But can improved reading fluency be achieved by older students, and should it be a target of remediation?

There are questions about reading fluency that are not so overtly instructionally pragmatic, at least not at first blush. These questions relate to the cognitive and linguistic processing components of reading competency and affect decoding and comprehension as well as reading fluency. Scientific literature has demonstrated the role of rapid automatized naming (RAN; Denckla & Rudel, 1976; Cutting & Denckla, 2001; Katzir et al., 2007) in decoding and reading fluency. Differing reading profiles can be seen in struggling readers who are slow but are accurate namers (according to RAN measures) versus those who are rapid and inaccurate or slow and inaccurate (Lovett, 1987). Practitioners who work with children can definitely identify children who read with these same characteristics (slow and accurate, fast and inaccurate, and slow and inaccurate). Of those three categories, it would seem that the latter two have the most deficient reading skills. But what if the child who reads accurately but slowly also has weak working memory abilities; perhaps the child's slow reading impedes his or her ability to remember what he or she read.

This brings another dimension into the alphabet soup of processing factors thought to affect reading competence—that of working memory. The literature has demonstrated the role of working memory in phonological awareness and processing (Alloway, Gathercole, & Willis, 2004; Baddeley, 2003; Baddeley & Hitch, 1974), reading and spelling (Gathercole, Lamont, & Alloway, 2006; Swanson, Howard, & Saez, 2006; Swanson & O'Connor, 2009), and written language (McCutchen, 1996; McCutchen, 2000; Ormrod & Cochran, 1988). Diagnosticians assess constructs such as RAN, working memory, and processing speed and relate these constructs to reading, academic skill development, and classroom intervention methods and strategies. Although there is strong evidence for the diagnostic value of RAN, working memory, and processing speed, is the evidence as strong for specific interventions, or are practitioners engaging in what they hope are "best practices"? Even though practitioners are confident that at least they "do no harm," is harm done due to lost time spent on programs or interventions that have weak or no evidence? Practitioners are concerned about whether intervention can improve the underlying cognitive and linguistic processes that science has shown contribute to reading competence. Questions related to processing are posed that could support practitioners' efforts to make a significant difference with struggling readers:

- Could an underlying cause for deficits in reading decoding, reading fluency, and reading comprehension, such as RAN and working memory, be effectively remediated to improve decoding, fluency, and reading comprehension?
- Is it reasonable to expect improvements in reading fluency if there are deficits in processing speed?
- Can underlying auditory processing abilities with respect to processing rapid speech, dichotic listening, and reduced ability to discern signal to noise be improved to the extent that improvements in reading decoding would be realized? If so, how could this be implemented in a school setting?
- Can the role of working memory in reading be further delineated diagnostically to help identify which students may demonstrate greater resistance to intervention?
- Can software programs designed to improve working memory actually achieve that objective with results evident for reading? If so, will that growth be sustained over time?

READING DEFICITS AND WRITTEN LANGUAGE

Practitioners who work with students who struggle with reading understand the interaction between reading and written language (Miller, McCardle, & Long, 2014). For students with dyslexia, deficits in written language are pervasive and encompass spelling, vocabulary usage, grammar and syntax, the organization and quality of thoughts and text structure, and the quantity of words used in writing samples (see Alves & Limpo, Chapter 17). Connelly and Dockrell (Chapter 16) provide insight into the compelling effect of poor spelling on written language output and discuss quality as measured by vocabulary usage. Practitioners also see additional challenges with written language and look to science to inform their practice for this group of learners:

- Could scientific inquiry for written language include an evidence base for the components of written language competence and ways to assess these components that include the differentiation of narrative and expository writing?

INTERVENTIONS BEYOND THE EVIDENCE BASE

Practitioners make decisions about interventions that are deemed "good," or maybe even "best," practice with respect to bypass strategies (accommodations) that *may* have a positive effect for those with reading difficulties. We use various means of presenting reading material to yield a positive effect on comprehension. We *think* that graphic novels level the comprehension playing field for some learners. We *believe* that technology aids instruction for struggling readers. We *trust* that presenting film or video versions of novels enhances comprehension of the printed form, so we *deliberate* about which should be introduced first: print or film. We *support* the use of recorded books or voice-to-text technologies to provide a multisensory presentation to aid access to print-driven information. Those of us who work with students know that some students find this use of technology life changing, yet some do not. It would be helpful to know at the front end of instructional planning which learners would benefit from this kind of assistive technology.

As a culture, we now *embrace* the use of tablet technology as a teaching and learning tool (see also Jodoin, Chapter 19), yet we do not know how technology affects reading comprehension in able readers, let alone in those who have difficulty. We do *observe,* however, that including tablets in the teaching/learning environment is highly motivational for students. Once again, practitioners frequently board the latest reading or educational bandwagon because they have been lulled by the practice at large, been persuaded by effective marketing strategies, or succumbed to the appeal of a quick fix or to the political will of our teaching environments. We *admit* that our practice is not consistently supported by evidence to drive our programming decisions.

In addition to technology, we *contemplate* whether non–language-based strategies have a place in the toolbox we use to help those who struggle with reading, so we ask the research community questions about practices that as yet do not have a strong evidence base:

- What effect do text variables, such as font, font size, and spacing, have on text readability separate from linguistic factors?
- What effect do strategies, such as the composition and size of instructional groupings, teacher training, pacing of instruction, and instructional orientation (such as project-based, multisensory discovery learning) have on reading improvement?
- What kinds of progress monitoring strategies are appropriate for what kinds of interventions, and with what frequency should these tools be used?
- In what ways will technology change how we intervene?

RESEARCH TO PRACTICE TO RESEARCH

Education professionals have matured into a culture that defines and seeks an evidence base, and by default, they are becoming competent consumers of research. It is this evolution of practice seeking research that naturally expands to practice helping to inform research. Neurobiological, genetic, and education research have provided volumes of information related to identifying struggling readers and what works for this population of learners. Perhaps there should be a shift from "what" to "how"—how to implement what works and how to adapt implementation from school setting to school setting, from public to independent schools, from individual to small-group to whole-class interventions, from resource room to inclusion service delivery models.

Many practitioners welcome research scientists into their schools, but often the research designs are not compatible with the format, structure, and even culture of the individual school. How can intervention research be designed to fit within the constructs of a variety of school settings in a way that is controlled yet ecologically valid? With rapid advances in data analyses and the technologies that support these, wouldn't it be beneficial for education research to include data analytics for student achievement across instructional areas? Very simplistically, such technology-based research strategies could use student learning profile data and a set of teaching objectives and associated teaching practices to predict the trajectory of learning based on student responses. In fact, some work is already moving in this direction (Connor et al., 2013; see Connor, Chapter 11). Consider the impact on the effectiveness of an RTI model for student improvement if this kind of continuous analytic data were to be used in all classrooms. Innovations such as data analytics are needed to propel the field of reading intervention forward and make significant differences in the lives of children. The ultimate question practitioners ask of researchers is, how do we innovate and expedite intervention research? Can we study important questions in a different way that yields faster knowledge accrual? Educators, practitioners, and researchers have to help children *today.* Does "a different way" mean different ways to conceptualize what defines good research design and good evidence? Does it mean different collaborations?

The Dyslexia Foundation's (TDF) Extraordinary Brain Symposia (EBS) have been very innovative through the years in the desire to blend silos of knowledge by bringing together diverse groups of research scientists who represent work in reading, education, communication sciences, neuroscience, genetics, research design, and technology. Participating professionals have always been charged with rethinking their work (in terms of traditional lines of inquiry and methodology) and thinking anew (in ways that step outside of "business-as-usual" research questions, comparisons, analyses, etc.) to propel reading research related to dyslexia and literacy development forward. TDF's focus has always been to promote rigorous science and to translate it to practice for educators, practitioners, and families. The EBS that informs this book has taken the research-to-practice mantra a step further and has added a third dimension: practice to research. Thus the symposium meeting and this volume also represent yet another blending of silos—the silos that define research and practice. Researchers have traditionally asked and studied important questions, and practitioners, the "doers," have implemented the important answers.

But in reality, we all ask, and we all do. The size of the question, the size of the thinking, or the size of the sample may vary. Practitioners are often innovators. They take a program, process, or procedure validated by science *or not* and tweak it to meet the needs of the student in front of them. How can this small-scale innovation be translated to large-scale research? I challenge my fellow practitioners to stay in the practice-to-research game, to keep their voices strong, and to engage in collaborative work with researchers to bring even greater impact to the field of reading intervention for students who have dyslexia and other reading difficulties. I challenge researchers to expand their scope of inquiry to ask, "What do you think?," "What more do you want to know?," or "What should we be doing differently?" And I challenge us all—practitioners and researchers—to live according to our new mantra in our daily work, to close the circle of research to practice to research because our struggling readers depend on us all.

REFERENCES

Alloway, T.P., Gathercole, S.E., & Willis, C. (2004). A structural analysis of working memory and related cognitive skills in young children. *Journal of Experimental Psychology, 87(2),* 85–106. doi:10.1016/j.jecp.2003.10.002

Alloway, T.P., Gathercole, S.E., & Willis, C. (2006). Working memory in children with reading disabilities. *Journal of Experimental Psychology, 93*(3), 265–281. doi:10.1016/j.jecp.2005.08.003

Baddeley, A. (2003). Working memory and language: An overview. *Journal of Communication Disorders, 36*(3), 189–208. doi:10.1016/S0021-9924(03)00019-4

Baddeley, A., & Hitch, G. (1974). Working memory. *Psychology of Learning and Motivation, 8,* 47–89. doi:10.1016/S0079-7421(08)60452-1

Castles, A., & Coltheart, M. (1993). Varieties of developmental dyslexia. *Cognition, 47*(2), 149–180. doi:10.1016/0010-0277(93)90003-E

Connor, C.M., Morrison, F.J., Fishman, B., Crowe, E.C., Al Otaiba, S., & Schatschneider, C. (2013). A longitudinal cluster-randomized controlled study on the accumulating effects of individualized literacy instruction on students' reading from first through third grade. *Psychological Science, 24*(8), 1408–1419. doi:10.1177/0956797612472204

Cutting, L.E., Clements-Stephens, A., Pugh, K.R., Burns, S., Cao, A., Pekar, J.J., . . . Rimrodt, S.L.(2013). Not all reading disabilities are dyslexia: Distinct neurobiology of specific comprehension deficits. *Brain Connectivity, 3(2),* 199–211.

Cutting, L.E., & Denckla, M.B. (2001). The relationship of Rapid Automatized Naming and word reading in normally developing readers. *Reading and Writing: An Interdisciplinary Journal, 14,* 673–705.

Cutting, L.E., Materek, A., Cole, G.A.S., Levine, T.M., & Mahone, E.M. (2009). Effects of fluency, oral language, and executive function on reading comprehension performance. *Annals of Dyslexia, 59,* 34–54.

Denckla, M.B., & Rudel, R.G. (1976). Rapid 'automatized' naming (RAN): Dyslexia differentiated from other learning disabilities. *Neuropsychologia, 14*(4), 471–479.doi:10.1016/0028-3932(76)900075-0

Eden, I.G.F., Jones, K.M., Cappell, K., Gareau, L., Wood, F.B., Zeffiro, T.A., . . . Flowers, D.L. (2004). Neural changes following remediation in adult developmental dyslexia. *Neuron, 44*(3), 411–422. doi:10.1016/j.neuron.2004.10.019

Gathercole, S., Lamont, E., & Alloway, T. (2006). Working memory in the classroom. In G. Phye & S. Pickering (Eds.), *Working memory and education.* (pp. 219–240). Burlington, MA: Elsevier.

Katzir, T., Kim, Y., Wolf, M., O'Brien, B., Kennedy, B., Lovett, M., & Morris, R. (2007). Reading fluency: The whole is more than the parts. *Annals of Dyslexia, 56*(1), 51–82.

Lovett, M. (1987). A developmental approach to reading disability: Accuracy and speed criteria of normal and deficit reading skill. *Child Development, 2*(1), 243–260.

McCutchen, D. (1996). A capacity theory of writing: Working memory in composition. *Educational Psychology Review, 8*(3), 299–325. doi:10.1007/BF01464076

McCutchen, D. (2000). Knowledge, processing, and working memory: Implications for a theory of writing. *Educational Psychologist 35*(1), 13–23. doi:10.1207/S15326985EP3501_3

Manis, F.R., Seidenberg, M.S., Doi, L.M., McBride-Chang, C., & Peterson, A. (1996). On the basis of two subtypes of development dyslexia. *Cognition 58*(2), 157–195. doi:10.1016/0010-0277(95)00679-6

Miller, B., McCardle, P., & Long, R. (Eds.). (2013). *Teaching reading and writing: Improving instruction and student achievement.* Baltimore, MD: Paul H. Brookes Publishing Co.

Ormrod, J.E., & Cochran, J.E. (1988). Relationship of verbal ability and working memory to spelling achievement and learning to spell. *Literacy Research & Instruction, 28*(1), 33–43. doi:10.1080/19388078809557956

Scammacca, N., Roberts, G., Vaughn, S., Edmonds, M., Wexler, J., Reutebuch, C.K., & Torgesen, J.C. (2007). *Interventions for adolescent struggling readers: A meta-analysis with implications for practice.* Portsmouth, NH: RMC Research Corporation, Center on Instruction.

Scarborough, H. (2009). Connecting early language and literacy to later reading (dis)abilities: Evidence, theory, and practice. In F. Fletcher, J., Campbell, J., Soler, & G. Reid (Eds.), *In approaching difficulties in literacy development: Assessment, pedagogy, and programmes* (pp. 23–38). London, UK: The Open University.

Swanson, H.L., & O'Connor, R. (2009). The role of working memory and fluency practice on the reading comprehension of students who are dysfluent readers. *Journal of Learning Disabilities, 42*(6), 548–575. doi:10.1177/0022219409338742

Swanson, H.L., Howard, C.B., & Saez, L. (2006). Do different components of working memory underlie different subgroups of reading disability? *Journal of Learning Disabilities, 39*(3), 252–269. doi:10.1177/00222194060390030501

Tighe, E.L., Barnes, A.E., Connor, C.M., & Steadman, S.C. (2013). Defining success in adult basic education settings: Multiple stakeholders, multiple perspectives. *Reading Research Quarterly, 48*(4), 415–435. doi:10.1002/rrq.57

Ziegler, J.C. (2011). Understanding developmental dyslexia through computational modeling. In P. McCardle, B. Miller, J.R. Lee, & O.J.L. Tzeng (Eds.), *Dyslexia across languages: Orthography and the brain-gene-behavior link.* (pp. 169–183). Baltimore, MD: Paul H. Brookes Publishing Co.

11

Literacy in the Early Grades

Research to Practice to Research

Carol McDonald Connor[1]

Across the world, literacy is considered a "fertile function" and among the ten human rights (see Alves & Limpo, Chapter 17). Research in neurology, genetics, linguistics, psychology, and education has revealed important characteristics of children who have serious difficulties learning to read, including children with dyslexia. Yet much of this research has not found its way into the classroom. Although a great number of reasons for this have been proposed, one likely reason is that translating basic science into meaningful and effective instructional practices is complex and, hence, very difficult. The associations between genotypes and phenotypes, for example, is multifaceted (see Hart, Chapter 9), and phenotypes for reading difficulty are related to many candidate genes that interact with the environment. Thus, although the skill of reading is highly heritable, there is no "reading gene" but rather an array of genes controlling the neurological processes that support the reorganization of the brain (see Del Tufo & Pugh, Chapter 8) that, in turn, interact with the environment (see Hart, Chapter 9) and underlie evolving individual child differences. One of the most important environments influencing children's learning is their school classroom environment and the instruction in which they participate. Individualizing Student Instruction (ISI) is an intervention that provides technology and professional development to teachers so

1. I thank the Individualizing Student Instruction Project team and Elizabeth Crowe, Frederick J. Morrison, Barry Fishman, and Christopher Schatschneider. I also thank the children, parents, teachers, and schools who participated in this project. Funding for this project was provided by the U.S. Department of Education, Institute of Education Sciences (R305H04013 and R305B070074) and the National Institute of Child Health and Human Development (R01HD48539, R21HD062834, and P50 HD052120).

that they can provide optimal amounts of different types of literacy instruction based on children's constellation of language and reading skills. Elucidating the constellation of malleable skills that interact with instruction to support proficient reading has led to classroom reading instructional practices that can make a true difference in students' literacy outcomes (Connor et al., 2013). Since 2001, we have been conducting research that exemplifies the premise of this book: how using research to inform practice and practice to inform research can lead to better classroom practice and stronger outcomes for students. The purpose of this chapter, then, is to provide a review of the research on ISI and the dynamic forecasting intervention (DFI) models used to compute the recommended amounts and types of literacy instruction, which can inform our understanding of literacy development in the early grades.

CHILD CHARACTERISTIC-BY-INSTRUCTION INTERACTIONS

Many children do not achieve proficient literacy skills because they do not receive the amount and types of reading instruction they require. One important reason for this is that there are child characteristic-by-instruction (CXI) interactions (also called *aptitude-by-treatment interactions*)—that is, the effect of a particular type of literacy instruction depends on children's developing language, decoding, and comprehension skills. First graders in whole language classrooms, for example, were observed (Connor, Morrison, & Katch, 2004) to receive widely varying amounts of code-focused instruction, including none at all. Children in classrooms in which teachers taught substantial amounts of code-focused instruction made no greater gains than did children whose teachers used primarily sustained, independent silent reading; student choice; and other whole language activities. Why not? It turns out that the weaker the students' decoding skills were in the fall of the school year, the greater were their gains as the amount of code-focused instruction increased; however, for those students who were already decoding well, greater time in decoding instruction was associated with weaker reading skill gains. There was a crossover CXI interaction rather than a main effect.

There might be many reasons for these kinds of CXI interaction effects on reading. To test whether these CXI interactions were causally implicated in the varying effectiveness of reading instruction, we created ISI as an instructional intervention (Connor, Morrison, Fishman, Schatschneider, & Underwood, 2007). ISI was designed to support teachers' use of assessment to guide instruction, which is difficult for many teachers (Roehrig, Duggar, Moats, Glover, & Mincey, 2008). These kinds of instructional regimes are generally more effective than instruction that does not accommodate the different skills and aptitudes children bring to the classroom (Raudenbush, 2005). Thus ISI encourages effective standards of practice that are supported by rigorous research, rather than the more typical, idiosyncratic practice observed in many schools in the United States. To test the efficacy of ISI and to understand the causal implications of CXI interactions, my colleagues and I conducted eight randomized controlled trials (RCTs) from 2005 to 2011 in two districts in Florida with children from kindergarten through third grade. We used an alternative treatment design (vocabulary in District 1 and math in District 2) and randomly assigned teachers within schools. Within districts, all teachers used the same core reading curriculum. About 50% of students qualified for the U.S. Free and Reduced Lunch program, a widely used indicator of family poverty.

To support effective standards of practice, ISI has two key components: 1) the Assessment to Instruction (A2i) technology platform and 2) teacher professional development. The focus of this chapter is on the A2i technology platform and what DFI algorithms (Connor et al., 2011) can tell us about the complex interactions among students' developing language, decoding, and comprehension skills and the literacy instruction they receive. Briefly, ISI teachers participated in two half-day workshops, monthly communities of practice, and biweekly classroom-based support during the literacy block. Research assistants with classroom experience provided this professional development.

THE INDIVIDUALIZING-STUDENT-INSTRUCTION/ ASSESSMENT-TO-INSTRUCTION FRAMEWORK

Our research on CXI interactions and the ISI/A2i framework rests on the Simple View of Reading, which holds that proficient literacy relies on fluent decoding and strong language skills (Hoover & Gough, 1990). Children's aptitudes differ in these skills, which, although related, are somewhat orthogonal—that is, some children can have strong language skills but struggle with decoding, whereas others may learn to decode but have limited language, which impedes comprehension. We also have found that some children have specific difficulty applying their adequate language skills to the task of comprehending text. Hence explicit meaning-focused and code-focused instruction are important components of effective literacy instruction and are the two main types of instruction in ISI.

Another critical dimension of instruction addresses *who* is focusing students' attention on the learning activity: teachers, students, and peers. There is a belief among many educators that, given rich and informative experiences, children can construct their own knowledge and that they learn better when forced to figure things out on their own (Fosnot, 2005). In these kinds of learning activities, students and their peers are focusing attention on the learning activity at hand, and hence ISI considers these kinds of learning activities to be *student/peer-managed (SPM) activities.* In contrast, when the teacher is directly interacting with the students, the teachers and students together are responsible for focusing attention on the learning activity. These kinds of activities are considered *teacher/student-managed (TSM) activities,* and research shows that many children require this kind of interactive but explicit and systematic instruction to learn key reading skills (e.g., Denton et al., 2010).

Another aspect of instruction considered in the ISI/A2i framework is the context of the instruction: whole class, small group, or individual. In general, all contexts of instruction contribute to learning, but to truly accommodate each student's unique constellation of skills, a minimum amount of TSM small-group instruction focused on learning needs is recommended.

These dimensions of instruction operate simultaneously to define the range of evidence-based literacy learning activities (see Table 11.1) and have been validated through careful classroom observation using videotaped observations of the literacy block and coding of the types of literacy instruction each individual student received (Connor, Morrison, et al., 2009). These data, in combination with assessments of each student's fall and spring vocabulary, decoding, and comprehension skills, allowed us to document CXI interactions and to conceptualize the classroom learning environment as a complex system (Yoshikawa & Hsueh, 2001) with interacting and reciprocal effects influenced by the teacher, the learning opportunity, and the students themselves. This, in turn, informed the development of DFI models (Connor et al., 2011) in which our computer algorithms allowed us to quantify this complexity.

THE ASSESSMENT-TO-INSTRUCTION DYNAMIC FORECASTING INTERVENTION COMPUTER ALGORITHMS

The inspiration for the DFI computer algorithms was the game SimCity (http://www.simcity.com), in which the player seeks to build a thriving metropolis through his or her control of taxes, buildings, and investments in infrastructure—all driven by computer algorithms. My family and I were living in Los Angeles when California passed a law mandating the use of whole language literacy instruction. My reaction was that it would have been nice

Table 11.1. Examples of instructional activities defined by the ISI dimensions of instruction

	Teacher/student managed	Student/peer managed
Code-focused instruction	The teacher is with a small group of students discussing how to decode multisyllabic words with prefixes and suffixes (i.e., building morphological awareness).	Students are working in pairs to practice sight word fluency of nondecodable words in short sentences (i.e., building word and sentence fluency).
Meaning-focused instruction	The teacher and students are discussing moral dilemmas found in the book *The Single Shard.* The teacher asks the students, "How can you tell when what you are doing is right or wrong, and how does this apply to Tree-ear's decision to tell the merchant about the spilling rice?"	Students are reading a book of their choice silently to themselves in the library corner (i.e., individual SPM meaning-focused instruction).

Key: ISI, Individualizing Student Instruction.

for lawmakers to see whether whole language instruction was effective using simulated children à la SimCity rather than *my* children.

The DFI algorithms essentially reverse engineer the hierarchical linear models (HLM) used to predict students' reading outcomes in correlational studies (e.g., Connor et al., 2004). The HLM equations take into account initial (i.e., fall or beginning of the school year) reading and vocabulary skills and the amounts and types of literacy instruction—TSM and SPM code- and meaning-focused instruction—as well as CXI interactions for vocabulary, decoding, and comprehension. For example, for kindergarteners, we set a target outcome (the Yij in the HLM equation) at 0.9 grade equivalents (GE), or a school year's gain from their fall scores (fall GE + 0.9 GE = target outcome). Then, using the students' assessed vocabulary, decoding, and comprehension scores, we solve for TSM-code focused, TSM-meaning focused, SPM-code focused, and SPM-meaning focused instruction.

The patented DFI models are analogous to the dynamic forecasting models used by meteorologists to predict the routes of hurricanes (Rhome, 2007). The idea is that every child has a range of potential trajectories of achievement that are influenced by genetics, neurological development, homelife, parenting, and classroom learning experiences, among other sources of influence. In schools, the purpose of instruction is to ensure that each student attains the highest level of achievement he or she possibly can while understanding that there will always be individual differences. By examining these DFI algorithms, we can begin to better understand the complex associations among students' language and literacy skills, the instruction they receive, and their development of proficient reading skills, as noted in the next section.

THE ASSESSMENT TO INSTRUCTION TECHNOLOGY PLATFORM

The DFI algorithms are a key part of the A2i technology platform designed to support teachers' efforts to use assessment effectively and to meet the instructional recommendations of the algorithms for each student (see Figure 11.1). We start with CXI interactions: The effect of particular types of literacy instruction depends on the vocabulary, decoding, and comprehension skills students bring to the classroom (Box 1 in Figure 11.1). The A2i platform uses students' scores to compute recommended amounts of each of the four types of instruction, and these are displayed in the classroom view (Boxes 2–3 in Figure 11.1). There are two built-in computer adapted assessments: Word Match Game, which assesses word knowledge, and Letters2Meaning, which assesses both decoding and comprehension; however, any valid and reliable assessments of vocabulary, decoding, and comprehension can be used. The RCTs used the Woodcock-Johnson III Tests of Achievement (Woodcock, McGrew, & Mather, 2001).

There are also grouping algorithms that recommend homogeneous reading skill groupings of students in the classroom view provided in the software program, which teachers can override. Teachers select how many small groups

(1)
Child-by-instruction interactions

Students bring unique constellations of strengths and weaknesses to the classroom that affect the impact of reading instruction on their outcomes in the following areas:

- Phonological processing, decoding, and fluency
- Oral language and vocabulary
- Reading comprehension

(2)
Using assessment to guide instruction

- Letter–word reading
- Vocabulary
- Comprehension

Conversion tables so that schools use their valid and reliable assessments and the A2i assessments:

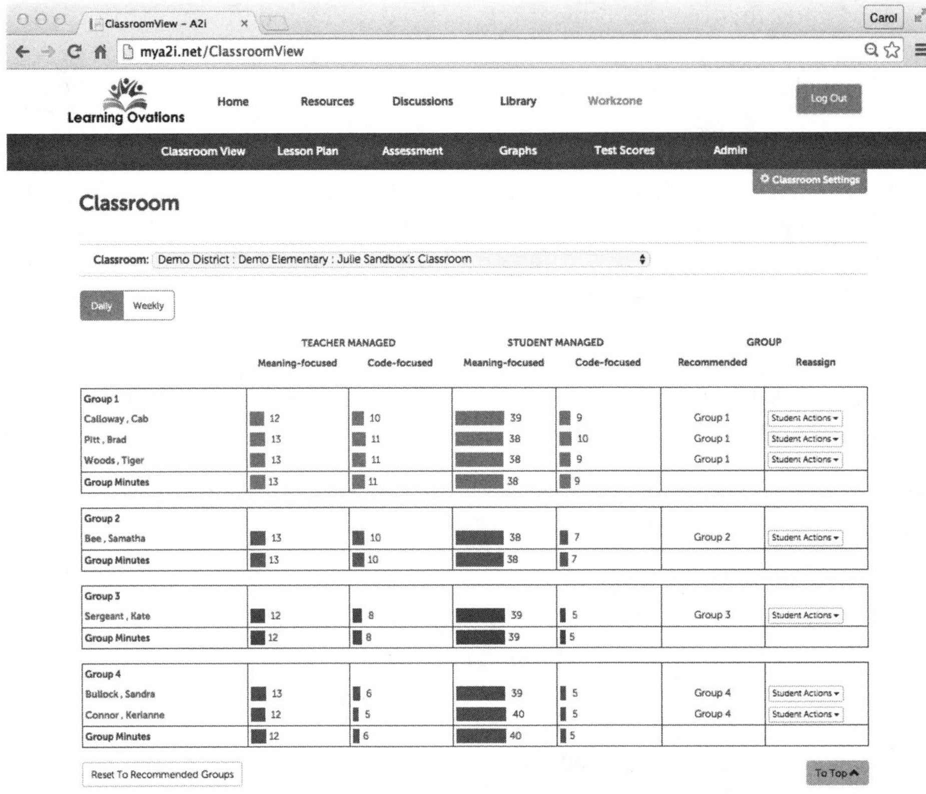

(3)
Assessment-to-instruction algorithms

- Set target outcome
- Compute recommended amounts of Instruction
- Teacher–student-managed code focused
- Teacher–student-managed meaning focused
- Student–peer-managed code focused
- Student–peer-managed meaning focused

Figure 11.1. Assessment to Instruction technology platform. (*Key:* CCSS, Common Core State Standards.)

(4)
Planning

- Recommended flexible learning groups that educators can change
- Literacy Minutes Manager to support organization of the Literacy Block
- A2i Lesson Plan focusing on the minutes and the match:
  - Recommended minutes for each type of instruction
  - Appropriate skill-matched activities

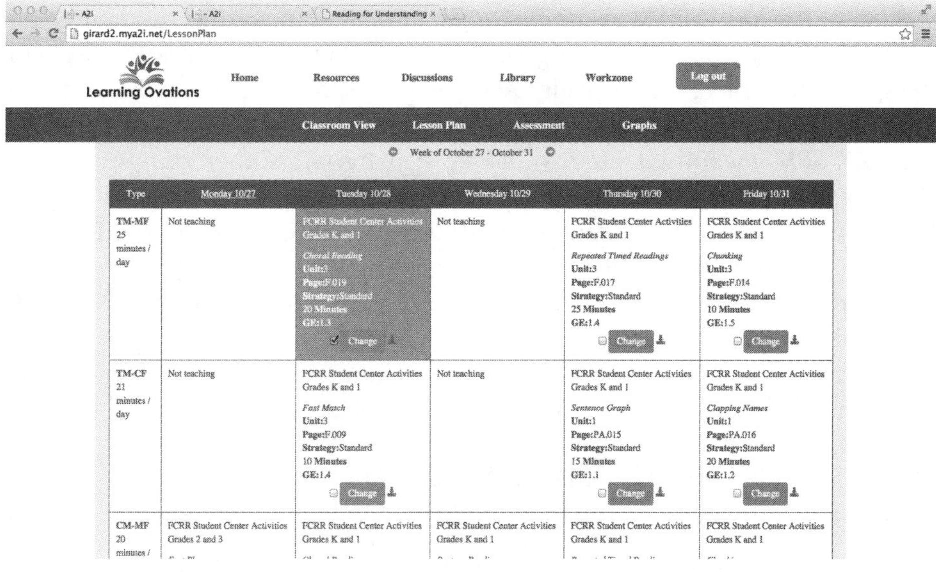

(5)
Implementation in the classroom

Professional development

- Face to face
- Online
- Train the trainer

Monitoring A2i use

- User logs and patterns of use

Evaluating teacher and/or special educator implementation

- Activities report of instruction implemented
- Alignment with CCSS

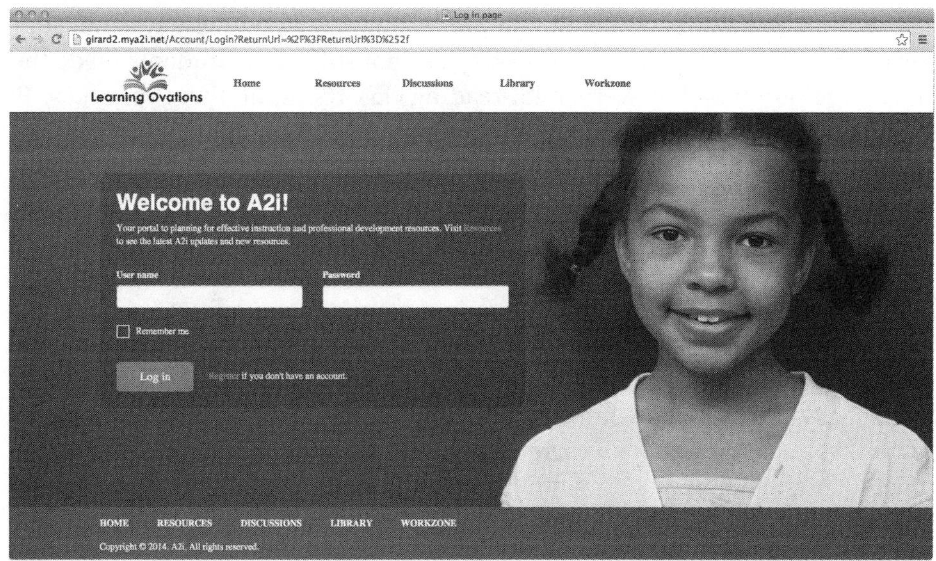

they want to use. A child information page is also accessible to the teacher from the classroom view within this software by clicking the student's name. This page shows the student's test scores and progress monitoring charts along with other information the teacher might want to access for the student.

A2i also has classroom organization features, including the ability for teachers to select the number of groups and the days of the week that each of the groups will meet. There is also a lesson plan (Box 4) in which the teacher's evidence-based resources are indexed by type of instruction (e.g., TSM code-focused, SPM meaning-focused) and leveled by GE. Other computer algorithms select activities for each group that are appropriate with regard to type, length (in minutes), and alignment with the groups' GE skill levels. Teachers can change activities within each type.

Implementation of ISI in the classroom is supported through online professional development resources (Box 5 in Figure 11.1). Resources include units on classroom organization, using assessment to guide instruction, and using research to inform instruction. Videos of master teachers are available as well.

RESULTS OF THE RANDOMIZED CONTROLLED TRIALS AND IDENTIFYING ACTIVE INGREDIENTS

Our research group has conducted eight RCTs since 2005—one in kindergarten, three in first grade, two in second grade, and two in third grade—and found significant effects of treatment in all but one second-grade study. From 2006 to 2011, we conducted a longitudinal efficacy trial (Connor et al., 2013). In this study, we recruited teachers and their students in first grade and randomly assigned them to an ISI intervention in reading (ISI-reading) or a comparable intervention in math (ISI-math). We then followed students into second grade and randomly assigned their teachers to ISI-reading or ISI-math. We did the same thing in third grade and found that the effects of ISI-reading accumulated from first through third grade. We had conjectured that there might be an inoculation effect of first grade, but that hypothesis was not supported. Rather, first grade was necessary but not sufficient. Students made the greatest gains when they were in ISI-reading classrooms all three years (d =.78; see Figure 11.2).

When we compared the observed amount of instruction with the recommended amounts, students whose *distance from recommendations* (*DFR;* equivalent to the recommended amount minus the observed amount) was smaller made significantly greater gains than did students whose DFR was greater. These DFR effects are published for first and third grade students (e.g., Connor, Piasta, et al., 2009); however, these are essentially post hoc correlational studies. Stronger evidence is found in the two second-grade studies; in the first second-grade study, the DFI algorithms were wrong and there was no treatment effect, but in the second study, with corrected DFI algorithms, there was a significant effect of instruction (d = .44).

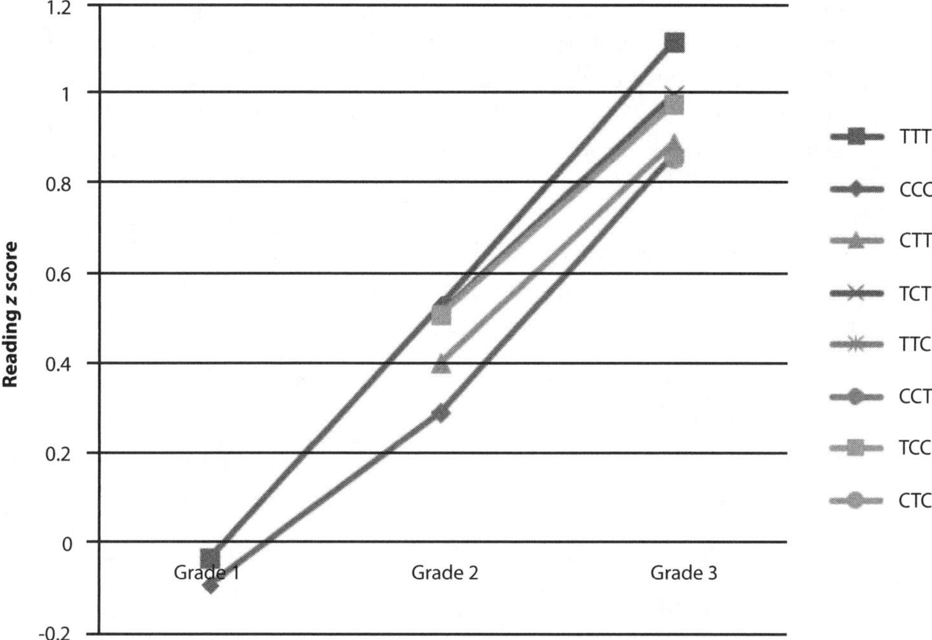

Figure 11.2. End-of-grade results from the longitudinal efficacy trial. For reading *z* scores, 0 = end of second grade mean, T = assigned to ISI, C = assigned to math control group. Hence TTT students received ISI all three years, CCC students received the math intervention all three years, and CTT students were in the math control group in first grade and in ISI in second and third grade. (*Key:* ISI, Individualizing Student Instruction.)

WHAT MIGHT THE DYNAMIC FORECASTING INTERVENTION MODELS TELL US ABOUT INTERACTIONS AMONG STUDENT SKILLS AND OPTIMAL INSTRUCTION?

Connectionist models have helped us understand how, for example, children learn to read words when there is a mismatch between their home dialect and the dialect they are expected to use at school (see Terry, Chapter 12). The DFI models serve the same purpose. In this section, I present the simple function between a key literacy skill (i.e., vocabulary, decoding, or comprehension) and the recommended amounts of each type of instruction. All of the DFI models depend on students' target outcomes, which vary depending on initial skill levels, the principal and secondary predictors for the particular type of instruction, and the month of the school year. In addition, recommendations are updated each time the students are reassessed. In order to graphically represent the function, all initial skills that are not manipulated are held constant at their mean, the target outcome is set at the end of the grade level, and the month, which is the second month of the school year, is set at 1. By fixing all but two of the variables, the results can be graphed two-dimensionally.

Explicit, systematic, code-focused instruction is particularly important for children with dyslexia (see Cutting, Bailey, Barquero, & Aboud, Chapter 7; Del

Tufo & Pugh, Chapter 8). Hence, for this chapter, I focus principally on the two types of recommended code-focused instruction: TSM, which is teacher/student-managed, systematic, and explicit; and SPM, which allows students to practice newly acquired skills and improve fluency and automaticity. The DFI algorithm functions for TSM and SPM code-focused instruction are presented in Figure 11.3. The meaning-focused functions are provided in Figure 11.4. Note that the functions vary from grade to grade. That makes sense for two reasons. First, at each grade, students are developmentally different—growing and learning as they progress through the grades. Second, the expectations for proficient reading

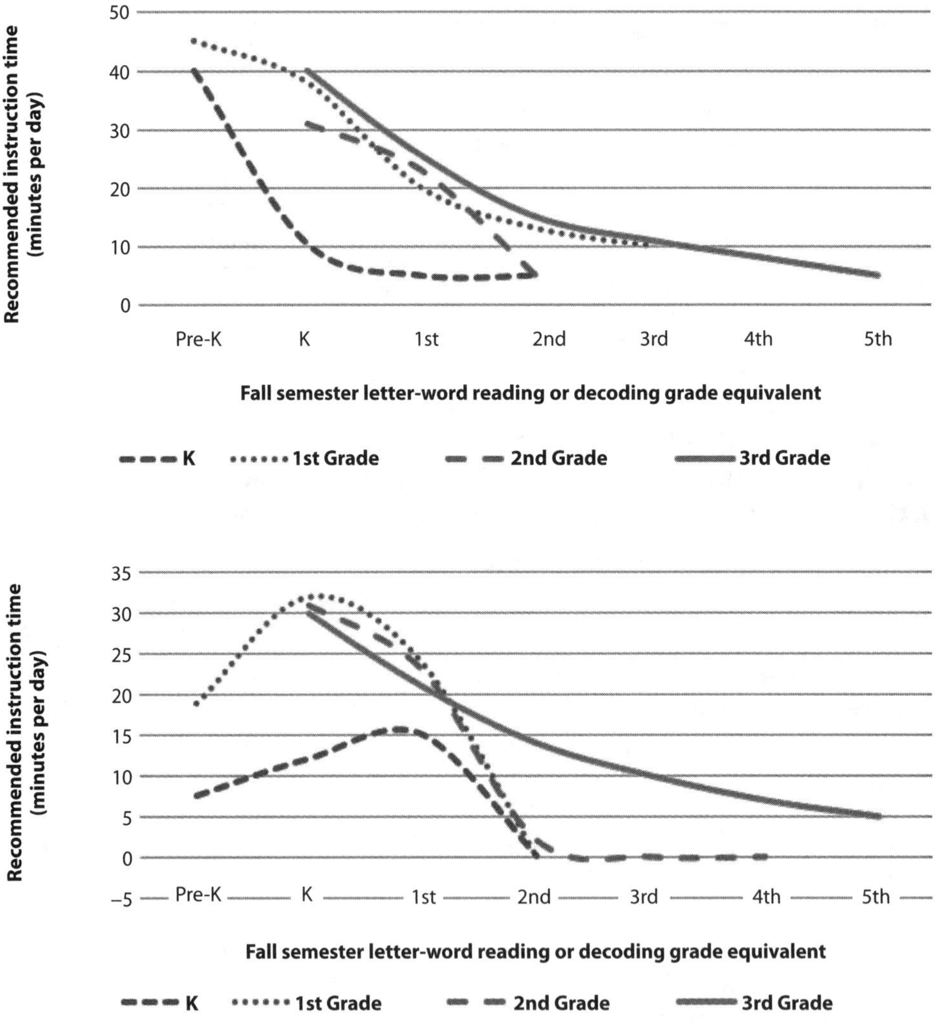

Figure 11.3. Recommended amounts of teacher/student managed code-focused instruction (top) and student/peer managed code-focused instruction (bottom) as functions of letter–word reading, fall grade equivalent in month 1 of the school year. All other variables are held constant.

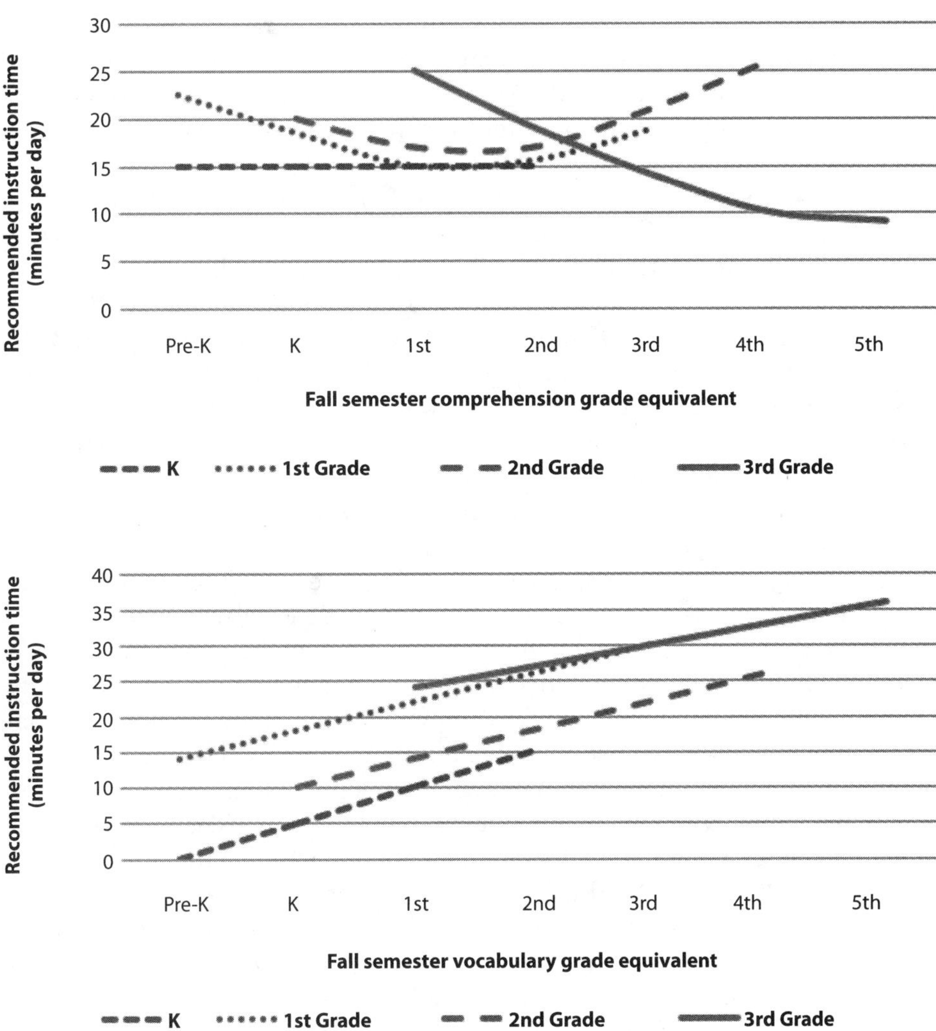

Figure 11.4. Recommended amounts of teacher/student managed meaning-focused instruction (top) and student/peer managed meaning-focused instruction (bottom) as functions of comprehension and vocabulary, respectively, fall grade equivalent in month 1 of the school year. All other variables are held constant.

vary from grade to grade, with decreasing focus on decoding and increasing focus on proficient reading for understanding by third grade, when most of the recommended amount of minutes per day are for meaning-focused instruction.

CODE-FOCUSED INSTRUCTION

TSM code-focused instruction. The key skills driving the code-focused DFI algorithms are letter–word reading and decoding skills, as might be expected. Although the shape of the curve for the TSM code-focused recommended amounts is somewhat similar across grades, a kindergartner reading at a kindergarten GE has substantially lower recommended amounts of TSM code-focused instruction than those of a first or third grader reading at a kindergarten level: 10 minutes per day compared with the first grader's 35 minutes per day. For the third grader reading at a kindergarten level, 40 minutes per day of TSM code-focused instruction is recommended to achieve a GE of 3.9 by the end of third grade.

If the kindergartner, the first grader, and the third grader are reading at grade-level expectations at the beginning of their respective grades, the recommended amount of TSM code-focused instruction, per day, for the kindergartner is still less than that of the first grader but equal to that of the third grader: about 10 minutes for kindergartners and third graders compared with 20 minutes for first graders. These may seem like small differences, but one should keep in mind that these are in minutes per day. If one were to compare minutes per week or per month, these differences would be more dramatic. The first graders' recommended TSM code-focused instruction amounts would be greater than the kindergartners' and third graders' by 50 minutes per week or about 200 minutes per month. The second-grade function shape differs substantially from the other three grades with recommended amounts steady but decreasing sharply as students begin to exceed grade-level expectations.

SPM code-focused instruction. When we consider the SPM code-focused instruction recommendation functions across grades, we see very similarly shaped functions for kindergarten through second grade with substantial amounts of code-focused practice (independently or with peers) recommended for students who are achieving at grade equivalents of kindergarten and first grade. Recommended amounts drop substantially once students reach second-grade GE levels, almost regardless of the student's actual grade. Except for in kindergarten, between 20 and 25 minutes per day of SPM code-focused instruction are recommended for students reading at a first-grade level. This includes second and third graders who are displaying difficulties achieving fluent decoding skills, including many children with dyslexia.

In third grade, the recommended amounts of SPM code-focused instruction are similar to those recommended for those first and second graders who start third grade reading at a kindergarten or first-grade level (i.e., many students with dyslexia). However, recommended amounts of code-focused instruction remain higher than those recommended for first and second graders reading at or above grade level—that is, for students in those actual grades who are doing well. According to our classroom observations, virtually all code-focused instruction in third grade focuses on the decoding of multisyllabic words, prefixes, suffixes, and morphological awareness. Hence more practice with abstract skills appears to be required for students to attain proficient literacy skills.

MEANING-FOCUSED INSTRUCTION

Figure 11.4 shows that substantial amounts of both TSM and SPM meaning-focused instruction are recommended from kindergarten through third grade, including for students who are reading below grade-level expectations. Thus building oral language skills and teaching students how to apply their oral language skills to understanding the text they have decoded are associated with stronger reading gains overall for all students from kindergarten through third grade (and likely beyond), regardless of their decoding skills. This includes students with dyslexia. Comprehension and vocabulary scores are generally the key predictors of recommended amounts of meaning-focused instruction.

CONCLUSION

The development and evaluation of ISI and A2i show how research can inform practice, which, in turn, can inform new research. The DFI models provide a direct translation of the basic science on CXI interactions into practice. The models reveal the complex and dynamic interactions among students' developing decoding, vocabulary, and comprehension skills and the amounts and types of reading instruction required to optimize their learning. ISI and A2i help teachers use assessment to better accommodate the various constellations of language and literacy skills that students bring to the classroom by individualizing or personalizing their instruction. Feedback from teachers and observation of their classroom practices revealed new questions and initiated research about sources of influence that might impact the classroom learning environment. For example, the expectations for self-regulated learning, which were inherent in ISI classroom practices, led to stronger development of students' self-regulation (Connor et al., 2010).

The DFI models show that the relationships among students' reading, language, and optimal amounts of instruction are nonlinear. As seen in Figure 11.4, for example, as students' decoding skills fall farther below grade level, exponentially more time is recommended for TSM code-focused instruction. The association is not a straight line, nor is it categorical (on or off). This has implications for teacher practice and multitiered, or RTI, systems of instruction. According to the DFI models, there is not a clear cutoff score indicating when students require more intensive interventions, although such cutoff scores are assumed in multitiered, or response-to-instruction, interventions (Al Otaiba et al., 2011). For example, if the cutoff score for a second grader requiring more intensive Tier 2 intervention is reading at a GE of 1.0, then what happens to a student reading at a GE of 1.1? According to dynamic systems intervention models, both students need about the same amount of small-group instruction each day, but the student reading at a GE of 1.1 will not receive this instruction.

The nonlinear and complex DFI models provide an explanation for why teachers find it so difficult to effectively use assessment to guide their instruction (Roehrig et al., 2008). These nonlinear associations are not intuitive. In addition, simple reading scores do not provide enough information. Information about oral language skills and comprehension are also important to consider, according to the DFI models. Many teachers do not have access to reliable progress monitoring measures of word knowledge and comprehension.

In sum, DFI models provide an example of basic science informing practice, which in turn, inspires new research. These models reveal complex associations among the constellations of students' skills and literacy instruction and help to simplify the interpretation of complex associations among students' language and literacy skills and the literacy instruction they receive. This allows teachers greater ability to use assessment to guide effective instruction for all students.

REFERENCES

Al Otaiba, S., Connor, C.M., Folsom, J.S., Greulich, L., Meadows, J., & Li, Z. (2011). Assessment data-informed guidance to individualize kindergarten reading instruction: Findings from a cluster-randomized control field trial. *Elementary School Journal, 111*(4), 535–560. doi:0013-5984/2011/11104-0003

Connor, C.M., Morrison, F.J., & Katch, E.L. (2004). Beyond the reading wars: The effect of classroom instruction by child interactions on early reading. *Scientific Studies of Reading, 8*(4), 305–336.

Connor, C.M., Morrison, F.J., Fishman, B., Crowe, E.C., Al Otaiba, S., & Schatschneider, C. (2013). A longitudinal cluster-randomized controlled study on the accumulating effects of individualized literacy instruction on students' reading from first through third grade. *Psychological Science, 24*(8), 1408–1419. doi:10.1177/0956797612472204

Connor, C.M., Morrison, F.J., Fishman, B., Ponitz, C.C., Glasney, S., Underwood, P., . . . Schatschneider, C. (2009). The ISI classroom observation system: Examining the literacy instruction provided to individual students. *Educational Researcher, 38*(2), 85–99.

Connor, C.M., Morrison, F.J., Fishman, B.J., Schatschneider, C., & Underwood, P. (2007). The early years: Algorithm-guided individualized reading instruction. *Science, 315*(5811), 464–465. doi:10.1126/science.1134513

Connor, C.M., Morrison, F.J., Schatschneider, C., Toste, J., Lundblom, E.G., Crowe, E., & Fishman, B. (2011). Effective classroom instruction: Implications of child characteristic by instruction interactions on first graders' word reading achievement. *Journal for Research on Educational Effectiveness, 4*(3), 173–207.

Connor, C.M., Piasta, S.B., Fishman, B., Glasney, S., Schatschneider, C., Crowe, E., . . . Morrison, F.J. (2009). Individualizing student instruction precisely: Effects of child by instruction interactions on first graders' literacy development. *Child Development, 80*(1), 77–100.

Connor, C.M., Ponitz, C.E.C., Phillips, B., Travis, Q.M., Day, S.G., & Morrison, F.J. (2010). First graders' literacy and self-regulation gains: The effect of individualizing instruction. *Journal of School Psychology, 48,* 433–455.

Denton, C.A., Kethley, C., Nimon, K., Kurz, T.B., Mathes, P.G., Shih, M., & Swanson, E.A. (2010). Effectiveness of a supplemental early reading intervention scaled up in multiple schools. *Exceptional Children, 76*(4), 394–416.

Fosnot, C.T. (Ed.). (2005). *Constructivism: Theory, perspectives, and practice* (2nd ed.). New York, NY: Teachers College Press.

Hoover, W.A., & Gough, P.B. (1990). The simple view of reading. *Reading and Writing, 2*(2), 127–160.

Raudenbush, S.W. (2005). How do we study what happens next? *Annals of the American Academy of Political and Social Science, 602*(1), 131–144.

Rhome, J.R. (2007). Technical summary of the National Hurricane Center track and intensity models. Retrieved from http://www.nhc.noaa.gov/modelsummary.shtml

Roehrig, A.D., Duggar, S.W., Moats, L.C., Glover, M., & Mincey, B. (2008). When teachers work to use progress monitoring data to inform literacy instruction: Identifying potential supports and challenges. *Remedial and Special Education, 29,* 364–382.

Woodcock, R.W., McGrew, K.S., & Mather, N. (2001). *Woodcock-Johnson-III tests of achievement.* Itasca, IL: Riverside.

Yoshikawa, H., & Hsueh, J. (2001). Child development and public policy: Toward a dynamic systems perspective. *Child Development, 72*(6), 1887–1903.

12

Addressing Dialect Variation in Early Reading Instruction for African American Children

Nicole Patton Terry[1]

In the United States, the persistent poor reading achievement of African American children is a longstanding, significant concern that influences the nation's health, education, and economic and social well-being. African American children are at greater risk for developing serious reading difficulties than their White or Asian American peers, and this has been a primary factor in the achievement gap reported for these children since the late 1960s. For example, the 2013 National Assessment of Educational Progress, an annual achievement assessment given randomly to school-age children throughout the United States, revealed that 83% of African American fourth graders were reading at or below "basic" levels when compared with 55% of White students (National Center for Education Statistics [NCES], 2013). Conversely, 15% of African American students and 34% of White students were "proficient" readers. Despite major advances in understanding reading development and instruction, achievement gaps like these have remained relatively stable over the years.

Meanwhile, given the level of reading difficulty observed in this student population, it is surprising that relatively few African American students are receiving special education services for reading or learning disabilities; however, African American children are disproportionately represented in special education for other reasons. In fact, more African American children tend to be served in special education than any other racial or ethnic group, and more African American children are served than would be expected based on the

1. Preparation of this article was supported by the *Eunice Kennedy Shriver* National Institute of Child Health and Human Development (grant R24D075454).

proportion of their representation within the general school-age population (Zhang, Katsiyannia, Ju, & Roberts, 2014); this population's overrepresentation tends to occur within the emotional–behavior disorders and mild intellectual disability categories (U.S. Department of Education, Office of Special Education and Rehabilitative Services, Office of Special Education Programs, 2012). Based on their overrepresentation in these categories, it is notable that African American children tend to be underrepresented in the learning disabilities category.

Given these trends, a somewhat obvious question begins to emerge: Why are so many African American children not receiving the support they need to develop proficient reading skills? And perhaps more importantly, what can we do to fix this? Multiple factors have been implicated in the quest to understand and alleviate reading difficulties among African American children; however, not all of these factors are equally amenable to treatment. Perhaps the focus should shift toward factors that are both malleable and educationally impactful. Thus the purpose of this chapter is to review some of these probable factors, focusing on one variable that could be a target of instruction: dialect variation. The literature on child African American English (AAE) use and its relation to reading will be reviewed briefly, followed by a discussion of implications for reading instruction, intervention, and future research.

WHY DO SO MANY AFRICAN AMERICAN CHILDREN HAVE DIFFICULTY LEARNING HOW TO READ?

The reading achievement gap is typically explained by two broad sociocultural factors: the schooling environment, including instructional quality, teacher quality, and the proportion of poor and minority students in a school and family and home environment, including poverty, parenting practices, and early care and education experiences (see Washington, Terry, & Seidenberg, 2013, for a more thorough review of the literature). A growing body of research has shown that education achievement gaps are evident at and even before school entry and that the gap widens the longer children are in school. For example, Fryer and Levitt (2004) found that achievement differences between White and African American students in kindergarten and first grade increased about one tenth of a standard deviation for every year children were in school. Burchinal and colleagues (2011) found a noticeable achievement gap between low-income White and African American children by age 3 that persisted throughout elementary school. Within this longitudinal sample, differences in family, child care, and schooling explained much of the achievement gap, with instructional quality being particularly important to African American children's academic performance.

Although it is clear that factors present in the schooling context influence achievement, the presence of an achievement gap before formal schooling suggests not only that out-of-school influences matter but also that schools alone may not be able to close the achievement gap. One of the most widely considered contributing factors that is separate from but related to schooling is poverty. African American children are more likely to come from and live with families with incomes well below the poverty threshold and, relatedly, with very low parent education levels (Federal Interagency Forum on Child and Family Statistics, 2012). Poverty begets several conditions that collectively impact educational achievement negatively, including limited economic and social resources, poor physical and mental health, unstable housing, and parenting and school engagement behaviors that are not particularly conducive to school success. For instance, Gutman, Sameroff, and Cole (2003) found that poor academic trajectories, such as lower grades and absenteeism, were more likely to occur among students in first through twelfth grades when four or more risk factors (e.g., low income, low parent education) were present in their lives at 4 years old.

Though potentially detrimental to academic achievement, the "usual suspects" related to schooling, home, and family factors are not sufficient in explaining why so many African American children have difficulty learning how to read. For instance, researchers have observed both African American children from low-income homes who perform well academically and African American children from middle-income homes who perform less well, especially when compared with their White, middle-income peers (e.g., Gosa & Alexander, 2007). Moreover, the extensive field of reading research has focused little on this population, leaving much to be discovered about the neurobiological, genetic, cognitive, and linguistic factors that African American children bring to the reading task. Thus other less commonly considered factors may prove particularly helpful in both understanding reading difficulty and promoting reading success. Two possible factors include special education eligibility and language variation.

Eligibility for Special Education Services in Schools

With regard to special education, it is curious that the number of African American students who experience reading failure is not commensurate with the number of African American children who receive support for reading disabilities. One source of this mismatch may lie in the Individuals with Disabilities Education Improvement Act (IDEA) of 2004 (PL 108-446). Enacted in 1975 and continuously revised thereafter, IDEA was created to ensure that all children with disabilities have the opportunity to receive a free and appropriate public education in the least restrictive environment, just like children without disabilities in U.S. schools. Criteria are established within IDEA for students to qualify to receive special education services in school. Specifically, support for learning disabilities (including reading disabilities) services are not permitted for students whose learning difficulties are thought to be due to environmental factors, cultural differences, economic disadvantage, or inadequate instruction. These criteria were intended to improve specificity in the diagnosis and treatment of specific learning disabilities; however, they also create a barrier to advancing both the understanding and the remediation of reading disabilities among African American children because they specifically exclude children who are disproportionately poor, who experience significant environmental risk factors, and who often present with cultural differences. None of these conditions preclude a learning or reading disability, yet as noted previously, African American children are more likely to grow up in poverty and to attend lower quality schools characterized by less well prepared teachers, poorer instructional quality, and greater impediments to academic achievement. Thus they may be less likely to be deemed eligible for special education services, or they may be identified for treatment of other disorders that are also associated with academic difficulties, such as emotional or behavior disorders or mild intellectual disabilities rather than a learning or reading disability. In either case, misidentification results in African American children not receiving appropriate support to treat reading difficulty. Many schools are implementing multitiered systems of support or response to intervention (RTI; Al Otaiba et al., 2014), which may help young African American students receive more appropriate interventions.

Language Variation

African American children also come to school with cultural differences that are related to academic achievement. For example, many African American children begin school speaking AAE fluently. AAE is a nonmainstream, cultural dialect of American English whose form, content, and use differ from mainstream American English (MAE) and from standard written English orthography (see Charity, 2008; Green, 2011; Washington & Craig, 2002, for comprehensive lists of AAE features). It is important to state that AAE, like other nonmainstream forms of American English, is not poor, incorrect, or bad English; it's just different. It is also just as systematic and rule governed as MAE. In fact, AAE and MAE share many overlapping features. Nevertheless, AAE's unique features and representation in popular culture tend to be very stigmatizing, and AAE is generally perceived as a low-prestige dialect of American English, especially when used in formal contexts like schools.

AFRICAN AMERICAN ENGLISH USE AND READING ACHIEVEMENT

It is well established that variation in children's oral language abilities is related to reading ability (National Reading Panel, 2000; Scarborough, 2001). Therefore, it is worth questioning whether or not the unique oral language patterns that many African American children bring to the task of learning how to read are not only related to their reading difficulty but also important to improved reading ability. With regard to reading difficulty among African American children, AAE is a particularly interesting factor to consider because it is common, it is uniquely related to reading ability, and it is malleable (see Terry, Brown, & Stuckey, 2014, for a thorough review of the literature).

African American English Production and Use

AAE is commonly used among African American adults and children. It can be heard among most African Americans across regional areas of the United States and across socioeconomic, age, and gender groups within the African American population (Wolfram & Schilling-Estes, 2006). Recent research has revealed much about the characteristics of child AAE use. For instance, African American children as young as 2 years old produce a wide variety of AAE features; however, children can vary greatly in the frequency with which they use these features. In general, higher frequency rates have been reported among children in the Southern United States, African American boys, and children from low-income households (Charity, 2007; Craig & Washington, 2002; Washington & Craig, 1998). Frequency rates can also differ by discourse context, with higher dialect feature production rates being observed, for example, in oral tasks than in written tasks (Craig, Zhang, Hensel, & Quinn, 2009) and a greater variety of AAE types being produced on a picture-description task as compared with a free-play task (Washington, Craig, & Kushmaul, 1998). Moreover, children generally shift from using more AAE to less AAE (and more MAE) in school contexts between preschool and first grade (Craig & Washington, 2004; Terry, Connor, Petscher, & Conlin, 2011). Finally, young AAE speakers appear to have underlying knowledge of both AAE and MAE forms despite high AAE frequency rates observed in overt speech (Mansour & Terry, 2014; Terry, 2014)—that is, while learning how to read, many young African American children have lexical knowledge of speech patterns that match what is found in printed text (e.g., MAE) and that do not match printed text (e.g., AAE). It is not clear if having knowledge of both forms creates confusion.

The Relationship Between African American English and Reading Ability

Spoken AAE use appears to be significantly related to reading ability but is also separable from other factors known to be associated with reading ability and disability, including family characteristics, school and home environment, and neurobiological, genetic, cognitive, and linguistic traits. A growing body of evidence has revealed significant associations among children's AAE production and various language, reading, and reading-related skills, including vocabulary, syntax, morphological awareness, phonological awareness, oral narration, decoding, word reading, spelling, reading comprehension, and text composition (e.g., Charity, Scarborough, & Griffin, 2004; Craig, Connor, & Washington, 2004; Craig et al., 2009; Kohleret al., 2007; Terry & Connor, 2010; Terry, Connor, Thomas-Tate, & Love, 2010).

It is important to note that the nature of these relationships has varied across studies. In many instances, negative linear associations have been found in which children who produce more AAE in speech perform more poorly on various language and reading measures (e.g., Craig et al., 2004); researchers have also found positive relationships between frequent AAE use and specific skills, such as complex syntax (e.g., Craig & Washington, 1994). Researchers have also found indirect relations in which children's AAE use explained some of the variance in reading ability, although these were not always significant when other factors, such as socioeconomic status or oral vocabulary, were considered (e.g., Terry & Connor, 2012). Finally, researchers have also observed *u*-shaped relationships (Connor & Craig, 2006; Terry et al., 2010; Terry, Connor, Petscher, & Conlin, C., 2012). In these instances, children who spoke AAE very little (e.g., 10% of the time) or very frequently (e.g., 75% of the time) performed better on language and reading measures than did children who spoke AAE moderately (e.g., 50% of the time).

The Malleability of African American English

Children's AAE use appears to be malleable. Change in dialect use is referred to as *style shifting* or *code switching*—a sociolinguistic phenomenon in which speakers vary their speech style by increasing, decreasing, or substituting features among dialects (Wolfram & Schilling-Estes, 2006). It is important to note that the ability to shift successfully depends at least partially on metalinguistic ability, as speakers would have to both recognize the contexts for using a specific dialect and adjust their dialect production accordingly. Researchers have found that many African American children appear to shift from more to less AAE production in school over time (e.g., between first and second grades; Terry et al., 2012) and across contexts (e.g., between oral and written contexts; Craig et al., 2009). In both instances, a decrease in AAE features has been associated with stronger reading performance, and this change was not provoked by explicit instruction to do so. Terry and colleagues (Terry et al., 2012) found not only that change in AAE use was predicted by children's oral language skills but also that children who did not decrease their AAE use by the end of first grade demonstrated less growth in reading skills during first and second grades. Interestingly, much of this change appears to happen during early schooling at the same time children are learning to read. It may be that learning to read is a catalyst for change in dialect use, that change in dialect use begets reading ability, or that both may be occurring reciprocally. In either case, it appears that children who begin formal reading instruction while continuing to use AAE frequently in school contexts may be at risk for reading difficulty.

In sum, the malleability of children's AAE use, combined with its significant relation to reading ability and frequent use among African American children, makes this factor particularly relevant to reading instruction and intervention. Although the reading difficulty that many African American children experience in school is likely due to multiple factors, many of those factors may go beyond those that can be changed by schooling. AAE use, however, may be both responsive to instruction and associated with improved reading achievement.

AFRICAN AMERICAN ENGLISH AND READING INSTRUCTION

Interest in the association between "dialect-informed" instruction and academic achievement is neither novel nor limited to the United States. Indeed, researchers in many countries with salient and distinct dialects have been grappling with the educational implications of language variation on achievement for years, especially for low-performing students from low-income households (e.g., see discussions of Arabic-speaking children in Israel in Saiegh-Haddad, 2003; Zuzovsky, 2010). In the United States, much of this work has focused on African American children who speak AAE and contrastive analysis approaches to increasing students' awareness of differences between AAE and MAE (see Siegel, 1999, for a more extensive review of the literature). Based on sociolinguistic and second-language acquisition theories, contrastive analysis approaches are thought to be effective with second-language learners because they require the learner to notice features of the second language (or language variety), compare those features to features that are a part of their native language, and integrate this newly developed comparative knowledge into their existing language system.

As it relates to dialects like AAE, this kind of awareness may actually be much harder to achieve because AAE and MAE share many overlapping features—that is, children use features of both dialects often, creating an intralanguage context that makes noticing and comparing differences less salient without explicit direction to do so. Most recent applications of dialect awareness that use contrastive analysis approaches have focused on the contexts of language use (e.g., Wheeler & Swords, 2010). Students are taught that language can be used formally and informally, with MAE being more appropriate for most formal contexts (e.g., at school, at work, on assignments) and AAE being more appropriate for most informal contexts (e.g., among friends, at home, in literary prose). Typically, this instruction is focused on morphosyntactic features because these are the features that are most often stigmatized and on writing because nonstandard forms are often present in students' writing samples. Most of this work consequently has been attempted with older students.

To date, very few experimental studies have been conducted to determine not only if dialect-informed instruction changes children's AAE use but also if these changes are associated with improved reading achievement. For example, Wheeler and colleagues have reported successful writing outcomes for students in second through sixth grades who were taught to use MAE forms in sentence composition through contrastive analysis (Wheeler & Swords, 2010). In one exception, Fogel and Ehri (2000) compared outcomes for third and fourth graders ($n = 89$) who participated in one of three 45-minute instructional conditions: exposure to MAE in written stories 1) alone, 2) followed by an explanation of MAE rules for use of specific features, and 3) followed by an explanation of MAE rules for use of specific features and practice applying those rules to transform sentences written in AAE into MAE. When later asked to translate sentences written in AAE into MAE and to respond to an extended story-writing prompt, the researchers found that students in the third condition outperformed students in the other two conditions significantly.

Because previous findings suggested that students who did not reduce their AAE use in school by second grade were most at risk for reading failure, Connor and colleagues (Connor, Thomas-Tate, Johnson, Underwood, & Terry, 2014) compared two approaches to building dialect awareness among second, third, and fourth graders (*n* = 116) who used AAE frequently in speech or writing. Students were randomly assigned to one of three 20-minute instructional conditions for 4 weeks: 1) business-as-usual untreated control, 2) an editing intervention in which students were taught to use specific grammatical forms in writing but in which differences between "home" and "school" English were not explicitly taught, and 3) an editing intervention in which "home" and "school" English were contrasted explicitly. Results indicated that students in the third condition used significantly less AAE in a speech sample on an extended story-writing prompt and on an editing task in which they had to identify grammatical errors and write the appropriate form.

Focusing instead on preventing reading failure, Craig and colleagues (Craig, 2014) have developed a similar program for younger children (i.e., kindergarten and first grade). In their program, children are taught differences between "formal" and "informal" language use explicitly through texts that were developed for the curriculum. In this manner, young students are not expected to write texts; rather, they examine sentences and stories for the use of specific features and consider the contexts in which the features are used. Preliminary pre- and posttest findings (*n* = 34) from 20 minutes of instruction that occurred twice a week for 8 weeks indicate moderate to large effect sizes on curriculum-based measures of recognition, elicited use, and translation between AAE and MAE use in speech as well as increases in standard scores on a standardized measure of letter and word reading.

Taken together, the results of these studies suggest that even relatively brief instruction that goes beyond simply teaching MAE grammar can have a robust effect on AAE speakers' grammatical writing proficiency and spoken dialect use. Much remains to be discovered, however, about the educational usefulness of dialect-informed instruction. It remains unclear, for instance, whether or not such instruction will generalize to improve reading achievement. It is plausible that such effects will be obtained: For example, Craig and colleagues (Craig et al., 2009) found that student's use of AAE forms in print (and not speech) was predictive of reading outcomes. In addition, there is evidence that writing can improve word reading, reading comprehension, and reading fluency (Graham & Herbert, 2011). It is also unclear if such instruction is best implemented with younger, beginning readers or older, struggling readers.

On the one hand, if most children appear to shift from more to less AAE use in the early grades without explicit instruction to do so, then perhaps it is not beneficial to prioritize dialect-informed instruction, especially as teachers struggle to fit everexpanding curriculum content into already full school days. On the other hand, if such instruction can be delivered in relatively brief but integrated and impactful ways, then why not deliver it to students who are already known to have several risk factors that may impede their reading achievement? Finally, the added value of such instruction is still in question. As noted previously, African American children are more likely to attend under-resourced schools in which they are less likely to be receiving effective instruction. It may be that although dialect-informed instruction supports reading achievement, it is not necessary if students are simply taught how to read well using evidence-based practices that are already known to support reading success, including language, reading, and writing instruction.

The answers to these questions are not trivial. Findings of decreased reading growth among children who do not change their AAE use by second grade are alarming, especially when one considers the large number of children in U.S. schools who likely speak AAE. Such findings compel practitioners, researchers, and educators to intervene, both to prevent and to treat reading difficulty. Evidence-based practices, however, can only improve reading outcomes if teachers can implement them with fidelity, and knowledge and expertise on dialects and dialect differences are specialized and not typically or easily acquired by many teachers (Godley, Sweetland, Wheeler, Minnici, & Carpeter, 2006). Historically, discussions of dialect-informed instruction in U.S. schools have not been well received by parents, teachers, policy makers, and other key stakeholders (e.g., the 1996 Oakland ebonics controversy; Adger, Christian, & Taylor, 1999). Although instruction that highlights spoken dialect differences may be beneficial for AAE speakers, it becomes useless if teachers cannot or will not implement it. Meanwhile, if the underlying benefit of dialect-informed instruction is improved language and literacy skill in general, then perhaps effective instruction that focuses on language and literacy proficiency more globally (without attention to dialect differences) may have the same effect and may be more readily implemented in schools. Providing high-quality language and literacy instruction to support reading performance, irrespective of dialect use, is neither a novel idea nor a controversial one.

CONCLUSION

The challenges facing many African American children, as well as researchers and practitioners who seek to improve their reading achievement, are daunting. The fields of both reading research and special education, in particular, have much work to do to better consider African American children in the identification and treatment of reading difficulty and disability. Recent research on spoken dialect variation presents a promising lens through which to understand and treat reading difficulty, but ongoing research, particularly training studies that allow for better causal explication, is needed. The empirical pursuit of reading interventions within this population will be helpful in preventing many African American children from having difficulty learning how to read proficiently, which will support stronger academic success and better life outcomes.

REFERENCES

Adger, C.T., Christian, D., & Taylor, O. (1999). *Making the connection: Language and academic achievement among African American students.* Washington, DC: Center for Applied Linguistics.

Al Otaiba, S., Connor, C.M., Folsom, J.S., Greulich, L., Wanzek, J., Schatschneider, C., & Wagner, R.K. (2014). To wait in Tier 1 or intervene immediately: A randomized experiment examining first grade response to intervention (RTI) in reading. *Exceptional Children, 81*(11), 11–27. doi:http://ecx.sagepub.com/content/81/1/11

Burchinal, M., McCartney, K., Steinberg, L., Crosnoe, R., Friedman, S.L., McLoyd, V., & Pianta, R. (2011). Examining the black-white achievement gap among low-income children using the NICHD study of early child care and youth development. *Child Development,* 82(5), 1401–1420.

Charity, A.H. (2007). Regional differences in low SES African-American children's speech in the school setting. *Language Variation and Change, 19,* 281–293.

Charity, A.H. (2008). African American English: An overview. *Perspectives on Communication Disorders and Sciences in Culturally and Linguistically Diverse Populations, 15*(2), 33–42.

Charity, A., Scarborough, H., & Griffin, D. (2004). Familiarity with school English in African American children and its relation to early reading achievement, *Child Development,* 75, 1340–1356.

Connor, C., & Craig, H. (2006). African American preschoolers' language, emergent literacy skills, and use of AAE: A complex relation. *Journal of Speech, Language, and Hearing Research, 49,* 771–792.

Connor, C.M., Thomas-Tate, S., Johnson, L., Underwood, P., & Terry, N.P. (2014). *An experimental investigation of dialect awareness instruction for African American children in second through fourth grade.* Manuscript under review.

Craig, H., Connor, C., & Washington, J. (2004). Early positive predictors of later reading comprehension for African American students. *Language, Speech, and Hearing Services in Schools, 34,* 31–43.

Craig, H.K. (2014). *Toggle talk: An evidence-based program for teaching young African American English speaking students to switch to Standard American English for academic purposes.* Ann Arbor, MI: The Regents of University of Michigan.

Craig, H.K., & Washington, J.A. (1994). The complex syntax skills of poor, urban, African American preschoolers at school entry. *Language, Speech, and Hearing Services in Schools, 25,*181–190.

Craig, H.K., & Washington, J.A. (2002). Oral language expectations for African American preschoolers and kindergartners. *American Journal of Speech–Language Pathology, 11,* 59–70.

Craig, H.K., & Washington, J.A. (2004). Grade related changes in the production of African American English. *Journal of Speech, Language and Hearing Research, 47,* 450–463.

Craig, H.K., Zhang, L., Hensel, S.L., & Quinn, E.J. (2009). African American English-Speaking students: An examination of the relationship between dialect shifting and reading outcomes. *Journal of Speech, Language and Hearing Research, 52,* 839–855.

Federal Interagency Forum on Child and Family Statistics. (2012). *America's children: Key national indicators of well-being.* Washington, DC: Government Printing Office.

Fogel, H., & Ehri, L.C. (2000). Teaching elementary students who speak Black English to write in Standard English: Effects of dialect transformation practice. *Contemporary Educational Psychology, 25,* 212–235.

Fryer, R.G., & Levitt, S.D. (2004). Understanding the black-white test score gap in the first two years of life. *The Review of Economics and Statistics, 86*(2), 447–464.

Godley, A., Sweetland, J., Wheeler, R., Minnici, A., & Carpenter, B. (2006). Preparing teachers for dialectally diverse classrooms. *Educational Researcher, 35,* 30–37.

Gosa, T.L., & Alexander, K.L. (2007). Family disadvantage and the educational prospects of better off African American youth. *Teachers College Record, 109*(2), 285–321.

Graham, S., & Herbert, M. (2011). Writing to read: A meta-analysis of the impact of writing and writing instruction on reading. *Harvard Educational Review, 81*(4), 710–744.

Green, L.J. (2011). *Language and the African American child.* Cambridge, UK: Cambridge University Press.

Gutman, L.M., Sameroff, A.J., & Cole, R. (2003). Academic growth curve trajectories from 1st grade to 12th grade: Effects of multiple social risk factors and preschool child factors. *Developmental Psychology, 39*(4), 777–790.

Individuals with Disabilities Education Improvement Act of 2004 (IDEA), PL 108-446, 118 Stat. 2647 (2004).

Kohler, C.T., Bahr, R.H., Silliman, E.R., Bryant, J.B., Apel, K., & Wilkinson, L.C. (2007). African American English dialect and performance on nonword spelling and phonemic awareness tasks. *American Journal of Speech-Language Pathology, 16*,157–168.

Mansour, S., & Terry, N.P. (2014). Phonological awareness skills of young African American English speakers. *Reading and Writing: An Interdisciplinary Journal, 27,* 555–569.

National Center for Education Statistics. (2013). *The nation's report card: A first look: 2013 mathematics and reading* (NCES 2014-451), Institute of Education Sciences, U.S. Department of Education, Washington, DC. Retrieved from http://nationsreportcard.gov

National Reading Panel. (2000). *Teaching children to read: An evidence-based assessment of the scientific research literature on reading and its implications for reading instruction* (NIH Pub. No. 00-4769). Washington DC: Department of Health and Human Services, Public Health Service, National Institutes of Health, National Institute of Child Health and Human Development.

Saiegh-Haddad, E. (2003). Linguistic distance and initial reading acquisition: The case of Arabic diglossia. *Applied Psycholinguistics, 24,* 115–135.

Scarborough, H.S. (2001). Connecting early language and literacy to later reading (dis)abilities: Evidence, theory, and practice. In S.B. Neuman & D.K. Dickinson (Eds.), *Handbook of early literacy research* (pp. 97–110). New York, NY: Guilford Press.

Siegel, J. (1999). Stigmatized and standardized varieties in the classroom: Interference or separation? *TESOL Quarterly, 33,* 701–728.

Terry, N.P. (2014). Dialect variation and phonological knowledge: Phonological representations and metalinguistic awareness among beginning readers who speak nonmainstream American English. *Applied Psycholinguistics, 35,* 155–176.

Terry, N.P., & Connor, C.M. (2010). African American English and spelling: How do second graders spell dialect-sensitive features of words? *Learning Disabilities Quarterly, 33*(3), 199–210.

Terry, N.P., & Connor, C.M. (2012). Changing nonmainstream American English use and early reading achievement from kindergarten to first grade. *American Journal of Speech Language Pathology, 21,* 78–86.

Terry, N.P., Brown, M.C., & Stuckey, A. (2014). African American children's early language and literacy learning in the context of spoken dialect variation. In R.H. Bahr & E.R. Silliman (Eds.), *Handbook of communication disorders.* (pp. 303–313). Abingdon, UK: Routledge.

Terry, N.P., Connor, C.M., Petscher, Y., & Conlin, C. (2012). Dialect variation and reading: Is change in nonmainstream American English use related to reading achievement in first and second grade? *Journal of Speech, Language, and Hearing Research, 55,* 55–69.

Terry, N.P., Connor, C.M., Thomas-Tate, S., & Love, M. (2010). Examining relationships among dialect variation, literacy skills, and school context in first grade. *Journal of Speech, Language, and Hearing Research, 53*(1), 126–145.

U.S. Department of Education, Office of Special Education and Rehabilitative Services, Office of Special Education Programs. (2012). *Implementation of the Individuals with Disabilities Education Act, 2009* (Report No. 31). Washington, DC: Author.

Washington, J.A., & Craig, H.K. (1998). Socioeconomic status and gender influences on children's dialectal variations. *Journal of Speech, Language, and Hearing Research, 41,* 618–626.

Washington, J.A., & Craig, H.K. (2002). Morphosyntactic forms of African American English used by young children and their caregivers. *Applied Psycholinguistics, 23,* 209–231.

Washington, J., Craig, H., & Kushmaul, A. (1998). Variable use of African American English across two language sampling contexts. *Journal of Speech, Language, and Hearing Research, 41,* 1115–1124.

Washington, J.A., Terry, N.P., & Seidenberg, M. (2013). Language variation and literacy learning: The case of African American English. In C.A. Stone, E.R. Silliman, B.J. Ehren, & G.P. Wallach (Eds.), *Handbook of language and literacy* (2nd ed., pp. 204–222). New York, NY: Guilford Press.

Wheeler, R.S., & Swords, R. (2010). *Code-switching lessons: Grammar strategies for linguistically diverse writers.* Portsmouth, NH: Heinemann.

Wolfram, W., & Schilling-Estes, N. (2006). *American English* (2nd ed.). Malden, MA: Blackwell.

Zhang, D., Katsiyannia, A., Ju, S., & Roberts, E. (2014). Minority representation in special education: 5-year trends. *Journal of Child & Family Studies, 23,* 118–127. doi:10.1007/s10826-012-9698-6

Zuzovsky, R. (2010). The impact of socioeconomic versus linguistic factors on achievement gaps between Hebrew-speaking and Arabic-speaking students in Israel in reading literacy and in mathematics and science achievements. *Studies in Educational Evaluation, 36,* 153–161.

13

Reading Development Among English Learners

Nonie K. Lesaux

In industrialized countries worldwide, the population of children growing up in linguistically diverse homes is on the rise (UNICEF Innocenti Research Centre, 2009). In the United States, the past several decades have seen a dramatic increase in the number of school-age children from homes in which English is not the primary language. Between 1980 and 2009, this population of children, English learners (ELs), rose from 4.7 to 11.2 million youth, or from 10% to 21% of school-age children (Aud et al., 2011). Approximately 73% of ELs come from Spanish-speaking households, but the remaining members of the population collectively speak 150 other languages at home (Batalova & McHugh, 2010). It is also important to recognize that although one might hear the term *English learner* and conjure up the notion of a recent immigrant, more than half of school-age ELs are born in the United States; the two largest and fastest growing subpopulations of U.S. ELs are students who immigrated before kindergarten and U.S.-born children of immigrants (Capps et al., 2005).

To be sure, many ELs in the United States thrive academically, and there is a considerable amount of research evidence suggesting that bilingualism may facilitate the development of reading skills in a second language, in part due to the fact that bilingual learners appear to have heightened metalinguistic awareness (e.g., Bialystok, Craik, & Luk, 2012). When compared with their majority-culture peers, however, this population, on average, demonstrates lower academic achievement and experiences higher rates of grade retention and school dropouts (August & Shanahan, 2006; Fry, 2007). Although there are many risk factors associated with academic outcomes, many of which ELs carry with them, one risk factor is unique to this population: Its members enter U.S. schools facing the challenge of simultaneously learning academic content and developing English language proficiency; they have to learn with enormous efficiency to catch up with their monolingual English-speaking classmates.

At the same time as having to learn to read in a language in which they are not fully proficient, other risk factors associated with the EL population often include household incomes at or near poverty levels, low parental education rates, and enrollment in underresourced, low-performing schools with high concentrations of students of color (Aud et al., 2011; Capps et al., 2005; Fry & Gonzales, 2008).

This chapter first describes trends and patterns in research focused on ELs' reading development and explores how their instructional environments might relate to these developmental findings. This chapter next reviews two emerging lines of research on developmental and contextual factors influencing ELs' reading development. Finally, it suggests future directions for research aimed at tightening the link between the understanding of reading development and today's linguistically diverse student population.

UNDERSTANDING THE INDIVIDUAL MULTILINGUAL LEARNER

Although ELs may share common characteristics, it is important to remember that no two students are the same. Second-language acquisition is an *uneven* process (Bialystok, 1991) and depends on many contextual factors. When taught in English, some ELs become more proficient in academic English than in their first language. Thus their relative proficiency in English and in their first language can fluctuate depending on the topic. Each student also differs in the degree of exposure to his or her first or second language. Some are *simultaneous bilinguals,* meaning that they speak both English and Spanish or another language in their homes and are in the process of learning two languages at once. Others are *sequential bilinguals,* in which case they are from homes in which they and their families almost exclusively speak their native language; they are fluent in their first language and are learning English as a second or additional language. Some ELs are from wealthy or middle-class families and others are from low-income households. Some have a lot of experience as students, whereas others have spent little time in the classroom. Indeed, we need to build from these experiences when designing effective EL instruction. Finally, whereas ELs' hesitancy to speak, syntactic errors, or accents are often misinterpreted as indicators of low language ability or learning problems (Cummins, 2000), ELs are clearly just as capable as their fluent English-speaking peers of engaging in higher level thinking, though it might take them longer to process language, especially when a task is cognitively demanding. Even when ELs seem fluent in oral English, they may be expending cognitive energy translating content into their first language.

TYPICAL READING DEVELOPMENT FOR ENGLISH LEARNERS

For all readers, including ELs, the process of reading development is both componential and cumulative (RAND Reading Study Group, 2002). By "componential," we mean that a number of separate but related skills are part of the process. Broadly speaking, and particularly relevant for understanding ELs' reading development, these component skills can be classified into two types: code based or meaning related (Duke & Carlisle, 2011; Lesaux, 2012; Paris, 2005). *Code-based skills* allow students to read words with accuracy and efficiency. These skills include, but are not limited to, phonological processing, letter knowledge, decoding, and fluency. *Meaning-related skills* involve the range of abilities and knowledge necessary for both extracting and making meaning from text. Many of these skills are associated with language development, such as oral language, vocabulary, and listening comprehension skills, as well as the background knowledge needed to access and apply a text's message. Also included in this broad group of skills are the cognitive strategies needed to facilitate meaning construction and learning, such as those focused on comprehension monitoring and making inferences.

By *cumulative,* we mean that the process of reading development begins at birth and continues through adulthood. By developing skills and knowledge while accumulating reading experiences over time, a reader is able to keep pace with the changing demands of the context and the purpose of reading. This continual development creates a foundation for learning across all school subjects (RAND Reading Study Group, 2002) with a curriculum largely mediated by oral and written language.

Research demonstrates that both code-based and meaning-related skills contribute to ELs' reading development and ultimately to their reading comprehension (Geva & Yaghoub Zadeh, 2006; Gottardo & Mueller, 2009; Mancilla-Martinez & Lesaux, 2010; Proctor, Carlo, August, & Snow, 2005). Yet there are still important qualifications to this generally similar trend. Research indicates that with sufficient exposure to English reading instruction—that is, when ELs are past the newcomer or recent-arrival stages—they attain similar amounts of code-based skills, whether assessed in elementary or middle school (Betts, Bolt, Decker, Muyskens, & Marston, 2009; Geva & Yaghoub Zadeh, 2006; Jean & Geva, 2009; Lesaux, Crosson, Kieffer, & Pierce, 2010; Mancilla-Martinez & Lesaux, 2011). These skills relate mostly to the "mechanics" of reading—the ability to map the letters onto their respective sounds in combinations and thus read words. At the same time, however, meaning-based literacy competencies (e.g., oral language) in ELs appear to be persistent sources of difficulty, and ultimately, these difficulties impede literacy outcomes (Betts et al., 2009; Geva & Yaghoub Zadeh, 2006; Jean & Geva, 2009; Lesaux, Koda, Siegel, & Shanahan, 2006; Lesaux et al., 2010; Mancilla-Martinez & Lesaux, 2011; Proctor et al., 2005; Swanson, Rosston, Gerber, & Solari, 2008). Therefore, by the upper elementary- and middle-school years, a common profile among ELs in the United States, a large number of whom were born here, is that of a reader who is both accurate and efficient in reading words and performing well within the average range on such measures but who struggles significantly to make meaning from text on account of underdeveloped vocabulary—often considered a proxy for background knowledge.

The challenges specific to having been considered "limited English proficient" at one time are not always clear. In the United States, many ELs also are raised in poverty, which has long been identified as a risk factor for later reading difficulties (for a review, see Snow, Burns, & Griffin, 1998). Emerging work using a comparative design demonstrates the role of poverty in reading difficulties, noting the similar literacy outcomes for children from low-income households schooled predominantly in the United States, irrespective of language background. For example, a recent study examined the nature of reading comprehension difficulties for struggling sixth-grade readers enrolled in 26 mainstream classrooms in a large, urban district (Lesaux & Kieffer, 2010). When comparing the sources of difficulty for ELs (schooled in the United States since the primary grades) and monolingual English speakers, my research colleagues and I found more similarities than differences. For the sample studied, low vocabulary knowledge was a profound source of weakness across linguistic groups, whereas the majority of these struggling readers had developed age-appropriate skills-based reading competencies.

Another study using the nationally representative Early Childhood Longitudinal Study-Kindergarten (ECLS-K) dataset showed that children who entered kindergarten with limited proficiency in English continued to demonstrate reading achievement below that of their monolingual English-speaking peers through fifth grade (Kieffer, 2010). The kindergarten ELs, however, had scores similar to those of monolingual English speakers from homes at comparable socioeconomic levels. Moreover, an in-depth comparison of adolescent ELs and their monolingual English-speaking classmates demonstrated that both groups knew key elements of text features known to influence comprehension but that both performed at rather low levels on measures of language and vocabulary (Lesaux, Gaméz, & Anushko Rizzo, 2014).

These findings suggest that many students who enter school with limited English proficiency, low scores on early literacy or "reading readiness" measures, or both don't necessarily "catch up." In turn, many educators are left with the impression that negotiating two languages may compromise overall learning ability. Performance growth rates for these vulnerable EL populations, however, are promising despite low reading performance levels. For example, a 10-year longitudinal study following Spanish-speaking children from early childhood (U.S.-born children of immigrants recruited from Head Start centers at age 4) through early adolescence finds that both skills-based and knowledge-based reading competencies grew at a rate equivalent to that of the average U.S. monolingual English-speaking student (Mancilla-Martinez & Lesaux, 2011). Kieffer's research using the ECLS-K similarly suggests that children who entered kindergarten with lower proficiency in English than that of their monolingual peers had significantly lower scores in fifth grade, even though they had slightly *faster* rates of growth in reading (Kieffer, 2008, 2010). Taken together, these studies suggest that although children entering school with limited English proficiency demonstrate age-appropriate or relatively rapid growth in English reading achievement from early childhood through early adolescence, the growth is not *sufficient* to compensate for the substantial early gaps.

INSTRUCTIONAL PRACTICES IN LINGUISTICALLY DIVERSE CLASSROOMS

Like all learners, ELs' development and achievement are inextricably intertwined with their classroom learning experiences. The line of research focused on typical instruction in linguistically diverse classrooms, therefore, sheds light on the developmental trends described in the previous section. Perhaps not surprisingly, classroom research using observational methods indicates that literacy instruction frequently tends to be much more heavily focused on developing code-based literacy competencies than on meaning-based skills (Gamse, Jacob, Horst, Boulay, & Unlu, 2008). In the average classroom, there is minimal time spent on explicit instruction in building vocabulary and oral language skills (Carlisle, Kelcey, & Berebitsky, 2013; Lesaux, Kelley, & Harris, 2014), and there is little emphasis on using reading and writing as platforms for deepening and extending thinking (Applebee & Langer, 2011; Lesaux, Kelley, & Harris, 2014).

This discrepant instructional focus is made salient by a 2014 study examining standard practice in 26 middle school English language arts classrooms in a large urban district serving large numbers of ELs. The authors of this study found that across hundreds of hours of instruction, a very modest amount of time was devoted to vocabulary teaching (8%) or to rich oral language development (6%; Lesaux, Kelley, & Harris, 2014). Furthermore, when vocabulary instruction did occur, the words taught were overwhelmingly of two types: rare words unlikely to be encountered again with much frequency (e.g., *gossamer, somnolence*) and content-specific words (e.g., *protagonist, tone, mood*). In part, the lack of focus on general service (i.e., more frequently used) academic language (e.g., *therefore, argument*) may have resulted from the increased emphasis placed on reading literary texts (28% of the instruction observed) versus informational texts (18%).

Research further suggests that existing comprehension instruction focuses primarily on developing strategies for comprehending text (e.g., Dewitz, Jones, & Leahy, 2009). This instructional focus, in the absence of strong language and knowledge building, has a potential unintended influence on ELs' reading comprehension outcomes. For example, a mixed-methods study conducted with 41 sixth- and seventh-grade ELs sheds light on how strategy use during the reading process unfolds for this group of readers who demonstrate below-average scores on assessments of reading comprehension and vocabulary knowledge (Harris & Lesaux, 2014). Based on students' responses during semistructured interviews focused on their reading of a particular passage, findings illustrated that the participants engaged in an active reading process focused on making meaning; students described using a suite of strategies, such as constructing inferences about the passage's content and connecting what they know to what appeared in the passage. Despite this active-learner stance, participants tended to construct inaccurate representations of the text. The authors interpret these results as suggesting that the value of reading strategies is better realized when other components of reading comprehension, including vocabulary and content knowledge, are similarly well developed.

Before continuing in this chapter, it is important to note here that the instructional answer to these developmental trends is not less time and emphasis on code-based literacy competencies but a commitment to being just as explicit and systematic with the approach to building meaning-based skills from the earliest years (i.e., learning to read *and* reading to learn).

BROADENING THE LENS ON DEVELOPMENTAL AND CONTEXTUAL FACTORS INFLUENCING READING DEVELOPMENT

In addition to discussing trends in ELs' reading development and reading instruction, this chapter presents two emerging lines of research that aim to broaden the lens through which researchers and educators view the developmental and contextual factors that influence ELs' reading development. This type of research is needed if we are to design a more comprehensive instructional model—one that responds to ELs' needs and successfully enacts the mission of the public education system.

Emerging Insights: The Role of Classroom Talk

As mentioned, ELs' development and achievement are inextricably intertwined with their classroom learning experiences. One of the more salient features of the classroom environment demanding study is the language that teachers use when engaging students—referred to as *classroom talk*. In the work discussed here, classroom talk is empirically described by examining the complexity of teachers' vocabulary and syntax as well as the overall amount of teacher talk.

Though relatively small, the research base examining classroom talk in classrooms serving ELs demonstrates that teachers' use of high-quality language forms is linked to individual differences in ELs' language and literacy skills (Bowers & Vasilyeva, 2011; Gámez & Lesaux, 2012, 2014; Gámez & Levine, 2013). For example, Bowers and Vasilyeva (2011) found a significant association between teachers' language input in linguistically diverse classrooms and their preschool sample's vocabulary gains during the course of the year. For both ELs and their monolingual classmates, they found that vocabulary growth was related to the total number of words produced by the teacher and to the diversity of teachers' speech. They found, however, that the mean number of words per utterance (i.e., a measure of structural complexity) was negatively associated with ELs' English vocabulary growth and not significantly associated with English monolinguals' vocabulary growth. Therefore, preschool ELs showed gains only from the increased quantities of language exposure, whereas their monolingual counterparts, who were presumably further along in language development, showed gains associated with the diversity of their teachers' vocabulary and syntactic complexity.

Moving up the developmental continuum, two studies conducted in urban middle schools serving a linguistically diverse population also examined the influence of classroom talk on ELs' literacy development (Gámez & Lesaux, 2012, 2014). The authors found a positive relation between English language arts teachers' use of high-quality language (i.e., use of sophisticated and complex linguistic forms) and the vocabulary (Gámez & Lesaux, 2012) and reading outcomes (Gámez & Lesaux, 2014) among their adolescent students, both ELs and monolingual English speakers. At the same time, teachers' syntactic complexity was differentially associated with ELs' and monolingual students' vocabulary skill gains: Monolingual English speakers evidenced greater gains in vocabulary in comparison to ELs. Follow-up analyses, however, showed a positive relation between teachers' syntactic complexity and vocabulary performance for a subset of the ELs—that is, the more complex the teachers' syntax, the greater the gains for ELs on the higher end of the vocabulary performance spectrum (i.e., above the 25th percentile) who had advanced English language proficiency.

Emerging Insights: Developmental Pathways to Reading Outcomes

A central barrier to progress in improving ELs' reading comprehension, and thus to their overall academic performance, is that our perspective is skewed almost exclusively toward understanding (strictly) reading-related factors, and research largely emphasizes this population's status as language learners—that is, as described previously, developmental research on ELs tends to focus on empirically describing their reading skills, motivated largely by the well-documented gap between this population's reading comprehension and that of children who speak English as a primary language. Although it is clearly valuable, such an approach overlooks the importance of broader psychosocial constructs known to influence the academic outcomes of monolingual English speakers, such as self-regulation (SR) and executive functioning (EF). EF refers to a set of cognitive processes that modulate attention, control, and the planning and execution of goal-directed behavior (Best, Miller, & Naglieri, 2011). SR refers to the competencies necessary for managing emotion, behavior, and successful interactions with others (Raver, 2004).

Research conducted with children who speak English as a primary language has shown that strong EF can play a protective role in children's reading and math development as well as in the ability to partake in general classroom learning (Blair & Razza, 2007; Howse, Calkins, Anastopoulos, Keane, & Shelton, 2003). Although there is some emerging research on the role of EF in ELs' academic outcomes, the findings are equivocal, likely in part because this research has been conducted with diverse populations of ELs (e.g., Bialystok et al., 2012; Carlson & Meltzoff, 2008; Lesaux, Lipka, & Siegel, 2006). Even when conducted with specific language groups, this research is traditionally cross-sectional and is focused on linguistically balanced bilinguals from advantaged socioeconomic backgrounds (for a discussion see Morton & Harper, 2007). Therefore, more research with different samples using a longitudinal approach is needed to further understand these relationships.

In the domain of SR, research conducted with children who speak English as a primary language has shown that difficulties in this domain contribute to their experiencing high levels of negative emotional arousal alongside concentration and recall difficulties that affect learning and retention. Notably, not unlike the findings from other lines of research that highlight the compromising role of poverty in development, it has been documented that children growing up in poverty show challenges in SR (Blair & Razza, 2007). Paradoxically, however, an emerging body of research using a comparative lens finds that ELs from immigrant families, who often reside in low-income households, often display enhanced SR (Crosnoe, 2007; Fuligni, 1997; Georgiades, Boyle, & Duku, 2007; Han, 2010). For example, Crosnoe (2007) studied school readiness for children from Mexican immigrant families participating in the ECLS-K cohort and found that Latino ELs entered school with levels of academic readiness that were slightly below those of their peers from English-speaking households. These same students, however, also entered school with somewhat higher social-emotional aptitudes as compared with their non-Latino peers. Similar findings were demonstrated in a longitudinal study conducted by Han (2010), also using the ECLS-K data set in which Latino children who spoke a language other than English at home did as well as or better than their white, monolingual English-speaking peers on measures of social and emotional development, even though they were from lower SES backgrounds.

My colleague Stephanie Jones and I are examining the nature and developmental course of EF, SR, and literacy skills for children growing up in low-income households, non-English-speaking households, or both. Descriptive statistics gleaned from the first wave of data ($n = 236$ prekindergarten children, 91 of whom are ELs) suggest variation in children's performance across all measures. On average, the participants demonstrated scores within the average range on measures of vocabulary and letter–word identification. Although ELs and their English-only peers performed similarly on the measures of cognitive and social-emotional skills, ELs were slightly more likely to demonstrate lower scores on the literacy-based measures. For all children, these skills appear to be interrelated—that is, when a child demonstrated strong skills in one area, she or he was more likely to demonstrate strong scores in other areas, providing insights into the potential benefits of a more comprehensive approach to reading instruction and intervention.

CONCLUSION

Going forward, there are many questions for the research and practitioner communities to address in order to better serve the growing population of students from linguistically diverse backgrounds entering today's classrooms, many of whom are at risk for reading difficulties. Primarily, the field would benefit from a research agenda driven by the goal of learning how to build ELs' meaning-based literacy competencies in the service of improved outcomes. This research may take many forms, as described in the following paragraph.

In the domain of reading development, future research should aim to generate a more precise understanding of how to accelerate early literacy development and prevent late-emerging reading difficulties. In addition, the complexities of reading and the heightened demands that sophisticated texts make of ELs call for research on the social-emotional characteristics and higher order cognitive abilities that guide self-regulation, planning, and complex thought. We also need to further understand the relations among these skills and competencies. Finally, research focused on describing classroom instruction and processes should focus on the role of high-quality language learning environments as a promising lever for improving ELs' outcomes. Such studies could advance existing research by characterizing the bidirectional nature of teacher–student language interactions and by generating an understanding of how aspects of the classroom language environment influence teacher–student communication feedback loops.

REFERENCES

Aud, S., Hussar, W., Kena, G., Bianco, K., Frohlich, L., Kemp, J., Tahan, K. (2011). *The condition of education 2011* (NCES 2011-033). U.S. Department of Education, National Center for Education Statistics. Washington, DC: U.S. Government Printing Office.

Applebee, A.N., & Langer, J.A. (2011). A snapshot of writing instruction in middle schools and high schools. *English Journal, 100*(6), 14–27.

August, D., & Shanahan, T. (Eds.). (2006). *Developing literacy in second-language learners: Report of the National Literacy Panel on Language-Minority Children and Youth.* Mahwah, NJ: Lawrence Erlbaum Associates.

Batalova, J., & McHugh, M. (2010). *Top languages spoken by English language learners nationally and by state.* Washington, DC: Migration Policy Institute.

Best, J.R., Miller, P.H., & Naglieri, J.A. (2011). Relations between executive function and academic achievement from ages 5 to 17 in a large, representative national sample. *Learning and Individual Differences, 21*(4), 327–336.

Betts, J., Bolt, S., Decker, D., Muyskens, P., & Marston, D. (2009). Examining the role of time and language type in reading development for English language learners. *Journal of School Psychology, 47*(3), 143–166.

Bialystok, E. (Ed.). (1991). *Language processing in bilingual children.* Cambridge, UK: Cambridge University Press.

Bialystok, E., Craik, F.I., & Luk, G. (2012). Bilingualism: Consequences for mind and brain. *Trends in Cognitive Sciences, 16*(4), 240–250.

Blair, C., & Razza. R.P. (2007). Relating effortful control, executive function, and false belief understanding to emerging math and literacy ability in kindergarten. *Child Development, 78*(2), 647–663.

Bowers, E., & Vasilyeva, M. (2011). The relation between teacher input and lexical growth of preschoolers. *Applied Psycholinguistics, 32*(1), 221–241.

Capps, R., Fix, M., Murray, J., Ost, J., Passel, J.S., & Herwantoro, S. (2005). *The new demography of America's schools: Immigration and the No Child Left Behind Act* (Research report). Washington, DC: Urban Institute.

Carlisle, J.F., Kelcey, B., & Berebitsky, D. (2013). Teachers' support of students' vocabulary learning during literacy instruction in high poverty elementary schools. *American Educational Research Journal, 50*(6), 1360–1391.

Carlson, S., & Meltzoff, A. (2008). Bilingual experience and executive functioning in young children. *Developmental Science, 11*(2), 282–298.

Crosnoe, R. (2007). Early child care and the school readiness of children from Mexican immigrant families. *International Migration Review, 41*, 151–182.

Cummins, J. (2000). *Language, power, and pedagogy: Bilingual children in the crossfire.* Clevedon, UK: Multilingual Matters Limited.

Dewitz, P., Jones, J., & Leahy, S. (2009). Comprehension strategy instruction in core reading programs. *Reading Research Quarterly, 44*(2), 102–126.

Duke, N.K., & Carlisle, J.F. (2011). The development of comprehension. In M.L. Kamil, P.D. Pearson, E.B. Moje, & P. Afflerbach (Eds.), *Handbook of reading research* (Vol. 4, pp. 199–228). London, UK: Routledge.

Fry, R. (2007). *How far behind in math and reading are English language learners?* Washington, DC: Pew Hispanic Center.

Fry, R., & Gonzales, F. (2008). *One-in-five and growing fast: A profile of Hispanic public school students.* Washington, DC: Pew Hispanic Center.

Fuligni, A.J. (1997). The academic achievement of adolescents from immigrant families: The roles of family background, attitudes, and behavior. *Child Development, 68*(2), 351–363.

Gámez, P.B., & Lesaux, N.K. (2012). The relation between exposure to sophisticated and complex language and early-adolescent English-only and language minority learners' vocabulary. *Child development, 83*(4), 1316–1331.

Gámez, P.B., & Lesaux, N.K. (2014). *Exposure to sophisticated vocabulary in urban middle school classrooms and early adolescents' reading comprehension.* Manuscript submitted for publication.

Gámez, P.B., & Levine, S.C. (2013). Oral language skills of Spanish-speaking English language learners: The impact of high-quality native language exposure. *Applied Psycholinguistics, 34*(04), 673–696.

Gamse, B.C., Jacob, R.T., Horst, M., Boulay, B., & Unlu, F. (2008). *Reading first impact study final report* (NCEE 2009–4038). Washington, DC: National Center for Education Evaluation and Regional Assistance, IES, U.S. Department of Education.

Georgiades, K., Boyle, M.H., & Duku, E. (2007). Contextual influences on children's mental health and school performance: The moderating effects of family immigrant status. *Child Development, 78*(5), 1572–1591.

Geva, E., & Yaghoub Zadeh, Z. (2006). Reading efficiency in native English-speaking and English-as-a-second-language children: The role of oral proficiency and underlying cognitive-linguistic processes. *Scientific Studies of Reading, 10*(1), 31–57.

Gottardo, A., & Mueller, J. (2009). Are first-and second-language factors related in predicting second-language reading comprehension? A study of Spanish-speaking children acquiring English as a second language from first to second grade. *Journal of Educational Psychology, 101*(2), 330–344.

Han, W. (2010). Bilingualism and socio-emotional well-being. *Children and Youth Services Review, 32*, 720–731.

Harris, J.R., & Lesaux, N.K. (2014). *Exploring the reading comprehension processes of adolescent language minority students who demonstrate reading difficulties.* Manuscript in preparation.

Howse, R., Calkins, S.D., Anastopoulos, A., Keane, S., & Shelton, T. (2003). Regulatory contributors to children's kindergarten achievement. *Early Education and Development, 14*, 101–119.

Jean, M., & Geva, E. (2009). The development of vocabulary in English as a second language children and its role in predicting word recognition ability. *Applied Psycholinguistics, 30*(1), 153–185.

Kieffer, M.J. (2008). Catching up or falling behind? Initial English proficiency, concentrated poverty, and the reading growth of language minority learners in the United States. *Journal of Educational Psychology, 100*(4), 851–868.

Kieffer, M.J. (2010). Socioeconomic status, English proficiency, and late-emerging reading difficulties. *Educational Researcher, 39*(6), 484–486.

Lesaux, N.K. (2012). Reading and reading instruction for children from low-income and non–English-speaking households. *The Future of Children, 22*(2), 73–88.

Lesaux, N.K., & Kieffer, M.J. (2010). Exploring sources of reading comprehension difficulties among language minority learners and their classmates in early adolescence. *American Educational Research Journal, 47*, 596–632.

Lesaux, N.K., Crosson, A., Kieffer, M.J., & Pierce, M. (2010). Uneven profiles: Language minority learners' word reading, vocabulary, and reading comprehension skills. *Journal of Applied Developmental Psychology, 31,* 475–483.

Lesaux, N.K., Gaméz, P.B., & Anushko Rizzo, A.A. (2014). Narrative Production Skills of Language Minority Learners and their English-only Classmates in Early Adolescence. Manuscript submitted for publication.

Lesaux, N.K., Kelley, J.G., Harris, J.R. (2014). *Instruction in the urban middle school English language arts classroom: Evidence from a district-wide observational study.* Manuscript submitted for publication.

Lesaux, N.K., Koda, K., Siegel, L.S., & Shanahan, T. (2006). Development of literacy of language minority learners. In D.L. August & T. Shanahan (Eds.), *Developing literacy in a second language: Report of the National Literacy Panel* (pp. 75–122). Mahwah, NJ: Lawrence Erlbaum Associates.

Lesaux, N.K., Lipka, O., & Siegel, L.S. (2006). Investigating cognitive and linguistic abilities that influence the reading comprehension skills of children from diverse linguistic backgrounds. *Reading and Writing: An Interdisciplinary Journal, 19*(1), 99–131.

Mancilla-Martinez, J., & Lesaux, N.K. (2010). Predictors of reading comprehension for struggling readers: The case of Spanish-speaking language minority learners. *Journal of Educational Psychology, 102*(3), 701–711.

Mancilla-Martinez, J., & Lesaux, N.K. (2011). The gap between Spanish speakers' word reading and word knowledge: A longitudinal study. *Child development, 82*(5), 1544–1560.

Morton, J.B., & Harper, S.H. (2007). What did Simon say? Revisiting the bilingual advantage. *Developmental Science, 10*(6), 719–726.

Paris, S. (2005). Reinterpreting the development of reading skills. *Reading Research Quarterly, 40*(2), 184–202.

Proctor, C., Carlo, M., August, D., & Snow, C. (2005). Native Spanish-speaking children reading in English: Toward a model of comprehension. *Journal of Educational Psychology, 97*(2), 246–256.

RAND Reading Study Group. (2002). *Reading for understanding: Toward a R&D program in reading.* Arlington, VA: RAND.

Raver, C.C. (2004). Placing emotional self-regulation in sociocultural and socioeconomic contexts. *Child Development, 75,* 346–353.

Snow, C.E., Burns, M.S., & Griffin, P. (Eds.). (1998). *Preventing reading difficulties in young children.* Washington, DC: National Academy Press.

Swanson, H.L., Rosston, K., Gerber, M., & Solari, E. (2008). Influence of oral language and phonological awareness on children's bilingual reading. *Journal of School Psychology, 46,* 413–429.

UNICEF Innocenti Research Centre. (2009). *Children in immigrant families in eight affluent countries: Their family, national and international context.* Florence, Italy: United Nations Children's Fund.

14

Students with Reading Difficulties Who Are English Learners

Melodee A. Walker, Philip Capin, and Sharon Vaughn

The population of English learners (ELs) in U.S. schools has increased by 60% in the last decade, whereas the overall school population has grown by less than 3% (U.S. Department of Education, 2008). Findings from the National Assessment of Educational Progress (NAEP) reflect the challenges educators have had in adequately meeting the learning needs of ELs. According to findings from the NAEP, only 35% of fourth-grade students, 11% of students with disabilities, and 7% of ELs are performing at or above the proficient level in reading (National Center for Education Statistics, 2013).

Instructional practices and reading interventions for ELs need further examination. Although much is known about reading interventions that prevent reading failure for monolingual readers, there is far less research regarding reading interventions for ELs at risk for reading difficulties (Mathes, Pollard-Durodola, Cardenas-Hagan, Linan-Thompson, & Vaughn, 2007; McCardle & Leung, 2006). Historically, the education community has indicated that ELs have distinct educational needs (e.g., see review by Fitzgerald, 1995). Specific curricula for ELs and distinct instructional practices point to the widely held understanding that ELs require unique instruction (Francis, Rivera, Lesaux, Kieffer, & Rivera, 2006; Gersten & Geva, 2003). Fewer researchers have examined the appropriateness of applying what is known about effective interventions for monolingual students to ELs (e.g., Kieffer & Vukovic, 2013).

One example of applying research-based programs to both ELs and non-ELs is the implementation of multitiered frameworks, such as response to intervention (RTI). RTI has been associated with a decline in reading failure in students not identified as ELs (Fletcher & Vaughn, 2009; Fuchs & Fuchs, 2006), as well as in ELs (Linan-Thompson, Vaughn, Prater, & Cirino, 2006), when implemented with high-quality, research-based instruction and frequent progress monitoring. Within RTI, effective Tier 1 reading instruction integrates critical content within the areas of language development, phonemic awareness, graphophonemic knowledge, word recognition, fluency, vocabulary, and comprehension. Some researchers indicate that these principles can be generalized when designing reading instruction for ELs (e.g., Mathes et al., 2007).

In a review of interventions for ELs (Spanish–English), implications for EL readers at risk for reading failure were identified, including the importance of recognizing the difficulty of learning to read in English as compared with Spanish due to the orthographic complexity of written English, capitalizing on background knowledge and vocabulary-building opportunities, and using common features of reading instruction to design reading interventions (Vaughn, Linan-Thompson, Pollard-Durodola, Mathes, & Cardenas-Hagan, 2006a; Vaughn et al., 2006b). In light of the complexity of adjusting instruction for the myriad learners that teachers instruct, and considering the applicability of principles and features of effective instruction across both ELs and those not identified as ELs within increasingly complex school contexts that are serving diverse student populations, we posit these questions: What would happen if we designed all instruction to ensure its success for ELs? By considering curriculum and instruction from the perspective of ELs, would we maximize learning for all students? Much of what we know about teaching reading to monolingual students applies to ELs, which potentially allows for greater efficiency when designing and implementing interventions. Conversely, the instructional practices and curricula foci that promote learning for ELs are also important to the academic advancement of students who are not identified as ELs. Specifically, we suggest that an emphasis on language development, vocabulary, and background knowledge is critical when designing instruction and developing interventions that will maximize reading outcomes for both ELs and students who are not identified as ELs.

This chapter describes components of interventions that we have implemented with ELs. We provide findings from efficacy studies describing the components of these interventions that may be beneficial for all students. We begin by reviewing the research conducted in a large-scale project involving students in Grades 1 and 2 and by identifying the critical features of an intervention for young ELs at risk for reading difficulty. We next review two experimental studies to improve vocabulary knowledge and comprehension among middle school students identified as ELs. The results of the middle school studies and other analyses provide initial support for the conclusion that all learners may benefit from instruction that supports the development of academic language and the development of oral and written language skills.

FIRST GRADE READING INTERVENTION FOR ENGLISH LEARNERS

Vaughn et al. (2006a, 2006b) conducted reading intervention research with the goal of identifying empirically supported features of interventions for ELs at risk for reading disabilities and to provide a foundation for developing interventions that promote reading development and prevent reading failure for all students. In the design of their intervention research, Vaughn and colleagues targeted first-grade ELs with reading difficulties who were identified for treatment and were receiving parallel reading interventions in their language of instruction, either Spanish or English, as determined by the schools. Two cohorts of students participated in the studies, as a second cohort was needed for the replication of the first study. The methods used in the studies for both cohorts were the same. Interventions were provided in addition to the primary reading instruction that was occurring in the classrooms, and they were provided in the same language as that of the students' core reading instruction. Students were taught in groups of 4 for 50 minutes a day for approximately 7 months. The reading intervention was implemented and taught to mastery each day, with an emphasis on explicit phonics instruction and the integration of fluency, decoding, and comprehension strategies. The scope and sequence of each intervention was designed to avoid confusion for participants. The lesson cycle included the three components of story retelling, synthetic reading instruction, and embedded language support. The story retelling oracy component consisted of previewing the book, making predictions, building background knowledge, building vocabulary, and retelling the story. The reading component included explicit instruction in synthetic phonics with an emphasis on fluency and mastery. The daily lessons included multiple intervention strands (see Figure 14.1). During each lesson, the amount of new information was kept to a minimum, and review and generalization components were implemented.

Interventionists were provided with scripts to teach embedded language support activities, which were integrated throughout lessons and took approximately 5 minutes of instructional time. The embedded language support activities aided students in understanding the vocabulary used in the reading activity directions as well as language central to the meaning of connected texts. Interventionists were trained to support students' vocabulary, language, and literacy needs using instructional behaviors found to be effective with ELs. Instructional behaviors included providing explicit instruction in language use, ensuring multiple opportunities for elaborated responses, and using gestures, facial expressions, and visual aids to support language understanding.

During the English intervention, the focus within phonemic awareness was on segmenting and blending sounds until the participants were sensitive to phonemes within blends. Mastery of reading monosyllabic consonant-vowel-consonant words was the interventionists' first area of focus before moving on to multisyllabic words. Sounding out words was the primary decoding strategy, but participants were taught to be flexible decoders due to the high occurrence of irregular words in English. Decodable stories were used to help students process connected text fluently, and basic comprehension strategies were taught daily.

The Spanish intervention, designed to parallel components of the English intervention, had less phonemic awareness instruction and a significantly

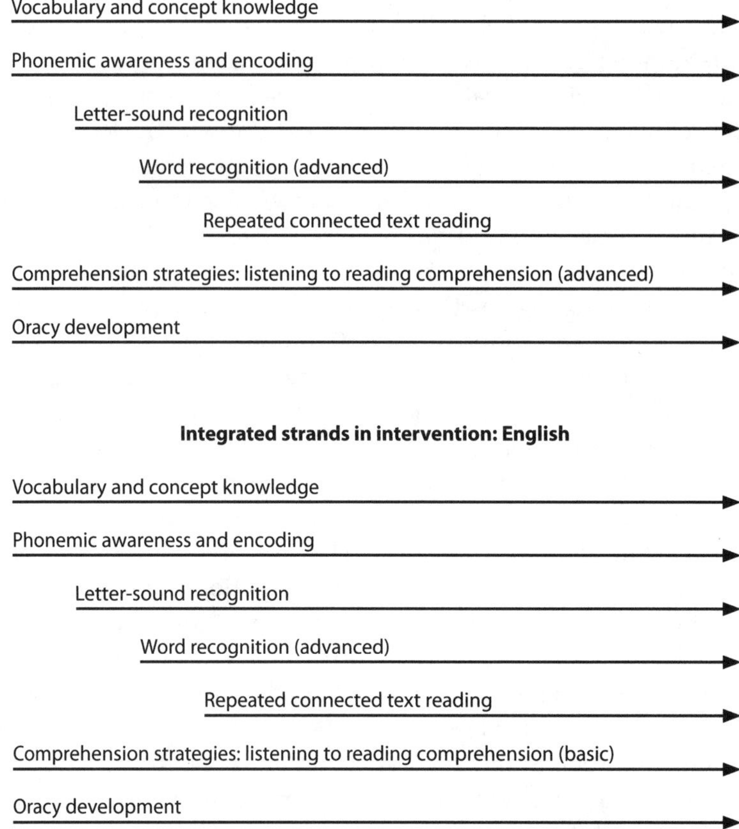

Figure 14.1. Spanish and English intervention strand comparison. (Adapted from "Effective intervention for English language learners [Spanish–English] at risk for reading difficulties," by S. Vaughn, L.R. Martinez, S. Linan-Thompson, C.K. Reutebuch, C.D. Carlson, and D.J. Francis, 2006, *Handbook of Early Literacy Research [Vol. 2],* New York: Guilford Press; and "Effectiveness of an English intervention for first-grade English language learners at risk for reading problems," by S, Vaughn, P.G. Mathes, S. Linan-Thompson, P.T. Cirino, C. D. Carlson., S.D. Pollard-Durodola, E. Cardenas-Hagan, D.J. Francis, 2006, *Elementary School Journal, 107:2,* pp. 153–181.)

revised phonics sequence with an emphasis on the consonant-vowel-syllable type (e.g., *gato, cama*) and reading multisyllabic words began almost immediately. Unlike the English intervention, the phonics elements were syllables within words; children did not sound out an entire multisyllabic word sound by sound, as processing words syllable by syllable was the primary decoding strategy. Because Spanish is more transparent (which means there is high consistency between phonology and orthography, unlike English), participants in the Spanish intervention read more complex word structures sooner than participants in the English intervention. Thus more advanced comprehension strategies could be included because the Spanish text contained more complex word types so that students could move to comprehension activities beyond decodable text more quickly.

First Grade Spanish Intervention Results

Vaughn et al. (2006a, 2006b) reported findings for the English and Spanish interventions in both cohorts. Effect sizes for both cohorts of the Spanish interventions are summarized in Table 14.1. In Cohort 1, statistically significant differences were found in favor of the Spanish intervention treatment group for outcomes in Spanish. Conversely, in Cohort 2 statistically significant differences were found in favor of the English intervention treatment group for outcomes in English. Time-by-treatment interaction effects in Cohort 1 were reported for the following: letter sounds, blending phonemes, word attack, oral reading fluency (words read correctly per minute), passage comprehension, and overall language development. This means that the students participating in the intervention performed statistically significantly better than the students in the control condition over time on outcome measures in reading related to letters, sounds, word reading, fluency, reading for understanding, and overall language development. In Cohort 2, time-by-treatment interaction effects were found for the following: phonemic awareness composite, letter-sound identification, word attack, and oral reading fluency. This means that the students receiving treatment significantly outperformed controls not only on basic skills, such as phonemic awareness and phonics, but also on oral reading fluency (reading words correctly in text). These findings are particularly meaningful because students in the treatment and control conditions were from the same teachers' first-grade classrooms.

Table 14.1. Effect sizes for Spanish intervention

	Effect size (Cohen's *d*)	
Spanish measure	Cohort 1	Cohort 2
Letter-name identification	+ 0.32	+0.26
Rapid letter naming	+0.46	+0.67
Letter-sound identification	+0.72	+0.53
Phonemic awareness composite	+0.73	+0.81
Oral language composite	+0.35	+0.23
Word attack	+0.85	+0.45
Passage comprehension	+0.55	+0.42
Oral reading fluency	+0.75	+0.28, +0.41

Adapted from "Effective intervention for English language learners (Spanish-English) at risk for reading difficulties," by S. Vaughn, L.R. Martinez, S. Linan-Thompson, C.K. Reutebuch, C.D. Carlson, and D.J. Francis, 2006, *Handbook of Early Literacy Research (Vol. 2).* New York: Guilford Press.

First Grade English Intervention Results

Effect sizes for both cohorts of the English interventions can be found in Table 14.2. In Cohort 1, statistically significant differences were found in favor of the English intervention treatment group for outcomes in English. In Cohort 2, similar statistically significant differences were found in favor of the English intervention treatment group for outcomes in English. In Cohort 1, students participating in the intervention performed statistically significantly better than the students in the control condition over time on the following outcome measures: letter-naming fluency, letter-sound identification, phonemic awareness, word attack, dictation, and passage comprehension. Students participating in the intervention in Cohort 2 performed statistically significantly better than control participants on the following measures: letter-sound identification, letter–word identification, phonemic awareness composite, word attack, and oral reading fluency.

First Grade Intervention Follow-Up: Grade 2 and Grade 4 Outcomes

Both cohorts of students were assessed at the end of Grade 2 and in the spring of Grade 4 or 5 to examine the impact of the intervention over time (Vaughn

Table 14.2. Effect sizes for English intervention

	Effect size (Cohen's *d*)	
Spanish measure	Cohort 1	Cohort 2
Letter-name identification	+0.59	−0.23
Rapid letter naming	+0.88	−0.16
Letter-sound identification	+1.01	+0.36
Phonemic awareness composite	+1.24	+0.38
Verbal analogies	+0.77	+0.11
Oral language composite	+0.43	−0.17
Word attack	+1.09	+0.42
Passage comprehension	+1.08	+0.06
Oral reading fluency	+0.16	+0.27, +0.32

Adapted from "Effective intervention for English language learners (Spanish-English) at risk for reading difficulties," by S. Vaughn, L.R. Martinez, S. Linan-Thompson, C.K. Reutebuch, C.D. Carlson, and D.J. Francis, 2006, *Handbook of Early Literacy Research (Vol. 2)*. New York: Guilford Press.

et al., 2008). Follow-up testing revealed few statistically significant differences in favor of intervention participants on Spanish measures, though the effect sizes generally favored the intervention students (median $d = +0.33$). Similarly, for the English study, few statistically significant differences favoring intervention students were detected. As with the Spanish group, effect sizes generally favored the intervention participants (median $d = +0.23$). Although the effects were small, there were no additional interventions or booster sessions implemented after the cessation of the Grade 1 treatment described previously. Thus the follow-up results are promising in terms of the long-term effectiveness of systematic and explicit small-group instruction.

The first-grade interventions revealed features of instruction that are beneficial for ELs, including explicit and systematic instruction, an emphasis on vocabulary development with repeated opportunities to learn words, and oracy development through routines such as those in the retell component of the interventions. We next report on selected reading interventions for ELs conducted in middle school to determine if these instructional implications hold in the upper grades.

SELECTED MIDDLE GRADE READING INTERVENTIONS FOR ENGLISH LEARNERS

Vaughn et al. (2009) conducted two experimental studies in two successive years with nonoverlapping samples to examine the efficacy of instructional practices implemented by social studies teachers to improve vocabulary knowledge and comprehension of native English speakers and ELs in middle school. The second study served as a replication of the first. The approach was a multicomponent treatment of integrated strategies from past research that were found to be effective for ELs, such as explicit vocabulary support and pairing students in heterogeneous groups (Arrega-Mayer, 1998; August & Shanahan, 2006). Nearly 900 total students participated in the two experiments, including more than 200 ELs from two central Texas school districts. Schools were purposively selected based on the substantial number of ELs identified as *limited English proficient* (*LEP*). Although not all of the same schools were involved in the replication study, all schools had relatively high proportions of students who qualified for the free or reduced lunch program (more than 65%) and who were Latino (more than 50%).

Each middle school social studies teacher's class sections were randomly assigned to treatment and control conditions. Thus the same teacher provided both treatment and comparison conditions. This procedure aimed to reduce the effects of differences in teacher quality and ensure that all students were provided equal access to important vocabulary and content. Teachers were trained to implement instructional practices only in their treatment classes and to continue with business-as-usual instruction in comparison classes. To support the effectiveness of the implementation and determine if there was any extension of the treatment in the comparison classes, teachers received materials, modeling, and support to assist them in delivering the intervention and were monitored while providing instruction in both conditions.

Intervention Features

The intervention took place daily in the students' 50-minute social studies class for 9–12 weeks. The lesson plans provided to teachers identified the "big ideas" and important vocabulary students needed to learn and provided direction on the specific instructional practices to teach core subject matter. The instructional routine within lessons was consistent across the intervention: 1) brief overview of the "big idea," 2) explicit vocabulary instruction, 3) viewing of a short video (2–4 minutes) and relevant discussion, 4) paired-student or teacher-led reading assignment with a discussion, and 5) prewriting or writing exercise to provide closure.

The scripted lessons included specific procedures to emphasize explicit concept and vocabulary instruction, structured collaborative learning opportunities, and the use of graphic organizers and short videos to improve understanding. During the overview of the "big idea," instructors provided clear and succinct explanations of key concepts. In addition, students were explicitly taught key vocabulary using student-friendly definitions, visual representations, and two appropriate uses of each word in context during the explicit vocabulary routine. The vocabulary routine also integrated opportunities for paired student practice, as students were provided an opportunity to apply their word knowledge with a student partner when given a prompt. After the vocabulary routine, students were engaged in responding to very brief videos (fewer than 3 minutes) that provided background knowledge and academic vocabulary related to the topic. Students were engaged in focused discussions to integrate the new information presented in the videos into the "big idea." The daily reading assignment was either teacher-led or performed in pairs. When performed in pairs, students were provided two to three specific questions related to the crucial concepts of the lesson. Last, students worked with their peer partners to complete a graphic organizer or other brief writing activity focused on the key concepts and were provided teacher feedback.

Findings

Although there were no significant differences between students in treatment and comparison conditions at pretest, results from Study 1 revealed that there were differences between conditions in both vocabulary and social studies knowledge in favor of the participants in the treatment sections (see Table 14.3). An interesting finding was the lack of interaction between student language status (i.e., EL or non-EL) and treatment effects, indicating that ELs and non-ELs benefitted analogously from participation in the treatment. Another encouraging finding is that the posttest means for ELs who received treatment were equal to or larger than the means for non-ELs in the comparison condition for

Table 14.3. Effect sizes for Studies 1 and 2

Study	Measure	Effect size (Hedge's *g*)
Study 1	Comprehension	+0.71
	Vocabulary	+0.49
Study 2	Comprehension	+0.47
	Vocabulary	+0.36

Note: As adopted by What Works Clearinghouse (Vol. 2), all effect sizes were calculated using the unadjusted posttest means and the pooled within-group standard deviation at the posttest as the measure of standard deviation.

Adapted from "Enhancing social studies vocabulary and comprehension for seventh-grade English language learners: Findings from two experimental studies," by S. Vaughn, L.R. Martinez, S. Linan-Thompson, C.K. Reutebuch, C.D. Carlson, and D.J. Francis, 2009, *Journal of Research on Educational Effectiveness, 2*(4), p. 297–324.

both vocabulary and comprehension. When we consider that the ELs had significantly lower scores in vocabulary and social studies knowledge than the non-ELs at pretest, this finding suggests that ELs can approximate or exceed their non-EL peers in reading comprehension and vocabulary related to social studies when provided high-quality instruction. Effect sizes for Studies 1 and 2 are reported in Table 14.3.

In Study 2, treatment students again outperformed comparison students on the measures of vocabulary knowledge and comprehension. As in Study 1, there was no interaction between student language status and either outcome. In conjunction, Study 1 and the replication suggest that the blending of explicit vocabulary and concept instruction with a focus on promoting students' language skills is effective in improving vocabulary and comprehension outcomes for ELs and non-ELs. This is particularly noteworthy considering that the treatment was crafted to meet the language needs of ELs. Also significant is the finding that ELs assigned to treatment in both years learned words and increased their comprehension scores at the same rate as their non-EL peers.

ADDITIONAL READING INTERVENTIONS WITH ENGLISH LEARNERS AND NON-ENGLISH LEARNERS

In addition to the previously discussed Vaughn et al. (2009) studies, we have identified three other studies with findings that indicate mutual benefits for ELs and non-ELs and identify key components of instruction for optimal language development, such as explicit vocabulary development and collaborative learning opportunities for improved oral language skills. August, Branum-Martin, Cardenas-Hagan, and Francis (2009) conducted a study of 40 sixth-grade science classrooms to evaluate the effectiveness of the Quality English and Science Teaching (QuEST) program in improving the vocabulary and science knowledge of ELs and students proficient in English. The QuEST program emphasizes the use of hands-on experimentation and incorporates language and learning scaffolds to make the science content more understandable for ELs. For example, the intervention includes the use of visuals, graphic organizers, teacher modeling, carefully planned discussions, explicit vocabulary instruction, student pairing, and a procedure for teachers to clarify and elaborate on student responses. After 9 weeks of instruction, students who received the QuEST intervention, on average, outperformed those in the comparison condition in both science and vocabulary knowledge, regardless of their language status.

Carlo et al. (2004) implemented a vocabulary enrichment intervention for ELs that was provided to both ELs and non-ELs in fifth grade to determine its efficacy. Students who received the treatment were taught academic vocabulary through explicit word instruction combined with instruction in word-learning strategies. Knowledge was gained through a multiday instructional routine that introduced students to new vocabulary in the context of engaging texts, provided students multiple exposures and opportunities for practice, and taught students how to analyze morphology and utilize cognates to identify word meanings. The results of the quasi-experimental study revealed that both ELs and non-ELs improved with the vocabulary intervention as evidenced by the similar improvements across subgroups.

Another example of a study evaluating the efficacy of a vocabulary intervention conducted with ELs and non-ELs examined Academic Language Instruction for All Students (ALIAS), a program developed for low-performing English language arts classrooms with high proportions of ELs (Lesaux, Kieffer, Faller, & Kelly, 2010). In this quasi-experimental study, 21 sixth grade classrooms were matched according to their pretest scores and assigned to treatment and comparison conditions. Students were introduced to vocabulary through short pieces of engaging expository texts and were taught words using student-friendly, informal definitions. Similar to previously discussed studies, treatment students were paired for small-group discussions, taught word-learning strategies related to morphology and contextual cues, and engaged in short writing activities to promote deep processing. Results indicated that the treatment students performed significantly better on measures of taught words than did comparison students, and the effects were comparable for ELs and non-ELs. Findings from these studies suggest that faster rates of gains in content-area and vocabulary knowledge are possible for both ELs and non-ELs when implementing interventions devised to meet the language and learning needs of ELs.

The findings from the middle-grade interventions suggest several effective instructional practices associated with positive outcomes for ELs and non-ELs. Components of effective middle-grade interventions include using the following:

- Explicit vocabulary and reading comprehension with modeling
- Short videos
- Graphic organizers

- Structured peer pairing and discussions
- Hands-on experimentation in science
- Instruction in strategies for word learning related to morphology and contextual cues
- Engaging texts

CONCLUSION

We now return to the guiding question in the context of the findings and implications from the studies reviewed: What would happen if we designed all instruction to ensure that it was successful for ELs? By considering curriculum and instruction from the perspective of ELs, would we maximize learning for all students? The findings presented in this chapter indicate that designing all instruction with research-based components linked to improved reading outcomes for ELs would concurrently maximize learning for students not identified as ELs. The recommendations set forth in *Teaching Academic Content and Literacy to English Learners in Elementary and Middle School,* a practice guide published by the Institute of Education Sciences, have been demonstrated to be effective for all learners (see Figure 14.2). The practice guide supports the notion of maximizing learning for all students by asserting, "Research suggests that effective teaching for English Leaners also benefits native English speakers" (Baker et al., 2014, p. 46).

In addition to informing current and future research agendas, there are practical considerations and implications related to conceptually shifting instructional design and implementation to address integrating a language focus that

EL Practice Guide	Would the recommendation benefit all learners?
1. Teach a set of academic vocabulary words intensively across several days using a variety of instructional activities.	✓
2. Integrate oral and written English language instruction into content-area teaching.	✓
3. Provide regular, structured opportunities to develop written language skills.	✓
4. Provide small-group instructional intervention to students struggling in areas of literacy and English language development.	✓

Figure 14.2. The benefits of the English Learner (EL) Practice Guide's recommendations for all learners. (Adapted from *Teaching academic content and literacy to English learners in elementary and middle school* [p. 6], by S. Baker, N. Lesaux, M. Jayanthi, J. Dimino, C.P. Proctor, J. Morris, R. Gersten, K. Haymond, M. J. Kieffer, S. Linan-Thompson, & R. Newman-Gonchar, 2014, Washington, DC: National Center for Education Evaluation and Regional Assistance [NCEE], Institute of Education Sciences, U.S. Department of Education.)

emphasizes vocabulary, background knowledge, and academic discourse. An emphasis on these elements could strategically shift instruction so that it supports all learners. Additionally valuable is the notion that teachers would not have to consider ways to weave instruction for ELs into their routines but rather could think about instructing all students in ways that benefit ELs. Teachers may consider it more feasible to implement instructional practices that would simultaneously help more of their students learn to read proficiently given the demands and toll of designing differentiated instruction for a range of learners.

In terms of future research agendas, additional research needs to be conducted to evaluate the efficacy and feasibility of implementing targeted instructional practices that are designed to enhance vocabulary, language, background knowledge, and academic discourse and help all learners. For example, specific mechanisms for promoting academic discourse across content-area instruction (e.g., science, social studies) that provide opportunities for expanding word and world knowledge and promote access to content for all learners. Currently, there are many classrooms in which content-area text plays a minimal role in enhancing content knowledge (Swanson et al., in press). Students spend little time reading text, comparing information in texts, and drawing inferences and conclusions from text. In part, this may be because content-area teachers have been inadequately prepared to effectively and efficiently integrate text into their instruction. With the push toward content coverage, many teachers may perceive that text-based learning and discourse slow down knowledge acquisition and therefore provide limited time for text reading and discussion. In addition to the range of content-area work needed to promote text learning for all students, particularly ELs with reading difficulties, we think future research addressing the relative effects of intervention components on outcomes such as academic vocabulary and comprehension would be useful.

The extant research reviewed in this chapter has limitations that are important to consider. The findings may be limited to schools with high levels of ELs and low-performing students. Future research should replicate the experiments we have discussed in schools with higher percentages of students who are performing at or above grade level. In addition, all of the vocabulary measures discussed were psychometrically well defined but were aligned with the treatments. Whether students will learn adequate numbers of words beyond those taught specifically through the treatment is unknown. Furthermore, we wonder whether it would be advantageous to study the additive effects of treatments over time and across teachers and content areas. For example, if students were provided research-based practices in all content areas for multiple years, would there be an additive effect? Multiyear interventions may reveal the effects of this instruction on standardized measures. Consideration of both the limitations and the potential promise of the research reviewed here can inform further investigations to identify instructional practices and interventions for ELs in order to identify the impactful practices that might be most beneficial to the greatest range of students.

REFERENCES

Arreaga-Mayer, C. (1998). Language sensitive peer-mediated instruction for culturally and linguistically diverse learners in the intermediate elementary grades. In R.M. Gersten & R.T. Jiménez (Eds.), *Promoting learning for culturally and linguistically diverse students* (pp. 73–90). Belmont, CA: Wadsworth.

August, D., Branum-Martin, L., Cardenas-Hagan, E., & Francis, D.J. (2009). The impact of an instructional intervention on the science and language learning of middle grade English language learners. *Journal of Research on Educational Effectiveness, 2*(4), 345–376.

August, D.L., & Shanahan, T. (2006). *Developing literacy in second-language learners: A report of the national literacy panel on language minority children and youth.* Mahwah, NJ: Lawrence Erlbaum Associates.

Baker, S., Lesaux, N., Jayanthi, M., Dimino, J., Proctor, C.P., Morris, J., . . . & Newman-Gonchar, R. (2014). *Teaching academic content and literacy to English learners in elementary and middle school* (NCEE 2014–4012). Washington, DC: National Center for Education Evaluation and Regional Assistance (NCEE), Institute of Education Sciences, U.S. Department of Education. Retrieved from http://ies.ed.gov/ncee/wwc/publications_reviews.aspx

Carlo, M.S., August, D., McLaughlin, B., Snow, C.E., Dressler, C., Lippman, D.N., . . . White, C.E. (2004). Closing the gap: Addressing the vocabulary needs of English-language learners in bilingual and mainstream classrooms. *Reading Research Quarterly, 39*(2), 188–215.

Fitzgerald, J. (1995). English-as-a-second-language learners' cognitive reading processes: A review of research in the United States. *Review of Educational Research, 65*(2), 145–190.

Fletcher, J.M., & Vaughn, S. (2009). Response to intervention: Preventing and remediating academic difficulties. *Child Development Perspectives, 3*(1), 30–37.

Francis, D.J., Rivera, M., Lesaux, N., Kieffer, M., & Rivera, H. (2006). *Practical guidelines for the education of English language learners: Research based recommendations for instruction and academic interventions* (Cooperative Agreement Grant No. S283B050034). Prepared for the U.S. Department of Education. Portsmouth, NH: RMC Research Corporation, Center on Instruction. Retrieved from http://www.centeroninstruction.org/files/ELL1-Interventions.pdf

Fuchs, D., & Fuchs, L.S. (2006). Introduction to response to intervention: What, why, and how valid is it? *Reading Research Quarterly, 41,* 93–99.

Gersten, R., & Geva, E. (2003). Teaching reading to early language learners. *Educational Leadership, 60*(7), 44–50.

Kieffer, M.J., & Vukovic, R.K. (2013). Growth in reading-related skills of language minority learners and their classmates: More evidence for early identification and intervention. *Reading and Writing, 26*(7), 1159–1194.

Lesaux, N.K., Kieffer, M.J., Faller, S.E., & Kelley, J.G. (2010). The effectiveness and ease of implementation of an academic vocabulary intervention for linguistically diverse students in urban middle schools. *Reading Research Quarterly, 45*(2), 196–228.

Linan-Thompson, S., Vaughn, S., Prater, K., & Cirino, P.T. (2006). The response to intervention of English language learners at risk for reading problems. *Journal of Learning Disabilities, 39*(5), 390–398.

Mathes, P.G., Pollard-Durodola, S.D., Cardenas-Hagan, E., Linan-Thompson, S., & Vaughn, S. (2007). Teaching struggling readers who are native Spanish speakers: What do we know? *Language, Speech, and Hearing Services in Schools, 38,* 260–271.

McCardle, P., & Leung, C.Y.Y. (2006). English language learners: Development and intervention. *Topics in Language Disorders, 26* (4), 302–304.

National Center for Education Statistics. (2013). *The nation's report card: Trends in academic progress 2012* (NCES 2013-456). National Center for Education Statistics, Institute of Education Sciences, U.S. Department of Education, Washington, DC.

Swanson, E.A., Wanzek. J., McCulley, L.V., Stillman-Spisak, S.J., Vaughn, S., Simmons, D., . . . Hairrell, A. (in press). Literacy and text reading in middle and high school social studies and English language arts classrooms. *Reading and Writing Quarterly.*

U.S. Department of Education, Office of English Language Acquisition, Language Enhancement, and Academic Achievement for Limited English Proficient Students. (2008). *The biennial report to Congress on the implementation of the Title III state formula grant program:*

School years 2004–05. Washington, DC: Author. Retrieved from http://www2.ed.gov/about/offices/list/oela/title3biennial0406.pdf

Vaughn, S., Cirino, P.T., Tolar, T., Fletcher, J.M., Cardenas-Hagan, E., Carlson, C.D., & Francis, D.J. (2008). Long-term follow-up of Spanish and English interventions for first-grade English language learners at risk for reading problems. *Journal of Research on Educational Effectiveness, 1*(4), 179–214.

Vaughn, S., Linan-Thompson, S., Pollard-Durodola, S.D., Mathes, P.G., & Cardenas-Hagan, E. (2006a). Effective intervention for English language learners (Spanish-English) at risk for reading difficulties. In D.K. Dickinson & S.B. Neuman (Eds.), *Handbook of early literacy research* (Vol. 2, pp. 185–197). New York, NY: Guilford Press.

Vaughn, S., Martinez, L.R., Linan-Thompson, S., Reutebuch, C.K., Carlson, C.D., & Francis, D.J. (2009). Enhancing social studies vocabulary and comprehension for seventh-grade English language learners: Findings from two experimental studies. *Journal of Research on Educational Effectiveness, 2*(4), 297–324.

Vaughn, S., Mathes, P.G., Linan-Thompson, S., Cirino, P.T., Carlson, C.D., Pollard-Durodola, S.D., . . . Francis, D. (2006b). Effectiveness of an English intervention for first-grade English language learners at risk for reading problems. *Elementary School Journal, 107*(2), 153–180.

15

The *Letra* Program

A Web-Based Tutorial Model for Preparing Teachers to Improve Reading in Early Grades

Juan E. Jiménez

The main purpose of this chapter is to provide an overview of research focused on professional development in scientifically based reading instruction using a web-based tutorial model for preparing teachers in Spanish-speaking regions to improve reading in the Spanish language in early grades. The two key goals were to determine 1) whether a web-based professional development course could improve teacher knowledge of phonemic awareness, systematic phonics instruction, fluency, vocabulary, strategies for comprehension as necessary components of quality reading instruction, and the multitiered system of support or response to intervention (RTI) model; and 2) whether such training would affect teachers' implicit theories (beliefs) about how children learn to read. Previous research was carried out for piloting and testing scientifically based materials through implementing Tier 2 (i.e., small group, more intensive) intervention in early reading skills for kindergarten, first-, and second-grade students at risk for underachievement in the Canary Islands. In addition, we explored teachers' beliefs, or implicit theories,[1] and knowledge about how children learn to read. Based on these studies, we designed a web-based tutorial model including tested, scientifically based materials, as well as an assessment of teacher beliefs and knowledge regarding the five core components of beginning reading identified by the National Reading Panel (NRP; NICHD, 2000). Many of these skills have also been identified as good predictors of reading in the Spanish language (Jiménez & O'Shanahan, 2008).

1. The terms *beliefs* and *implicit theories* are used interchangeably throughout this chapter.

The main purpose of the e-tool the *Letra* Program[2] is to provide preschool, elementary, and special education teachers with online education, instructional materials, and tutorials about how to teach reading based on the scientific investigations highlighted in the NRP report (NICHD, 2000) and those conducted since 2000. This e-tool is composed of e-learning modules, stopping points for self-assessment, web-based tutorials for preparing teachers, and an interactive discussion forum. The e-learning modules of the *Letra* Program provide the teacher with information about the RTI model and the theoretical foundations of early reading skills. The web-based tutorials offer structured materials based on explicit and systematic instruction, and these materials are complemented by models of high-quality classroom practices in the forms of virtual animations and video recordings. A large amount of research suggests that teachers have a hard time implementing techniques that have only been described theoretically and that using video or animation modeling is quite helpful (Dede, Ketelhut, Whitehouse, Breit, & McCloskey, 2009; DeWert, Babinksi, & Jones, 2003; Fisher, Schumaker, Culberston, & Deshler, 2010; Ritterband, Gonder-Frederick, Cox, Clifton, West, & Borowitz, 2013).

Furthermore, instructions for the use of progress monitoring and assessment are provided. To our knowledge, there are no other technological resources that respond to the need to educate and train teachers in reading education based on an RTI model in the Spanish-language domain, or in general, with a developing country orientation. This e-tool has recently been piloted with in-service and preservice teachers from different Ibero-American countries (e.g., Spain, Guatemala, Ecuador, México; Jiménez & O'Shanahan, 2015). The *Letra* Program has demonstrated potential at a large scale and provides every teacher, regardless of his or her geographic location, the possibility to receive an online education about how to teach reading based on scientific evidence. As of 2014, the *Letra* Program is included in a postgraduate teacher certification program offered by the University of La Laguna in the Canary Islands that is needed for students to qualify as reading specialists.

TRAINING TEACHERS TO TEACH READING

Teachers play a key role in helping children learn to read, particularly for those children who are at risk for failing to learn to read (Brady & Moats, 1997). In their meta-analysis, Marzano, Pickering, and Pollock (2001) concluded that teacher effectiveness is one of the most important factors in explaining learning progress, not only in reading but also in mathematics and other school areas. In some countries, such as the United States, federal legislation has recognized that teacher quality is essential to student success in reading (e.g., the No Child Left Behind Act of 2001 [PL 107-110]). In Europe, a recent report from

2. This e-tool was funded by the *Plan Nacional I+D+i (Ministerio de Economía y Competitividad). Ref.: PSI2009–11662, Spain.*

the Education, Audiovisual, and Culture Executive Agency (EACEA) about teaching reading concluded the following:

> A key aspect in reading instruction is teachers' ability to adopt the stance of research-oriented practitioner towards reading difficulties. Therefore, teachers need to receive appropriate initial training which provides them with solid foundations in educational research and methodology. In particular, coupling the development of theoretical knowledge with field experience appears to be very effective in reconstructing any prior beliefs inconsistent with effective reading instruction, such as attributing reading difficulties solely to home background. Continuing professional development (CPD) also has a fundamental role to play in helping teachers to adopt research-oriented and reflective practices. How to promote more effective CPD in the area of reading instruction is a challenge for the future. (2011, p. 134)

Therefore, the following questions may arise: Are teachers sufficiently prepared to teach and improve reading skills, especially in the case of children who are struggling with reading? Why do teachers need to acquire knowledge from scientific studies? How can we appropriately prepare teachers to teach reading in accordance with suggestions from scientific research?

It is important to properly train teachers who are responsible for student learning (including reading) and for the prevention and correction of reading and other learning disabilities. It has been found, however, that many preservice and in-service teachers lack the knowledge of how children learn to read and write or why many of their students have learning difficulties (Bos, Mather, Dickson, Podhajski, & Chard, 2001). This lack of knowledge often goes hand in hand with incorrect teacher beliefs regarding what they need to know and do in order to help their students learn (Moats & Lyon, 1996). Recent studies show that many teachers lack sufficient knowledge regarding language, as well as good teaching practices, to effectively help their students acquire these basic reading skills, particularly in phonemic awareness (PA) and grapheme–phoneme correspondences (GPC; Moats, 2009).

In addition to the importance of teacher knowledge of reading development and instruction in effectively teaching reading, teacher beliefs are also important. Teacher beliefs may create obstacles when it comes to incorporating improvements or good practices into their classroom practices (Cunningham, Zibulsky, Stanovich, & Stanovich, 2009). In the absence of knowledge regarding the essential components of reading instruction, teachers base their teaching decisions on their own beliefs, which most likely were formed during their own educational experiences or in their training experiences (Joshi et al., 2009). It has been found that teachers create theories based on different domains of their experience, constituting a sort of implicit knowledge, which serves as the basis of their decisions and actions (Tirta-Seputro, 1998). Consequently, those designing online teacher training programs and testing their efficacy should consider not only including scientifically based materials but also assessing teachers' existing knowledge and beliefs.

TEACHING STUDENTS TO READ: SCIENTIFIC RESEARCH–BASED INSTRUCTION

Scientifically based materials to be included in the *Letra* Program e-tool were tested in the Canary Islands, implementing Tier 2 early reading skills for K–2 students at risk for learning difficulties. This initiative was possible because the Canary Islands legislation (BOC, 2010a; 2010b; 2011) has left the door open to the use of RTI-based models, which, in the text of its own legislation, refers to the student who, "after undergoing intervention programs, exhibits resistance to improving processes." (Al-Yagon et al., 2013). During the 2009–2010 period, an initial study was designed to examine the effectiveness of Tier 2 intervention for at-risk readers within the context of an RTI approach (Jiménez et al., 2010). A sample of 1,123 Spanish children from 14 school districts were given the Spanish adaptation of The Hong Kong Specific Learning Difficulties Behavior Checklist (Ho, Chan, Tsang, & Lee, 2002); children who scored at or above the 75th percentile on the test were classified as at risk for early reading difficulties. Half of these students were randomly assigned to a project-based intervention condition in which they received small-group supplementary intervention for 30 minutes per day using the *Letra* Program's instructional materials from mid- to late December and continued until mid-June. The other half received whatever remedial services were available at their schools. Treatment effects on measures from the Early Grade Reading Assessment (EGRA; RTI International, 2009) were analyzed using two-way multivariate analyses of covariance (MANCOVA) of grade (kindergarten, first, and second grade) and treatment program, with experimental treatment versus control as a between-subjects factor. The sets of dependent measures included posttests of 1) phoneme segmentation, 2) initial sound identification, 3) listening comprehension, 4) letter-name knowledge, 5) letter-sound knowledge, 6) familiar word reading, 7) unfamiliar nonword reading, 8) oral passage reading and comprehension, and 9) dictation. The pretest measures for these variables were included as the covariates.

Results indicated that children who received the *Letra* Program's instructional materials had higher scores on the EGRA on initial sound identification, listening comprehension, letter-sound knowledge, and oral reading fluency when compared with the control group. After this experience, during the 2010–2011 school year, Crespo, Jiménez, Baker and Park (2015) designed a new study to examine the effects of a Tier 2 intervention for K–2 Spanish monolingual speakers at risk for reading difficulties. The authors were specifically interested in knowing whether the use of a Tier 2 intervention that follows guidelines similar to the interventions conducted in the United States was also effective in a Spanish monolingual setting, taking the differences in the Spanish and English orthographic systems into account.

The authors used *Indicadores Dinámicos del Éxito Lector* (*IDEL*, Dynamic Indicators of Reader Success; Cummings, Baker, & Good, 2006) measures to examine students' initial statuses and growth on letter-sound and letter-name knowledge, understanding of the alphabetic principle, oral reading fluency, story retelling, and vocabulary. All students who received Tier 2 instruction in the treatment group also received progress monitoring five times during the school year; students in the control group were monitored three times during the school year. All special education teachers in the treatment group received 10 days of professional development.

On the first day, teachers were trained on the RTI approach and the core components of beginning reading: phonemic awareness, the alphabetic principle, fluency, vocabulary, and comprehension. On the second day, teachers received training on the intervention program. Teachers received training on the main structure of the program, how to use it, how to introduce the sequence of letters, and how they should construct the daily lessons. On days 3 and 4, teachers received training on how to administer and score our screening measure, The Hong Kong Specific Learning Difficulties Behavior Checklist and the *IDEL* progress monitoring measures. Throughout the year, members of the *Dificultades de Aprendizaje, Psicolingüística y Nuevas Tecnologías* (*DEAP&NT*, Learning Difficulties, Psycholingusitics, and New Technologies) research team from the University of La Laguna met with teachers every 3 weeks to help and advise them on issues of program implementation, student progress monitoring, and any other discussions or challenges they may have had.

Spanish monolingual K–2 students who were at risk for reading difficulties and received a Tier 2 systematic and explicit intervention significantly increased their beginning reading skills when compared with at-risk students who received the typical remedial intervention provided by the school. The major findings derived from this study were that significant differences were found between the treatment and the control groups in vocabulary in kindergarten, in phonemic awareness in kindergarten and first grade, and in oral reading fluency and story retelling in second grade.

THEORIES, BELIEFS, AND LEARNING TO READ

In an earlier study, some colleagues and I analyzed the bodies of work describing scientific theories on the acquisition of reading skills (Jiménez, Rodríguez, Suárez, & O'Shanahan, 2014a). Using historical research techniques, we reviewed a series of scientific theories that have been practiced throughout the years and are still utilized (for a review, see Tracey & Mandel, 2012)—constructivist, sociocultural, nativist, maturation, behaviorist, and cognitive-psycholinguistic theories—and determined the basis of each of these theories. We then held teacher brainstorming sessions that included a series of regulatory questionnaires to determine the principal ideas presented by teachers of early childhood and primary education and linked those to these major theories.

At this point, it is important to note that we are discussing scientific theories, which are based on social-scientific conventions and have explicit verbal formulations and logically structured arguments, as opposed to beliefs, which are implicit and do not have systematic verbal formulations (Rodrigo, 1993). Based on this framework, we should consider how individuals mentally store the most relevant characteristics of each of these theories. Rodrigo suggests that individuals do not store scientific theories in their minds; rather, they store systems of experiences based upon which they synthesize a determined theory for distinct purposes at specific moments. Thus it is necessary to differentiate between two functional levels of representation: the knowledge level and the belief level. Theories operate at a conscious or knowledge level when individuals, using the theory to recognize or discriminate between different ideas, produce verbal expressions regarding that theory. When dealing with their own beliefs, however, individuals use theories in a practical way to interpret situations, making practical inferences to understand and predict successes and to plan their behavior. The distinction between these two levels consists of whether or not the demand is theoretical or pragmatic in nature.

Theories and Knowledge Level

Jiménez et al. (2014) selected a sample of 16 teachers from different educational centers in northern and southern Tenerife (in the Canary Islands) to participate in a study. They worked in early childhood education—first and second grades of primary school—and had considerable experience in the area of reading. For the first phase of the study, various sessions were held addressing several issues. The moderator began by introducing key statements representing different epistemological theories, refocusing the discussion whenever it deviated from the topic. Initially, the moderator indicated that this was a study related to reading and that the researchers were seeking teachers' opinions based on their experiences, that there were no right or wrong answers, and that he would facilitate but not state opinions of his own. The teachers were then asked to freely express opinions on the following questions: How do you think children learn to read? What variables make it possible for children to learn to read? Do children learn to read based on some specific strategies? The moderator next told the participants that in order to expand upon the topic, they would be presented with some statements on which they could offer their points of view. The moderator began by introducing key statements for selected theories (e.g., "When we teach a child to read, we should base this on their prior knowledge"; "To learn to read, a child should first develop the skill of recognizing the phonemes of the oral language [not the names of the letters] because each grapheme corresponds to a sound"; "Children learn to read at an early age").

The conversation regarding the phrases corresponding to each theory was exhausted before moving on to the next theory. Teachers explained their points of view, and their opinions were recorded. A literal transcription was made from the recorded material of this brainstorming session, and analysis of the content from each theory was conducted later; using a system of experts, the most characteristic and prototypical statements from each theory were analyzed. The expert participants were teachers and researchers working in distinct study areas related to the different theories of reading acquisition (i.e., psychology, pedagogy, psychopedagogy, and teaching). The ideas of each teacher were evaluated and included for each of the theories based on the basic assumptions of the theories. A sample of representative statements from the group discussion and proposals for their evaluation by experts is presented in Table 15.1.

Table 15.1. Some representative statements from the group discussion that have been included for each theory based on expert opinion

Theory	Statement
Constructivist theory	• In order for new learning to occur, it must be based on previous learning, which creates conflicts and dissonances in order to restructure knowledge. • The child should construct his or her own learning experience. • In early grades, it is better to let children discover their own mistakes by rereading than it is to correct them. • If the child discovers his or her own mistakes, he or she will remember this. Systematic correction does not have this same effect. • To strengthen the child's ability to learn to read, it is important to create spaces and contexts that stimulate them.
Sociocultural theory	• Although learning to read tends to emphasize the teaching of skills, the child's environment should also be considered. • When interacting with others, children improve and gain reading skills. • A child in a stimulating environment will learn to read before others who are in less favorable conditions. • When families interact with children, this favors and strengthens reading acquisition. • When schools have resources such as libraries in the classroom and make use of them, this motivates the child to read.
Nativist theory	• Some children discover reading on their own at an early age. • Learning to speak and read at the same time is possible because these skills are connected. For instance, some children cannot yet speak correctly but are already able to read a bit. • If early reading occurs naturally and pleasantly, it will always be very advantageous. • Children between ages 3 and 5 may learn to read in a relaxed, unforced manner; those who are prepared will learn to read, whereas those who are not prepared will take a bit longer. • Some children learn to read by 4 years of age.
Maturation theory	• It is necessary to learn to read to have a specific psychomotor maturity. • Some children do not acquire the maturity needed to learn to read until reaching 7 years of age. • Mastering spatial orientation will help children learn to read. • Children in early childhood education and the early grades of primary school are unable to fully internalize the difference between right and left, and this causes them to confuse letters. • Ideally, the child will learn to read when it is his or her "correct time."

(continued)

Table 15.1. *(continued)*

Behaviorist theory	• Children should always be encouraged when they are doing things; positive motivation is very important because it will allow them to grow and work much better. • Children tend to repeat what the teacher does, copying him or her. • Correcting children helps them realize the errors that they make while reading. • Repeating words over and over when children have misread them is a good method to follow. • Immediate correction is necessary when children make mistakes while reading.
Cognitive-psycholinguistic theory	• To learn to read, it is important to begin with phonemes. • Oral language is the basis of early childhood education; reading is something that comes later in a complementary manner. • Children with a large vocabulary may understand texts that are adapted to their age once they have reached the age of deciphering signs. • In the early grades, fluidity in reading should be emphasized so that children understand what they are reading. • It is important to work with those phonemes that are the easiest to identify.

The following expert criteria were used to select the items considered to be the most representative of each theory: statement length (conciseness), statement clarity, its relationship to and inclusion in the reference theory, and its grammatical aspects.

In order to determine if all of the scientific theories identified by the sociohistorical analysis have a representative body, if some of them have disappeared, or if some of them overlap with others, a normative study was conducted. In this way, it was possible to study the relations between the representational structure of the subjects and the theories analyzed while also determining the degree of coherence of the statements making up each reading-acquisition theory. A sample of 497 students of psychology, pedagogy, and education (in all possible specialty areas) was selected. We used "critical episodes" that were typical of each of the theories to serve as triggers, including a description of practical situations in which predetermined individuals (i.e., teachers) expressed perceptions that coincided with those of a specific theory. Using critical episodes instead of presenting conceptual arguments is consistent with the idea that individuals do not store theories as abstract concept networks but rather as sets of experiences based upon which they synthesize a theory when specifically required to do so. Thus theories tend to be activated by experiences and not by the presentation of concepts (Rodrigo, 1993).

Booklets were made for each of the theories, and a web application was used to complete them. In the first page of the booklet, participants filled in their personal information. Next, they were presented with a critical episode, a description of an everyday situation in which specific individuals express points of view that coincide with those of a specific theory (Correa & Camacho, 1993). Table 15.2 presents examples of the critical episodes.

Table 15.2. Critical episodes

Critical episode: Constructivist theory
At the start of the school year, two teachers speak about their plans for teaching their students to read during the coming school year:
Clara: I don't believe in forcing it, we should wait until they understand what reading involves. There is no purpose in explaining it, since this just ruins the illusion of their discovering it for themselves.
María: While it seems that children at these ages need many explanations, almost the opposite is actually true, they need for us to give them space and contexts where they can discover these explanations for themselves. For example, Jorge (a child in their class that they both know) discovered for himself that the "c" although always the same, changes its sound when followed by different vowels.
Critical episode: Sociocultural theory
At the start of the school year, two teachers speak about their plans for teaching their students to read during the coming school year:
Mercedes: This year I have decided to continue to use the same methodology that I used last year since the children learned and had a lot of fun. Even though last year parents already participated actively, I am going to try to get them even a bit more involved. I will have them be in charge of creating the classroom library, with our help of course, since they know the most about their children's interests.
Alicia: Absolutely, I also plan to do that. Although I think that parents first have to understand what we mean by "reading." They expect their children to recognize words that they can say, that they can identify "a," "e," and so forth. But really, the most important thing is that their children understand the value of reading, even if they can't read many of the words yet.
Critical episode: Nativist theory
At the start of the school year, two teachers speak about their plans for teaching their students to read during the coming school year:
María: There are some children that seem to have been born with a great ability to learn how to read. It is as if they were born with the ability! They are alert and learn how to read words immediately. They are like sponges and have an innate ability to learn these skills.
Carmen: I know. They are like sponges and have an innate ability to learn these skills. In fact, believe it or not, Julia (a girl in her class) is only three and she can already recognize a lot of words.
Critical episode: Maturation theory
At the start of the school year, two teachers speak about their plans for teaching their students to read during the coming school year:
Ana: You know you are right, but it is almost impossible for me to teach them to read because they still confuse their right from their left, they haven't assimilated their body schema, and they haven't got a grasp of spatial orientation yet.
Nieves: Don't get too upset about this. They set their own rhythm to follow. It isn't so straightforward; there are certain psycho-motor aspects that limit their progress, and we have to wait until they have matured a bit.

(continued)

Table 15.2. *(continued)*

Critical episode: Behaviorist theory
At the start of the school year, two teachers speak about their plans for teaching their students to read during the coming school year:
Isabel: Although it is something that we always do—correcting students right after they make a mistake when reading—making them repeat the words over and over is the best way to make sure that they learn to read correctly. And it is even better if you have them imitate you.
Elena: It's true. If you correct children when they make the mistake, they realize that they have made an error and will immediately correct it, reading the word again correctly. I think that it is a good idea to correct them and also to encourage them, applauding them when they have read well, making them feel good and encouraging them to make a greater effort.

Critical episode: Cognitive-psycholinguistic theory
At the start of the school year, two teachers speak about their plans for teaching their students to read during the coming school year:
Noelia: This year, I am going to follow the same strategies as last year for teaching my students to read since they had very good results. I will focus mainly, on an oral level, on having them recognize that sentences are made up of words, that words are made up of syllables, and that syllables are made up of phonemes. This will help them to later discover the relationship between sounds and letters.
Carolina: I also think that it is important to stimulate oral language, and that is why I will emphasize phonological segmentation of words. You know, I will give them exercises to make them more aware of the fact that words are made up of sounds while also helping them to understand why reading is important.

After reading the critical episode, participants were informed that teachers acting as the main characters in the scene were asked to convey a specific concept regarding how children learn to read and that teachers reading the scene may have different perspectives. The participants were informed that they were not being asked for their own perspectives but for the opinions of these characters regarding how children learn to read. Thus the researchers strongly suggested that prior to filling out the questionnaire, the participants attempt to put themselves in the positions of the characters from the scene and assess the degree of similarity between each verbal statement and the concept that the individual in the scene holds regarding reading acquisition in children.

Participants were next presented with three examples of how they might respond to the questionnaire. The resolved examples were presented in order to demonstrate how to score the statements as having high, intermediate, or low degrees of similarity. Each verbal statement was scored 0–10. A score of 0 meant that the phrase did not correspond at all with the ideas expressed by the characters; a score of 10 was given when the statements corresponded greatly to the previously stated ideas. Intermediate scores were given to those statements having average correspondence to the ideas. A total of 139 items were included for each critical episode.

The data obtained from the normative questionnaire were analyzed based on typicality and polarity to determine the similarity of the statements to the tenets of a specific theory, independent of the others, as well as whether or not the most typical statements of one theory were also representative of other theories.

In examining the relation that exists between typicality and polarity for each theory, the correlations between typicality and polarity were statistically significant ($r > .80$), and the greatest positive correlations were always obtained between the typicality and polarity corresponding to the same theory. The typicality and polarity analysis also revealed that some statements that are typical and characteristic of a theory do not share the assumptions of the other analyzed theories. These results corroborated the idea that the analyzed theories exist in the minds of the participants who assess whether or not the statements belong to the same theory.

Belief Level

The study of the theories and their representational function has enabled researchers to analyze the implicit theories or beliefs attributed to the teacher. Jiménez, Rodriguez, Suárez, and O'Shanahan (2014) analyzed the implicit theories or beliefs of in-service teachers regarding learning to read and determined whether these implicit theories or beliefs differed based on the cultural and geographic contexts of the teachers.

By analyzing these main theories, it was possible to identify those that were ascribed to by the teachers. It was found that many of these implicit theories or beliefs correspond to certain scientific theories that were identified in a prior study examining representational bodies of the scientific theories (i.e., nativist, behaviorist, maturational, constructivist, sociocultural, and cognitive psycholinguistic; see Jiménez et al., 2014). The study sample consisted of 591 in-service teachers from various Latin American countries (i.e., Spain, Mexico, Guatemala, Colombia, and Ecuador). They analyzed attributional structure or teacher beliefs regarding learning to read using a principal components analysis. Findings revealed that many of the teachers' implicit theories about learning to read correspond to the historiographical analysis and representational structure identified in previous studies. Significant differences were found, however, in the learning theories of the teachers as a function of geographical and cultural contexts. In addition, the theoretical approaches underlying different national curricula were not related to the teachers' implicit theories about learning to read.

In an effort to both provide high quality, evidence-based professional development and study the impact of this on teacher beliefs regarding theories of learning, the *Letra* Program was developed and tested. It is a tutorial learning system that uses the Moodle platform to create a virtual educational environment that is based on this scientific evidence (Jiménez et al., 2012). Moodle is a flexible, web-based, open-source piece of software that enabled us to provide a dynamic, interactive online means of providing this professional development training to teachers over a wide geographic area. Creation of the *Letra* Program was made possible thanks to the support of the Spanish National Plan of the Ministry of Economy and Competitiveness. It focuses on the five core components of beginning reading identified by the NRP (i.e., phonemic awareness, phonics, vocabulary, reading fluency, and reading comprehension; NICHD, 2000). In addition to scientific, research-based instructional materials tested in the Spanish language, this e-tool also includes teacher-belief and teacher-knowledge assessments.

The *Letra* Program was designed to offer teachers a model of how to teach these skills in their daily classroom practice. The multimedia design created by the authors represents a virtual library in which users see a row of books in the upper corner, which contain all of the necessary content and resources for teacher training. When users visit the first volume of the library (i.e., theoretical foundation), they will have the opportunity to browse different tutorials that will help them understand what it means for a child to attain a good level of phonological awareness, alphabetical knowledge, fluency, vocabulary, and comprehension and how to implement the RTI model. In the second volume (i.e., structure), the organization of the material is presented for intervention with the student. It includes five books for teachers and five notebooks for students.

Book I (for the teacher) is devoted to the proper instruction of letter sounds; the identification of the sound at the beginning, middle, and end of a word; instruction on the spelling of upper- and lowercase vowels; and the use of oral and written vocabulary. Books II, III, IV, and V (for the teacher) contain upper- and lowercase consonants and interconnected syllables that are structured based on various classification criteria. In addition to the articulatory modes of each of the consonants, sound–spelling transparency, the difficulty of writing, and syllable structure are also considered to achieve a learning sequence that facilitates the child's identification of the phonemes. In the third volume of the library (i.e., implementation), the user may consult both the instructional materials of the teacher and the student materials in order to work on all of the skills that should be encouraged when teaching a child how to read, including the following:

- *Phonological awareness through tasks requiring that the child manipulate phonemes:* For example, children are asked to listen closely and try to distinguish those words beginning with a given phoneme, or they are asked to lift or lower their thumb, depending on whether or not the word stated by the teacher begins with a given phoneme.
- *Phonics and alphabetic knowledge in order to strengthen the grapheme–phoneme and phoneme–grapheme correspondence:* In some activities, this requires asking the child to write the letters that the teacher says and, at the same time, pronounce the letter being written.
- *Vocabulary, to support reading fluency and comprehension:* Children are offered different topics about which they can learn new vocabulary, in both written and oral forms, with the understanding that the better their oral and

written vocabulary, the easier it will be for them to maintain a good level of fluency and comprehension.

- *Comprehension developed through the use of illustrated albums:* This type of book allows the child to access comprehension via two elements—illustrations and the mediator's voice upon reading the text, particularly if the child is unable to read them by him or herself. It is necessary for children to continue working on comprehension, along with other illustrated albums that are adapted to the ages and characteristics of the children.
- *Fluency:* Although there is also specific training on quick reading of multisyllabic words, it is understood that reading fluency is improved as all other components of reading improve.

When visiting the fourth volume of the library (i.e., evaluation), the user learns to use the evaluation materials for both the initial screening of children who are at risk for presenting difficulties in learning to read as well as the control of the students' learning progress. In the fifth volume (i.e., experiences), video recordings are presented on how to implement good teaching practices when teaching children about phonological awareness, phonics and alphabetic knowledge, fluency, vocabulary, and comprehension. In the sixth and final volume (i.e., resources), users will find a bibliography that will help them learn more about reading instruction based on empirical evidence, focusing on the predictive variables of reading success; a bibliography of educational legislation; and some related web sites of interest.

Conclusion: Effects of the *Letra* Program on Teachers' Knowledge and Teachers' Beliefs

The *Letra* Program was piloted with 697 participants: 265 Spanish preservice university students majoring in education at the University of La Laguna in the Canary Islands and 432 Spanish-speaking in-service teachers from public and private institutions in various Ibero-American countries (i.e., Mexico, Guatemala, Ecuador, and Spain; Jiménez & O'Shanahan, 2015). The in-service teachers had registered with the *Letra* online training tutorial through a research project, and the sample of preservice teachers had registered with the *Letra* Program through a language didactics course in which they were enrolled at the University of La Laguna. Findings suggest that teachers can improve their knowledge of phonemic awareness, systematic phonics instruction, fluency, vocabulary, strategies for comprehension as necessary components of quality reading instruction, and the RTI model. Upon completion of the training, effects were also found on the teachers' beliefs. We found that in-service teachers scored significantly higher on the posttest than on the pretest in the cognitive-psycholinguistic theory that was more in line with *Letra* Program. In addition, Jiménez, O'Shanahan, González, Frugone, and Barrientos (2014) analyzed the preservice students and in-service teachers' rating of the *Letra* Program.

A sample of preservice students from the Canary Islands and in-service teachers from México, Guatemala, and Ecuador who received the *Letra* Program gave positive ratings, which were not mediated by previous experiences in receiving online professional courses.

REFERENCES

Al-Yagon, M., Cornoldi, C., Cavendish, W., Fawcett, A.J., Grünke, M., Hung, L.Y., . . . Vio, C. (2013). The proposed changes for DSM-5 for SLD and ADHD: International perspectives—Australia, Germany, Greece, India, Israel, Italy, Spain, Taiwan, and the United Kingdom. *Journal of Learning Disabilities, 46,* 1, 58–72.

Boletín Oficial de Canarias. (2010a). *Decreto de 29 de julio de 2010, por el que se regula la atención a la diversidad del alumnado en el ámbito de la enseñanza no universitaria de Canarias* (BOC nº 154, de 06.08.10).

Boletín Oficial de Canarias. (2010b). *Orden de 13 de diciembre de 2010, por la que se regula la atención al alumnado con necesidades específicas de apoyo educativo en la Comunidad Autónoma de Canarias* (BOC nº 250, de 22.12.10).

Boletín Oficial de Canarias. (2011). *Resolución de 9 de febrero de 2011, por la que se dictan instrucciones sobre los procedimientos y los plazos para la atención educativa del alumnado con necesidades específicas de apoyo educativo en los centros escolares de la Comunidad Autónoma de Canarias* (BOC nº 40, de 24.2.11).

Bos, C., Mather, N., Dickson, S., Podhajski, B., & Chard, D. (2001). Perceptions and knowledge of preservice and inservice educators about early reading instruction. *Annals of Dyslexia, 51,* 97–120.

Brady, S., & Moats, L.C. (1997). Informed instruction for reading success: Foundations for teacher preparation. Spring issue. *Perspectives: A position paper of the International Dyslexia Association.* Baltimore, MD: International Dyslexia Association.

Correa, A.D., & Camacho, J. (1993). Diseño de una metodología para el estudio de las teorías implícitas. In M.J. Rodrigo, A. Rodríguez, & J. Marrero. *Las teorías implícitas. Una aproximación al conocimiento cotidiano* (pp. 123–163). Madrid, Spain: Visor.

Crespo, P., Jiménez, J.E., Rodríguez, C., Baker, D., & Park, Y. (2015). *Differences in growth reading patterns for at-risk Spanish-monolingual children as a function of a Tier 2 intervention.* Manuscript submitted for publication.

Cummings, K.D., Baker, D.L., & Good, R.H. (2006). Guía para la administración y calificación de IDEL. In D.L. Baker, R.H. Good, N. Knutson, & J.M. Watson (Eds.), *Indicadores Dinámicos del Éxito en la Lectura* (7th ed.). Eugene, OR: Dynamic Measurement Group. Retrieved from http://dibels.uoregon.edu

Cunningham, A.E., Zibulsky, J., Stanovich, K.E., & Stanovich, P.J. (2009). How teachers would spend their time teaching language arts. *Journal of Learning Disabilities, 42,* 418–430.

Dede, C., Ketelhut, D.J., Whitehouse, P., Breit, L., & McCloskey, E.M. (2014). A research agenda for online teacher professional development. *Journal of Teacher Education, 60,* 8–19.

DeWert, M.H., Babinski, L.M., & Jones, B.D. (2003). Providing support to beginning teachers. *Journal of Teacher Education, 54,* 311–320.

Education, Audiovisual, and Culture Executive Agency. (2011). *Teaching reading in Europe: Contexts, policies and practices.* Brussels, Belgium: Euridyce.

Fisher, J.B., Schumaker, J.B., Culberston, J., & Deshler, D.D. (2010). Effects of a computerized professional development program on teacher and student outcomes. *Journal of Teacher Education, 6,* 302–312.

Ho, C.S.H., Chan, D.W.O., Tsang, S.M., & Lee, S.H. (2002). *The Hong Kong Test of Specific Learning Difficulties in Reading and Writing (HKT-SpLD).* Hong Kong: Hong Kong Specific Learning Difficulties Research Team.

Jiménez, J.E., & O'Shanahan, I. (2008). Enseñanza de la lectura: De la teoría y la investigación a la práctica educativa. *Revista Iberoamericana de Educación, 45*(5), 1–22.

Jiménez, J.E., & O'Shanahan, I. (2015). *Effects of web-based training on Spanish pre-service and in-service teacher knowledge and implicit beliefs on learning to read.* Manuscript submitted for publication.

Jiménez, J.E., O'Shanahan, I., González, J.A., Frugone, M., & Barrientos, P. (2014). Pre-service students and teachers in-service rating of Letra program: A piloting experience in Latin American countries. *Estudios de Psicología, 35,* 605–624.

Jiménez, J.E., Rodríguez, C., Crespo, P., González, D., Artiles, C., & Afonso, M. (2010). Implementation of response to intervention (RTI) model in Spain: An example of a collaboration between Canarian universities and the department of education of the Canary Islands. *Psicothema, 22,* 935–942.

Jiménez, J.E., Rodríguez, C., González, D., O'Shanahan, I., Guzmán, R., Suárez, N., . . . Morales, C. (2015). Programa "LETRA": Sistema de aprendizaje tutorial para la formación del profesorado en la enseñanza de la lectura. Secretariado de Publicaciones. Universidad de La Laguna. Retrieved from http://www.programaletra.ull.es

Jiménez, J.E., Rodríguez, C., Suárez, N., & O'Shanahan, I. (2014). ¿Coinciden nuestras ideas con lo que dicen las teorías científicas sobre el aprendizaje de la lectura? *Revista Española de Pedagogía, 259,* 395–412.

Jiménez, J.E., Rodríguez, C., Suárez, N., O'Shanahan, I., Villadiego, Y., Borjas, M., . . . Rodas, P. (2015). *Teacher's implicit theories of learning to read: A cross-cultural study in Ibero-American countries.* Manuscript submitted for publication.

Joshi, R.M., Binks, E., Hougen, M., Dahlgren, M.E., Ocker-Dean, E., & Smith, D.L. (2009). Why elementary teachers might be inadequately prepared to teach reading. *Journal of Learning Disabilities, 42,* 392–402.

Marzano, R.J., Pickering, D.J., & Pollock, J.E. (2001). *Classroom instruction that works: Research-based strategies for increasing student achievement.* Alexandria, VA: Association for Supervision and Curriculum Development.

Moats, L. (2009). Still wanted: Teachers with knowledge of language. *Journal of Learning Disabilities, 42,* 387–391.

Moats, L.C., & Lyon, G.R. (1996). Wanted: Teachers with knowledge of language. *Topics in Language Disorders, 16,* 73–86.

National Institute of Child Health and Human Development (NICHD), National Reading Panel. (2000). *Teaching children to read: An evidence-based assessment of the scientific research literature on reading and its implications for reading instruction; Reports of the subgroups* (NIH Publication No. 00-4754). Retrieved from http://www.nichd.nih.gov/publications/nrp/upload/report_pdf.pdf

No Child Left Behind Act of 2001, PL 107-110, 115 Stat. 1425, 20 U.S.C. §§ 6301 *et seq.*

Research Triangle Institute International. (2009). *Early grade reading assessment toolkit* (Contract No. 7141961). Prepared for the World Bank, Office of Human Development. Research Triangle Park, NC: RTI International. Retrieved from http://pdf.usaid.gov/pdf_docs/PNADS441.pdf

Ritterband, L.M., Gonder-Frederick, L.A., Cox, D.J., Clifton, A.D., West, R.W., & Borowitz, M. (2013). Internet interventions: In review, in use, and into the future. *Professional Psychology: Research and Practice, 34,* 527–534.

Rodrigo, M. (1993). Representaciones y procesos en las teorías implícitas. In M.J. Rodrigo, A. Rodríguez, & J. Marrero (Eds.), *Las teorías implícitas: Una aproximación al conocimiento cotidiano* (pp. 95–117). Alianza Editorial: Madrid.

Tirta-Seputro, T. (1998, August). *The influence of the teacher's subject matter knowledge and beliefs on teaching practices: A case study of an Indonesian teacher teaching Graph Theory in Indonesia.* Paper presented at the 13th Annual Western Australian Institute for Educational Research Forum, University of Notre Dame, Fremantle, IN.

Tracey, D.H., & Mandel, L. (2012). *Lenses on reading: An introduction to theories and models.* London, UK: Guilford Press.

16

Struggling with Writing

The Challenges for Children with Dyslexia and Language Learning Difficulty When Learning to Write

Vincent Connelly and Julie E. Dockrell

Poor writing, like poor reading, can result from a multitude of causes. Individuals who have developmental or learning difficulties such as dyslexia or a language learning disorder (LLD), however, will often have challenges in learning to write. In this chapter, we review some recent research on the writing difficulties of children with dyslexia and LLD and consider the information available about interventions to help these children make progress in their writing.

Research on writing has lagged behind research on reading and oral language development despite many concerns about students' ability to produce written text; however, the past two decades have witnessed an increased focus on the development of children's writing processes and recognition of the specific difficulties experienced by some students.

MAPPING DEVELOPMENTAL DISORDERS TO EXPRESSIVE WRITING PROBLEMS

One potential approach to understanding written-expression difficulties is to examine the extent to which particular patterns of difficulty can be linked to specific diagnostic categories of developmental difficulties. If students with dyslexia or LLD experience unique patterns of difficulty with written expression, this would inform both models of writing development and intervention approaches. Approaches to writing difficulties that follow a diagnostic approach first identify groups of children that meet diagnostic criteria and then profile the writing difficulties experienced by these children, often in comparison to typically developing children or peers with other developmental disabilities.

This is very often seen in the reading literature and has led to some notable findings, but it is much less prevalent for writing, with notable exceptions (see Connelly, Dockrell, & Barnett, 2011).

MODELS OF WRITING DEVELOPMENT

In order to clearly understand how developmental difficulties can constrain writing development, a clear theoretical framework is necessary (Connelly & Dockrell, in press). A number of theories in this area are based on adult models of writing, so they incorporate multiple writing processes that are developed over time. For example, in Hayes and Berninger's (2014) model, the first of these processes to develop in children is usually transcription, the act of physically representing writing by hand or by keyboard, including the selection of the appropriate spelling. Translation is also a key process whereby ideas are translated into appropriate language for writing; ideas are generated through a proposer mechanism, and all of the processes are monitored by an internal evaluator mechanism. This development is influenced by other cognitive skills, including language, reading, and long-term and working memory, as well as attention. In time, a control level also develops beyond the evaluator process to incorporate planning and the application of writing schemas. Many other models of writing development are similar in structure, but there are also complex models of spelling and handwriting development that stand apart from the more general writing literature (e.g., Kandel, Peereman, Grosjacques, & Fayol, 2011).

DYSLEXIA

Dyslexia is a learning disorder characterized by a specific difficulty in learning to read and spell (see *Diagnostic and Statistical Manual of Mental Disorders, Fifth Edition* [*DSM-5*], American Psychological Association, 2013). A substantial amount of literature has shown that the majority of children with dyslexia have difficulties with the phonological aspects of reading and spelling. The coding and translation of phonological information into orthographic codes is difficult for these children (Berninger, Neilson, Abbott, Wijsman, & Raskind, 2008). Many individuals with dyslexia also have problems with the rapid naming of letters, and their working memory spans appear to be smaller, although the causes of these difficulties remain a matter of debate. Most researchers argue, however, that the difficulties faced by the majority of children with dyslexia affect their writing at the word or subword level (Berninger et al., 2008).

There is strong evidence that children with dyslexia do not progress as well as their peers in composing written language. They find it difficult to do well in timed written assessments, achieving lower levels of success than other students. Moreover, writing continues as a long-term barrier to progress, with 80% of a childhood sample with dyslexia reporting difficulty with writing and spelling in adulthood (Maughan et al., 2009). Even university students with dyslexia continue to do less well (Richardson & Wydell, 2003).

There are good reasons to hypothesize that the primary barrier to producing good writing in children with dyslexia is their poor spelling. For example, the spelling knowledge contained in their long-term memory is less fine-grained than that of their typically developing peers and takes longer to extract. When composing, this will have an impact on the transcriber, slowing down his or her writing and using up his or her cognitive resources. Spelling was found to be the strongest predictor of compositional quality from a sample of 122 nine-to-twelve-year-olds and 200 adults in a recent study in the United States (Berninger et al., 2008), and similar findings have been reported in the United Kingdom (Sumner, Connelly, & Barnett, 2013, 2014a).

Other aspects of composition will also suffer as a result of poor spelling skills. Many children with dyslexia report having to substitute words in composition with words they know they can spell; this places a demand for extra resources on the translation aspect of composition as children search for the item they can spell. As a result, children are also likely to rely on a smaller set of lexical items. Free of the constraint of spelling, children with dyslexia have been shown to produce an oral version of a narrative with no difference in lexical diversity compared with that of their same-age peers. By contrast, lexical diversity was poorer in the equivalent written version but was equivalent to children matched for spelling skills (Sumner, Connelly, & Barnett, in press). There is also further evidence that adults with dyslexia show less lexical diversity in their writing compared with that of their peers (Tops, Callens, Van Cauwenberghe, Adriaens, & Brysbaert, 2013).

More recent research has begun to focus on the process of writing by analyzing keyboard logs for students who are typing and digital writing tablets for students who are handwriting compositions. These studies have shown that children and adults with dyslexia quite literally struggle over individual words when writing. For example, when keyboarding, adults with dyslexia will often show long pauses within words and will retype the same word many times while trying to spell the word accurately (Wengelin, Johansson, & Johansson, 2014). Children with dyslexia also show longer and more frequent pauses within words when handwriting text. The lengths of these within-word pauses are predicted by spelling ability, and more of these pauses are associated with misspelling than they are in typically developing children of the same age. Children and adults with dyslexia are very slow composers, taking longer to complete a writing task despite writing much shorter texts than their peers; this extra time is almost entirely attributable to the amount of pausing during the process. The actual speed of handwriting across the page, minus the pauses, is actually no different from their same-age peers, but the amount of pausing is at the same level as that of typically developing children matched for spelling ability (Sumner et al., 2013).

The impact of poor spelling on the temporal aspects of writing is not limited to composing tasks. More than 50% of the variability in performance of children with dyslexia on a sentence copying task was predicted by spelling ability, and again the children were slower than their same-age peers but were no slower than a group of children matched for spelling ability (Sumner et al., 2014a). Thus poor spelling can limit the efficiency of the transcriber, even on copying tasks in which there are markedly fewer working memory demands.

LANGUAGE LEARNING DISORDER

In the *DSM-5*, language disorders are included under the wider spectrum of communication disorders. Practitioners, policy makers, and researchers use a range of different terms to describe LLD (Dockrell, Lindsay, Letchford, & Mackie, 2006). Children with LLD experience difficulties with both phonological and nonphonological aspects of oral language (i.e., lexicon, morphology, and syntax), although they do not necessarily experience difficulties in both of these domains, and there is considerable heterogeneity within the population (Dockrell, Lindsay, Letchford, & Mackie, 2006). As a consequence, children with LLD have significant difficulties in developing adequate literacy skills. They struggle to learn to read, to spell, and to produce written compositions. How these difficulties within the language system affect writing is currently underexplored despite clear associations between oral language skills and written text production (see Shanahan, 2006, for a review) and the fact that increased oral language facility is associated with increased written language proficiency (e.g., Silverman et al., in press).

It is not surprising then that difficulties in the production of written text have been reported for children with LLD. Texts written by children with LLD are shorter and more error prone with fewer ideas and more spelling errors than those of their typically developing peers (Broc et al., 2013; Larkin, Williams, & Blaggan, 2013) and, for some aspects of text production, than those of their language-matched peers (Mackie & Dockrell, 2004; Mackie, Dockrell, & Lindsay, 2013). It has been demonstrated that oral language measures of vocabulary and written-language assessments of spelling contribute to text production for students with LLD throughout primary and secondary school (Critten, Connelly, Dockrell, & Walter, 2014; Dockrell & Connelly, 2013; Dockrell, Lindsay, & Connelly, 2009).

Children with LLD also have difficulties with the grammatical components of language, as evidenced by grammatical errors in their writing. Studies have also reported difficulties with written syntax in children with LLD (Mackie et al., 2013). These findings would appear to provide confirmatory evidence of direct influences of specific difficulties with language on the production of written text; however, there are some problems interpreting results in this area due to interactions with spelling knowledge.

Using digital writing tablet data to capture online writing processes, it was demonstrated that children with LLD wrote sustained bursts of text that were equivalent in length to those of language ability–matched children but were significantly shorter than those of same-age peers (Connelly, Dockrell,

Walter, & Critten, 2012). Spelling competence and language level were independent predictors of the length of the bursts of text writing. The pauses between bursts in children with LLD were associated with more misspellings than those of the same-age peers, and the children with LLD paused for longer when writing. Shorter bursts of writing were associated with poorer text quality ratings. Thus, although children with LLD do have spelling difficulties that lead to similar difficulties with transcription, as with children with dyslexia, they also have problems with translation in terms of finding the appropriate language to translate their ideas into written text. Finally, due to the interaction between task demands and skill level putting heavy demands on cognitive resources, children with LLD also have problems simultaneously coordinating transcription and translation processes, and this makes writing very difficult.

INTERVENTIONS FOR CHILDREN WITH WRITING DIFFICULTIES

The children we have described in the previous section present with profiles of writing difficulties that hinder progress in writing when compared with those of their same-age peers; however, the problem for the classroom teacher is that on examining the final writing product, most of these children also will appear to be weak across most areas of assessment. Given the integrated nature of writing, this is not unexpected, but it does give rise to challenges in supporting children with potentially different profiles. Lack of clarity concerning the nature of the diagnoses of dyslexia and LLD contributes to this difficulty, as do complications arising from comorbidity across many developmental disorders. As such, diagnostic labels may provide indicative information about the difficulties students have with producing written text, but they may not be sufficient to guide general interventions. Yet children with dyslexia or LLD do not generally appear to be worse than expected at writing, given their spelling and language abilities. Therefore, interventions that are useful for typically developing children will likely also be useful for children with dyslexia and LLD. These interventions may need to be more intensive, carefully targeted, and ability appropriate (for example, see Lewis & Norwich, 2005, for a detailed taxonomy of pedagogic strategies relevant to supporting and developing interventions for children with LLD). A key to developing effective interventions is a detailed profile of each child's writing skills (Limpo & Alves, 2013).

ACCURATE FORMATIVE ASSESSMENT

To date, studies of writing development and the ways in which writing products are assessed have been relatively neglected (Miller & McCardle, 2011). Intervention to improve students' academic skills is necessarily premised on the identification of the core components, or dimensions, of the academic skill targeted for intervention. This suggests that writing assessments should encapsulate performance at the word, sentence, and text levels to capture the key dimensions of both productivity and accuracy. These assessments should be sensitive to small changes over time and involve uncomplicated scoring techniques to aid their regular and reliable administration. This will provide the educator the detailed writing profile of the learner in order to monitor progression (see Sumner, Connelly, & Barnett, 2014b).

Students need to be assessed on reliable and valid measures, and high-stakes national tests often do not provide this information (Graham, Harris, & Hebert, 2011). Therefore, formative assessment can be used especially when examining interventions to monitor change. Two basic elements are required: First, students need to be assessed over time, and second, the writing task needs to be tailored to the competencies that are being examined. In addition, wherever possible, comparisons should be made across different writing genres (Olinghouse & Wilson, 2013).

A curriculum-based measurement (CBM) approach to profiling writing may be useful here and could also provide the basis for ongoing measurement during an intervention. CBMs measure a child's academic progress through direct assessment of academic skills and have been well established for reading and numeracy. They are also argued to be a sensitive index of students' productivity and accuracy with regard to written text production and have been successfully used to examine the skills of English language learners (Campbell, Espin, & McMaster, 2013). These assessments involve students writing for short periods (between 3 and 7 minutes) in response to a probe; they have been shown to be valid and reliable measures of writing proficiency for students between 7 and 12 years of age, including those who struggle with writing (Dockrell, Connelly, Walter, & Critten, in press).

The use of CBM for writing has not gone unchallenged. There are a number of significant criticisms of the use of such measures. For example, Costa and colleagues concluded that only the CBM variables of total words written, words spelled correctly, and correct word sequences showed clear developmental trends and argued that CBM should be used in combination with other forms of assessment (Costa, Hooper, McBee, Anderson, & Yerby, 2012; Dockrell et al., in press).

SUMMATIVE ASSESSMENT AND ACCOMMODATIONS FOR SLOW SPEED

Students with writing problems are generally slow writers and are slow to improve. Therefore, accommodations, such as extra time to complete a written summative assessment, can allow these students time to proofread, revise, and edit their texts when other children with stronger skills have already completed the task. Even those individuals in the population who overcome difficulty and go on to higher education, for example, have some persisting difficulties with timed written assessments (Connelly, Campbell, MacLean, & Barnes, 2006), and adult students with dyslexia perform better on exams when given extra time (Gibson & Leinster, 2011). As noted earlier, speed is a particular long-term difficulty when both children with dyslexia and those with LLD compose written text, and even simple tasks, such as copying, take longer for children with dyslexia (Sumner et al., 2014a).

IMPROVING SPELLING AND HANDWRITING

Spelling, evidently a prime difficulty for both students with dyslexia and those with LLD, might be expected to have an impact on writing beyond the single-word level. Therefore, what can be done to improve spelling in these groups of learners? There are a number of spelling interventions that can achieve some success with children diagnosed with dyslexia and LLD (e.g., see Brookes, 2013). A recent meta-analysis by Graham and Santangelo (2014) has shown that direct and explicit instruction in spelling leads to greater gains than more implicit programs of spelling instruction and is good for all learners at all grades and at all levels of literacy skills. Six studies showed that spelling instruction focused on word-level skills leads to improved spelling within written text, with moderate to large effect sizes reported. It has been reported that effective spelling instruction should include common patterns, frequently used words, strategies for studying new words, the application of spelling knowledge (e.g., spelling by analogy), and proofreading (Graham, Harris, & Loynachan, 1996). Children with LLD up to age 11, in particular, seem to struggle with morphological spelling (Critten et al., 2014), but there have also been a number of interventions showing positive effects on morphological spelling in older children in this area (see Nunes & Bryant, 2009).

Given the assumption that difficulties in spelling may overload a vulnerable writing system, it would seem to be a reasonable assumption that improving spelling performance would free up cognitive resources for writing. Thus improving and/or automating spelling should improve writing more generally in light of cognitive resource capacity theories of writing; however, the evidence showing that improving spelling leads to wider improvements in written composition is limited. Whereas Berninger and colleagues (2002) showed some improvements in written composition in third graders who were slow learners, when explicit spelling and writing instruction were combined, the overall effect sizes were small (Graham & Santangelo, 2014). A larger effect size was gained when explicit spelling instruction was given to struggling first-grade spellers in the United States for a 16-week period. Here children showed gains in spelling words, and these gains lasted for 6 months, along with impressive gains in writing sentences after spelling instruction, although the difference in writing sentences washed out at the 6-month follow-up (Graham & Harris, 2005). A study examining the efficacy of different approaches to invented spelling in typically developing first graders found large effects of spelling instruction that generalized to writing skills, but the data were not clear for those students with poor spelling skills (Sussman, 1998). Moderately sized positive effects for writing were found in a study that attempted to improve both the spelling and writing skills of children with dyslexia in Grades 4–9, although these treatment effects could have been accounted for by the additional writing instruction (Berninger et al., 2008).

Fluent and legible handwriting is another necessary, but not sufficient, factor for developing good writing skills. There are a number of studies showing that interventions to improve the fluency of handwriting can help remove a key constraint on the development of quality composition (e.g., Berninger et al., 1997; Jones & Christensen, 1999).

TEACHING WRITING AND COMPOSITION SKILLS

Throughout recent years, Graham and his colleagues have completed a range of meta-analyses examining the ways in which writing can be successfully supported in schools (Graham & Hebert, 2010; Graham & Perin, 2007; Morphy & Graham, 2012). Many of the interventions they reviewed offer effective approaches to teaching students with writing difficulties. It is increasingly clear that the teaching of explicit writing strategies for planning, revising, and editing provides students a powerful boost in all genres of writing. Furthermore, a self-regulated strategy development approach to developing these skills is particularly effective. (For example, see Torgerson & Torgerson, 2014, for a recent randomized, controlled trial intervention achieving large effect sizes using this approach with low-achieving writers.) Setting clear product goals and explicitly teaching summarization and sentence combination also worked well (e.g., Saddler, 2012). In the classroom, carefully organized collaborative writing, structured inquiry activities, prewriting tasks, the study of writing models, and the process writing approach in general were good for children struggling with writing. Although these approaches have been shown to be successful with typically developing younger writers, teachers may find that additional and intensive scaffolding opportunities are required for students with LLD to succeed (Dockrell, Lindsay, Roulstone, & Law, 2014).

In order to implement these effective writing strategies for students with writing difficulties, teachers require a sound knowledge of the processes that underpin writing development and an understanding of the specific difficulties that will challenge students and account for periods when progress may be slow. Flexibility in approach and regular progress monitoring should be considered essential. Finally, teachers should be aware of ways in which poor spelling and handwriting can negatively affect their perceptions of the quality of written work (Meadows & Billington, 2005). This can be a potential barrier for students with writing problems in secondary and higher education when being taught by subject-specific teachers who use writing for learning within a subject area.

CONCLUSION

We are now beginning to understand the writing difficulties of children with dyslexia and LLD. On the surface, they have much in common, and teachers will note their slow speed when composing, their many spelling errors, and their generally poorer compositions when compared with those of same-age peers. Our research suggests, however, that children with dyslexia are primarily constrained by their poor spelling skills, whereas both poor spelling and poor oral language doubly affect the writing of children with LLD. The value of simple, detailed assessment that is administered regularly should not be overlooked nor should the necessity for accommodations that take into account these children's slow pace of composition writing. Interestingly, the use of spelling- and language-matched control groups indicates that writing progress is delayed to a level explained by poor spelling in the case of children with dyslexia and poor language in the case of children with LLD. This tendency toward delay rather than difference indicates that typical instructional interventions that work for all children should be useful for children with dyslexia and LLD. However, these interventions will likely have to be more intense and finely targeted with regular monitoring of small amounts of progress as well as rigorous assessments of efficacy.

In order to make further detailed progress, more interventions need to be carried out on the writing skills of children who struggle with writing. This work is needed to clarify, both theoretically and practically, the links between what is taught and what is learned in the classroom so that research can discern what is most effective and most parsimonious at different points in the development of the writing process (Dockrell & Connelly, in press). We also should consider what combinations of writing intervention practices that have already been identified work best and why. Longitudinal studies to chart progress and instruction over time will also be informative. Finally, we will want to consider the impact of instructing and intervening with new and emerging digital technologies. The development of advanced speech-to-text applications and the potential to individualize writing instruction through personalized online instruction programs based on response to intervention principles could transform the writing of children with difficulties in the near future.

REFERENCES

American Psychological Association. (2013). *Diagnostic and Statistical Manual of Mental Disorders* (5th ed.). Arlington, VA: American Psychiatric Publishing.

Berninger, V.W., Nielsen, K.H., Abbott, R.D., Wijsman, E., & Raskind, W. (2008). Writing problems in developmental dyslexia. *Journal of School Psychology, 46,* 1–21.

Berninger, V., Vaughan, K., Abbott, R., Abbott, S., Brooks, A., & Rogan, L., . . . Graham, S. (1997). Treatment of handwriting fluency problems in beginning writing: Transfer from handwriting to composition. *Journal of Educational Psychology,* 89, 652–666.

Berninger, V.W., Vaughan, K., Abbott, R.D., Begay, K., Byrd, K., Curtin, G., . . . Graham, S. (2002). Teaching spelling and composition alone and together: Implications for the simple view of writing. *Journal of Educational Psychology, 94,* 291–304.

Berninger, V.W., Winn, W.D., Stock, P., Abbott, R.D., Eschen, K., Shin-Ju, L., . . . Nagy, W. (2008). Tier 3 specialized writing instruction for students with dyslexia. *Reading and Writing,* 21, 95–129.

Broc, L., Bernicot, J., Olive, T., Favart, M., Reilly, J., Quémart, P., & Uzé, J. (2013). Lexical spelling in children and adolescents with SLI: Variations with the writing situation. *Research in Developmental disabilities, 34,* 3253–3266.

Brookes, G. (2013). *What works for children and young people with literacy difficulties* (4th ed.). London, UK: Dyslexia SPLD Trust.

Campbell, H., Espin, C.A., & McMaster, K. (2013). The technical adequacy of curriculum based writing measures with English learners. *Reading and Writing, 26,* 431–452.

Connelly, V., & Dockrell, J.E. (in press). Writing development and instruction for students with learning disabilities. In C. MacArthur, S. Graham, & J. Fitzgerald (Eds.), *Handbook of writing research* (2nd ed.). New York, NY: Guilford Press.

Connelly, V., Campbell, S., MacLean, M., & Barnes, J. (2006). Contribution of lower order skills to the written composition of college students with and without dyslexia. *Developmental Neuropsychology, 29,* 175–196.

Connelly, V., Dockrell, J.E., & Barnett, A. (2011). Children challenged by writing due to language and motor difficulties. In V. Berninger (Ed.), *Cognitive psychology of writing handbook* (pp. 217–245). New York, NY: Psychology Press.

Connelly, V., Dockrell, J.E., Walter, K., & Critten, S. (2012). Predicting the quality of composition and written language bursts from oral language, spelling and handwriting skills in children with and without SLI. *Written Communication, 29,* 278–302.

Costa, L.J.C., Hooper, S.R., McBee, M., Anderson, K.L., & Yerby, D.C. (2012). The use of CBM in young at-risk writers: Measuring change over time and potential moderators of change. *Exceptionality, 20,* 199–217.

Critten, S., Connelly, V., Dockrell, J.E., & Walter, K. (2014). Inflectional and derivational morphological spelling abilities of children with specific language impairment. *Frontiers in Psychology: Cognitive Science, 5,* 948.

Dockrell, J.E., & Connelly, V. (2013). The role of oral language in underpinning the text generation difficulties in children with specific language impairment. *Journal of Reading Research.* doi:10.1111/j.1467-9817.2012.01550.x

Dockrell, J.E., & Connelly, V. (2014). The relationships between oral and written sentence generation in English speaking children: The role of language and literacy skills. In J. Perera, M. Aparici, E. Roado, & N. Salas (Eds.), *Learning to read and write across European orthographies.* Barcelona, Spain: University of Barcelona Press.

Dockrell, J.E., Connelly, V., Walter, K., & Critten, S. (2014). Assessing children's writing products: The role of CBM. *British Journal of Research in Education.* doi:10.1002/berj.3162

Dockrell, J.E., Lindsay, G., & Connelly, V. (2009). The impact of specific language impairment on adolescents' written text. *Exceptional Children, 75,* 427–446.

Dockrell, J.E., Lindsay, G., Connelly, V., & Mackie, C. (2007). Constraints in the production of written text in children with SLI. *Exceptional Children, 73,* 147–164.

Dockrell, J.E., Lindsay, G., Letchford, B., & Mackie, C. (2006). Educational provision for children with specific speech and language difficulties: Perspectives of speech and language therapy service managers. *International Journal of Language & Communication Disorders, 41*(4), 423–440.

Dockrell, J.E., Lindsay, G., Roulstone, S. and Law, J. (2014). Supporting children with speech, language and communication needs. *International Journal of Language & Communication Disorders.* doi:10.1111/1460-6984.12089

Gibson, S., & Leinster, S.J. (2011). How do students with dyslexia perform in extended matching questions, short answer questions and observed structured examinations? *Advances in Health Science Education, 16*(3), 395–404.

Graham, S., & Harris, K.R. (2005). Improving the writing performance of young struggling writers. *The Journal of Special Education, 39,* 19–33.

Graham, S., & Hebert, M. (2010). *Writing to read: Evidence on how writing can improve reading.* Washington DC: Carnegie Trust.

Graham, S., & Perin, D. (2007). A meta-analysis of writing instruction for adolescent students. *Journal of Educational Psychology,* 99(3). 445–476.

Graham, S., & Santagelo, T. (2014). Does spelling instruction make students better spellers, readers, and writers? A meta-analytic review. *Reading and Writing: An Interdisciplinary Journal, 27,* 1703–174.

Graham, S., Harris, K., & Hebert, M. (2011). *Informing writing: The benefits of formative assessment.* Washington, DC: Alliance for Excellent Education.

Graham, S., Harris, K.R., & Loynachan, C. (1996). The directed spelling thinking activity. *Learning Disabilities Research and Practice, 11,* 34–40.

Hayes, J.R., & Berninger, V. (2014). Cognitive process in writing. In B. Arfé, J.E. Dockrell, & V.W. Berninger (Eds.), *Writing development in children with hearing loss, dyslexia or oral language problems* (pp. 3–15). New York, NY: Oxford University Press.

Jones, D., & Christensen, C. (1999). The relationship between automaticity in handwriting and ability to generate written text. *Journal of Educational Psychology, 91,* 44–49.

Kandel, S., Peereman, R., Grosjacques, G., & Fayol, M. (2011). For a psycholinguistic model of handwriting production: Testing the syllable-bigram controversy. *Journal of Experimental Psychology: Human Perception and Performance, 37*(4), 1310–1322.

Larkin, R.F., Williams, G.J., & Blaggan, S. (2013). Delay or deficit? Spelling processes in children with SLI. *Journal of Communication Disorders, 46,* 401–412.

Lewis, A., & Norwich, B. (Eds.). (2005). *Special teaching for special children? Pedagogies for inclusion.* Maidenhead, UK: Open University Press.

Limpo, T., & Alves, R.A. (2013). Modeling writing development: Contribution of transcription and self-regulation to Portuguese students' text generation quality. *Journal of Educational Psychology, 105*(2), 401–413.

Mackie, C., & Dockrell, J.E. (2004). The nature of written language deficits in children with SLI. *Journal of Speech Language and Hearing Research, 47*(6), 1469–1483.

Mackie, C., Dockrell, J.E., & Lindsay, G. (2013). An evaluation of the written texts of children with SLI. *Reading and Writing, 26,* 865–888.

Maughan, B., Messer, J., Collishaw, S., Pickles, A., Snowling, M., Yule, W., & Rutter, M. (2009). Persistence of literacy problems: Spelling in adolescence and at mid-life. *Journal of Child Psychology and Psychiatry, 50*(8), 893–901.

Meadows, M., & Billington, L. (2005). *A review of the literature on marking reliability.* Manchester, UK: Assessment and Qualifications Alliance.

Miller, B., & McCardle, P. (2011). Reflections on the need for continued research on writing. *Reading and Writing, 24*(2), 121–132.

Morphy, P., & Graham, S. (2012). Word processing programs and weaker writers/readers: A meta-analysis of research findings. *Reading and Writing, 25,* 641–678.

Nunes, T., & Bryant, P. (2009). *Children's reading and spelling: Beyond the first steps.* Chichester, UK: Wiley-Blackwell.

Olinghouse, N.G., & Wilson, J. (2013). The relationship between vocabulary and writing quality in three genres. *Reading and Writing, 26,* 45–65.

Richardson, J.T.E., & Wydell, T.N. (2003). The representation and attainment of students with dyslexia in UK higher education, *Reading and Writing, 16,* 475–503.

Saddler, B. (2012). *Teachers guide to effective sentence writing: What works for special needs learners.* New York, NY: Guilford Press.

Shanahan, T. (2006). Relations among oral language, reading and writing development. In C. MacArthur, S. Graham, & J. Fitzgerald (Eds.), *Handbook of writing research* (pp. 171–183). New York, NY: Guilford Press.

Silverman, R.D., Coker, D.L., Proctor, P.C., Harring, J.R., Piantedosi, K., & Meyer, A.G. (in press). The relationship between language skills and writing outcomes for linguistically diverse students in upper elementary school. *Elementary School Journal.*

Sumner, E., Connelly, V., & Barnett, A. (2014a). The influence of spelling ability on handwriting production: Children with and without dyslexia. *Journal of Experimental Psychology: Learning Memory and Cognition, 40*(5), 1441–1447.

Sumner, E., Connelly, V., & Barnett, A. (2014b). Dyslexia and expressive writing in English. In B. Arfe, J.E. Dockrell, & V.W. Berninger (Eds.), *Writing development and instruction in children with hearing, speech, and oral language difficulties* (pp. 188–200). Oxford, UK: Oxford University Press.

Sumner, E., Connelly, V., & Barnett, A. (2014). The influence of spelling ability on written vocabulary choices for children with dyslexia. *Journal of Learning Disabilities.* doi: 10.1177/0022219414552018

Sussman, G.L. (1998). *The effects of phonological constructed spelling on first graders' literacy development* (Unpublished doctoral dissertation). Fordham University, New York.

Tops, W., Callens, M., Van Cauwenberghe, E., Adriaens, J., & Brysbaert, M. (2013). Beyond spelling: The writing skills of students with dyslexia in higher education. *Reading and Writing, 26,* 705–720.

Torgerson, D., & Torgerson, C. (2014). *Improving writing quality: Evaluation report and executive summary.* London, UK: Educational Endowment Foundation.

Wengelin, Å., Johansson, R., & Johansson, V. (2014). Expressive writing in Swedish 15-year-olds with reading and writing difficulties. In Arfé, B., Dockrell, J., & Berninger, V. (Eds.), *Writing development and instruction in children with hearing, speech and oral language difficulties* (pp. 244–256). Oxford, UK: Oxford University Press.

17

Fostering the Capabilities that Build Writing Achievement

Rui A. Alves and Teresa Limpo[1]

Literacy is a special capability that includes competence with a written language; this implies mastering reading and writing and skillfully using a wealth of written documents. Literacy is an important skill in many present-day complex societies (Olson, 1999). In fact, it adds a new layer of complexity to human societies and, by itself, creates a new world to be inhabited, navigated, and acted upon (Bazerman, 2013). As noted by Olson, in such societies, "archival texts play a central authoritative role" (2000, p. 60), which is managed by literate elites. This emphasizes the importance of writing as a key part of literacy and underlines the importance of its instruction.

Sen describes capability as "a kind of freedom: the substantive freedom to achieve alternative functioning combinations (or, less formally put, the freedom to achieve various lifestyles)" (1999, p. 75). Functioning is the active realization of capabilities: the things people value doing or being. Nussbaum further clarified that capabilities do not reside in individuals but encompass the "freedoms and opportunities created by a combination of personal abilities and the political, social, and economic environment" (2011, p. 20). In this sense, literacy is truly a capability, as it depends critically on the existence of a literate culture that teaches (or does not teach) people to read, write, and use documents. No individual learns to read and write without a teacher and a script.

Literacy is special because it allows for the creation of a multitude of other capabilities or richer and more in-depth capabilities (Wolff & de Shalit, 2007). For instance, in modern societies, literacy opens the doors to full participation in institutions and is critical for human and societal development. It is

1. The study reported in this chapter was supported by the Portuguese Foundation for Science and Technology (grant FCT PTDC/PSI-PCO/110708/2009) and benefited from the emerging COST Action IS1401/European Literacy Network.

no wonder then that a report from the European Union High Level Group of Experts on Literacy celebrated literacy as

> a crucial life competence which empowers the individual citizen to develop capacities of reflection, oral expression, critical thinking and empathy, boosting personal development, self-confidence, a sense of identity and full participation in a digital and knowledge economy and society. (2012, p. 21)

Even if this statement lacks definitive scientific evidence, it speaks to the valuable role and aspirations that societies ascribe to literacy—to texts and the capabilities required to effectively produce and understand them.

Producing an effective text is a paramount literacy skill, which, as we noted earlier, can be hugely consequential but has traditionally been seen as too complex to research, too difficult to teach, and too effortful to master. This has meant that writing research, writing instruction, and writing achievement typically lagged behind reading research, instruction, and achievement principally because they have been viewed as more difficult problems to tackle within the literacy domain. Fortunately, in the last 30 years, research on writing has been met with considerable progress (Bazerman, 2008; Beard, Myhill, Riley, & Nystrand, 2009; Berninger, 2012; MacArthur, Graham, & Fitzgerald, 2006), evidence has been accumulating on how to inform effective writing instruction (Graham & Hebert, 2010; Graham, McKeown, Kiuhara, & Harris, 2012; Graham & Perin, 2007a, 2007b), and the sources of writing achievement are beginning to be understood (Berninger & Abbott, 2010; Graham, Berninger, Abbott, Abbott, & Whitaker, 1997; Limpo & Alves, 2013a). In this review, we briefly highlight the relevant research trends, and from our research effort, we focus on four capabilities that may build writing skill. This list of critical ingredients to writing achievement is not new and it should seem like common sense to researchers and practitioners alike. Still, what might be considered new is the conceptualization of these ingredients as substantive freedoms with which writers can perform successfully in a literate world. Specifically, we adopt a developmental stance through which we look at motivation, language skill, transcription, and self-regulation as the key capabilities that need to be fostered for effective writing to be achieved.

MOTIVATION TO WRITE

Motivation to write is probably not different from motivation to perform other deeds. Still, we would argue that it is more fragile than other drives. At least four things account for the fragility of motivation to write: Writing is complex, it requires great effort, it is unpredictable, and it is social.

The cognitive approach to writing has exposed the very complex and demanding nature of writing (Hayes, 1996; Kellogg, 1994). Writing builds on many cognitive processes. A famous synthesis by Hayes and Flower (1980, 1986) emphasizes three of the many complex cognitive processes on which writing builds: planning, translating, and revising. Each one of these processes comprises an array of subprocesses that operate recursively throughout composition. Moreover, most of them operate necessarily under the constraints of limited working memory capacity and in interaction with long-term memory, motivational aspects, and the social and physical elements of the writing environment (Hayes, 1996). Characteristically, most of the generative processes in writing need to resist automatization if writing mastery is to be achieved (McCutchen, 1988; Torrance & Jeffery, 1999). Writing does not get easier with expertise. In fact, as Bereiter and Scardamalia (1987) noted, it seems to be the other way around, with higher levels of ability pushing the individual to deal with tougher problems. This highlights the inherently effortful nature of writing skill development and, consequently, the need for sustained motivation over extensive periods of practice.

Engaging in writing implies the will to expend considerable amounts of energy, of the impetus to strive toward uncertain results and rewards. For most writers, the final text is not entirely predictable from the initial ideas a writer might have about it (Rau & Sebrechts, 1996); many writers ascribe to notions of "discovery through writing" (Galbraith, 2009). Usually, from plan to text, the initial idea of the text expands considerably (Kaufer, Hayes, & Flower, 1986), so that the final text is crafted rather than dictated in perfect form from the muse. Writing is hard work toward an uncertain end product. Even if the constructive, craft-like nature of writing can be a source of apparent isolation, writing is inherently social, as it implies a reader, an audience, and a response. In writing, reward from the audience is hardly guaranteed and usually is quite removed in time from the writing itself. Reward is neither certain nor predictable. This stands for both the child writing to her parents and the world-class novelist. Thus writing is risky business.

Such risk calls for great care in handling emerging writing skills. Specifically, establishing a positively charged, well-scaffolded, affective environment wherein writing skills can be nurtured and adequately challenged might be a prime undertaking for those interested in fostering writing achievement. Positive affect and valuing writing can start in the family. Based on this set of ideas, Camacho and Alves (2014) devised an intervention to foster parents' involvement in writing. Parents of second graders were invited to take part in a discussion group as part of their engagement with the school; some parents were immediately enrolled in the group, and others were assigned to a waiting list (control group). Before and after running the parent intervention group, all children performed a set of tasks that included a narrative text composition. Over a period of 10 weeks, the parents met four times with an educational psychologist who facilitated group dynamics. The group met for hourly sessions, typically after a day's work. In the first session, the group discussed the importance of parental involvement in schoolwork and the benefits of praising a child's effort as opposed to praising his or her ability (see Dweck, 2006). During the intervention period, the schoolteacher asked all children to write four stories as homework. The children whose parents were in the discussion group performed those homework compositions in interaction with their parents.

During the second meeting of the group, the psychologist trained the parents to use the homework assignment as a basis for a specific parent–child interaction about writing. The interaction started with the child writing the story alone and then showing it to his or her parent. The parent read the story aloud and, immediately afterward, praised one of three features (i.e., handwriting, spelling, or text quality) and gave the child two suggestions for improving the text. (One fix was to "write a little more"; another was selected from among the features of handwriting, spelling, or quality.) Then the child and parent rewrote a final version of the story, which the child read aloud, followed by final praise from the parent. After training on the use of this interaction sequence and its written record, the parent group meeting ended with an individual expressive writing assignment (for a description, see Wilson, 2011).

In the third session, the group reviewed the child–parent interactions that had already occurred and discussed ways to further nurture writing motivation. In the last session, the group reflected on and evaluated the program. Finally, some of the stories written over the 10-week period were shared among parents and read aloud. After the parent training had ended, all children participating in the study were asked to write a story responding to a written prompt, and all texts were blindly evaluated by two independent judges. The texts collected at posttest from the children whose parents attended the discussion group were of better quality than those of the children whose parents had been assigned to the waiting list. This preliminary result is important, as it shows that positive interactions about text production might feed into children's ability to write better stories and, critically, might drive a positive, self-reinforcing cycle through which children can motivate themselves to write, spend effort, practice, improve their writing, and be rewarded by their achievements.

Another critical element that can fuel this positive reinforcement cycle is the beliefs of parents, teachers, and students about the nature of writing. Dweck and collaborators have extensively shown that from an early age humans tend to adopt one of two beliefs about intelligence (for reviews, see Dweck, 1999, 2006): that it is a fixed entity that cannot be changed or that it is incremental and can be cultivated through practice and effort. These beliefs are consequential in academic achievement, wherein they are at the foundation of distinct motivational frameworks of goals (i.e., performance goals versus learning goals) and learning patterns (i.e., helplessness versus mastery orientation). Limpo and Alves (2014) reasoned that analogous beliefs might hold true with regard to writing skill—that is, some children might view writing ability as fixed, others as incremental. To test this hypothesis, they developed the Implicit Theories of Writing Scale and used it to evaluate the beliefs of 192 children. The children participated in planning instruction based on either the Self-Regulated

Strategy Development (SRSD) model (Harris & Graham, 1996, 2009) or standard Portuguese writing instruction. Although the SRSD group outperformed the standard instruction group in several writing measures, Limpo and Alves also found that the students who held an incremental view of writing skill were those who showed the greatest increase in text quality. This result is important, as it clearly shows that a motivational element mediates the response to this writing intervention. Those providing writing instruction need to have a better grasp of the many motivational aspects that can co-occur with writing and that might show similar effects. This will surely come as research advances in this area, which, to a great extent, remains unexplored (Alves, 2012; Boscolo & Hidi, 2007; Troia, Shankland, & Wolbers, 2012).

LANGUAGE ABILITY IN WRITING

Clearly, writing is a linguistic activity and a unique one, we would argue, as its main, distinctive feature might be to bring language into consciousness (Olson, 1994). Writing shares several components with spoken language (Grabowski, 1996), and speech is a natural foundation of writing skill. Berninger (2000) suggested that language is not a unitary system but the developmental overlap of four independent language systems (i.e., language by ear, mouth, eye, and hand), each with its own developmental trajectory. What might be particular to writing is that it allows for the explicit distinction and representation of different language levels (i.e., sublexical, lexical, syntactic, and discourse), which seem to require independent skill learning. Berninger and collaborators have consistently found not only that individuals differ in their abilities to produce language across levels (Abbott & Berninger, 1993) but also that children Grades 4–6 show intraindividual differences in their ability to produce language at distinct levels—that is, a child's ability to produce words does not generally predict his or her skill to produce at the sentence level or paragraph level, nor does his or her competence at the sentence level predict his or her competence at the paragraph level (Berninger, Mizokawa, Bragg, & Cartwright, 1994; Whitaker, Berninger, Johnston, & Swanson, 1994). These findings clearly point to a need to address distinct language levels when designing and delivering writing interventions to children.

One level that many assume to be critical in fostering writing skill is that of the sentence level (Landon, 2013). Specifically, a proven instructional method that enhances syntactic complexity and overall compositional quality is sentence combining (Saddler, 2007; Saddler & Graham, 2005; Strong, 1986). Through sentence combining, a novice writer learns that two basic, somewhat repetitive sentences can be combined into a single, sophisticated sentence that expresses the writer's message more efficiently and is also more appealing to the reader. Limpo and Alves (2013b) have coupled sentence-combining instruction with self-regulation procedures derived from the SRSD model (Harris & Graham, 1996, 2009) and compared its effectiveness with that of a practice control group and with that of a planning strategy instruction group that was also coupled with SRSD. Whereas both intervention groups outperformed the control group in most measures (e.g., critically in opinion essay quality), both showed specific effects at different language levels. Specifically, stronger effects for sentence combining were found at the word (e.g., vocabulary diversity) and sentence (e.g., syntactic complexity) levels, and effects for planning were stronger at the discourse level (e.g., presence and elaboration of functional essay elements). These results highlight the importance of designing writing interventions tailored to cover and integrate specific levels of language. Thus oral language skills, verbal reasoning, vocabulary, reading, reading comprehension, sentence construction, grammar, and genre knowledge all seem to be important elements in a literacy-rich environment that ought to nurture language ability in all learners.

TRANSCRIPTION IN WRITING

Transcription is a defining and necessary condition of writing. Writing is typically characterized by the permanence and visibility that language achieves when it is inscribed on a surface. Cognitive models usually distinguish between two main processes in transcription: spelling retrieval and programming of the fine finger movements required to make language visible. Both are necessarily intertwined as learners master transcription (Berninger & Swanson, 1994; Jones & Christensen, 1999). In contrast to the more creative aspects of writing, such as capturing ideas in text, which require conscious attention and mindfulness, transcription is highly automatic in more proficient writing. In behavioral observations of writers producing texts, it was also noted that transcription does not proceed continuously from start to finish (Kaufer et al., 1986); instead, it proceeds through a series of fast-paced bursts of transcription activity interspersed by long pauses (typically well above 2 seconds each). A common result is that adult writers who are composing spend about half of their on-task time pausing (Alves, Castro, Sousa, & Strömqvist, 2007; Strömqvist & Ahlsén, 1999). Kaufer et al. (1986) compared the average burst length of professional writers with that of college students. They found that the professionals had longer bursts than students (11 versus 7 words per burst, respectively) and argued that differences in language skill between expert and novice writers accounted for that difference.

More recent studies support the contention that language skill is a key source of bursts (Hayes & Chenoweth, 2007) but also point to the critical role of transcription skill in determining burst length (Alves, 2013). Chenoweth and Hayes (2001) found that writers composed more fluently and had longer bursts in their first language than in their second language. In a subsequent study (Chenoweth & Hayes, 2003), they also showed that bursts of language are kept online in verbal working memory, as articulatory suppression clearly reduced burst length by 34% (from about 12 to about 8 words per burst). Alves et al. (2007), who also studied adult writers, argued that transcription skill played a role in determining burst length. They compared high- against low-skilled typists and found that the former had longer bursts. In a subsequent experimental study, Alves (2013) manipulated transcription modality (handwriting versus typing) and transcription skill (high versus low). As expected, he found that hampering transcription skill in both modalities (writers composed with either an uppercase script or a scrambled keyboard, in which the letter positions on the keyboard are rearranged from the standard positions) had a detrimental impact on burst length.

The role of language and transcription in determining burst length was further confirmed by a series of studies with school-age children. Connelly, Dockrell, Walter, and Critten (2012) studied bursts in children with specific language impairment (SLI) as compared with two groups, matched with the SLI children for chronological age (10 years old) and language ability (8 years old). They found that SLI children had shorter bursts than their age-matched peers but had similar burst lengths to language-matched controls. Alves, Branco, Castro, and Olive (2012) found that fourth graders (9 years old) with high handwriting skill composed with longer bursts than children with low or average handwriting skill. Alves and Limpo (2014) tracked the development of bursts from Grades 2 to 7, and as expected for their incremental skills in language and transcription, burst length increased steadily from grade to grade. Bursts increased from about two words per burst in Grade 2 to about six words per burst in Grade 7. Alves et al. (2014) conducted a randomized, controlled intervention study in which three groups of second graders received 20 hours of training in handwriting, spelling, or keyboarding. Even though all groups showed increases in their trained skill, only the handwriting group showed a noticeable increase in burst length, text length, and text quality. This result shows that children's handwriting, but not spelling, ability is causally related to burst length. Taken together, these results conform well to the known foundational role that transcription plays in writing development (for a review see, Graham & Harris, 2000).

SELF-REGULATION IN WRITING

Writing is so utterly complex that it seems to require regulation. There is compelling evidence that, to a great extent, a writer's expertise relies on his or her capability to strategically regulate his or her environment, behavior, and self (Zimmerman & Risemberg, 1997). Teaching self-regulation strategies to novice writers is among the most powerful aids that one can offer them to improve their writing (Graham & Perin, 2007a; Graham et al., 2012; Harris, Graham, Mason, & Friedlander, 2008). Particularly, self-regulation interventions targeting cognitive processes such as planning or revising appear to be important to improve writing skill and, over time, to build a sense of self-efficacy in writing. Still, for child writers, it is unlikely that self-efficacy can be derived from planning or revising because these are activities in which children seldom engage (Limpo, Alves, & Fidalgo, 2014) unless explicitly taught, and self-efficacy's metacognitive nature makes difficult its observation and awareness. It is more likely that the visibility of transcription skills makes them a likelier prime source of self-efficacy in writing.

To test this and the well-accepted notion that transcription automaticity frees cognitive resources that can then be used by other cognitive processes (Bourdin & Fayol, 1994; Fayol, 1999; Kellogg, 1996; McCutchen, 1996; Olive & Kellogg, 2002), Limpo and Alves (2013a) assessed 376 children, Grades 4–9, with a comprehensive set of transcription, planning, revision, self-efficacy, and text-generation measures. They used multiple-group structural equation modeling to test the contribution of transcription and self-regulation to writing quality over two developmental periods (Grades 4–6 and Grades 7–9). Figure 17.1 summarizes their main findings.

Limpo and Alves found that in the early grades, transcription contributed to planning, revision, and self-efficacy and had a direct effect on text quality. Transcription was actually the sole contributor to text quality in that age group. Interestingly, in the older grades, the path from transcription to text quality became nonsignificant, but transcription showed indirect effects on text quality through both planning and self-efficacy. These results are important because they corroborate a foundational role for transcription skill in setting the stage for both cognitive processes (e.g., planning and revision) and motivational elements (e.g., self-efficacy) that are critical for skill improvement and persistence, respectively.

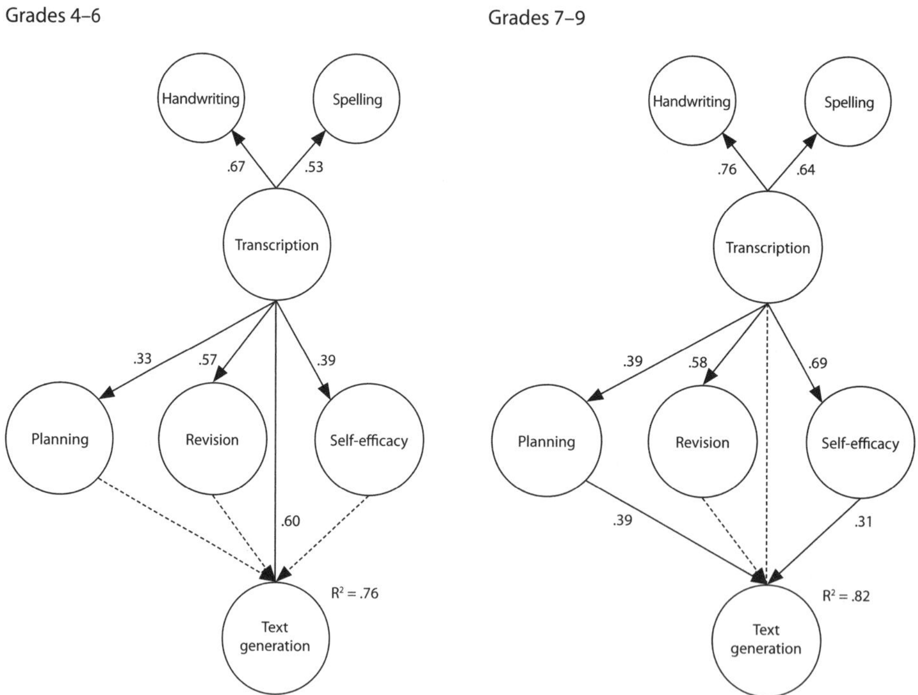

Figure 17.1. Structural models of the relationship among transcription, planning, revision, self-efficacy, and text generation in Grades 4–6 (left) and in Grades 7–9 (right). Dashed lines represent nonsignificant paths.

CONCLUSION

These are positive and optimistic times for literacy research (Alves, 2012), as the field moves toward cross-disciplinary integration of the traditional research topics of writing, reading, and oral language (Miller & McCardle, 2011), and several key ingredients that promote literacy achievement are now empirically well documented. In this chapter, we highlighted four capabilities that we propose are the foundational blocks of writing achievement: motivation to write, transcription skills, language ability, and self-regulation. These foundations might be thought of as substantive freedoms through which humans can exert their choices and move toward mastering literacy skills. To the extent that this happens, we should see human and societal developments and greater life success for all students.

REFERENCES

Abbott, R.D., & Berninger, V.W. (1993). Structural equation modeling of relationships among developmental skills and writing skills in primary- and intermediate-grade writers. *Journal of Educational Psychology, 85*, 478–508. doi:10.1037/0022-0663.85.3.478

Alves, R.A. (2012). The future is bright for writing research. In V.W. Berninger (Ed.), *Past, present, and future contributions of cognitive writing research to cognitive psychology* (pp. 593–599). New York, NY: Psychology Press.

Alves, R.A. (2013). *A mente enquanto escreve: A automatização da execução motora na composição escrita [The mind while writing: The automatization of motor execution in written composition].* Lisboa, Portugal: Fundação Calouste Gulbenkian.

Alves, R.A., & Limpo, T. (2014). *Development of bursts of written language: Their reliance on transcription and contribution to writing performance.* Manuscript under review.

Alves, R.A., Branco, M., Castro, S.L., & Olive, T. (2012). Effects of handwriting skill, handwriting and dictation modes, and gender of fourth graders on pauses, written language bursts, fluency, and quality. In V.W. Berninger (Ed.), *Past, present, and future contributions of cognitive writing research to cognitive psychology* (pp. 389–402). New York, NY: Psychology Press.

Alves, R.A., Castro, S.L., Sousa, L., & Strömqvist, S. (2007). Influency of typing skill on pause-execution cycles in written composition. In M. Torrance, L. van Waes, & D. Galbraith (Eds.), *Writing and cognition: Research and applications* (pp. 55–65). Amsterdam: Elsevier.

Alves, R.A., Limpo, T., Fidalgo, R., Carvalhais, L., Pereira, L.A., & Castro, S.L. (2014). *The impact of promoting transcription on early text production: Effects on bursts and pauses, levels of written language, and writing performance.* Manuscript submitted for publication.

Bazerman, C. (Ed.). (2008). *Handbook of research on writing: History, society, school, individual, text.* Mahwah, NJ: Lawrence Erlbaum Associates.

Bazerman, C. (2013). *A theory of literate action: Literate action* (Vol. 2). Anderson, SC: Parlor Press and WAC Clearinghouse.

Beard, R., Myhill, D., Riley, J., & Nystrand, N. (Eds.). (2009). *The SAGE handbook of writing development* (pp. 65–79). London, UK: Sage Publications.

Bereiter, C., & Scardamalia, M. (1987). *The psychology of written composition.* Mahwah, NJ: Lawrence Erlbaum Associates.

Berninger, V.W. (2000). Development of language by hand and its connections with language by ear, mouth, and eye. *Topics in Language Disorders, 20*, 65–84.

Berninger, V.W. (Ed.). (2012). *Past, present, and future contributions of cognitive writing research to cognitive psychology.* New York, NY: Psychology Press.

Berninger, V.W., & Abbott, R.D. (2010). Listening comprehension, oral expression, reading comprehension, and written expression: Related yet unique language systems in grades 1, 3, 5, and 7. *Journal of Educational Psychology, 102*, 635–651. doi:10.1037/a0019319

Berninger, V.W., & Swanson, H.L. (1994). Modifying Hayes and Flower's model of skilled writing to explain beginning and developing writing. In E.C. Butterfield (Ed.), *Children's writing: Toward a process theory of the development of skilled writing* (Vol. 2, pp. 57–81). Greenwich, CT: JAI Press.

Berninger, V.W., Mizokawa, D.T., Bragg, R., & Cartwright, A.C. (1994). Intraindividual differences in levels of written language. *Reading & Writing Quarterly: Overcoming Learning Difficulties, 10,* 259–275.

Boscolo, P., & Hidi, S. (2007). The multiple meanings of motivation to write. In S. Hidi & P. Boscolo (Eds.), *Writing and motivation* (pp. 1–14). Amsterdam: Elsevier.

Bourdin, B., & Fayol, M. (1994). Is written language production more difficult than oral language production? A working memory approach. *International Journal of Psychology, 29,* 591–620.

Camacho, A., & Alves, R.A. (2014, February). *Fostering parent involvement in writing: Development and empirical test of an intervention program for parents.* Paper presented at the 7th Meeting of the Young Researchers at University of Porto, Porto, Portugal.

Chenoweth, N.A., & Hayes, J.R. (2001). Fluency in writing: Generating text in L1 and L2. *Written Communication, 18,* 80–98. doi:10.1177/0741088301018001004

Chenoweth, N.A., & Hayes, J.R. (2003). The inner voice in writing. *Written Communication, 20,* 99–118. doi:10.1177/0741088303253572

Connelly, V., Dockrell, J.E., Walter, K., & Critten, S. (2012). Predicting the quality of composition and written language bursts from oral language, spelling, and handwriting skills in children with and without Specific Language Impairment. *Written Communication, 29,* 278–302. doi:10.1177/0741088312451109

Dweck, C. (1999). *Self-theories: Their role in motivation, personality and development.* Philadelphia: Psychology Press.

Dweck, C. (2006). *Mindset: The new psychology of success.* New York, NY: Random House.

EU High Level Group of Experts on Literacy. (2012). *Final report.* Luxembourg, Luxembourg: Publications Office of the European Union.

Fayol, M. (1999). From on-line management problems to strategies in written composition. In M. Torrance & G. Jeffery (Eds.), *The cognitive demands of writing: Processing capacity and working memory effects in text production* (pp. 13–23). Amsterdam: Amsterdam University Press.

Galbraith, D. (2009). Writing as discovery. *British Journal of Educational Psychology Monograph Series, 2*(6), 5–26. doi:10.1348/978185409X421129

Grabowski, J. (1996). Writing and speaking: Common grounds and differences toward a regulation theory of written language production. In C.M. Levy & S. Ransdell (Eds.), *The science of writing: Theories, methods, individual differences, and applications* (pp. 73–91). Mahwah, NJ: Lawrence Erlbaum Associates.

Graham, S., & Harris, K.R. (2000). The role of self-regulation and transcription skills in writing and writing development. *Educational Psychologist, 35,* 3–12.

Graham, S., & Hebert, M. (2011). Writing to read: A meta-analysis of the impact of writing and writing instruction on reading. *Harvard Educational Review, 81,* 710–744.

Graham, S., & Perin, D. (2007a). A meta-analysis of writing instruction for adolescent students. *Journal of Educational Psychology, 99,* 445–476. doi:10.1037/0022-0663.99.3.445

Graham, S., & Perin, D. (2007b). What we know, what we still need to know: Teaching adolescents to write. *Scientific Studies of Reading, 11,* 313–335.

Graham, S., Berninger, V.W., Abbott, R.D., Abbott, S.P., & Whitaker, D. (1997). Role of mechanics in composing of elementary school students: A new methodological approach. *Journal of Educational Psychology, 89,* 170–182. doi:10.1037/0022-0663.89.1.170

Graham, S., McKeown, D., Kiuhara, S., & Harris, K.R. (2012). A meta-analysis of writing instruction for students in the elementary grades. *Journal of Educational Psychology, 104,* 879–896. doi:10.1037/a0029185

Harris, K.R., & Graham, S. (1996). *Making the writing process work: Strategies for composition and self-regulation* (2nd ed.). Cambridge, MA: Brookline Books.

Harris, K.R., & Graham, S. (2009). Self-regulated strategy development in writing: Premises, evolution, and the future. *British Journal of Educational Psychology Monograph Series, 2*(6), 113–135. doi:10.1348/978185409X422542

Harris, K.R., Graham, S., Mason, L.H., & Friedlander, B. (2008). *Powerful writing strategies for all students.* Baltimore, MD: Paul H. Brookes Publishing Co.

Hayes, J.R. (1996). A new framework for understanding cognition and affect in writing. In C.M. Levy & S. Ransdell (Eds.), *The science of writing: Theories, methods, individual differences, and applications* (pp. 1–27). Mahwah, NJ: Lawrence Erlbaum Associates.

Hayes, J.R., & Chenoweth, N.A. (2007). Working memory in an editing task. *Written Communication, 24,* 283–294. doi:10.1177/0741088307304826

Hayes, J.R., & Flower, L. (1980). Identifying the organization of writing processes. In L.W. Gregg & E.R. Steinberg (Eds.), *Cognitive processes in writing* (pp. 3–29). Mahwah, NJ: Lawrence Erlbaum Associates.

Hayes, J.R., & Flower, L. (1986). Writing research and the writer. *American Psychologist, 41,* 1106–1113. doi:10.1037/0003-066X.41.10.1106

Jones, D., & Christensen, C.A. (1999). Relationship between automaticity in handwriting and students' ability to generate written text. *Journal of Educational Psychology, 91,* 44–49. doi:10.1037//0022-0663.91.1.44

Kaufer, D.S., Hayes, J.R., & Flower, L. (1986). Composing written sentences. *Research in the Teaching of English, 20,* 121–140.

Kellogg, R.T. (1994). *The psychology of writing.* Oxford, UK: Oxford University Press.

Kellogg, R.T. (1996). A model of working memory in writing. In C.M. Levy & S. Ransdell (Eds.), *The science of writing* (pp. 57–71). Mahwah, NJ: Lawrence Erlbaum Associates.

Landon, B. (2013). *Building great sentences: How to write the sentences you love to read.* New York, NY: Plume.

Limpo, T., & Alves, R.A. (2013a). Modeling writing development: Contribution of transcription and self-regulation to Portuguese students' text generation quality. *Journal of Educational Psychology, 105,* 401–413. doi:10.1037/a0031391

Limpo, T., & Alves, R.A. (2013b). Teaching planning or sentence-combining strategies: Effective SRSD interventions at different levels of written composition. *Contemporary Educational Psychology, 38,* 328–341. doi:10.1016/j.cedpsych.2013.07.004

Limpo, T., & Alves, R.A. (2014). Implicit theories of writing and their impact on students' response to a SRSD intervention. *British Journal of Educational Psychology.* Advance online publication. doi:10.1111/bjep.12042

Limpo, T., Alves, R.A., & Fidalgo, R. (2014). Children's high-level writing skills: Development of planning and revising and their contribution to writing quality. *British Journal of Educational Psychology, 84,* 177–193. doi:10.1111/bjep.12020

MacArthur, C.A., Graham, S., & Fitzgerald, J. (Eds.). (2006). *Handbook of writing research.* New York, NY: Guilford Press.

McCutchen, D. (1988). "Functional automaticity" in children's writing: A problem of metacognitive control. *Written Communication, 5,* 306–324.

McCutchen, D. (1996). A capacity theory of writing: Working memory in composition. *Educational Psychology Review, 8,* 299–325. doi:10.1007/BF01464076

Miller, B., & McCardle, P. (2011). Reflections on the need for continued research on writing. *Reading & Writing, 2,* 121–132. doi:10.1007/s11145-010-9267-6

Nussbaum, M.C. (2011). *Creating capabilities: The Human Development approach.* Cambridge, MA: Harvard University Press.

Olive, T., & Kellogg, R.T. (2002). Concurrent activation of high- and low-level production processes in written composition. *Memory & Cognition, 30,* 594–600. doi:10.3758/BF03194960

Olson, D.R. (1994). *The world on paper: The conceptual and cognitive implications of writing and reading.* Cambridge, UK: Cambridge University Press.

Olson, D.R. (1999). Literacy. In R.A. Wilson & F.C. Keil (Eds.), *The MIT encyclopedia of the cognitive sciences* (pp. 481–482). Cambridge, MA: MIT Press.

Olson, D.R. (2000). Literacy. In A.E. Kasdin (Ed.), *Encyclopedia of psychology* (pp. 60–63). New York, NY: Oxford University Press.

Rau, P.S., & Sebrechts, M.M. (1996). How initial plans mediate the expansion and resolution of options in writing. *The Quarterly Journal of Experimental Psychology, 49A,* 616–638.

Saddler, B. (2007). Improving sentence construction skills through sentence-combining practice. In S. Graham, C.A. MacArthur, & J. Fitzgerald (Eds.), *Best practices in writing instruction.* New York, NY: Guilford Press.

Saddler, B., & Graham, S. (2005). The effects of peer-assisted sentence-combining instruction on the writing performance of more and less skilled young writers. *Journal of Educational Psychology, 97,* 43–54.

Sen, A. (1999). *Development as freedom.* Oxford, UK: Oxford University Press.

Strömqvist, S., & Ahlsén, E. (Eds.). (1999). *The process of writing: A progress report* (Gothenburg Papers in Theoretical Linguistics No. 83). Gothenburg, Sweden: University of Göteborg, Department of Linguistics.

Strong, W. (1986). *Creative approaches to sentence combining.* Urbana, IL: ERIC Clearinghouse on Reading and Communication Skills and the National Council of Teachers of English.

Torrance, M., & Jeffery, G. (1999). Writing processes and cognitive demands. In M. Torrance & G. Jeffery (Eds.), *The cognitive demands of writing: Processing capacity and working memory effects in text production* (pp. 1–11). Amsterdam: Amsterdam University Press.

Troia, G.A., Shankland, R.K., & Wolbers, K.A. (2012). Motivation research in writing: Theoretical and empirical considerations. *Reading & Writing Quarterly, 28,* 5–28. doi:10.1080/10573569.2012.632729

Whitaker, D., Berninger, V.W., Johnston, J., & Swanson, H.L. (1994). Intraindividual differences in levels of language in intermediate grade writers: Implications for the translating process. *Learning and Individual Differences, 6,* 107–130.

Wilson, T. (2011). *Redirect: The surprising new science of psychological change.* London, UK: Allen Lane.

Wolff, J., & de Shalit, A. (2007). *Disadvantage.* Oxford, UK: Oxford University Press.

Zimmerman, B.J., & Risemberg, R. (1997). Becoming a self-regulated writer: A social cognitive perspective. *Contemporary Educational Psychology, 22,* 73–101.

18

Effectiveness of a Beginning Reading Intervention

Compared with What? Examining the Counterfactual in Experimental Research

Michael D. Coyne

In education, and more specifically in reading research and practice, many educators aspire to make the profession more evidence based. A central and essential tenet of an evidence-based profession is the assumption that some practices are more effective or efficacious than others and that, through rigorous scientific research, researchers have the ability to reliably identify those practices. As evidence about effective practices accumulates, members of the profession can access and use this knowledge base to make informed decisions about adopting and implementing specific practices that are more likely to produce positive and desirable reading outcomes for students.

Experimental research is the primary method used for identifying effective practices in an evidence-based profession (Feuer, Towne, & Shavelson, 2002). In education, there has been a growing emphasis on conducting experiments, or randomized controlled trials (RCTs), to investigate efficacy (e.g., Educational Sciences Reform Act of 2002 [PL 107-279]). At a basic level, RCTs are relatively easy and straightforward to understand and interpret. Participants, or groups, are randomly assigned to either the practice of interest (i.e., the treatment) or a control group. This design provides a direct test of the intervention while controlling for any other differences between the treatment and control groups. Results indicate whether or not participants in the treatment group outperformed those in the control group—that is, whether the practice was effective or not.

The purpose of this chapter is to suggest that although RCTs play an essential role in identifying effective practices in reading research, both designing and interpreting the results of RCTs are more complex and multifaceted processes than is often thought. There are two essential components of an RCT: the practice or intervention that is being evaluated and what researchers compare it to—the control condition or counterfactual. This chapter will describe two RCTs that serve as illustrations of the important and complex role of the counterfactual (i.e., control groups) in experimental reading research and the implications they have for informing practice.

THE COUNTERFACTUAL

The goal of RCTs is to evaluate the impact of a treatment or intervention on the outcomes of participants when compared with what those outcomes would be if they had not received the treatment. Because it is not possible to observe and measure the same participants simultaneously receiving the treatment and not receiving the treatment, however, researchers use a randomly assigned control group to estimate what the outcomes of the participants in the experimental group would be if they had not received the treatment. This estimated conceptual construct used to characterize the absence of the treatment or intervention is referred to as *the counterfactual* (Shadish, Cook, & Campbell, 2002).

Because RCTs determine the effects of an intervention based on a comparison between the treatment and the counterfactual, intervention effects are always relative, not absolute. In other words, researchers are always comparing their interventions to something else: the counterfactual. Although it is often thought that the counterfactual represents a fixed and unchanging baseline or control, there is actually significant variability in the experiences of students in control groups in experimental research (Lemons, Fuchs, Gilbert, & Fuchs, 2014). The following two studies provide examples of that variability in the counterfactual, particularly related to the differences in instructional contexts across schools and districts.

THE EARLY READING INTERVENTION

The intervention evaluated in both RCTs was the Early Reading Intervention (ERI; Foresman, 2004).[1] ERI is a supplemental small-group beginning reading intervention program that explicitly teaches phonologic, alphabetic, decoding, spelling, and sentence-reading skills for kindergarten students identified as at risk for experiencing early reading difficulties. The 126-lesson program comprises four units that systematically progress from early phonemic and alphabetic skills to more complex regular and irregular word-reading, spelling, and sentence-reading skills.

---

1. The development and evaluation of the ERI program was funded by a series of grants from the U.S. Department of Education, Office of Special Education Programs (H324C980156) and Institute of Education Sciences (IES; R324E060067).

A typical 30-minute lesson consists of seven activities, each designed to last 3–5 minutes. The first 15 minutes of the lesson focus on phonemic awareness (phoneme isolation, blending, and segmenting), alphabetics (letter names and sounds), and word reading (decoding and irregular words); the second 15 minutes integrate writing, dictation, and spelling with previously taught phonemic and alphabetic skills. The final 30 lessons in the intervention program begin to combine alphabetic skills and strategies with irregular word reading to read sentences and short decodable storybooks.

Intervention lessons are highly specified and include detailed scripting to ensure extensive teacher modeling, consistent communication of information, and careful integration of skills and strategies. Scheduled instruction, review, and feedback are systematically incorporated into the program. In addition, the intervention provides teachers with explicit instructional language and procedures for correcting errors and extending practice for difficult items.

EVALUATING THE EFFICACY OF THE EARLY READING INTERVENTION: TWO RANDOMIZED CONTROLLED TRIALS

The efficacy of ERI was evaluated in a series of two RCTs (Coyne et al., 2013; Simmons et al., 2011).[2] The first study was conducted in schools in Texas and Connecticut during the 2006–2007 school year. Students were screened at the beginning of the year on measures of phonemic awareness and letter knowledge to identify students at risk for experiencing early reading difficulties (i.e., students performing below the 30th percentile). Kindergarten students ($n = 206$) from 48 classrooms who were identified as at risk for experiencing early reading difficulties were assigned randomly at the classroom level either to receive ERI (experimental group) or a school-designed typical practice intervention (counterfactual).

Students in the experimental group received ERI, and students in the control group received the type of beginning reading intervention that was generally provided to kindergarten students in those schools. The counterfactual was business as usual because we were interested in whether ERI had positive effects when compared with typical school practice. Both ERI and the school-designed intervention supplemented general classroom literacy instruction and were taught in small groups of three to five students by school-identified interventionists. Interventionists taught groups for 30 minutes per day for approximately 100 sessions.

In the spring of the school year, hierarchical linear modeling (HLM) analyses were conducted that revealed effects favoring ERI on all measures, with a majority of effect sizes representing a substantive and educationally meaningful impact (as defined by the U.S. Department of Education; What Works Clearinghouse, 2014) for students who received ERI. Effect sizes are summarized

2. Both funded by IES (R324E060067).

in the first column of Table 18.1. We were pleased with these results and concluded that the evidence suggested that ERI was an effective intervention when compared with typical practice. We were confident in the findings of our RCT because of the rigor of our experimental methodology.

The following year, an identical RCT was conducted in schools in Florida. We believed that replicating the effects of our initial study with different students in different schools would strengthen the evidence of effectiveness of ERI.

Table 18.1. Comparisons between ERI students and control students across Study 1 and Study 2: Effect sizes (Hedges's *g*)

Measure	ERI study 1 versus control Study 1[a]	ERI study 2 versus control Study 2[a]	ERI study 2 versus ERI Study 1[a]	Control study 2 versus control Study 1[a]
Alphabet knowledge				
WRMT-R/NU supplementary letter	0.19	−0.11	−0.17	0.24
Checklist: Name				
Letter sound knowledge				
WRMT-R/NU supplementary letter	**0.44**	−0.04	−0.02	**0.45**
Checklist: Sounds				
Phonemic awareness				
CTOPP sound matching	**0.43**	0.15	−0.09	0.30
CTOPP blending words	**0.40**	−0.07	0.19	**0.80**
DIBELS phonemic segmentation	**0.46**	−0.08	**0.50**	**1.06**
Fluency				
Word attack				
DIBELS nonsense word fluency	0.36	−0.21	0.25	**0.77**
WRMT-R/NU word attack	**0.51**	0	−0.05	0.51
Word identification				
WRMT-R/NU word identification	0.25	−0.18	0.22	**0.77**

[a] Reference group.

Note: Bolded data indicates significant effect.

Key: ERI, Early Reading Intervention; CTOPP, Comprehensive Test of Phonological Processing; WRMT-R/NU, Woodcock Reading Mastery Test–Revised–Normative Update; DIBELS, Dynamic Indicators of Basic Early Literacy Skills.

All procedures in the second study were the same as those in the initial study. Kindergarten students ($n = 162$) at risk for reading difficulty from 48 classrooms were assigned randomly at the classroom level to receive either ERI or a school-designed typical practice intervention. Student pretest performance, fidelity of implementation, and amount of instructional time were also consistent across the two studies. Similar HLM analyses were conducted, but this time no differences were found between the outcomes of students who received ERI and the controls. These effects are displayed in the second column in Table 18.1.

These results were unexpected. ERI, which produced consistent, meaningful effects in our initial study, had no discernable impact in the second study conducted the following year. Our first thoughts were that ERI was just not effective for students in the second study; for some reason, students didn't respond to the intervention as they had during the first study. To investigate this, we compared the end-of-year literacy outcomes of students who received ERI during the initial study to the outcomes of students who received ERI during the second study. These results are displayed in the third column in Table 18.1. Findings indicated that students who received ERI across both studies responded similarly to the intervention and had generally equivalent end-of-year literacy outcomes. In fact, students who received ERI experienced significant growth in literacy skills in both studies. Whereas all students were performing below the 30th percentile at the beginning of kindergarten, a majority of students in the ERI groups were achieving well above the 40th and even 50th percentiles on our end-of-year measures of reading and literacy.

These findings did not support our hypothesis that ERI did not work for students in the second study because students receiving ERI achieved similar positive outcomes across both studies. Finally, we wondered if there were any differences in the outcomes of students in the control groups across the two studies. We thought this unlikely because control-group students in both studies belonged to comparable demographics, exhibited similar pretest scores, and received business-as-usual, typical practice. These analyses, however, revealed that students in the control groups demonstrated very different end-of-the year literacy outcomes across the two studies, even though they entered kindergarten with similar skills. This comparison is displayed in the fourth column in Table 18.1. Control group students in the Florida schools substantially outperformed control group students in the Texas and Connecticut schools with moderate to large effect sizes on all measures.

Differences in the Counterfactual

We then investigated whether "business as usual" in the Florida schools in our second study was different from what was done in the Texas and Connecticut schools during the first study. In fact, the differences were significant. First, there were differences in the schools' overall approach to beginning reading instruction. In the Florida schools, which were all in the same district, kindergarten teachers had participated in comprehensive and coordinated professional development over the previous years, which focused on evidence-based beginning reading theory and instruction. These schools also implemented the same core instructional program with support from school-based literacy coaches. These efforts resulted in a coordinated focus on supporting beginning reading, a consistent approach to classroom instruction, and a common understanding of evidence-based practices in early literacy.

In contrast, the schools in Texas and Connecticut were from six different districts and took a more eclectic and individualized approach to reading instruction. Although some schools used published core programs, most schools used a combination of published materials, district-developed curricula, and guided-reading strategies. In addition, implementation varied across classrooms. The approach to and content of professional development in beginning reading also differed among schools and across districts.

There were also differences in the type and quality of beginning reading intervention provided to kindergarten students across the two studies. The Florida schools had been providing supplemental intervention to kindergarten students at risk for reading difficulties as part of their larger coordinated approach to beginning reading instruction and intervention (i.e., Just Read, Florida!, 2005). School-based interventionists in the Florida schools were familiar and fluent with the intervention strategies they provided to students in the business-as-usual control group. In contrast, ERI was new to the Florida interventionists. Many of the schools in Texas and Connecticut, however, had not been providing kindergarten intervention consistently. Interventionists in these schools, thus, had less experience providing any school-designed interventions. The structure of the ERI program likely provided support for interventionists in these schools even though the program was new to them. Hence their practices were generally more effective than the more idiosyncratic practices observed in the control classrooms.

We also observed the instructional content of the intervention provided to students in the control groups across both studies. As we had intended, the instruction in all of the intervention groups in the control conditions focused on early literacy and beginning reading content; however, our observations revealed that the control-group interventionists in the Florida schools and the Texas and Connecticut schools differed. Content in the Florida schools focused on reading and spelling sounds and words as well as phonological skills of blending and segmenting at the phoneme level, which are more advanced reading and spelling skills, similar to ERI. In contrast, content in the Texas and Connecticut schools included a greater emphasis on identifying and writing letter names and on phonological skills at the word and syllable levels, which are more basic skills.

Summary

To summarize results across the two studies, the impact of the ERI beginning reading intervention observed in an initial randomized, controlled study was not replicated in an experimental study conducted a year later in a different geographical location. Multiyear analyses suggest, however, that the divergent findings across the two studies were not the result of students' differential response to ERI—students in both studies responded equally well to ERI. Instead, differences were largely explained by the different experiences of the students who were in the counterfactuals, or control conditions.

This pattern of findings illuminates an essential aspect of experimental research: When conducting RCTs, we always compare our interventions to something else—the counterfactual. In other words, we make determinations about the effectiveness of our interventions based not on the absolute level of achievement attained by students who receive the treatment but on whether students who receive the treatment outperform students in the counterfactual. In our first study, students who received ERI outperformed the students in the control condition. In our second study, students who received ERI did not outperform students in the control condition, even though they experienced reading growth similar to that of students in the first study. Our observations showed that the interventions provided by the Florida control group teachers were generally more effective than the interventions provided by the Texas and Connecticut control group teachers.

CONCLUSION

The combined findings of these two RCTs highlight interesting and important implications for both researchers and practitioners when conducting and interpreting the results of experimental research studies in beginning reading.

Implications for Researchers

First, because RCTs always involve a comparison between a treatment and a control condition, researchers should carefully attend to the specific nature of the counterfactual. We often think that the control condition, or counterfactual, represents a static, fixed, or unchanging baseline, whereas it is much more likely to be a moving target. This is particularly true when the counterfactual consists of "business as usual." The findings from our two studies provide clear evidence that business as usual is not the same thing as a no-treatment control. Especially in an area such as beginning reading in which there have been significant advances in instruction and intervention, typical practice can, in fact, vary dramatically across settings and time (Lemons et al., 2014). For example, business as usual in the Florida school district, where we conducted our second study, consisted of high-quality beginning reading instruction and intervention that significantly accelerated the literacy achievement of kindergarten students at risk for reading difficulty. The accelerated achievement of the students in the business-as-usual control group made the effects of ERI appear weaker than those in an earlier study, in which ERI was compared to a less powerful counterfactual.

One possible solution is designing RCTs in which we compare beginning reading interventions with pure no-treatment controls; however, even though evaluating the effects of an intervention compared with those of a no-treatment control may provide a cleaner estimate of impact, this type of comparison rarely mirrors the realities in schools. In schools, interventions are often replacing and/or supplementing existing practices or are being implemented as one of many possible alternatives. Comparing the effects of a reading intervention to those of a no-treatment control would likely provide an inflated estimate of intervention effectiveness in actual, applied school settings. Finally, it is difficult to make a case for withholding reading intervention supports for students in control groups.

A comparison condition that consists of a no-treatment control is usually impractical and unrealistic in applied RCTs of beginning reading interventions, so it becomes essential to carefully and systematically describe the experiences of students in the counterfactual. These descriptions include monitoring and documenting different dimensions of instruction, such as content focus, quality of instructional delivery, and dosage (Dane & Schneider, 1998; Gersten et al., 2005). This information allows for careful examination of actual differences and similarities across the treatment and counterfactual (Cordray & Pion, 2006).

The broader implication is that *context matters* in reading research, even when conducting carefully controlled RCTs. Even beyond the experience of students in the counterfactual, the larger instructional context of a school or district can affect research findings. Contextual factors, such as the general instructional approach, philosophical orientation toward reading development, type and quality of professional development, and alignment between core instruction and different supplemental interventions, can influence the effect of a treatment, especially in comparison to a counterfactual that is also context-dependent. In sum, researchers may never be able to get a pure estimate of the absolute effectiveness of a reading intervention. What they can get is gradually accumulating evidence about the relative effectiveness of the intervention in particular contexts.

Because the results of individual RCTs are contextually dependent, the role of replication studies in reading research is critical. Replication studies strengthen external validity and provide converging evidence about the relative efficacy of an intervention in different contexts—for example, in different geographical settings with students who have different profiles or in different instructional environments. In educational research, varied replication studies are particularly useful. Varied replications "systematically vary one or more parameters of the original study to see whether its outcome remains stable or changes in a predictable way" (van Ijzendoorn, 1994, p. 57). The goal of varied replications is to isolate and identify the contextual factors that are most highly associated with differences in impact as well as the extent to which interventions are robust to contextual variability. Although replication studies are essential for understanding the effectiveness of reading interventions across different applied settings, very few replication RCTs are conducted in social science research, and findings are often difficult to publish (Cook, 2014; Makel,

Plucker, & Hegarty, 2012). However, new research outlets are emerging that encourage the submission of replication studies, such as the *Journal of Research in Educational Effectiveness* (http://www.sree.org/pages/publications/journal.php).

Implications for Practitioners

Teachers and administrators have to make decisions about adopting and implementing beginning reading practices in their schools and districts. Findings from experimental research provide practitioners with rigorous and trustworthy evidence about the efficacy of interventions and enable more informed decision making—and the field is increasingly encouraging practitioners to rely on this evidence base. Interventions, however, are not evaluated or implemented in a vacuum: Practitioners should understand that context matters. Important questions include the following: What is the overall instructional context in which we are implementing this intervention? What is it replacing or supplementing? How will this intervention align with other beginning reading practices in our school or district?

Although it may be difficult to review all aspects of the research design of RCTs, practitioners could examine portions of studies that describe the nature of the counterfactual, as well as the larger instructional context in which interventions were evaluated, to determine whether the setting is similar to their school or district. For example, if practitioners discover that their current practice is more similar to a less effective counterfactual, they likely will want to change their practice. If their practice is more similar to the effective intervention (as was the case for the Florida teachers in our study), however, then they may want to proceed more slowly, assessing students' progress along the way. Finally, practitioners and researchers alike should understand that the idea of an effective or evidence-based practice may not be as straightforward or absolute as they would like but that instead it is complex, multifaceted, and contextually dependent.

REFERENCES

Cook, B.G. (2014). A call for examining replication and bias in special education research. *Remedial and Special Education, 35*(4), 233–246.

Cordray, D.S., & Pion, G.M. (2006). Treatment strength and integrity: Models and methods. In R.R. Bootzin & P.E. McKnight (Eds.), *Strengthening research methodology: Psychological measurement and evaluation* (pp. 103–124). Washington, DC: American Psychological Association.

Coyne, M.D., Little, M.E., Rawlinson, D.M., Simmons, D.C., Kwok, O., Kim, M., . . . Civetelli, C. (2013). Replicating the impact of a supplemental beginning reading intervention: The role of instructional context. *Journal of Research on Educational Effectiveness, 6,* 1–23.

Dane, A.V., & Schneider, B.H. (1998). Program integrity in primary and early secondary prevention: Are implementation effects out of control? *Clinical Psychology Review, 18,* 23–45.

Education Sciences Reform Act of 2002, PL 107-279, 116 Stat. 1940 (2002).

Feuer, M.J., Towne, L., & Shavelson, R.J. (2002). Scientific culture and educational research. *Educational Researcher, 31*(8), 4–14.

Gersten, R., Fuchs, L.S., Compton, D., Coyne, M., Greenwood, C., & Innocenti, M.S. (2005). Quality indicators for group experimental and quasi-experimental research in special education. *Exceptional Children, 71,* 149–164.

Florida Department of Education. (2005). *Just Read, Florida!* Retrieved from http://www.justreadflorida.com/docs/6A-6–053.pdf

Lemons, C.J., Fuchs, D., Gilbert, J.K., & Fuchs, L.S. (2014). Evidence-based practices in a changing world: Reconsidering the counterfactual in education research. *Educational Researcher, 43*(5), 242–252.

Makel, M.C., Plucker, J.A., & Hegarty, B. (2012). Replications in psychology research: How often do they really occur? *Perspectives on Psychological Science, 7*(6), 537–542.

Scott Foresman. (2004). *My sidewalks on Scott Foresman Reading Street: Early reading intervention.* Glenview, IL: Pearson.

Shadish, W.R., Cook, T.D., & Campbell, D.T. (2002). *Experimental and quasi-experimental designs for generalized causal inference.* Boston, MA: Houghton Mifflin.

Simmons, D.C., Coyne, M.D., Hagan-Burke, S., Kwok, O., Simmons, L., Johnson, C., . . . Crevecoeur, Y. (2011). Effects of supplemental reading interventions in authentic contexts: A comparison of kindergartners' response. *Exceptional Children, 77,* 207–228.

van Ijzendoorn, M.H. (1994). *A process model of replication studies: On the relation between different types of replication.* Leiden, The Netherlands: Leiden University Library.

What Works Clearinghouse. (2014). *Procedures and standards handbook, version 2.0* [Electronic Version]. Retrieved from http://ies.ed.gov/ncee/wwc/pdf/wwc_procedures_v2_standards_handbook.pdf

Integrative Summary 2

Translating Reading Research into Effective Interventions for All Children Who Struggle with Reading

Julie A. Washington

> Literacy is truly a capability, as it depends critically on the existence of a literate culture that teaches (or does not teach) people to read, write, and use documents. No individual learns to read and write without a teacher and a script. (Alves & Limpo, Chapter 17)

This quote from Alves and Limpo highlights the importance of acquiring reading and writing skills. Reading and writing must be taught and learned, and, importantly, they rely on the presence of a sociocultural context that values and promotes the acquisition of literate skills for its citizenry. In addition, as Mele-McCarthy (Chapter 10) notes, the development of literacy also requires the cooperation of scientists who explore and explain the process of learning and teaching these important skills, practitioners who translate these explanations into action in the classroom, and child and adult learners who are receptive, motivated, and prepared to tackle the task of learning to read.

The importance of reading and writing for success in school, employment, and life generally has been affirmed and reaffirmed by the research and education communities. Phyllis Hunter, a champion of literacy (noted author, former administrator of the Houston Independent School District, and former board member of the National Institute for Literacy), declared reading to be the "civil right" of every child. Beyond the classroom, there is a movement, driven in large part by the employment sector, which is focused on "college and career readiness." Reading, writing, and oral language have been identified as critical skills for success beyond the classroom. In a Child Trends report on college and workplace readiness, Lippman, Atienza, Rivers, and Keith (2008) identified reading and writing as key competencies for a successful life. In a similar vein, the American Diploma Project identified poor reading, writing, and communication skills as significant barriers to high school completion and college attendance for a growing number of students who ultimately will drop out of school. These large-scale surveys and reports point to the importance of "getting it right" when children are young and first learning to read.

READING AND WRITING: COMPLEX SKILLS

Learning

What has not always been appreciated about reading and writing is the complexity of the acquisition process. Complexity is a consistent theme across the chapters in this section. For example, Connor (Chapter 11) points out that for reading, the acquisition process involves important interactions among teachers, instruction, and child characteristics that significantly impact the effectiveness of reading acquisition for many students—in particular, for those who will struggle with learning to read. These complex interactions can make it difficult for teachers to identify instructional materials and practices that will meet the needs of a diverse group of students. Similarly for writing, Connelly and Dockrell (Chapter 16) assert that the interactions among teaching, child characteristics, and key writing processes, spelling in particular, complicate the acquisition of strong writing skills, especially for children with dyslexia. These children do not make the same progress in writing as their nondyslexic peers, and there is little guidance in the extant literature for reasoned decision making about teaching these skills at key developmental junctures.

As the country becomes more diverse, the range of child-level variables that interact with classroom-level variables further increases the complexity of teaching children to read and write. Lesaux (Chapter 13) points to the growing numbers of English learners (ELs) as one of these factors. These children bring language differences to the reading process that seem to interfere most with their ability to develop solid reading comprehension skills. Their decoding skills are frequently very similar to those of their native English-speaking peers, but developing meaning from text is a source of persistent difficulty. Terry (Chapter 12) identifies language differences as a source of difficulty for African American children as well. Unlike their EL counterparts, African American children are native English speakers but often use a dialect of English, African American English (AAE), that contrasts with mainstream American English in its use of phonology and morphosyntax. This contrast has been identified as a significant variable in reading-skill development for those African American children who do not learn to code switch to the language of the classroom. In the cases of both ELs and AAE speakers, attention to the impact of their linguistic differences on the reading acquisition process appears to be critical for developing competent readers. Furthermore, these two populations of students are also disproportionately impoverished, increasing these students' linguistic distance from the mainstream instructional code and contributing to the complexity of literacy acquisition.

Teaching

Moats (1999) famously asserted that "teaching reading *is* rocket science" (emphasis in original in the title of the publication). Indeed, growing evidence suggests that teaching reading can be as hard for teachers as learning to read can be for many students. Since Moats's 1999 publication, the variables that she identified as contributing to the difficulty instructors have with effectively teaching reading have not changed much. In particular, she cites as a primary reason for these instructional difficulties the significant gap between instructional practices and a research knowledge base that does not make its way into the classroom consistently. Mele-McCarthy (Chapter 10) interjects the voices of practitioners who understand how important the research base is for improving reading instruction and laments the absence of research focusing on many pressing needs in the classroom context. She identifies the researcher–practitioner "partnership" as a key variable for improving reading instruction. Connor (Chapter 11) also discusses the importance of utilizing research knowledge to assist teachers directly with individualizing instruction for students who struggle with reading (see also Lovett, Chapter 2). Importantly, Connor is part of a growing group of researchers that is working to translate the research base into effective intervention approaches designed to improve instruction for children experiencing difficulty with learning to read.

TRANSLATING RESEARCH INTO EFFECTIVE INTERVENTIONS

Justice cites the "current educational-policy climate" (2006, p. 284) as a driving factor in the present focus on evidence-based practice in U.S. schools. These policies implore researchers to consider classroom instruction when developing new interventions and to test these methods in classrooms, using primarily randomized controlled trials (RCTs). Policies also require teachers to use evidence-based practices for decision making. In particular, the No Child Left Behind (NCLB) Act of 2001 (PL 107-110) represented a federal mandate that teachers should engage in evidence-supported instruction in classrooms, and the Race to the Top (RTT; U.S. Department of Education, 2009) legislation currently rewards the development and use of research-based innovation in education.

Like many federal policies, NCLB and RTT have had a significant impact on the approach to both instruction and learning by tying performance to financial incentives for both school districts and researchers alike. As Mele-McCarthy points out, however, the time that it takes to bring a research-supported intervention from the laboratory to the classroom can frustrate practitioners who have children sitting in front of them daily who need immediate intervention support. Several of the authors in this section have tried to be responsive to this need and present research-based interventions that have wound their way through the research process and been found to be promising for use with children who are reading below grade level. It is encouraging that a common feature of all of these interventions is their explicit focus on being inclusive, working to meet the needs of all children, regardless of the complex factors that they bring to the reading process.

Connor (Chapter 11) and Jiménez (Chapter 15) present technology-based approaches to addressing the needs of teachers. Connor presents a very creative and exciting new approach, Individualizing Student Instruction (ISI), which is designed to increase the effectiveness of instruction while taking into account the individual characteristics that students bring to the instructional task. The Assessment to Instruction (A2i) technology platform, which directly supports ISI, utilizes algorithms developed by Connor and colleagues to help teachers in their decision making as it relates to the transition from assessment to instruction, as well as providing important professional development for teachers. The algorithm includes many of the child characteristic-by-instruction interactions that have been identified as critical to consider. Student scores are used to develop recommendations for the amount and type of instruction.

Jiménez presents a web-based tutorial model for teacher professional development called the *Letra* Program. The program is based on an RTI model and is designed to prepare teachers to teach reading more effectively with preschool, elementary, and special education students. This research-based program seeks to address the "preparation gap" between preservice teachers and their practicing colleagues. Connor and Jiménez are among a growing group of researchers who appear to recognize the potential of technology to support teachers in their efforts to meet the needs of all children. In particular, technology presents a way to deliver professional development in a manner that allows teachers to participate on their own time and in an independent way.

Coyne (Chapter 18) and Walker, Capin, and Vaughn (Chapter 14) examine two reading interventions and challenge some of the assumptions that both researchers and practitioners currently have about intervention research. Specifically, Coyne raises the importance of context in RCT research, even when a study is very tightly controlled. Control groups are central to the conduct of RCTs and are designed to provide a fixed baseline condition. Yet Coyne found that the larger instructional context of a school district significantly altered the outcomes of his intervention study, particularly the control conditions, suggesting that in addition to matching obvious variables, such as age, socioeconomic status, location (i.e., urban versus rural), and grade level, researchers should pay closer attention to the implementation practices of the school districts in which they conduct research.

Walker and colleagues present an intervention conducted with Spanish-speaking ELs. These researchers challenge the common assumption that interventions need to be adjusted when used with this population of students. They propose instead that if researchers designed interventions to be effective for all students (ELs and monolingual English speakers), implemented them with fidelity, and focused on the skills that have been identified through research to be important for developing strong reading skills, they could improve reading outcomes for these students without the need to adjust the interventions. Interestingly, the skills that they emphasize—vocabulary, background knowledge, and academic discourse—are among the skills identified by Lee (1933) as important for reading achievement more than 80 years ago.

Despite the success of the interventions presented by these authors, there are always additional caveats and considerations that need to be addressed in future research and interventions. Terry (Chapter 12) identifies dialectal variation as a potentially malleable skill that, if addressed, could improve reading outcomes for thousands of African American children, particularly those being raised in poverty and who are heavy dialect users. Lesaux (Chapter 13) identifies self-regulation as an area of focus that warrants further consideration in research on reading instruction for ELs; self-regulation has already been identified as an important consideration in the classroom for children growing up in poverty (Raver, 2012). These children are at a higher risk for emotional and behavior difficulties that influence their ability to maintain focus on goal-directed activities. Lesaux suggests that self-regulation skills might represent an important next step for understanding the performance of EL children, just as they have proven to be informative for monolingual children. (See also Morrison, Chapter 3, for additional information on self-regulation.)

Finally, as Alves and Limpo (Chapter 17) and Connelly and Dockrell (Chapter 16) point out, scientifically based writing interventions have simply not kept pace with reading interventions. Alves and Limpo refer to writing as a "substantive freedom," identifying motivation, language skill, transcription, and self-regulation as key capabilities for developing writing skills. Connelly and Dockrell add spelling to this list as an important skill that frees cognitive resources for use in the writing process. Overall, there is much work to be done to understand the relationship between reading and writing and the potential to use one skill to build capacity in the other. Connor, Ingebrand, and Dombek (2014) and Costa and colleagues (2014) present current and cogent discussions about the relationships between these two important skills and the need for research addressing them.

CONCLUSION

Translating research into practice and allowing input from practice to inform the next steps in research could further refine instructional programs and interventions and do much to improve reading outcomes for students by encouraging partnerships between those who ask the questions and those who implement the answers. At their core, that is what this volume and the 14th Extraordinary Brain Symposium on Research to Practice to Research are all about. Going forward, it will be important to initiate these studies with concern about how and who will be able to access this new knowledge. In doing so, researchers will get emerging research into as many hands as possible and perhaps effectively reduce the global reading and writing gaps during our lifetimes.

REFERENCES

Connor, C.M., Ingebrand, S., & Dombek, J. (2014). The reading side. In B. Miller, P. McCardle, & R. Long (Eds.). *Teaching reading & writing: Improving instruction & student achievement* (pp. 7–20). Baltimore, MD: Paul H. Brookes Publishing Co.

Costa, L., Unber, A., Edwards, C., Vanselous, S., Yerby, D., & Hooper, S.R. (2014). The writing side. In B. Miller, P. McCardle, & R. Long (Eds.), *Teaching reading & writing: Improving instruction & student achievement* (pp. 21–33). Baltimore, MD: Paul H. Brookes Publishing Co.

Justice, L. (2006). Evidence-based practice, response to intervention and prevention of reading difficulties. *Language, Speech, and Hearing Services in Schools, 37,* 284–297.

Lee, D.M. (1933). The Importance of reading for achieving in grades four, five, and six. *Teachers College Record, 35*(2), 145–146.

Lippman, L., Atienza, A., Rivers, A., & Keith, J. (2008). *A developmental perspective on college and workplace readiness.* Washington, DC: Child Trends.

Moats, L. (1999). *Teaching is rocket science: What expert teachers should know and be able to do.* Washington, DC: American Federation of Teachers. Retrieved from http://www.aft.org/sites/default/files/br_teachingreadingisrocketscience_1999.pdf

No Child Left Behind Act of 2001, PL 107-110, 115 Stat. 1425 (2002).

Raver, C.C. (2012). Low-Income children's self-regulation in the classroom: Scientific inquiry for social change. *American Psychologist, 67*(8), 681–689.

U.S. Department of Education. (2009). *Race to the top executive summary.* Washington, DC: U.S. Department of Education. Retrieved from http://www2.ed.gov/programs/racetothetop/executive-summary.pdf

IV

Finale

Looking to the Future

19

Innovation and Technology that Can Inform Reading Interventions

David J. Jodoin

Even with the debates on how best to serve students with developmental reading difficulties, consensus exists among educational practitioners and researchers that solving the problem of reading difficulties among children and adults alike is of paramount importance. Significant research has been conducted on the causes of reading impairment across a spectrum of potential contributors, ranging from genetics, to neural processing deficiencies, to biological, physiological, and environmental factors. Yet relatively little of this research has contributed to getting intervention and remediation programs into schools. Although interventions do exist that are proven by research to be effective in the diagnosis and treatment of reading difficulties, this is only half the battle. Figuring out where these interventions best fit into curricula and how to get schools to adopt them is too often not occurring. This leaves schools open to the marketing hype of "snake oil" salespeople and any others who have the money to promote themselves. Getting a school to adopt an intervention that isn't already widely known is a challenge and requires any school that does adopt said intervention to defend its decision. Schools typically seek to get as much scientific support and evidence as possible to justify using a specific approach and are cautious if there is not enough support to protect them when adopting an intervention for widespread implementation. Unfortunately this may lead schools to adopt programs that are popular (but not necessarily research based) to avoid having their decision questioned.

There is a popular perception that scientific research on teaching and learning lacks a holistic connection among the varying factors that contribute to the real problems confronting teachers. This, combined with the extensive time and resources required to perform rigorous longitudinal and randomized controlled studies, results in a disconnect between the scientific data from such studies and their effectiveness in contributing to solutions that educational practitioners can employ in their day-to-day practices. This disconnect between research and practice has created a needs gap among parents and educators, which has allowed proprietors of "snake oil" solutions to present themselves and prey on the desperate people who yearn for a way to help children in distress. In addition, there are many remediation and intervention techniques used by educators today that seem to be assistive, yet due to the lack of scientific studies demonstrating the efficacy of such programs, a trust issue has developed that prevents such programs from experiencing widespread adoption. The result is that little progress has been made over the last few decades to address the needs of students with reading difficulties; this is reflected in long-term National Assessment of Educational Progress (NAEP) results—the national reading proficiency scores for 17 year olds have moved minimally since 1971 (NAEP, 2013).

The question raised is this: Why, with such extensive scientific research on educational programs to advance the proficiency of readers, typical and disadvantaged alike, do the results seem to have little if any impact on education? By comparison, during that same period of time from the early 1970s, there have been magnificent and extraordinary advances in technology that have fundamentally changed the way people learn and communicate, creating a global explosion of freely accessible information. These technological innovations have infused themselves into every one of our daily lives. The private sector, which is responsible for a large majority of these innovations, does not rely on scientific research as a means of driving adoption among consumers. The result is that innovation in the private sector has more influence on the way we develop as individuals (arguably good or bad) than any formal research in reading or education. Both researchers and educators need to know whether the lack of significant movement in national rates of reading proficiency is attributable to reading and intervention programs having low adoption rates, or that the study maybe got it wrong (which means multiple studies are needed to replicate results), or there are problems with implementation in classrooms and/or teacher background and depth of knowledge, or the programs are being delivered without sufficient targeting to the students who would most need them and could benefit from those types of programs. Whereas all these factors are important, enlisting the private-sector influence and current technology might move the process forward faster, with potentially better results.

As we seek ways to bridge the gap between research and education, is there an opportunity to understand how the process of technological innovation works and whether similar methods could be infused into the science–practitioner relationship? Could educators develop and implement better methods of diagnosis, intervention, and remediation for students with reading difficulties in a rapid fashion, similar to private innovation, in ways that can be backed by the scientists who could help ensure the efficacy of such methods?

Scientific research is sponsored and funded in ways that can make it challenging to incorporate innovation methodologies into its process. The grant funding process and the limited availability of grants, along with the strict guidelines on how grant funds are to be used, do not necessarily provide scientific researchers a lot of flexibility in how they conduct their research. Competition for grants is fierce, which pressures the entire system in a number of ways: Researchers may narrow down their area of study very specifically to stand out against others in the application process, or their patron organizations (usually universities and dedicated research facilities) may exert increased demands as to how the information is used, disseminated, and owned. The strict intellectual property ownership regulations of the universities who support the researchers, along with the (not entirely unjustified) fear of releasing unpublished data, do not promote the free exchange of research data early on in the development process. The idea is that the failure to move research to practice or even to get research on new approaches and programs done more rapidly could possibly be attributed to the pressures on the scientific community to "deal with the system." Therefore, even if they want to conduct studies that address the research-to-practice gap, researchers often have to accommodate and compromise just to get funded. Many scientists also have a perception that private-sector innovation methodologies are products of a chaotic and ill-organized environment not well suited to the regimented approach scientists adhere to in order to have the academic rigor necessary to ensure approval through the peer review process.

Taking these issues to heart, one could theorize that something is broken in the current methods of sponsorship and funding that adversely influences the implementation of the scientific process. It should not be unreasonable to expect stringent research methods to produce better results than the more chaotic and ill-structured methods used by the private sector focused on innovation. Yet this is not the case, and although scientific research has yielded some interesting data, there has yet to be any impact on the way reading-challenged learners are treated.

DEMYSTIFYING INNOVATION

Very often the terms innovation and creativity are used interchangeably. And although creativity contributes to innovation, the two are quite different. The biggest difference lies in the goals. Creativity is significantly weighted toward the aesthetic in which a desired outcome is not necessary and arguably adversely affects the process of creativity. Yes, creativity is a process. Perhaps people approach their creative process in different ways, but through research, it has been found that there are common ingredients as to how people express their creativity.

Process drives innovation as well. However, the process of innovation is usually driven by the desire to achieve a specific outcome or outcomes. Creativity may contribute to innovation, whereby something new and unique is an ingredient, but innovation also applies to the process of achieving improvements or enhancements to something that already exists. Because innovation builds on what exists, and often the novelty of innovation is in the unique combination or application of multiple things that have been done before, it becomes readily apparent that significant innovation requires a free and open exchange of ideas and invention.

AN EXAMPLE

In order to innovate, one needs to be able to tie the intended outcome and the ingredients used to achieve that outcome to an event that has happened in the past. History plays a major role in innovation. Prior discoveries may have seemed novel at the time, but they also may not have found their true impact in the era in which the discovery occurred. Take for example the work of the 19th-century English physicist Sir Charles Wheatstone. His most prominent and well-known work was the development, improvement, and popularization of what became known as the Wheatstone bridge, a device invented by British mathematician Samuel Hunter Christie, which is used to measure electrical resistance and has become widely used by scientists today. Sir Charles Wheatsone is also known for his own inventions, including the Playfair cipher, the stereoscope, the concertina, and paper tape data recording, and he can arguably be credited as coinventor of the electric telegraph (Science Museum Group, n.d.; Sir Charles Wheatstone, 2015).

How is the work of Sir Charles Wheatstone relevant to innovation? Many of his inventions and work (inadvertently or not) drove further innovations, continuing until today, and without his work, Apple may never have been able to create the iPhone: The Wheatstone bridge enabled further developments in the field of electronics, and the paper tape was one of the earliest forms of digital data storage and retrieval by a machine. The Playfair cipher contributed to the ability to encrypt sensitive information, which contributed to the development of the methods of securing data used in most communication protocols today. What this shows is that innovation drives the advance of technologies over time. It is not one leap forward but a sequence of leaps that drive innovation. This is not dissimilar to the scientific research performed by those working to understand the cause of reading difficulties; for without such research, there would be no foundation for building assessment and intervention planning strategies. Considering the works of inventors of the past, it shows that much of what drives innovation is a process of experimentation and trial and error. There is an awareness within private industry, though, that the failures in experimentation are just as important, if not more so, than the development of successes.

UNDERSTAND THE PROBLEM AT HAND

Innovation for the sake of innovation often leads to mediocre results. When this happens, it is often the case that the teams who were asked to innovate either did not have a clear understanding of the problem they needed to solve or were tasked with a problem set that was masking the real problem that needed to be solved.

Early in my career, I worked for a company in which my job was to supply and support the computers and software for other employees within our company. One day I received a phone call from an accounting supervisor who asked if I could provide a larger screen for one of the accountants, as the employee was not able to see the data that needed to appear on a report displayed on the existing screen. I originally thought this was an easy problem to solve, so I had a computer monitor brought down that was 3 inches larger than the one that the employee was currently using. A few days later, I received a call from the same accounting supervisor stating that the computer monitor was still not large enough and asked if I could send down a larger one. I was rather dismayed because I had already sent the largest computer monitor that we had available at the time; I couldn't understand why that had not fixed the problem the user was experiencing.

I decided to investigate, so I went to visit the employee who was using the computer monitor. After speaking with him, I realized that the problem wasn't the size of the monitor but rather that the report he needed to display required 120 characters per line when the computer was set to only display 80 characters per line. I then merely went into the monitor configuration and changed the number of display characters from 80 to 120 and the problem was solved. What I had failed to do was to understand the problem the user was encountering, and as a result, I could not solve the problem without further research.

FAIL EARLY, FAIL OFTEN

The realization that innovation requires frequent experimentation, allowing us to learn from failure, has led to a concept commonly known today as *fail early, fail often*. But how does one know which things to experiment with so that the many failures will help point to those things that won't fail? This is where the processes of creativity and innovation intersect. Both innovation and creativity rely heavily on divergent thinking and the ability to identify remote associations. Yet everyone has limitations in their capacity to think outside the box. Much of this is due to habits that are ingrained in individuals' day-to-day lives. But just as individuals can exercise to increase their abilities in other aspects of their lives, they can also work to develop the ability to think creatively.

One common exercise I like to employ that helps build skills in creative thinking is what I call reverse designing. This experience will be familiar to anyone who has ever needed to solve a problem and was unable to generate many ideas despite concentrating on possibilities. As much as people try to concentrate on possibilities, they often seem to stumble along with very few ideas generated. When writers experience this phenomenon, they call it writer's block. Writers often employ a similar technique to the exercise I am suggesting, in that they will sit there and just write about anything. Often just the act of beginning to write helps free the mind of the block that was preventing the person from writing about the topic they desired. Our exercise is very similar. But in our example, instead of trying to come up with ideas on how to design a solution that results in the desired outcome, we instead turn it into a fun game of coming up with design ideas that result in the worst possible outcome.

An example that I commonly employ involves picking a product that people use every day, such as a calculator. Let's say that an individual's desired outcome is to design the best possible calculator. Instead of jumping into the problem set directly, he or she should start by spending some time coming up with ideas on how to make the worst possible calculator. That person will find that he or she can come up with quite a few bad ideas. Now, rather than approaching the problem set as a chore, we are instead engaging in something fun. We have created an intrinsic motivator that allows us to start thinking freely. There are two benefits to this: Now that we have started thinking freely, we have overcome that block that normally works against us when we know we have difficult work to do. Second, we benefit from this exercise because often we are enlightened by the types of things we know we shouldn't do, as they point to areas of design that perhaps we should be focused on improving.

For instance, a bad idea for a calculator may be to make the screen size very small so that the user cannot read the numbers or perhaps to make the button labels using the same color ink that was used for the button plastic. In these two simple examples, we have now identified that we want to make the calculator as easy to read as possible, on both the screen and the buttons. And the result is an understanding that we need to be concerned with the size of the font and the contrasting color of the numbers and symbols. Starting with these simple requirements can lead us to explore ideas such as whether we should use green ink on buttons or not, as the end user of the calculator could be color blind. Or perhaps we should consider that the size of the calculator needs to be altered to accommodate a more suitable font size for the LCD display.

DIVERSITY IS ESSENTIAL

Creating a diverse team with varied skills and domains of knowledge is essential to innovation. Building a team of people that all have similar life experiences and similar knowledge sets will make that team far more limited in its ability to come up with unique and creative ways to address the desired outcome.

Exercises like these need to involve many thinkers, as ideas from one person may trigger ideas from other participants that would not have resulted if fewer people were involved. People have limits in their ability to think divergently or draw relationships in remote associations; by expanding the number of people involved in the exercise, they will expand their ability to create results. There are many ways to inspire more creative results in these tasks. One can open the conversation to as many people as possible, holding knowledge across myriad domains.

When I assemble teams to work on innovation projects, I require that a portion of the team includes people with different skill domains that have nothing to do with the industry for which we are trying to develop outcomes.

People looking at the problem for the first time require the people with the related domain expertise to explain the problem set in a way that those without that domain knowledge can understand. This process alone can elicit positive results for the experienced domain experts; articulating what they are trying to achieve in simplified terms often generates great insight. Also, someone with a different domain of knowledge brings to the exercise myriad ideas that can bring a fresh set of possibilities on how to approach the problem.

THE BABY AND THE BATH WATER

Innovation exercises produce a plethora of results that do not fit within the design of a solution to achieve the desired outcome. Yet, because we have built our teams to include people from varying domains, we can now recognize that even though some of our ideas may not fit the design parameters that constrain our solution, those ideas may be innovative solutions to problems that others are trying to solve. Thus we are really creating intellectual property from such ideas that can be used as bargaining capital. We now have an advantage, something with which to entice other groups or firms to participate on our innovation teams, because we can provide them with potential value to their work. This approach requires an acceptance that helping others with their problem sets while teaming to solve ours cannot be a protected exercise. Free and open access to the results of innovation fosters collaboration among various companies within the private sector. In the computer industry, this is evidenced by the prevalence of open source technology and free use patents. Such agreements hold requirements that the use of others' solutions to solve one's problem sets may require that he or she provide innovations back to the group for use in other solution sets.

CAN INNOVATION HELP CLOSE THE GAP?

I cannot claim to be an expert on scientific research. In fact, I have spent my entire career in private industry. I explained the value of having people from diverse backgrounds on innovation teams, and in fact, I am one of those non-domain participants in the exercise of exploring how to help close the gap between researchers and practitioners and improve outcomes for people with reading difficulties. However, what I can share is my perspective based on the conversations I had with those who participated at the 14th Extraordinary Brain Symposium.

I do believe that innovation can help address the gap between research and practice. However, there are challenges and obstacles that need to be overcome in order for this to occur. Regarding the processes of grants administration and research methods, it seems clear that scientists and researchers are working within a system that was designed in a way that does not optimally promote the freedom that private industry enjoys in several ways. The limitation of funds for grants to support such important research has caused the award-granting organizations to impose stringent requirements on the use of funds in ways that limit a researcher's ability to experiment freely and practice the concept of fail early, fail often.

There are so many applicants competing for grant awards from the same pool of money that in order to differentiate themselves, the researchers create narrowly defined research proposals to be considered unique and relevant to the agency objectives. As such, there remains very little research that provides holistic benefit to the overall problem set in ways that allow the application of that research to effectively promote broad-based solutions that can maximize real social change. The narrowness of such research also creates a condition whereby researchers are hesitant to say that their results can be used to support interventions or implementations of programs that were not specifically studied as part of their core research.

There exists the problem of stable and valid control groups whereby efficacy for new interventions can be measured. Control groups within schools are problematic, as families who have students participating in these studies can move either during the school year or over the course of a longitudinal study. Teachers do not always follow the same methods for teaching and may or may not implement an intervention as prescribed in the study, so that linking results to the actual intervention or educational program may be difficult (see Coyne, Chapter 18). In addition, many researchers and scientists, being bound by the "do no harm" principle, are reluctant to endorse an intervention program that does not have qualified research supported by a longitudinal study.

Longitudinal studies and holistic research programs, however, are precisely the backing that the practitioners I was exposed to at the Extraordinary Brain Symposium felt they needed in order to inspire confidence in and provide credibility to the programs they are looking to implement to address the needs of their students today. It seems that the issue is that practitioners feel they need scientific research to help them decide on diagnostic techniques and intervention program selection and data to help them determine ongoing remediation programs that ensure impactful results. Many practitioners feel that they are already teaching and intervening with effective practices, yet their methods are not endorsed by researchers or backed by research and scientific data. At least at the symposium, practitioners felt that there is a significant amount of opportunity to work in collaboration with scientists to improve what they do.

In trying to suggest ways in which innovation might be used to address problems in reading and education, I would first like to discuss whether the problems voiced by the practitioners are really the right problems to solve. Is it merely credible endorsements by the scientific community that the educational practitioners need to promote programs that they are already implementing, or are they looking for answers to bring their programs to a new level of efficacy that has not been achieved before? What is apparent is that there are many programs being implemented today that vary greatly from one another, many of which are not scientifically backed.

I would argue that the challenge of innovation should be to first attack the problems that are inherent in the system within which both researchers and practitioners operate. For researchers, innovation can be used to develop new technologies that help them collect better data in nonintrusive ways that could improve their ability to identify atypical reading behavior while mapping that to a more holistic collection of data describing what was happening at the time the problems were encountered. But such data are only of optimal value if a larger and more stable control group is built. In order to understand influencing factors for both typical and disadvantaged readers, common tools should be built that can be used in a general education setting and give instructors the ability to assess the results of students experiencing reading difficulties. With the technology advances that exist today, these tools could be exercised to collect data that is needed to support multiple studies from the same set of students. If one can then promote adoption of these tools in a widespread fashion, a large enough sample can be built to provide a holistic "control" group that can be used for comparison with any specific intervention program being investigated.

This requires a partnership across domains. Researchers and scientists need to be able to describe both the data they need to collect as well as how it needs to be collected to be valuable. Then these design parameters can be used in conjunction with practitioners' input on how to implement a common tool that is universally useful in their educational programs. Practitioners then need to promote the use of the tools in order to achieve the sample size necessary to give meaningful data sets to the researchers. This may not solve the problems inherent in the grant funding system, and it may not lead to immediate improvements in readers with difficulties. However, it could promote greater collaboration between researchers and practitioners and begin building a better set of research data that could be used across domains and contribute to the open exchange of information similar to that enjoyed by the private sector today.

Innovation is something that requires active engagement. It is not a passive activity that just happens when one puts people in a room. To exercise creativity, even within the stringent parameters that scientists face today (as imposed by the systems they have to follow), a good start is to use innovative exercises such as the ones discussed earlier. By exercising creativity in other areas of our lives, our approaches to the areas in which we cannot apply creativity are enhanced purely by the fact that we can now look at problems differently with an expanded lens. The gap between research and practice can be closed rapidly when all parties embrace the art of the possible instead of being artificially constrained by the systems in which we work.

REFERENCES

National Assessment of Education Progress. (2013). *The nation's report card.* Retrieved from http://nces.ed.gov/nationsreportcard/subject/publications/main2012/pdf/2013456.pdf

Science Museum Group. (n.d.). Charles Wheatstone (1802–1875). *Science Museum.* Retrieved from http://www.sciencemuseum.org.uk/onlinestuff/people/charles%20wheatstone.aspx

Sir Charles Wheatstone. (2015). In *Encyclopedia Britannica.* Retrieved from http://www.britannica.com/EBchecked/topic/641626/Sir-Charles-Wheatstone

20

Reading Intervention in Perspective

Donald L. Compton and Laura M. Steacy

It was a pleasure to spend a week in the city of Horta, on the island of Faial, discussing interventions for children with significant reading and writing difficulties with leaders from the worlds of research and practice. The Azores are entirely of volcanic origin, with the most recent volcanic activity having occurred on Faial in 1957 when the Capelinhos Volcano on the western coast of Faial destroyed 300 houses and engulfed a lighthouse on the westernmost point of the island. That lighthouse now stands reborn as part of the Interpretation Center of Capelinhos Volcano to preserve the existing landscape of the area affected by the eruption and remind all of the volcano's power.

The creation of the Azores archipelago as a volcanic formation serves as a fitting metaphorical reference to help us conceptualize the theories and ideas proposed at the 14th Extraordinary Brain Symposium and presented in this volume. During the initial formation of the Azores, uncontrolled lava flows spewed from the sea, pushing up to the sky. This relatively short period of fierce evolution was followed by long periods of calm refinement in which the elements were allowed to sculpt the island's topography into a tropical paradise able to support the vast array of plants and animals that now inhabit the islands. This is also true in the field of reading, which experiences times of explosive scientific discovery in which ideas and theories evolve at a speed that outpaces our ability to fully analyze and evaluate efficacy. Periods of discovery are often followed by long periods of refinement in which theories are sculpted and refined through scientific evaluation, clinical trials, and adoption in the field. This process leads to the development of reading/writing interventions able to support the literacy needs of our most vulnerable learners.

This chapter attempts to identify a set of unifying themes that cut across the chapters in this volume and to classify emerging ideas within themes into *fast evolution* (think lava flows) or *steady refinement* (think sculpting trade winds) phases. Distinctions between evolution and refinement will signal intervention ideas that are ready for practice and those emerging ideas of promise that warrant closer attention. The major themes across chapters include the following:

- The search for new and meaningful subgroups of children with unique instructional needs
- Identification of the neurological substrates and systems that support learning
- Evaluation of the efficacy of new and innovative instruction that meets the needs of individual children
- Consideration of ways to leverage technology and innovation to improve the reading and writing of all students

NEW AND MEANINGFUL SUBGROUPS OF STUDENTS

The process of comprehending written material requires the coordination of a complex set of skills, and as a consequence, there are a number of potential sources of reading failure (e.g., Cain, Oakhill, & Bryant, 2000; Gersten, Fuchs, Williams, & Baker, 2001; Perfetti, Marron, & Foltz, 1996; Rapp, van den Broek, McMaster, Kendeou, & Espin, 2007). This view of reading development has led to the common assumption that literacy difficulties (including both reading and writing) result from heterogeneous sets of student characteristics, which indicate the existence of distinct subgroups of learners. Subgroups of students that are at elevated risk for poor literacy outcomes are classified as such when a continuous variable (e.g., phonemic awareness, oral language skill, dialect use, self-regulation) thought to be causally related to literacy development is cut along the distribution at a point considered to be of clinical relevance (see Torgesen, 2002). The use of cut scores to form clinically relevant subgroups is predicated on the assumption that these subgroups represent a discrete set of children with unique phenotypes, neurobiologies, and instructional needs (Fletcher et al., 1997). Although there are problems associated with dichotomizing a continuous variable representing a dimensional disorder (e.g., reading disabilities) to form a clinical subgroup (see Fletcher, Denton, & Francis, 2005; Francis et al., 2005), this is an approach typically taken in schools and clinics. The importance of identifying and effectively treating various subgroups of children with reading and writing difficulties is a strong theme that runs through many of the contributions in this volume. These subgroups are of theoretical interest to the field and represent distinct clinical challenges for practitioners.

The subgroup data presented across multiple chapters represents a healthy mix of well-known (i.e., refining) and newly proposed (i.e., evolving) subclasses with significant, and perhaps unique, instructional needs in the area of literacy. For instance, Lovett and Connelly and Dockrell focus on the well-established subgroups of children representing responders versus nonresponders to validated interventions (Lovett, Chapter 2) and children with dyslexia and language learning disabilities (Connelly & Dockrell, Chapter 16). The work of Lovett and colleagues has demonstrated that intensive early intervention has the capacity to significantly improve the reading outcomes of even students who have the most impaired reading skills but that treatment effects are moderated and mediated by grade and individual child characteristics. Lovett and colleagues continue the search for important components that can help bolster the effects of multicomponent interventions on the reading performance of children who traditionally fail to respond adequately to our most powerful interventions.

In Chapter 16, Connelly and Dockrell explore the writing difficulties associated with subgroups of children defined as having dyslexia and language learning disabilities (LLD). The authors point out that on the surface, children with dyslexia and LLD share a common behavioral phenotype represented by slow composition speed, many spelling errors, and generally poor compositions when compared with same-age peers; however, children with dyslexia are primarily constrained by their poor spelling skill, whereas both poor spelling and poor language impact the writing of children with LLD. Although these results indicate that the two subgroups clearly need interventions tailored to remediate specific differences, Connelly and Dockrell suggest that interventions useful for typically developing children will likely also be useful for children with dyslexia and LLD. These interventions will of course need to be more intensive and carefully targeted for the detailed taxonomy of skills associated with dyslexia and LLD, thus suggesting that distinct pedagogic solutions are needed for dyslexic and LLD children to help ameliorate their writing difficulties.

Several of the chapters focus on important linguistic subgroups related to second-language acquisition (Lesaux, Chapter 13; Walker, Capin, & Vaughn, Chapter 14) and the use of African American English (AAE; Terry, Chapter 12). Both Lesaux and Walker and colleagues grapple with whether it makes sense to consider English learners (ELs) as having distinct educational needs when compared with monolingual students. As they point out, there is a prevailing belief within the field of education that ELs have distinct educational needs and therefore require specific curricula with distinct instructional practices. This is supported by the ELs' phenotype of accurate and efficient word reading but significant struggles comprehending text due to underdeveloped vocabulary and background knowledge (see Lesaux, Chapter 13). However, Walker and colleagues explore some intriguing questions: What would happen if we designed all instruction to ensure it was successful for ELs? By considering curriculum and instruction from the perspective of ELs, would we maximize learning for all students? These ideas fly in the face of conventional wisdom that ELs require specific curricula with distinct instructional practices. Instead, results presented by Walker and colleagues suggest that designing all classroom instruction with research-based components linked to improved reading outcomes for ELs concurrently maximizes learning for students not identified as ELs. Lesaux echoes their recommendations by suggesting that a focus on meaning-based literacy competencies (e.g., oral language) is most appropriate for both ELs and monolingual speakers who are at risk for poor reading outcomes.

Turning to a different linguistic dimension, a growing body of evidence reveals strong relationships among children's use of AAE, poverty, and reading ability. As Terry points out, "AAE is a nonmainstream, cultural dialect of American English whose form, content, and use differs from mainstream American English (MAE) and from standard written English orthography" (Chapter 12). Research suggests that children who show the ability to code switch between AAE and MAE generally exhibit better long-term reading outcomes when compared with those who have difficulty with code switching. The ability to code switch likely depends on metalinguistic abilities that are related to reading development (Terry, 2014), with code switching tending to increase at the same time students are learning to read. Thus results suggest a reciprocal relationship between the metalinguistic skills associated with code switching and reading development. Research suggests that children who begin formal reading instruction using AAE frequently in school contexts and who fail to develop code-switching skills during instruction may be at pronounced risk for developing reading difficulty. Fortunately code switching has been shown to be malleable in African American children (Terry, Chapter 12); however, very few experimental studies have been conducted to determine if AAE changes associated with dialect-informed instruction are associated with improved reading achievement. This is a fascinating area of inquiry that is *evolving* quickly and certainly deserves further exploration.

Finally, moving away from subgroups based on linguistic differences, Morrison's chapter (Chapter 3) explores an interesting new and potentially important subgroup of at-risk children based on early differences in self-regulation. According to Morrison, "self-regulation has been conceptualized as a complex skill, comprised of three fundamental components: attention control/flexibility, working memory, and response inhibition" (Morrison, Chapter 3). Self-regulation in young children has been found to vary substantially across individuals, change markedly with development, and predict children's emergent literacy skills. From a subgrouping standpoint, Morrison identified a subset of very young males who comprise the lower end of the distribution of self-regulation skills and who may be at risk for poor developmental outcomes. Perhaps most significant is that this group of the lowest performing children is almost exclusively male. Certainly, continued work examining the evolution of self-regulation skills in this group of at-risk boys along with concomitant development of academic skills, patterns of health, socioeconomic status, and criminality across childhood and adolescence is warranted. In addition, evaluations of the efficacy of new interventions designed to improve the self-regulation skills of young children at high risk for poor academic and psychological outcomes are sorely needed.

With many of the chapters focusing on important subgroups of children who are at elevated risk for poor literacy outcomes, we are reminded that a "one size fits all" educational system will fail to adequately serve a diverse population of children. The present chapters certainly reinforce the idea that researchers are busily working to identify subgroups of children with unique phenotypes and instructional needs. Children with dyslexia and LLD are already benefitting from specialized intervention protocols that significantly improve their long-term literacy development. As researchers learn more about the needs of children who are ELs, use AAE, or have low levels of self-regulation, we will hopefully be able to provide practitioners with the tools necessary to significantly impact the literacy development of these children.

NEUROLOGICAL SUBSTRATES AND SYSTEMS SUPPORTING LEARNING

With the advent of modern neuroimaging techniques, we can literally open the minds of developing readers to examine how the brain processes written language. To date, most of the neuroimaging work in reading development has focused on word recognition, contrasting typically developing children with children with dyslexia using functional magnetic resonance imaging. During word recognition in typically developing readers, brain activation takes place in three areas in the temporal and parietal areas of the left hemisphere, roughly corresponding to the superior temporal gyrus, Wernicke's area, and the angular gyrus. In contrast, children with dyslexia tend to activate the same areas but in the right hemisphere (see Pugh et al., 2000). More recent studies using pre- to postintervention imaging have shown convergence around normalizing changes in the neural network of dyslexic children, in which response to intervention is accompanied by increased activation in areas of the left hemisphere supporting word recognition, as well as apparent compensatory changes (Fletcher, 2009), suggesting that the neural systems underlying word recognition are malleable. This implies that learning to read has the potential to literally rewrite the organization of the brain.

Studies have begun to move past identifying differences in gray matter regions of typically developing and dyslexic readers to examinations of white matter tracts and neurotransmitters. In addition, there has been recent focus on using neuroimaging techniques to explore reading comprehension differences among good and poor readers. Two of the chapters focus on the use of neuroimaging techniques to explore neurochemical differences in children with dyslexia (Del Tufo & Pugh, Chapter 8) and the white matter tracks underlying word reading and comprehension in good and poor readers (Cutting, Bailey, Barquero, & Aboud, Chapter 7). These chapters represent the leading edge of the quickly *evolving* science exploring the neurobiological bases of reading difficulties.

In Chapter 8, Del Tufo and Pugh focus on the neurochemistry of dyslexia using magnetic resonance spectroscopy, a noninvasive technique used to measure the brain's metabolic activity using the resonances of frequencies of neurometabolites. This chapter is extremely timely, as the authors stress that little is known about the relationship of neurotransmitters to successful literary learning. Thus far, evidence suggests that individuals with dyslexia tend to have raised levels of choline and glutamate as well as elevated lactate and metabolic abnormalities. These findings of elevated choline and glutamate are consistent with what has been found in other neurodevelopmental disorders—including attention-deficit/hyperactivity disorder and autism. Although these are exciting findings indeed, the causal mechanism underlying these relationships has yet to be established. We agree with Del Tufo and Pugh, however, that future theories of dyslexia should consider the role of neurotransmitters, particularly choline and glutamate.

Cutting, Bailey, Barquero, and Aboud (Chapter 7) present results examining white matter tracks that appear critical to multiple levels of text comprehension with the hope of improving our understanding of struggling readers. Specifically this group has focused on the overlap between important word- and comprehension-level processes during discourse processing. Diffusion tensor imaging, a neuroimaging technique examining structural connectivity of white matter bundles, allows differences in the density and integrity of connectivity tracks to be identified across groups of readers. Previous studies suggest that individuals with dyslexia have either smaller or more dispersed white matter bundles compared with those of typical readers. In looking at the overlap between the white matter bundles supporting word- and comprehension-level processes, findings from the Cutting group suggest that words and passages show overlapping areas of activation in key nodes. However, white matter tracts from these nodes diverge to support separate word and comprehension processes. Thus these common nodes appear to have a role in both word-level and discourse processing and are presumably related to poor reading skills in adolescents struggling to read connected text.

The chapters by Cutting and colleagues (Chapter 7) and Del Tufo and Pugh (Chapter 8) are excellent examples of the incredible potential of modern neuroimaging techniques to help illuminate the basic brain mechanisms and processes involved with typical and atypical reading development. Hypotheses regarding the relationships among gray matter, white matter, neurochemistry, reading development, and response to instruction are *evolving* rapidly. Continued work in this area focusing on replication and extension is critical for the field of reading and disability. As Cutting and colleagues have stressed, understanding these basic relationships will allow researchers and educators to better develop and provide effective reading instruction to developing readers, particularly those resistant to current interventions, and to older struggling readers for whom origins of reading difficulties are heterogeneous.

EFFICACY OF NEW AND INNOVATIVE INSTRUCTION

Several decades of intervention research have resulted in a fierce *evolution* of our knowledge base regarding effective interventions for children who struggle to learn to read and write (Fletcher, Lyon, Fuchs, & Barnes, 2006). In light of this expanded understanding, a strong theme throughout the contributions in this volume is a focus on the efficacy of new and innovative approaches to teaching reading and writing that serve the needs of all students. Several contributions focus on the results of research on intervention elements that promote success in students with diverse instructional needs. In addition to these critical intervention elements, several contributions have focused on the need to tweak these interventions in new and innovative ways to increase the impact and efficiency of interventions for students with the highest needs.

Lovett (Chapter 2) offers a useful metaphor for the future of reading interventions when she notes that students and teachers require a detailed road map for the course of instruction in order to experience success. She further contends that this road map must be deeply rooted in reading theory, with a particular focus on an understanding of the reading system we are trying to build within students. With this goal in mind, she highlights a need for us to shift our focus to the processes that we hope to promote in students. Lovett draws our attention to the need for interventions that promote automatic and efficient word recognition but acknowledges that "exclusive focus on explicit instruction may have caused us to miss an aspect of intervention that could be important to achieving gains in the quality of lexical representations and greater word reading efficiency" (Lovett, Chapter 2). Lovett goes on to highlight the need to focus on the issue of implicit learning and the building of robust lexical representations in poor readers. By promoting transfer of skills and by building strong lexical representations, we may be able promote greater word reading skills and word reading efficiency in students with and at risk for disabilities. If interventions can successfully promote such transfer, we may be able to address the consistent finding that word reading accuracy can be more easily remediated than word reading efficiency and that we typically see students demonstrating more gains in decoding than on the identification of real words (Torgesen et al., 2001). The same relationship can be argued for reading comprehension. We must understand the underlying mechanisms of reading comprehension and apply this understanding to intervention. More specifically, we must focus on the process by which there is the simultaneous activation of semantic representations and access to background knowledge and how we can use our knowledge of these processes to help students with and at risk for disabilities. Lovett suggests that there is also a need for new and innovative approaches to comprehension measurement that could have important implications for assessing and intervening with children with poor reading comprehension. She calls for a shift in focus from measuring the product of reading comprehension to measuring the process of reading comprehension through new techniques that could possibly include neuroimaging and eye-tracking technology (Miller, Chapter 6).

Like Lovett, Connor (Chapter 11) acknowledges the critical elements of current interventions as well as a vision for how we can modify these interventions to serve students with the highest needs. Within the framework of the Simple View of Reading (Hoover & Gough, 1990), Connor suggests that interventions should include activities that promote fluent decoding and strong language skills. Connor further suggests that these interventions should have a strong focus on sustaining student attention. She acknowledges that the most pressing task of intervening with students at risk is to ensure that the right services are provided to the right students at the right time. Connor offers insight into innovations for meeting the complex needs of struggling readers. With her discussion of child characteristic-by-instruction interactions (or aptitude-by-treatment interactions), she aptly highlights the need to consider the complex learner profiles of students at risk. As we move toward a multitiered system of support or response to intervention (RTI) model of reading instruction, with increasing demand for individualized instruction at Tier 3, an immediate demand for tools to support teachers has become apparent. Connor offers such a tool with her Assessment to Instruction (A2i) technology platform, which brings a new perspective and technological framework for individualizing instruction.

Although the field of reading has moved toward the individualization of instruction for students who struggle to learn to read, there is still much to be learned about what constitutes evidence-based practices in writing and how that can be individualized across children. As Alves notes, "this has meant that writing research, writing instruction, and writing achievement typically lagged behind reading, as the harder problems to tackle within the literacy domain" (Alves & Limpo, Chapter 17). Alves highlights four capabilities that form the foundational building blocks of writing: motivation, language skills, transcription, and self-regulation. These components of effective writing instruction require further exploration, particularly with children who struggle to learn to write.

As we acknowledge the impact that several decades of research have had on interventions for students with and at risk for disabilities, so too must we acknowledge the process and challenges that accompany research on evidence-based practices. For example, we must acknowledge the issue of the counterfactual. As evidence-based practices make their way into mainstream instruction, our evaluations of new interventions are necessarily affected. No longer are we concerned with comparing interventions to instructional practices that are not evidence-based. As noted by Coyne (Chapter 18), research using randomized controlled trials is considered the gold standard for determining the efficacy of new intervention practices. The interpretation of these results, however, is greatly affected by the relative comparison group, or the counterfactual. Coyne cites two studies that highlight the great variability that can exist in the counterfactual, thereby greatly impacting interpretation. By looking more closely at the counterfactual across these studies, he and his colleagues determined that control groups in some areas (Florida) were receiving professional development and supports that changed the content of their counterfactual group, yielding no discernable differences between the experimental treatment and the control group. Teachers in other areas (Texas and Connecticut) who did not receive the training and supports had control groups that performed lower than the treatment groups. As a result of these findings, Coyne makes the important point that the contents of the interventions used in "business as usual" control groups must be carefully considered as researchers analyze their results and draw conclusions from their data.

TECHNOLOGY AND INNOVATION

In keeping with the discussion of new and innovative ways to serve the needs of diverse learners, a strong theme throughout this volume is the role of technology and innovation in serving children with and at risk for disabilities. In her discussion of child characteristic-by-instruction interactions, Connor (Chapter 11) highlights the need to provide teachers with tools that will assist them in individualizing (*refining*) instruction for students with the highest needs. This is particularly important for students in Tier 3 who require instruction that is qualitatively different from the instruction they previously received in Tiers 1 and 2. According to Connor, the Individualizing Student Instruction (ISI) platform provides teachers with a tool that allows them to employ effective standards of practice using the Assessment to Instruction (A2i) technology platform and teacher professional development. Using innovative technology and a theoretical perspective based on the Simple View of Reading, the A2i technology allows teachers to determine whether instruction should be code-focused or meaning-focused, whether it should be student-managed or teacher managed, and whether it should be administered to the whole class, in small groups, or individually. A computer algorithm inspired by the game SimCity and similar to those developed by meteorologists to predict the path of hurricanes allows teachers to input assessment information on students and provides individualized instructional programs that focus on areas in which students need focused support. This tool is one creative approach that allows teachers to incorporate research-based methods for identification with the support of technology. Another promising use of technology for implementing RTI is the *Letra* Program offered by Jiménez (Chapter 15), providing teachers with online education, instructional materials, and tutorials about how to teach reading based on the most recent scientific investigations. This tool is composed of e-learning modules, self-assessed stopping points, web-based tutorials for preparing teachers, and an interactive discussion forum to support the implementation of RTI within Spanish-speaking regions. This approach to professional development allows evidence-based practices to be distributed to teachers in the field who may not have access to the most up-to-date training and professional development opportunities.

In an interesting exploration of the role that technology can play in assessment, Connelly and Dockrell (Chapter 16) offer an innovative take on writing assessments. In their examination of how children with dyslexia and LLD learn to write, they try to capture the online writing process through technology. Using writing tablets, the researchers were able to explore how the writing behaviors of children with LLD were different from those with dyslexia or their age-matched peers. With this technology, they were able to track pause and writing times, spelling mistakes, and areas of difficulty in the writing process.

Another promising yet underutilized technology for investigating individual differences in text processing across developing readers is the use of eye movements. As Miller (Chapter 6) points out, the study of readers' eye movements can provide an additional source of information to better our understanding of reading as a developmental process for students with and without reading disabilities. Another form of innovation is the adoption of new statistical tools and concepts to inform research. Bartlett, Yates, Flax, and Brzustowicz (Chapter 4) effectively argue that new statistical methods are needed when the basic relationships being investigated do not meet the linear model assumptions. One new technique introduced by Bartlett's group is the use of distance correlations to investigate nonlinear dependence. The distance correlation quantifies the dependence of two variables without assuming a linear relation and therefore allows important threshold relationships to be explored in developing readers. In addition, Sideridis, Georgiou, Simos, Mouzaki, and Stamovlasis (Chapter 5) introduce the cusp catastrophe model to explain the nonlinear relationship between RAN, decoding, and word reading. The model is used to evaluate the "generic shutdown" hypothesis that predicts discontinuity in the impact of RAN scores on word reading scores, which is particularly evident among struggling readers. New techniques such as these have the potential for providing new insights into factors related to reading disability and dyslexia.

An area of rapid *evolution* has been the study of genetic factors in disability profiles and the role of genetics in the classroom. Hart (Chapter 9), in an innovative approach to the discussion of genetics, discusses how findings from genetics studies can impact instruction for students. She notes evidence from twin studies (Smith, Kimberling, Pennington, & Lubs, 1983; Stevenson, Graham, Fredman, & Mcloughli, 1987) that genetics and the shared environment are important for initial reading skill and likely for reading growth. She further notes that these twin studies suggest that these results are true across reading component skills, age, and ability and that genetic influences account for approximately 50% of the variance in reading outcomes. Hart highlights the need to acknowledge individual differences in response to classroom instruction and suggests that individual differences can be informed, at least in part, by behavioral genetics. In particular, she suggests that family history could be used as a proxy for genetic influences to form a risk index that could be predictive of child performance in school and could be used to inform recommendations for treatment. In keeping with the need for individualization noted earlier, Hart suggests using behavioral genetics to inform individualization and emphasizes the need to perform further assessments and progress monitoring.

CONCLUSIONS

The 14th Extraordinary Brain Symposium and this resulting volume offer multiple perspectives on the current state of literacy research and practice for students with diverse needs. We have identified important themes across the chapters: 1) the search for new and meaningful subgroups of children with unique instructional needs, 2) identification of the neurological substrates and systems that support learning, 3) evaluation of the efficacy of new and innovative instruction that meets the needs of individual children, and 4) consideration of ways to leverage technology and innovation to improve the reading and writing of all children. In keeping with our volcano analogy, we identified approaches to improving the literacy outcomes of children that are ready to make significant impacts for teachers and practitioners (i.e., refined) and those that are in their infancy and still require further scientific evaluation (i.e., evolving). Just as islands like the Azores appear, disappear, and change shape, so must our research and practice continue to evolve through eruptions of new ideas as well as continued refinement of those ideas that have solidified and become part of the existing terrain.

REFERENCES

Cain, K., Oakhill, J., & Bryant, P. (2000). Investigating the causes of reading comprehension failure: The comprehension-age match design. *Reading and Writing: An Interdisciplinary Journal, 12,* 31–40.

Fletcher, J.M. (2009). Dyslexia: The evolution of a scientific concept. *Journal of the International Neuropsychological Society, 15*(4), 501–508.

Fletcher, J.M., Denton, C., & Francis, D.J. (2005). Validity of alternative approaches for the identification of learning disabilities: Operationalizing unexpected underachievement. *Journal of Learning Disabilities, 38*(6), 545–552.

Fletcher, J.M., Lyon, G.R., Fuchs, L.S., & Barnes, M.A. (2006). *Learning disabilities: From identification to intervention.* New York, NY: Guilford Press.

Fletcher, J.M., Morris, R., Lyon, G.R., Stuebing, K.K., Shaywitz, S.E., Shankweiler, D.P., . . . Shaywitz, B.A. (1997). Subtypes of dyslexia: An old problem revisited. In B. Blachman (Ed.), *Foundations of reading acquisition and dyslexia: Implications for early intervention.* (pp. 95–114). Mahwah, NJ: Lawrence Erlbaum Associates.

Francis, D.J., Fletcher, J.M., Stuebing, K.K., Lyon, G.R., Shaywitz, B.A., & Shaywitz, S.E. (2005). Psychometric approaches to the identification of LD: IQ and achievement scores are not sufficient. *Journal of Learning Disabilities, 38,* 98–108.

Gersten, R., Fuchs, L.S., Williams, J.P., & Baker, S. (2001). Teaching reading comprehension strategies to students with learning disabilities: A review of research. *Review of Educational Research, 71*(2), 279–320.

Hoover, W.A., & Gough, P.B. (1990). The simple view of reading. *Reading and Writing, 2*(2), 127–160.

Perfetti, C.A., Marron, M.A., & Foltz, P.W. (1996). Sources of comprehension failure: Theoretical perspectives and case studies. In C. Cornoldi & J. Oakhill (Eds.), *Reading comprehension difficulties: Processes and interventions* (pp. 137–165). Mahwah, NJ: Lawrence Erlbaum Associates.

Pugh, K.R., Mencl, W.E., Shaywitz, B.A., Shaywitz, S.E., Fulbright, R.K., Skudlarski, P., . . . Gore, J.C. (2000). The angular gyrus in developmental dyslexia: Task specific differences in functional connectivity in posterior cortex. *Psychological Science, 11,* 51–56.

Rapp, D.N., van den Broek, P., McMaster, K.L., Kendeou, P., & Espin, C.A. (2007). Higher-order comprehension processes in struggling readers: A perspective for research and intervention. *Scientific Studies of Reading, 11*(4), 289–312.

Smith, S.D., Kimberling, W.J., Pennington, B.F., & Lubs, H.A. (1983). Specific reading disability: Identification of an inherited form through linkage analysis. *Science, 219*(4590), 1345–1347.

Stevenson, J., Graham, P., Fredman, G., & Mcloughli, V. (1987). A twin study of genetic influences on reading and spelling ability and disability. *Journal of Child Psychology and Psychiatry, 28*(2), 229–247.

Torgesen, J.K. (2002). Empirical and theoretical support for direct diagnosis of learning disabilities by assessment of intrinsic processing weaknesses. In R. Bradley, L. Danielson, & D. Hallahan (Eds.), *Identification of learning disabilities: Research to practice* (pp. 565–650). Mahwah, NJ: Lawrence Erlbaum Associates.

Torgesen, J.K., Alexander, A.W., Wagner, R.K., Rashotte, C.A., Voeller, K.K.S., & Conway, T. (2001). Intensive remedial instruction for children with severe reading disabilities: Immediate and long-term outcomes from two instructional approaches. *Journal of Learning Disabilities, 34*(1), 33–58.

21

Moving Forward in Reading Intervention Research and Practice

Peggy McCardle and Carol McDonald Connor

Clearly the focus of this volume, and of the discussions and presentations at the 14th Extraordinary Brain Symposium, is intervention. But the subtitle ("Research to Practice to Research") reflects the undergirding and overriding philosophy that was the basis of these undertakings—that is, that research can, should, and must inform practice if we are to truly find ways to help all children become literate, competent, and successful readers and writers. However, those engaged in designing and conducting research can also be informed by practice. Research questions and study designs can be informed by the needs of practitioners, and refinements of interventions can and should be informed by interaction with practitioners as studies are planned, implemented, and adapted for future studies and for replication studies. So once research makes it to the practice stage, it should cycle back from practice to additional research, and the reciprocity should continue.

This cycle proposes an alternative to the all-too-frequent "vicious cycle" of frustration in which practitioners are not using what research produces and researchers are not listening to what practitioners need or want; rather, this volume proposes a collaborative cycle that works for trust across communities—so that those working in schools and clinics are learning from and communicating with researchers. In turn, researchers should be listening to the needs of not only teachers and service providers in the schools and clinics but also administrators and policy makers, who also have needs in terms of training for staff, time to allow research or implementation of new approaches, and cost-benefit considerations. These administrators and policy makers also need to better understand the goals, rationale, and outcomes of research; the *hows* and *whys* of what researchers are recommending for their schools and practitioners; and how to choose among interventions and instructional programs that are shown to be effective with students like those they serve (in other words, to become informed consumers of research to inform policy and practice).

Thus as we share recommendations for future research, there are recommendations to be undertaken with this collaboration as a background, as a guiding framework that we believe can help both researchers and practitioners make a difference for today's learners and future generations of learners. The analogy that Compton and Steacy (Chapter 20) present in their thoughtful analysis of volcanic activity, of evolution and refinement, is itself a cycle that can be either destructive or beneficial. Disruption, as Jodoin (Chapter 19) also points out, can be good—to force us to think in new ways, to shift paradigms, and to consider old and new problems from different perspectives in order to find innovative and feasible solutions. As we build on what we know, we can and must be innovative, whether it is with the use of new technologies or simply by rethinking how we combine what is known in traditional instructional approaches that have been shown to be effective—integrating components of interventions to better meet the needs of students but not losing sight of the fact that some students will need focused attention on specific components. Some examples include teaching to mastery and offering sufficient repetition to enable learning without frustrating and boring students (Walker, Capin, & Vaughn, Chapter 14) or incorporating ways to bolster the self-efficacy and self-regulation of students (Lovett, Chapter 2; Morrison, Chapter 3).

Research has demonstrated that specific techniques work well for teaching reading (see such works as National Institute of Child Health and Human Development, 2000; August & Shanahan, 2006; and National Early Literacy Panel, 2008) and have advanced our understanding of reading comprehension (RAND Reading Study Group, 2002; Sabatini, Albro, & O'Reilly, 2012a, 2012b; Miller, Cutting, & McCardle, 2014). Although the science of teaching writing lags behind that of reading, there is also a lot we know about what is helpful for teaching writing (for meta-analyses and reviews, see Graham & Herbert, 2011; Graham & Santangelo, 2014; Graham, McKeown, Kiuhara, & Harris, 2012; Graham & Perin, 2007; Miller, McCardle, & Long, 2014). And using that evidence base to build interventions has been in many ways successful. For example, it has become clear that earlier is better for interventions, that older students require greater intensity over longer periods, and that for many students who are struggling with reading, even with a successful intervention at one point in their education, ongoing support will be needed to ensure that they continue to learn—literacy is not "finished" when early intervention ends. Learning and enhancing reading and writing continues throughout the K–12 educational process and beyond. Lovett's overview (Chapter 2) of past decades of literacy intervention research gives us perspective—we've come a long way but still have further to go. She cites our need for multifaceted interventions grounded firmly in tested and supported theory and empirical evidence, interventions that address not only literacy but broader learning needs and that include consideration of motivation, social-cognitive, and self-efficacy needs of the struggling reader. Lovett's "wish list" includes better road maps to the "construction of an efficient reading system"—more evidence on how best to help those with weak vocabulary and limited language experiences to attain deeper comprehension, the harnessing of technologies to provide more and better practices for struggling readers, and assessments to measure vocabulary and comprehension growth over time.

BASIC CONSIDERATIONS: BEHAVIOR, NEUROBIOLOGY, AND GENETICS

Given what we know about the importance of each of the components of reading (decoding, fluency, vocabulary, comprehension) and of language skills (Phonology, syntax, morphology, semantics, listening comprehension) in creating successful readers and writers, the job now is to refine and combine and to tailor those combinations for students who learn differently. Section II of the volume—"Basic Considerations for Reading Intervention: Behavior, Neurobiology, and Genetics"—lays out the tools and some of the issues that must be considered as we seek to understand what underlies and influences learning to read so that we can tailor interventions to accommodate the individual variations in learning that students bring to the task, with the ultimate goal of personalized interventions that are tailored to the needs and the unique characteristics—genetic, neurological, and behavioral—of students with dyslexia.

The behavior of the reader or future reader is an important consideration. One perspective that, particularly in the last 15 years, has been a focus in learning, especially in early childhood, is that of executive control or executive functions, which generally are defined as including planning, organization, working memory, and self-regulation (Carlson, Zelazo, & Faja, 2013). In Chapter 3, Morrison discusses the growing body of evidence on the importance of self-regulation for students for educational and general life success and its malleability, especially during early development. Clearly, the relation to literacy should be investigated, and the impact of self-regulation or executive function interventions on literacy and the impact of reading and writing difficulties and interventions on self-regulation and other areas of executive functioning should be explored.

Among the basic research considerations in Section II are novel analytic approaches, which two chapters address. Bartlett, Yates, Flax and Brzustowicz (Chapter 4) present a correlation metric—the distance correlation—new to reading research. Using it to examine the Simple View of Reading (oral language and decoding as components of comprehension), they posit a threshold relationship that drives the linear correlation that is found—that is, below-average scores in decoding are weak predictors of language, but average scores strongly predict above-average language ability. They conclude that nonlinear models offer a novel approach for the study of reading comprehension and that the relationship between the components of reading comprehension—oral language and decoding—involves additional factors such as phonological short-term memory. They call for longitudinal studies to further explore this threshold relationship.

Also presenting a novel analytic approach, Sideridis, Georgiou, Simos, Mouzaki, and Stamovlasis (Chapter 5) use the cusp catastrophe model (Thom, 1975) to demonstrate support for their view of reading as a self-organizing, dynamic system that alters depending on the complex interplay of cognitive abilities and affective or motivational states. Under this theory, working memory, processing speed, attention, crystallized knowledge, decoding, verbal retrieval, and visuomotor coordination are pulled into the process as needed, over time, and the system builds on itself. This process can be disrupted or interfered with by external and internal factors such as negative feedback and dysfunctional beliefs but may be robust depending on the level of task difficulty and available cognitive resources. Without the necessary prerequisites, general reading breakdown can occur. They call for studies using this model, using more direct measures of the components of rapid automatized naming (RAN) and with various subpopulations of at-risk students.

Section II also includes the basic considerations of imaging/biological research—eye tracking, neuroimaging, neurochemistry, and genetics. Some of these have been used for many years, but improvements in technology and in research methods now offer greater potential for use in intervention research. Miller (Chapter 6) provides an overview of a demonstrated tool, eye tracking, highlighting new potential for intervention research. Recent advances make this much more feasible than in the past and will require both a different approach to eye movement research itself (more interdisciplinary and team based) and efforts to link it to developmental literature on the cognitive and linguistic aspects of reading development. He urges a strong focus on experimental questions and methodologies that complement behavioral and neurobiological data and an examination of individual differences across experiments, with well-characterized samples to facilitate cross-study comparison. Studying both typical readers and those with reading disabilities across diverse populations and studying them within the classroom context should provide invaluable data. Miller urges data integration—eye movement with neuroimaging as well as behavioral data, which could help overcome some of the challenges faced in neuroimaging studies. To quote Miller, "the time is right for eye movement research to be more fully integrated into interdisciplinary developmental studies of reading" (Chapter 6).

Although neuroimaging has been a tool of choice for many studies on reading and reading disabilities for more than a decade, it has moved beyond simply documenting differences between good and poor readers. Cutting, Bailey, Barquero, and Aboud (Chapter 7) offer a review of the cognitive and neurobiological components of reading comprehension and discuss their own research in this area. Looking ahead, they focus on examining the implications of distinct versus common substrates of word- and comprehension-level processing and assert that we could better understand students struggling with reading comprehension if we could identify brain regions critical to multiple levels of text comprehension—which would also require careful examination of text characteristics themselves. They believe these efforts should lead to more finely tuned definitions and instructional and intervention strategies and potentially allow for interventions tailored to individual reader profiles.

Del Tufo and Pugh (Chapter 8), after a brief review of neuroimaging work in reading and reading disability, address the somewhat neglected area of neurochemistry in reading research. They also offer an explanation of the importance of animal models in this area and call for continued work in this area, as well as additional work integrating neurochemistry, neuroimaging, genetics, and behavioral data to ground practice for both reading disability identification and intervention.

Hart (Chapter 9) brings genetics to the classroom, with futuristic goals that mirror those of personalized medicine. Her clear presentation of behavioral genetics and the findings on components of reading leads to her brief mention of her own new applied study of familial genetic risk as a moderator of response to intervention, which will be followed by a randomized controlled trial of intervention dosages based on familial risk. Hart calls for more such programs of research as a means of implementation of personalized education—for example, to investigate student profiles that might be used to group students for interventions that would match their risk status.

Gaab, in her integrative summary, seconds the call for research that in its design, implementation, and analysis of the development and evaluation of reading interventions will take seriously the concepts, tools, and perspectives offered in this section. Gaab asserts that such a multifaceted approach should help the field move toward a clear understanding of what's on the market now and replace approaches that have no basis in science with intervention and instruction grounded in scientific findings.

INTERVENTION: RESEARCH TO INFORM PRACTICE

The questions and issues that practitioners raise (represented by Mele-McCarthy, Chapter 10) challenge us to think differently, to view our research from different perspectives, and to combine theory and real world practicalities (as most of the authors in this volume do) in order to find solutions for teaching literacy in the classroom with "typical students"—because today's typical classroom is diverse. Most of today's teachers will definitely find themselves instructing children with disabilities, children from differing socioeconomic situations, children with different racial and ethnic backgrounds, and children from different cultures who may speak different dialects of English or even different home languages. We need to enable teachers to actively adapt within those classrooms so that a response to intervention approach can be functionally used as it was intended—to prevent learning problems or to catch them early enough to not let them escalate. This way, we no longer have to ask students and parents to wait to fail or to show a severe enough problem to qualify for special services. Mele-McCarthy highlights several questions that are important and for which answers would be immensely helpful to practitioners attempting to meet the needs of struggling readers: How can we best predict who will be nonresponders (via behavioral, neural signatures, genetics/family history) in order to appropriately tailor instruction and intervention? Are there subtypes of reading comprehension difficulty, and how might motivation, interest, and self-confidence affect reading comprehension and inform intervention? What are the foundational components of reading comprehension, and how should they be combined or integrated instructionally? What is the role of reading fluency, and how does this relate to issues such as auditory processing and working memory? What is the evidence base for writing instruction and assessment, and how can we best use technology for instruction and intervention? She ends with what we hope is a question all practitioners and researchers will attend to and embrace: How do we innovate and expedite intervention research? This is at the heart of this volume and the reciprocal *research-to-practice-to-research* collaboration it calls for.

Four chapters in this section address intervention work with students who might be termed "linguistically different"—those who speak a nonmainstream dialect or a language other than English as their first or home language. Each contains recommendations for moving forward in reading intervention research. In Chapter 11, addressing research on Individualizing Student Instruction (ISI), Connor describes models that dynamically forecast the amounts and types of literacy instruction specific students need as an example of how research can inform practice. This work highlights the need for ongoing research that follows the implementation of such forecasts, that develops and makes available the necessary progress monitoring measures (e.g., those needed for word knowledge and reading comprehension), and additional work on providing, explaining, and improving the technology that enables teachers to obtain and use these forecasts and similar procedures.

Terry (Chapter 12), reminding us of the dismal statistics for African American students' reading achievement, explores why so many of these students have difficulty learning to read and what role dialect usage might play in reading. Terry concludes that the malleability of dialect use and the frequency of its use, together with the significant relation of dialect use to reading ability, make it a likely target for instruction and intervention. Clearly this will need to be done in an enlightened way that begins with teacher education and that values both mainstream and African American English dialects.

Lesaux (Chapter 13) describes research trends addressing English learner (EL) reading development, with a special focus on developmental and contextual factors. Of particular note, in this chapter and Gámez and Lesaux (2012, 2014), work on teacher talk in the classroom indicates strongly that researchers should be working with teachers to study not only their students' behaviors but also how their own teacher language and performance influences student learning—as Lesaux terms it, the bidirectional nature of teacher–student language interactions. She also calls for research on how best to build meaning-based literacy competencies in ELs, especially emerging reading difficulty identification and prevention and the relationship of the demands of complex, sophisticated text and students' social-emotional characteristics and their higher order cognitive functions.

Walker, Capin, and Vaughn (Chapter 14) also address reading intervention in ELs. As they (and Lesaux) suggest, instructional interventions that work well with ELs may well be just as helpful to all students, especially those who struggle with literacy. Although what works for a native English-speaking group of students may not be optimal for English learners who are proficient readers, the explicitness, clarity, repetition and practice, and scaffolding that work for ELs can boost the skills of many struggling readers and writers whose native language is English. Such a focus might even help teachers more deeply and fully understand their subject matter and the impact of their own behaviors in the classroom. Walker and colleagues note that providing an emphasis on vocabulary, background knowledge, and academic discourse in a language-focused literacy intervention could strategically shift the focus on instruction that would both benefit all students and would help teachers address both their EL and native English-speaking students together. They call for research to evaluate the efficacy and feasibility of such targeted instruction that uses academic course content, both overall and by the relative effects of the intervention components (e.g., academic vocabulary).

Jiménez (Chapter 15) describes a web-based tutorial program that has been used in a variety of countries to help teachers gain greater depths of knowledge in the components of reading and enable them to better instruct early grade students. In studying this program, he examined both teacher knowledge and beliefs. Jiménez found indications that (at least for in-service teachers) as they gained knowledge, their beliefs in how best to teach reading also tended to change; clearly additional research on the relationship and interaction between teacher knowledge and beliefs is important and could be facilitated by a strong research–practice collaboration. Jiménez also illustrates one use of existing technology to extend the reach for building teacher knowledge in those in remote areas.

Two chapters (Connelly & Dockrell, Chapter 16; Alves & Limpo, Chapter 17) in this section address the "other side" of literacy—writing. Alves and Limpo examine writing instruction from a cross-disciplinary perspective that views writing as part of literacy—that is, reading, writing, and oral language. They focus on four key areas that they see as the foundation of writing achievement—motivation, transcription, language, and self-regulation—with the hope that future research will examine the integration of these areas in writing instruction and intervention. Connelly and Dockrell outline an approach to examining the writing difficulties of students with dyslexia and language learning disorders by diagnostic category, in order to identify targets for intervention. They advocate the use of formative and summative assessments to carefully track progress, discuss the value of accommodations that take into account the speed/slower rate of composing for these students, and review recent work on interventions to improve spelling and handwriting. They call for additional writing intervention research, with detailed frequent progress assessment and specific work to clarify the theoretical and practical links between teaching and learning in the classroom, following students longitudinally to track both progress and instruction over time. They advocate the exploration of emerging technologies to individualize instruction.

Finally, this section ends with Coyne's (Chapter 18) caution that as we conduct rigorous research with randomly selected control and treatment and control groups, we must carefully consider the counterfactual (i.e., the control)—that is, intervention research must take into account the context in which the intervention is delivered and the context and dynamic nature of any control or comparison conditions. In fact, his message aligns with considerations for intervention research as well as how research can inform (and learn from) practice. Washington, in her integrative summary, emphasizes how important such studies can be and that we need to get their results into the hands of teachers and educators if we are to effectively reduce literacy learning gaps.

OVERALL THEMES OR MESSAGES FOR MOVING FORWARD

This volume clearly invokes many of the usual suspects that everyone mentions when discussing intervention research—rigorous design and analysis; response to intervention; assessment and progress monitoring; the triad of behavior, neurobiology, and genetics; and the use of new technologies. We could also add teacher knowledge and education, although these are generally less frequently found in discussions of intervention research. However, we believe the chapters in this volume bring novelty to these areas as well.

In our rigorous designs, we need to consider, as Coyne points out, what else is happening contextually in the schools and districts and what our comparison students and teachers are doing; we also need to carefully examine and interpret our data in light of those factors. Without a doubt, in many schools and districts, too many students are still not succeeding in reading and writing only because they do not receive the types, amount, and intensity of intervention and instruction they require. Although many educational leaders and teachers do not appreciate the importance of research, there are schools in which teachers and administrators understand the advantages of working with researchers; many of them are also using research to inform their practice. Hence they may provide control conditions that are "hard to beat," as Coyne points out. At the same time, the very schools that most need to use research findings to improve their students' achievement are also often reluctant to partner with researchers. Indeed, during the 14th Extraordinary Brain Symposium, there was a general sense among the practitioners that they have an obligation to reach out to these research-resistant schools but acknowledge that it is challenging. We hope that the concept of reciprocity—of research-to-practice-to-research partnerships, some of which are already happening but still needed in many areas—will help more schools understand, collaborate with researchers, and use research findings to inform the instruction and interventions they provide their students.

In addition, the analytic techniques we use are important. Both Bartlett (Chapter 4) and Sideridis (Chapter 5) and their colleagues provide novel analytic approaches that reveal new information about learning and intervention outcomes. These should be invaluable to research going forward, and the efforts of these researchers should inspire others to explore innovative approaches as well.

We always need new and better measures that can be used repeatedly to track progress in areas that have proven to be measurement challenges, such as phonological processing, reading comprehension, and writing. The fact that valid and reliable assessment is an ongoing challenge does not diminish its importance. Indeed, as we learn more about the time and intensity required for interventions with students in the upper elementary and higher grades, the need for additional rigorous and useful assessments becomes even more important. The use of technology to make assessment faster and more valid and reliable has tremendous promise. Keeping in mind that time used for assessment is time taken away from instruction and intervention, online and adaptive assessment can facilitate administration, data recording, and interpretation. Whether by helping teachers better monitor student reading progress, using the data to adjust instruction (as with Connor's A2i tool), or by diagnosing writing difficulties more accurately (as noted in Connelly & Dockrell, Chapter 16), we need to be tracking and recognizing progress over time in our struggling students.

The promise of neuroimaging, eye tracking, and genetics means that we may be better able to not only understand how the brain organizes and reorganizes with intervention success but also predict who will struggle—even eventually who will respond best to which types of intervention. Identifying the potential "nonresponders" should help us eventually eliminate the issue of nonresponse to treatment as we more carefully tailor treatment to the student.

The great consensus is that as we study student interventions, we should also assist and conduct research with teachers: Our interventions must include professional development that can help teachers understand what underlies the intervention and how best to implement it (see Chapter 15 for Jiménez's web-based professional development that impacted teacher beliefs and philosophies as well as knowledge about literacy), how best to use the data they gather as they assess and monitor progress (e.g., Connor, Chapter 11), and how we can develop (with their "user" input) technologies that will help them extend their ability to move all students forward. In addition, as Lesaux noted, there are teacher characteristics—the complexity of their sentences and the nature of the vocabulary they use—that influence student learning; most teachers are not even aware of the ways these characteristics affect their students. It would likely be very fruitful to measure how malleable these characteristics are and how they can be made conscious tools to enhance student learning. Giving teachers tools and approaches that work well with today's diverse classrooms of dialect speakers and English learners (and also enhance the literacy skills of all students) is a worthy goal and one that appears well within reach, given the work presented here by various authors (Terry, Chapter 12; Lesaux, Chapter 13; Walker, Capin, & Vaughn, Chapter 14).

MOVING FORWARD

We know how to intervene and enable many struggling readers and writers to improve. How do we sustain those gains and build on them? We need a universal instructional approach from which everyone can benefit, with well-trained teachers who know how and when to intervene, who know how to supplement and tailor instruction for all students and their varying constellation of skills and aptitudes. Education is a long-term investment, so expecting a quick fix is unrealistic. If we intervene in early childhood, we should be able to prevent many students from struggling, but we cannot simply "fix" students and then set them in motion and expect them to succeed, or remediate them in second grade and, once they can decode, expect them to read and learn without continued support. They are learners, not wind-up toys or clocks to set in motion—they need ongoing education, which is why we have a K–12 and beyond system of education. There is no inoculation or vaccination to prevent reading and writing difficulties. Learning is a lifetime occupation, and if there are risk factors, such as poverty or learning difficulties, those will not go away once we intervene and see a student making progress. These students need ongoing support, and we must help teachers be better able to determine when to decrease or when to intensify that support, without major disruption of the learning process. It may be that a student needs greater intensity at different points, so that the support and scaffolding that a student needs may fluctuate, not just from more to less intense but back to more intense at times. We need to monitor and try to predict the roller-coaster ride so that we smooth it out for students and can keep their learning trajectories rising—perhaps not closing the gap entirely but always increasing their learning and mastery. And we need to do so without making them feel less competent or less hopeful when supports are changed. If we do this, then we will have succeeded in providing good educational services to these students. This sounds much easier than it is or will be, but there is reason for hope, for all of us—researchers, practitioners, and students.

Here is a proposed research agenda in reading intervention based on the symposium and the chapters in this volume:

1. Look for answers that may come from high-tech approaches such as neuroimaging, brain neurochemical analyses, eye tracking, and genetics. Look for solutions from the innovative use of technologies with students in the classroom (via individualized assessment, assistive technology, or interactive smart tutoring), from the use of technologies with teachers (via professional development online, as Alves & Limpo [Chapter 17] describe, or real-time data informing classroom instruction), and from good interpersonal instructional interactions in the classroom.

2. Conduct research to better understand what motivates students and what aspects of their cognition, learning, and self-regulation can be improved and how to do that—and how that in turn affects classroom learning

and what role teachers play in actively guiding or indirectly influencing that learning. Finally, the more we all communicate and collaborate—in a research-to-practice-to-research reciprocity—the closer we can come to the ideal wherein we can predict in advance who will struggle; personalize intervention early to head off or minimize dyslexia, literacy difficulties, and writing problems; maintain the right amount and kind of intervention to sustain success; and discover approaches to support student learning that benefit the greatest number of students through individualized (or personalized) instruction and intervention.

REFERENCES

August, D., Shanahan, T. (Eds.). (2006). *Developing literacy in second-language learners: Report of the National Literacy Panel on Language-Minority Children and Youth.* Mahwah, NJ: Lawrence Erlbaum Associates.

Carlson, S.M., Zelazo, P.D., & Faja, S. (2013). Executive function. In P.D. Zelazo (Ed.), *The Oxford handbook of developmental psychology* (Vol. 1, pp. 706–743). New York, NY: Oxford University Press.

Gámez, P.B., & Lesaux, N.K. (2012). The relation between exposure to sophisticated and complex language and early-adolescent English-only and language minority learners' vocabulary. *Child development, 83*(4), 1316–1331.

Gámez, P.B., & Lesaux, N.K. (2014). *Exposure to sophisticated vocabulary in urban middle school classrooms and early adolescents' reading comprehension.* Manuscript submitted for publication.

Graham, S., & Herbert, M. (2011). Writing to read: A meta-analysis of the impact of writing and writing instruction on reading. *Harvard Educational Review, 81*(4), 710–744.

Graham, S., & Perrin, D. (2007). A meta-analysis of writing instruction for adolescent students. *Journal of Educational Psychology, 99*(3), 445–476.

Graham, S., & Santangelo, T. (2014). Does spelling instruction make students better spellers, readers, and writers? A meta-analytic review. *Reading and Writing, 27,* 1703–1743.

Graham, S., McKeown, D., Kiuhara, S., & Harris, K. (2012). Meta-analysis of writing instruction for students in elementary grades. *Journal of Educational Psychology, 104*(4), 879–896.

Miller, B., Cutting, L., & McCardle, P. (Eds.). (2013). *Unraveling the behavioral, neurobiological, and genetic components of reading comprehension.* Baltimore, MD: Paul H. Brookes Publishing Co.

Miller, B., McCardle, P., & Long, R.L. (Eds.). (2014). *Teaching reading and writing: Improving instruction and student achievement.* Baltimore, MD: Paul H. Brookes Publishing Co.

National Early Literacy Panel. (2008). *Developing early literacy: Report of the National Early Literacy Panel.* Washington DC: National Institute for Literacy and the National Center for Family Literacy.

National Institute of Child Health and Human Development. (2000). *Report of the National Reading Panel. Teaching children to read: An evidence-based assessment of the scientific research literature on reading and its implications for reading instruction.* (NIH Publication No. 00-4769.) Washington, DC: US Government Printing Office.

RAND Reading Study Group. (2002). *Reading for understanding: Toward an R&D program in reading comprehension.* Santa Monica, CA: RAND.

Sabatini, J., Albro, E., & O'Reilly. T. (2012a). *Measuring up: Advances in how we assess reading ability.* Lanham, MD: Rowman & Littlefield.

Sabatini, J., Albro, E., & O'Reilly, T. (2012b). *Reading and understanding: Innovations in how we view reading assessment.* Lanham, MD: Rowman & Littlefield.

Thom, R. (1975). *Structural stability and morphogenesis.* Reading, MA: W.A. Benjamin.

Index

Tables, figures, and notes are indicated by *t*, *f*, and *n*, respectively.

Academic achievement, dialect-informed instruction and, 149
Academic Language Instruction for All Students (ALIAS), 176
Adenosine triphosphate (ATP), 91
ADI-R, *see* Autism Diagnostic Interview-Revised
ADOS, *see* Autism Diagnostic Observation Schedule
Adult skilled readers, fixations for, 64
African American children
  addressing dialect variation in early reading instruction for, 143–151
  eligibility for special education services in schools, 145–146
  language variation and, 146
  reading achievement by, 266
  reasons for difficulties in learning to read, 144–146
African American English
  malleability of, 148
  reading ability and, 147–148
  reading achievement and use of, 146–148
  reading instruction and, 149–150
ALIAS, *see* Academic Language Instruction for All Students
Animal models of dyslexia, 93
Aptitude-by-instruction interactions, in behavioral genetics, 104
Aptitude-by-treatment interactions, 131
Archival texts, central authoritative role of, 209
Assessment
  formative, in writing, 201–202
  importance of individualized, 119
  summative in writing, 202
Assessment-to-instruction dynamic forecasting intervention computer algorithms, 132–133
Assessment to instruction technology platform, 133, 134–135*f*, 136
Association studies, 92
ATP, *see* Adenosine triphosphate
A2i technology platform, 133, 136
Auditory dyslexia, 121
Autism Diagnostic Interview-Revised (ADI-R), 40
Autism Diagnostic Observation Schedule (ADOS), 40

Background knowledge, in reading comprehension intervention, 13–15
Behavioral genetics
  aptitude-by-instruction interactions in, 104
  child characteristic-by-instruction interactions in, 104
  Cholesky decomposition and, 101
  decoding in, 100
  DeFries-Fulker analysis in, 103
  familial genetic risk index in, 105, 106
  field of, 99
  Florida Twin Project on Reading in, 101
  in informing education, 99–106
  personalized education in, 105
  phonological awareness in, 100
  Project KIDS in, 106
  reading comprehension and, 101
  reading fluency and, 100–101
  Simple View of Reading in, 101
  twin studies in, 99–100, 102
Behaviorist theory, 188*t*, 190*t*
Bifurcation, 57
Bilingualism, development of reading skills and, 155
Bilinguals
  sequential, 156
  simultaneous, 156

California, whole language literacy instruction in, 132–133
Candidate gene studies, 92
Capabilities
  defined, 209
  fostering, in building writing achievements, 209–217, 216*f*
CDI, *see* Children's Depression Inventory
CELF-4, *see* Clinical Evaluation of Language Fundamentals, Fourth Edition
Centrality, sensitivity to, 81
Child characteristic-by-instruction interactions, 130–131
  in behavioral genetics, 104

Children's Depression Inventory (CDI), 53
Cholesky decomposition in behavioral genetics, 101
Choline, *n*-acetylaspartate and, 88–90
Chronic fatigue syndrome, 91
Classroom talk, influence on reading development, 160–161
Clinical Evaluation of Language Fundamentals, Fourth Edition (CELF-4), 40
Code switching, 148
Code-based skills, 157
Code-focused instruction, 139–140
  for children with dyslexia, 137–138
  Student/peer-managed (SPM), 140
  Teacher/student-managed (TSM), 139–140
Cognitive approach in writing, 210–211
Cognitive blueprint of skilled readers, 8, 9*f*
Cognitive information processing, reading fluency, decoding, comprehension and, 122–124
Cognitive-psycholinguistic theory, 188*t*, 190*t*
Collaborative Strategic Reading approach, 14
Comprehension, *see also* Reading comprehension
  language, 73
  reading fluency, decoding, cognitive information processing and, 122–124
  word-level reading and discourse, 75–81, 76*f*, 78*f*, 79*f*, 80*f*
  see also Text comprehension
Comprehension development, 7
  learning mechanisms involved in, 10–11
Comprehension processing, eye-movement research and, 66
Comprehensive Test of Phonological Processing (CTOPP), 40, 43
Consonant dyslexia, 121
Constructionist theory, 187*t*, 189*t*
Correlation metric, 263
Counterfactual in reading interventions, 222, 225–226
Crossover (CXI) interactions, 130, 131, 132, 133, 141
CTOPP, *see* Comprehensive Test of Phonological Processing
Curriculum-based measurement approach to profiling writing, 202
Cusp catastrophe model, 49–58, 263–264

DCDC2 expression, in Gray matter, 94
Decodable stories, 169
Decoding, 122
  in behavioral genetics, 100
  integration with spelling, 7
  reading fluency, comprehension, cognitive information processing and, 122–124
  in Simple View of Reading, 44
  sounding out words as strategy in, 169
DeFries-Fulker analysis in behavioral genetics, 103
Depression, 91
Developmental disorders, mapping, to expressive writing problems, 197–198
Developmental pathways to reading outcomes, 161–162
Developmental reading disabilities, 62*n*
DFR, *see* Distance from recommendations
Diagnostic and Statistical Manual of Mental Disorders, Fifth Edition
  dyslexia in, 198
  language disorders in, 200
Dialect use, malleability of, 266
Dialect variation in early reading instruction for African American children, 143–151
Dialect-informed instruction, association between academic achievement and, 149
Diffusion tensor imaging (DTI), 77, 87
Discourse comprehension, word-level reading and, 75–81, 76*f*, 78*f*, 79*f*, 80*f*
Distance correlation, 263
  quantile regression as adjunct to, 44–45, 46*f*
Distance from recommendations (DFR), 136
DTI, *see* Diffusion tensor imaging
Dual Purkinje Image (DPI) eye tracker, 62
Dual Purkinje systems, 63
Dynamic forecasting intervention (DFI) models, 130, 131, 132, 133, 141–142
  interactions among student skills and optimal instruction and, 137–139
Dyslexia, 129
  animal models of, 93
  auditory, 121
  characteristics of, 85
  code-focused instruction for children with, 137–138
  consonant, 121
  emotional repercussions of, 85
  eye movements in, 67–68
  functional connectivity and, 87
  functional magnetic resonance imaging and, 86
  genetics of reading disability and, 92–93
  as hereditable disorder, 85
  heritability of, 92
  integrating neurobiological findings in search of neurochemical signature of, 85–95
  link to oculomotor control, 67